LIVING IN OUR WORLD

North Carolina

NC STATE UNIVERSITY

LIVING IN OUR WORLD

North Carolina

HUMANITIES EXTENSION/PUBLICATIONS PROGRAM

North Carolina State University

Raleigh, North Carolina

Cover: A hiking family stops for a rest at a mountain waterfall in the Shining Rock Wilderness Area of the Nantahala National Forest in North Carolina. Photo by Chip Henderson/Picturesque Stock Photos.

Design and Production: DECODE, Inc.

ISBN 1-885647-27-1
Printed in the United States of America.

1 2 3 4 5 6 7 8 BN 04 03 02 01 00 99 98 97

Series Authors, Editors, and Staff

North Carolina State University Humanities Extension/Publications

Dr. James W. Clark
Director & Professor of English

Dr. Burton F. Beers
Chief Executive Editor, Humanities Publications & Professor of History

Christian P. Garcia
Editor
Humanities Publications

Gail S. Chesson
Associate Editor
Humanities Publications

Nancy McAllister
Production/Rights Chief, Humanities Publications

Michael Rothwell
Electronic Publishing Specialist

James Alchediak
Chief Videographer & Lecturer in Communications

Neal Hutcheson
Videographer & Photographer

Pamela H. Ellis
Administrative Assistant

Rita Sears
Bookkeeper

Editorial Support

Bryan Smithey
Copy Editor
Warrenton, NC

Lynn P. Roundtree
Senior Photo Researcher
Chapel Hill, NC

Roger Harris
Photo Researcher
Chapel Hill, NC

Content Specialists

Area Specialists

Dr. David Phelps
Professor of Anthropology & Associate Director of the Institute of Historical and Cultural Research,
East Carolina University

Dr. William S. Price
Head, North Carolina Division of Archives and History & Professor of History, Meredith College

Dr. Douglas C. Wilms
Professor Emeritus, Geography, East Carolina University

Dr. James Young
Associate Professor of Geography,
Appalachian State University

Contributing Writer

Dr. Gary Freeze
James F. Hurley Scholar-in-Residence & Director of the Institute for Community Preservation,
Catawba College

Curriculum Specialists

Mary Vann Eslinger
Social Studies Consultant (ret.)
N.C. Department of Public Instruction

John Ellington
Social Studies Consultant (ret.)
N.C. Department of Public Instruction

Jacqueline Boykin
Social Studies Consultant
Williamston, NC

Steve Harvel
Social Studies Consultant
Wilkesboro, NC

Joe Webb
Social Studies Consultant
Jacksonville, NC

Consulting Teachers

Jane M. Davis
West Buncombe Elementary School
Asheville, NC

Patsy Hill
Allen Jay Elementary School
High Point, NC

Linda W. Peterson
E.C. Brooks Elementary School
Raleigh, NC

Dee Schmid
Bradley Creek Elementary School
Wilmington, NC

Lynne L. Welborn
Elmhurst Elementary School
Greenville, NC

Cathleen T. Wilson
Bradley Creek Elementary School
Wilmington, NC

Michele L. Woodson
Elon College Elementary School
Elon College, NC

Contents

UNIT 2 Linking the Past to the Present 78

SLUSH

North Carolina Today and Tomorrow 316

Skill Lessons

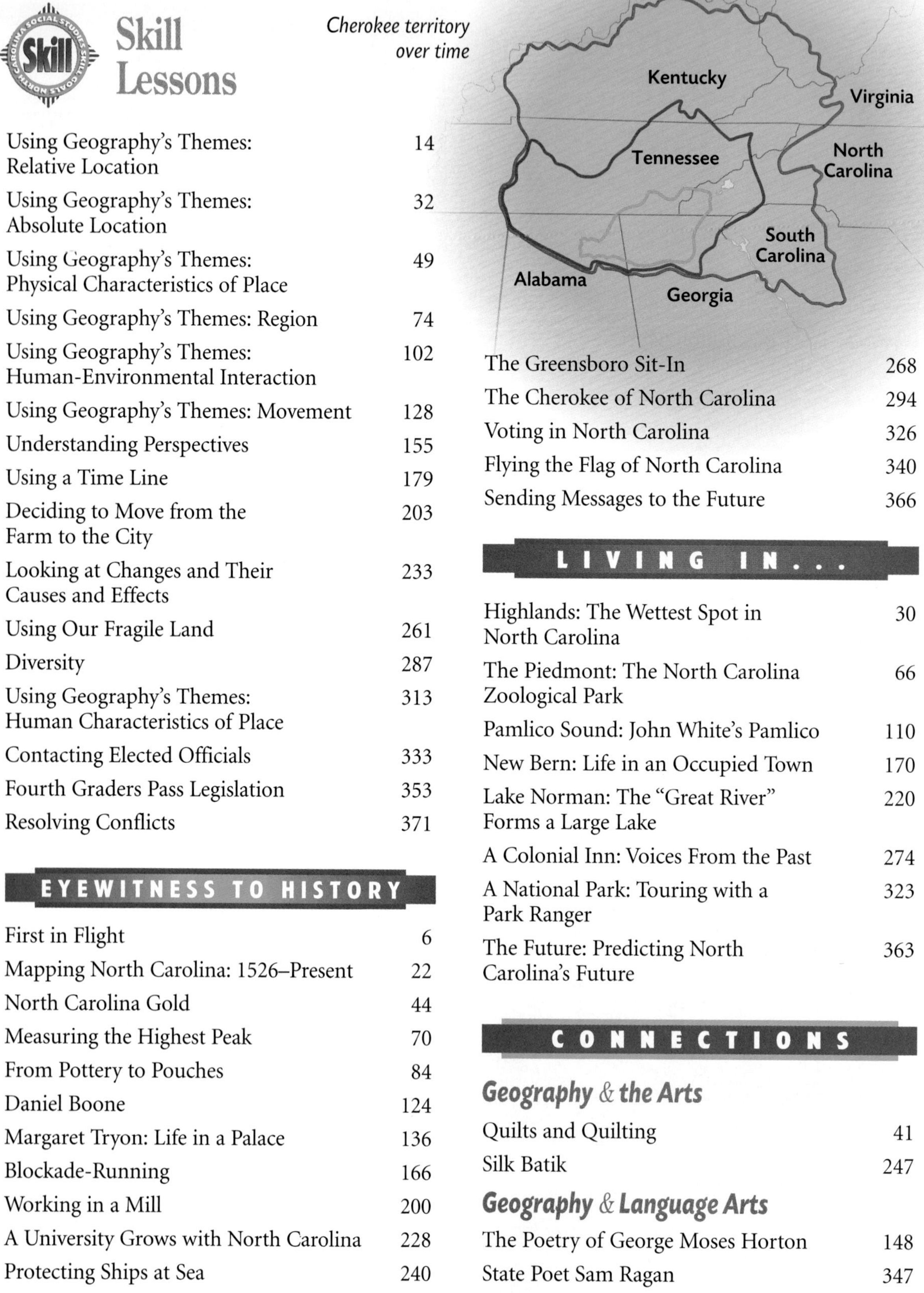

Cherokee territory over time

EYEWITNESS TO HISTORY

LIVING IN...

CONNECTIONS

Geography & the Arts

Geography & Language Arts

Geography & Math

Geography & Science

Maps

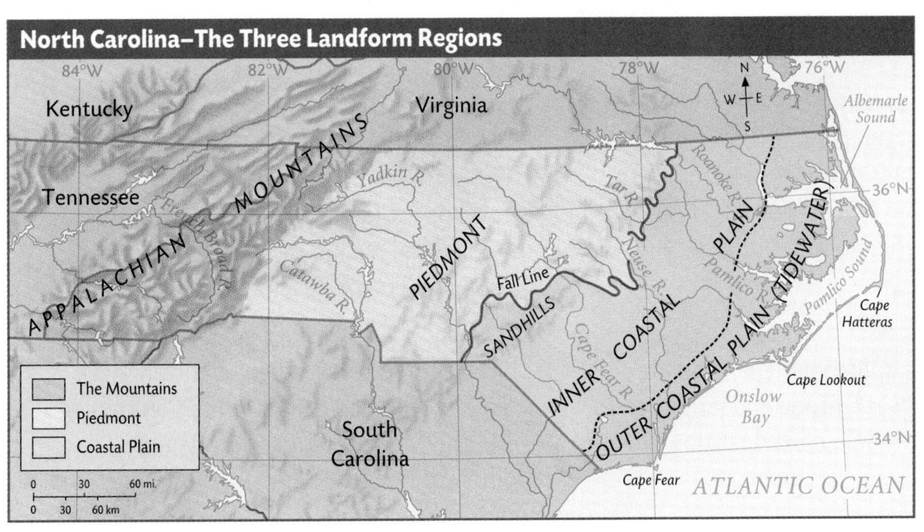

North Carolina–Location and Place

North Carolina is one of 50 states in the United States. Each state is different because of its location, landforms, and climate.

North Carolina is a place of great variety.

The flat Coastal Plain stretches to the water's edge. Beaches and sounds offer fun, jobs, and resources.

Cities of the Piedmont rise from the plateau. Newcomers from throughout the state and the world arrive daily.

Mountains stand against the dawn sky. Rivers and streams ripple through green valleys.

UNIT PREVIEW

CHAPTER 1

North Carolina in the United States

The geographic theme of relative location helps locate places in North Carolina and locate North Carolina in the United States.

CHAPTER 2

North Carolina in the World

The geographic theme of absolute location uses latitude and longitude to locate North Carolina. Location affects North Carolina's climate.

CHAPTER 3

North Carolina's Physical Characteristics

The physical characteristics of North Carolina include a variety of vegetation and natural resources.

CHAPTER 4

North Carolina's Regions

North Carolina has three major physical regions—the Coastal Plain, the Piedmont, and the Mountains. Landforms are different in each region.

The regions of North Carolina: Coastal Plain (right), Piedmont (bottom inset), Mountains (top inset)

North Carolina in the United States

How would you like to go bowling in your house? Most people do not have homes with rooms large enough to roll a heavy ball 60 feet (18 meters).

The Biltmore House in Asheville has more than 250 rooms—including a bowling alley—and acres of gardens.

Getting to Biltmore House depends upon knowing its location in North Carolina. Someone from outside North Carolina would have to know the state's location within the United States. In this chapter you will learn about North Carolina's location in the United States.

The Biltmore House gardens

CHAPTER PREVIEW

LESSON 1
Locating Your Home Using Relative Location
By describing what your home is near, you are using relative location to locate your home.

LESSON 2
Locating North Carolina Using Relative Location
By describing what North Carolina is near, you are using relative location to locate the state.

The Biltmore House

North Carolina in the United States

The Appalachian Trail

If you wanted, you could hike from Georgia to Maine using one trail. Think of it as you would an interstate highway. People drive on Interstate 95 from Maine to Florida. On the Appalachian Trail, you travel on foot.

This trail winds its way through North Carolina's Great Smoky Mountains. You will pass Clingmans Dome. Clouds might hide it the day you walk by. You will go through deep woods. Forest animals will surprise you and you might surprise them.

Locating Your Home Using Relative Location

LESSON PREVIEW

Key Ideas

- Relative location can be used to describe locations of places.
- Landmarks and directions can help you use relative location.

Key Terms

Location, Five Themes of Geography, relative location, landmark, cardinal directions, intermediate directions

If you were asked, "Where are you?" how would you answer the question? You might say you are in a classroom or you might say you are in school. You might answer you are in North Carolina or you might name your county or city. You might even say you are in the United States.

You might want to tell someone how to find where you are. Many people want to visit North Carolina. They like to hike in the mountains, swim in the ocean, or watch a sporting event in Charlotte or Greensboro. When you know about the theme of **Location**, you can help someone find your home, your school, or other places in the state.

Location is one of the **Five Themes of Geography**. These themes help geographers organize information about places. The other four themes are Place, Human-Environmental Interaction, Movement, and Region. Each will help you learn about North Carolina.

The location of a school's street, building, and even one classroom can be found by using relative location. *Can you describe what is near those places in your school?*

Relative Location

You can give the location of your home by describing places near it. When you describe the location of your home *in relation* to other places, you are using **relative location**.

To use relative location, first describe what is near your home. Then give directions from those nearby places.

Landmarks

We use landmarks to give the relative location of places. A **landmark** is a reference point people use to find other places. A landmark can be big or small, but it must be easily seen.

North Carolina has many famous landmarks. Some are natural parts of the land, such as mountains, rivers, or beaches. Other landmarks are built by people. Depending on where you live, you could use many landmarks to give a location.

WORD ORIGINS

Pilot Mountain did not get its present name until the late 1700s. Settlers chose the name because *pilot* is an old word that means "to act as a guide." Airline pilots guide people to their destinations. Pilot Mountain still helps people find where they are going. Native Americans called the mountain *Jomeokee,* which means "the Great Guide."

Famous Landmarks

A natural landmark can help a visitor find you. If you live in the Appalachian Mountains, you might give the name of a nearby mountain. Grandfather Mountain or Mount Mitchell are examples. Or you could say you live near the Fontana Dam, a landmark made by people.

If you live in the central part of the state, you might give Pilot Mountain, north of Winston-Salem, as a landmark. It rises so high above the surrounding hills that you can see it as far away as 30 miles (48 kilometers). You would not be the first person to use Pilot Mountain as a landmark. Native Americans used it. Early settlers used its peak as a guide.

A longstanding landmark is the Cape Hatteras Lighthouse. It sits so close to the water in Dare County, there is danger that the ocean may soon surround it.

Pilot Mountain in Surry County has been a landmark for travelers for thousands of years. *What places near your home are landmarks?*

Not far off the coast, the Gulf Stream and the Labrador Current meet in the Atlantic Ocean. Ships sail in these ocean currents along the east coast of the United States. Captains of ships at sea searched for lighthouses. The Cape Hatteras lighthouse and others let them know their location and warned of dangerous sandbars.

Landmarks Near Your Home

Landmarks do not have to be big or famous. Once a landmark is recognized, it helps guide people to your home.

A crossroads store near your home could be a landmark.

EYEWITNESS TO HISTORY

First In Flight

Flying was left to the birds until two brothers came to North Carolina. Orville and Wilbur Wright (right) of Ohio came to North Carolina in 1900 to test the flight of gliders, planes without motors. They chose Kitty Hawk, North Carolina, because of its location.

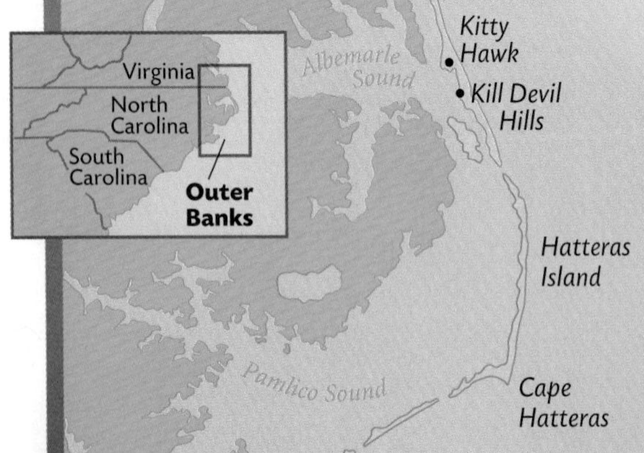

The Outer Banks of North Carolina provided steady wind, which the Wrights needed to test their glider. The cold wind was bitter, but did not hurt the 12-horsepower engine attached to their glider. Kitty Hawk did not have many people living there in 1900, so the brothers had the space to fly.

On December 17, 1903, Orville Wright stayed aloft 12 seconds in the first powered flight (right) of a heavier-than-air vehicle. Later that day, Wilbur flew 852 feet (256 m) in 59 seconds. You can see where they flew when you go to the Wright Brothers National Museum at Kill Devil Hills.

Tall buildings near the center of your city would help people from out of town find their way. An odd-shaped tree in a field near your driveway might alert your visitors that they have located you.

Directions

After describing a landmark near your home, you would need to tell a visitor the direction of your home from that landmark. There are four main directions—north, south, east, and west. These main directions are called **cardinal directions**.

GAMES People Play

Orienteering is a game to find locations in a forest or campground by matching land features with a map. When orienteers find the exact spots, a leader punches a hole in a card. The winner is the first one to match locations on the map with the land features.

The Wright Brothers flight began the rapid progress of aviation in the United States. Within ten years, Georgia Thompson Broadwicke (right) from Henderson, North Carolina, became the first woman to parachute from an airplane.

In 1927, Charles A. Lindbergh (left) flew alone across the Atlantic Ocean from New York to Paris. After Lindbergh returned, he flew his plane, the *Spirit of St. Louis,* around the country. One of his stops was at Greensboro.

By the 1930s, airplanes had become common. Charlotte and other cities in North Carolina built airports (above). Soon people could fly throughout the country. It all began in Kitty Hawk because of its favorable location!

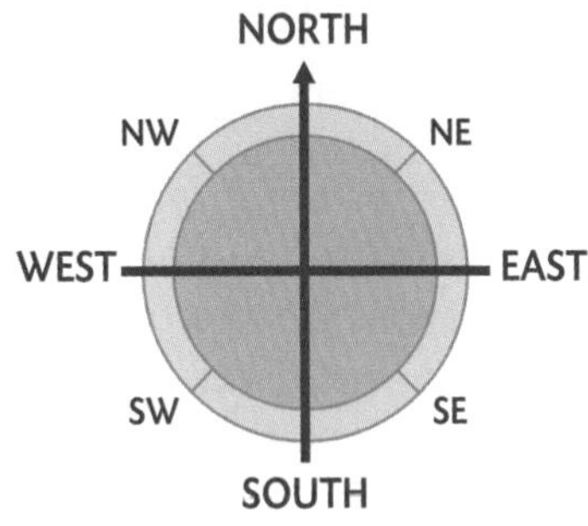

The cardinal directions of north, south, east, and west are shown on the diagram above. *What are the intermediate directions?*

What would YOU do?

Every year someone gets lost in the woods. Would you know what to do?

Before hiking or camping, you should be prepared. Have a compass and a map to keep you on the right path. Wear bright colors or carry a flashlight. But most people do not plan on getting lost. If you are lost, try to figure direction and time by looking at the location of the sun or the North Star.

Sometimes places are not directly north, south, east, or west from a landmark. Directions that are in between the cardinal directions are called **intermediate directions.**

Look at the diagram to the left. It shows the cardinal directions and the intermediate directions. For example, southwest is between south and west. Northeast is between north and east. What are the other intermediate directions?

Geographers, sea captains, and truck drivers use cardinal and intermediate directions. What other people use directions in their work?

Using Directions

You can use directions to guide a person to a certain place. For example, imagine you live near Greensboro. You would describe the direction of your town from Greensboro to give your town's relative location.

If you want to meet someone at the zoo in Asheboro, you would tell a new resident of Greensboro to go south. If your friend just moved to Siler City, you would tell that person to head southeast of Greensboro. Your friend would need to know more than the intermediate direction toward the zoo.

You might say, "Go west on U.S. Route 64 through Asheboro. At State Road 159, turn south. Drive eight miles until you reach the sign that says North Carolina Zoological Park. Turn left." You would have led your friend to meet you at the zoo.

LESSON 1 REVIEW

Fact Follow-Up

1. What is relative location?
2. What is a landmark?
3. What are cardinal directions?
4. What are intermediate directions?

Think These Through

5. Describe the location of your school relative to your home. Use directions to help you tell its relative location.
6. What are the most important landmarks in the community where you live? Why are they the most important ones?
7. How are cardinal and intermediate directions useful in locating places?

Locating North Carolina Using Relative Location

Do you remember why the Wright brothers went to Kitty Hawk? The Wrights found a steady wind and empty dunes. Kitty Hawk's location provided the ideal climate for flight.

Families move to North Carolina every day. They learn about their new homes the way the Wright brothers did. They ask questions about location. If we buy this house, will we be near work, schools, places to shop? By learning location, people begin to learn about a place.

Our first job is to locate North Carolina. Then we can learn more about the state.

LESSON PREVIEW

Key Ideas

- You can find North Carolina's relative location by describing the states it borders.
- Because North Carolina is both an East Coast state and a southern state, it shares landforms with other states.

Key Terms

landform, key, elevation, Coastal Plain, Piedmont, Appalachian Mountains

North Carolina in the United States

North Carolina is one of 50 states in the United States (see map, page 3). You can see the relative location of North Carolina within the United States.

Grandfather Mountain is located in Avery County. *What is Grandfather Mountain's relative location within North Carolina?*

There are different ways to describe North Carolina's relative location. It lies on the East Coast of the United States, bordering the Atlantic Ocean. This makes North Carolina both an eastern state and an Atlantic Coast state. North Carolina is also a southern state. Because North Carolina is a southern and an eastern state, the map below shows

The Southeast Region of the United States

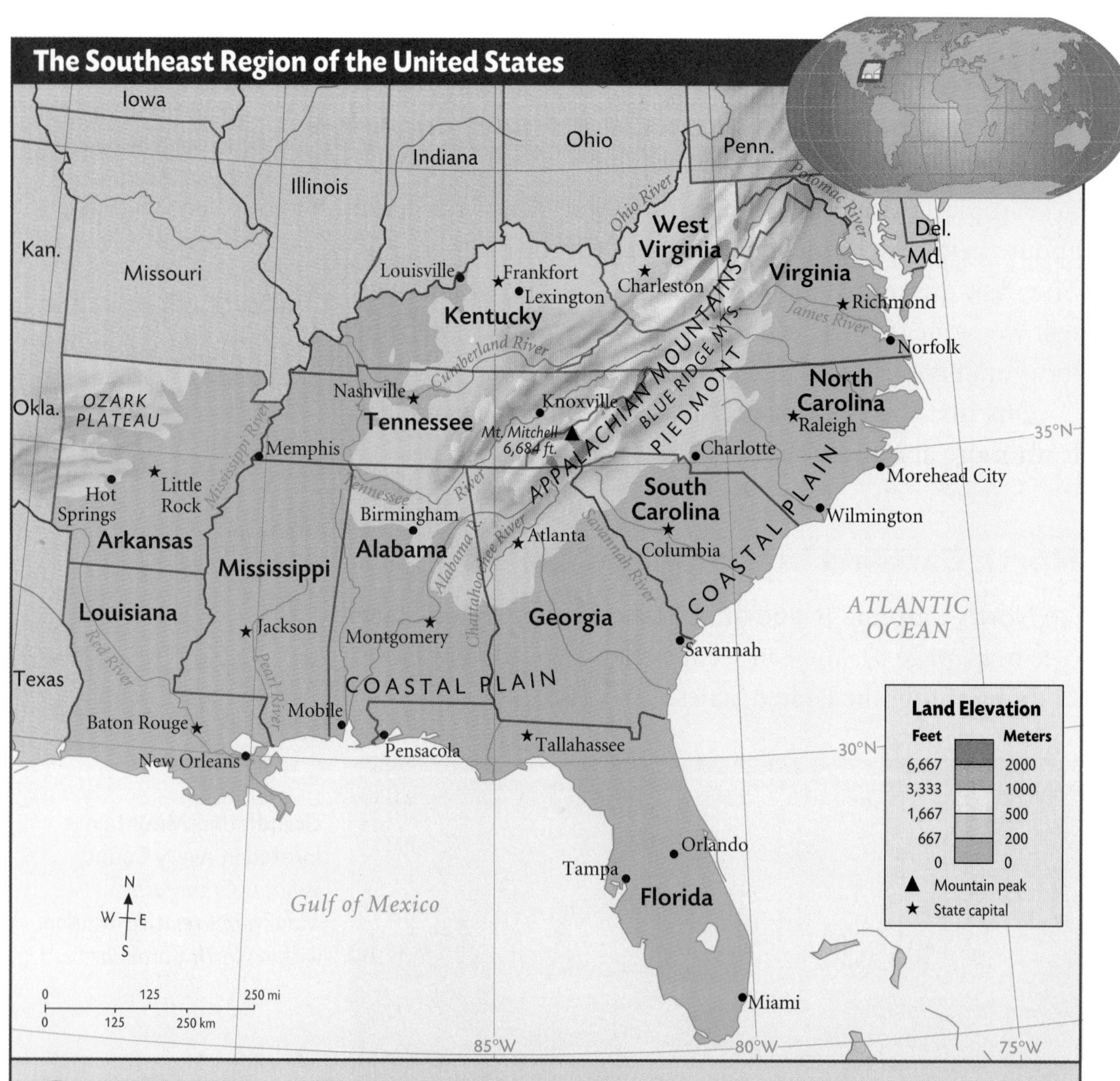

Location You can describe the relative location of North Carolina by describing the directions of the states it borders. *North Carolina is east of which state? North Carolina is south of which state? North Carolina is north of which state? North Carolina is southeast of which state?*

CONNECTIONS

Geography & Science

Butterfly Migration

Monarch butterflies have an urge to travel in the fall. These small, bright orange-and-black insects seek a warmer climate. Monarchs from North Carolina and other eastern states fly south to Mexico.

With a wing span of from 2 to 4 inches (5.1 to 10.2 centimeters), the monarch might fly more than 1,800 miles (2,898 km) to reach its destination.

Scientists are still looking for answers about monarch migration. We do know that these insects instinctively know when and where to fly. We don't yet understand *how* they know.

During the summer, the monarchs feed on milkweed in Canada and the northern United States. Then, the monarchs set out on their journey.

In late fall, monarchs migrate from northern regions. Most fly overland to Mexico. Some fly to Florida and go across the Gulf of Mexico to their hibernating grounds.

North Carolina's habitat supports the breeding of monarchs. Native monarchs join those from the northern regions and fly to warmer winter quarters.

You can look for these colorful travelers around the end of October and the first part of November.

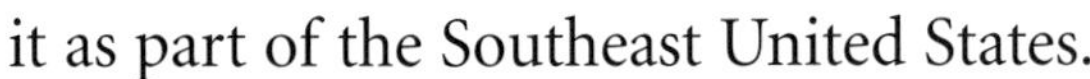

it as part of the Southeast United States.

The states bordering North Carolina are Virginia, Tennessee, Georgia, and South Carolina. These states and other southeastern states share physical characteristics of climate and landforms with North Carolina.

Major Landforms in the Southeast

A **landform** is a physical feature of the land. The Appalachian Mountains, the Piedmont, and the Coastal Plain

The Appalachian Mountains extend through western North Carolina. The mountains are one of three major landforms in North Carolina. *What are other landforms in the state? How are they shown on the map?*

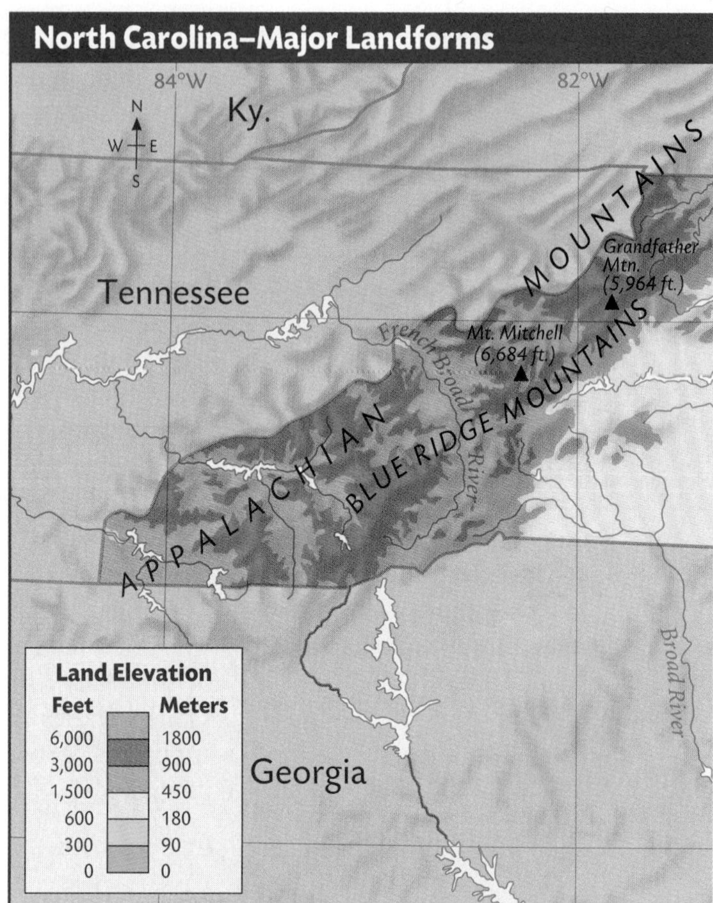

are the major landforms of the Southeast and of North Carolina. The map above shows those landforms through labels and the colors in the key. The **key** is a box on a map. It explains the symbols used on the map. The map key above explains how the colors on the map show **elevation**, or height of land above sea level. The different colors show the changing elevations of the landforms.

The **Coastal Plain** is flat or gently sloping land that extends inland from the Atlantic Ocean and the Gulf of Mexico. The Coastal Plain covers most of the Southeast from Virginia through Louisiana.

Bordering the Coastal Plain is the **Piedmont**. The hilly, rolling land of the Piedmont is narrow in Virginia but widens in the two Carolinas. It extends southward to Alabama.

Finally, many southeastern states share the largest mountain range in the eastern United States. The **Appalachian Mountains** extend from Canada, the country north of the

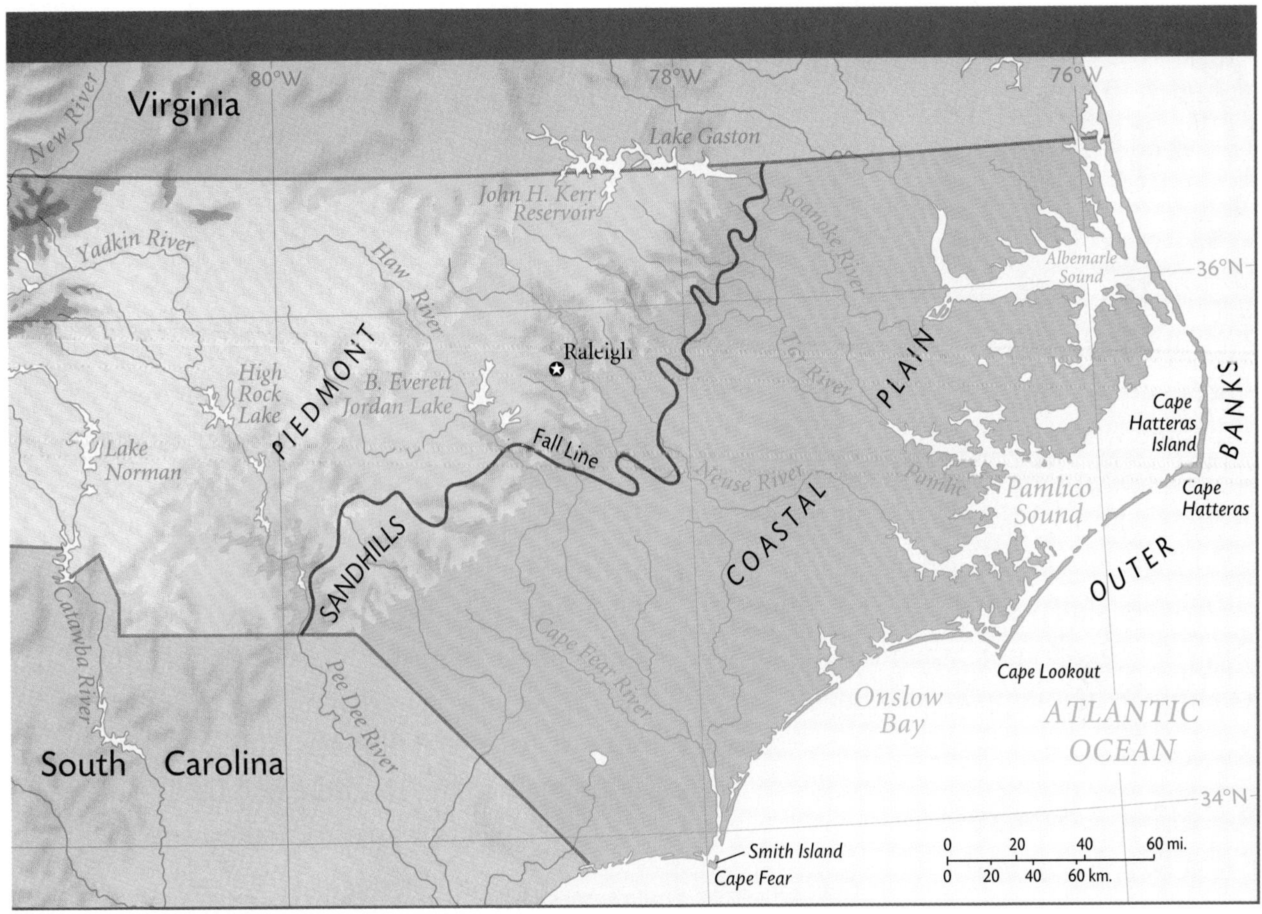

United States, to northern Alabama. In the Southeast, the Appalachians rise in parts of West Virginia, Virginia, Kentucky, Tennessee, South Carolina, Georgia, and Alabama. As the map above shows, the mountains also cover the western part of North Carolina. The three major landforms of North Carolina make up the three major regions of the state.

LESSON 2 REVIEW

Fact Follow-Up

1. What is the relative location of North Carolina within the Southeast?
2. What body of water borders North Carolina to the east?
3. What are the major landforms in North Carolina?

Think These Through

4. How can North Carolina be described both as an eastern and a southern state?
5. Use the map on page 3 to describe the location of North Carolina relative to the United States outside of the Southeast.
6. Describe how the landforms of the Southeast change from Virginia to Louisiana. Use the map on page 10 to help you write your description.

Using Information for Problem Solving, Decision Making, and Planning

Using Geography's Themes: Relative Location

Knowing the relative location of places can help you give clear directions to people who need them.

Imagine you have a new classmate. He needs to know his way around school, including the playground.

In this skill lesson you will practice using the geographic theme of relative location by helping your classmate.

Relative Location on a Playground

Look at the sketch to the right. It shows a playground seen from the air as though someone had flown overhead and made a drawing of it.

Notice the arrow in the upper right corner of the sketch. This symbol shows the cardinal directions of north, south, east, and west. The arrow is pointing north. The symbol does not give the intermediate directions, but you can figure those out because they are the directions in between the cardinal directions.

A tree is directly south of the arrow. In what cardinal direction from the arrow is the ball field? In what direction is the sandbox from the swing set? In what intermediate direction is the sandbox from the ball field?

The simple sketch you see can be made into a map if you use symbols for the drawings. What symbols can you think of for the swing sets, the sandbox, the track, the trees, and the ball field?

Use a sheet of paper to make a simple

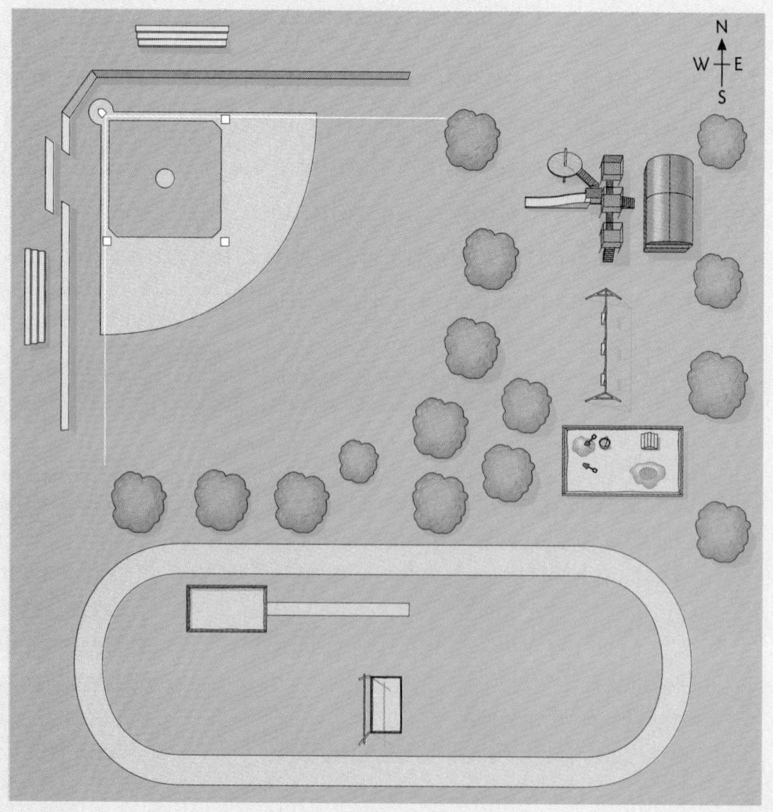

United States–Physical

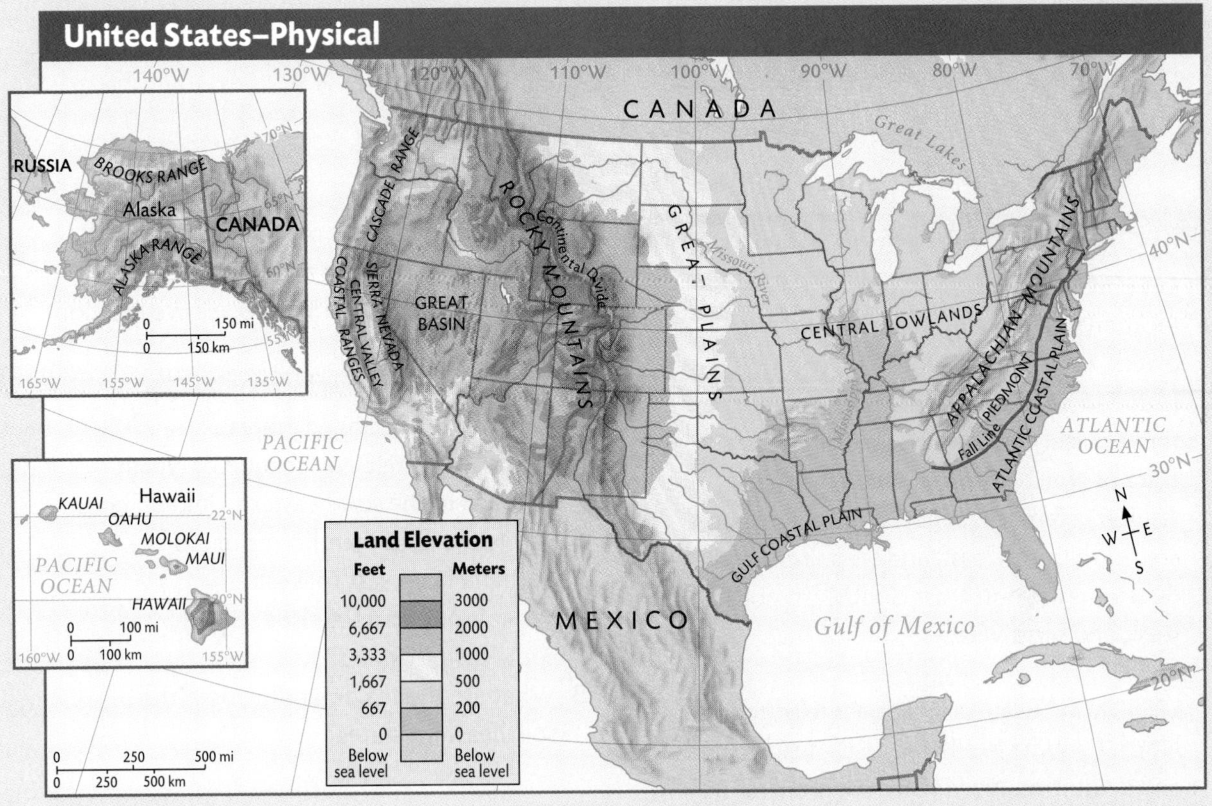

map of the sketch. Compare your map with one made by a classmate. How alike are they?

Using Relative Location on a Map of North Carolina

Now look at the map of North Carolina on pages 12–13. What symbols are used on that map to show different features? The directional arrow can be used to describe the relative locations of different places on the map. Choose a place in North Carolina and describe its relative location from Raleigh. What is the relative location of Cape Fear from Raleigh? What is the relative location of Lake Norman from the Sandhills? Can a classmate find other places you describe?

Using Relative Location on a Map of the United States

Next, look at the physical map of the United States above. Notice the location of North Carolina relative to landforms in the country.

Use the north arrow to describe the locations of landforms relative to North Carolina. Use cardinal and intermediate directions!

Describe North Carolina's location relative to the Great Plains. Describe North Carolina's location relative to the Central Lowlands, the Gulf Coastal Plain, and the Great Basin. Name and describe the location of mountains outside of North Carolina. Use the land elevation key (above) to find those landforms.

Chapter 1 Review

CHAPTER PREVIEW

LESSON 1 Relative location describes the location of a place by describing nearby places. To use relative location, you would use landmarks and directions to help someone find a place, whether it is your home or the state of North Carolina. A landmark is a familiar reference point. Cardinal directions are north, south, east, and west. Intermediate directions are northeast, southeast, northwest, and southwest.

LESSON 2 Relative location is used to locate North Carolina in relation to its nearby states and landforms. North Carolina is one of 50 states in the United States. It is an eastern state because it borders the Atlantic. It is a southern state bordered by Virginia, Tennessee, Georgia, and South Carolina. North Carolina shares major landforms with the rest of the Southeast.

TIME FOR TERMS

Location	Five Themes of Geography
relative location	landmark
cardinal directions	intermediate directions
landform	key
elevation	Coastal Plain
Piedmont	Appalachian Mountains

FACT FOLLOW-UP

1. How can landmarks help you describe the relative location of a place?
2. What are two types of landmarks?
3. How do the cardinal and intermediate directions help describe the relative location of places?
4. Describe the relative location of North Carolina in the United States.
5. Describe the relative location of North Carolina in the southeastern United States.
6. Name the major landforms of North Carolina from east to west.
7. What is one characteristic shared by all southeastern states?
8. What are the major landforms in the southeastern states?

THINK THESE THROUGH

9. What is the difference between landmarks and landforms?
10. Give directions from your home to the nearest service station. Remember to use landmarks and cardinal or intermediate directions.
11. Why is it important to be able to give accurate directions for reaching places?
12. What would the Southeast be like if it did not have one of its major landforms, the Appalachian Mountains?

SHARPENING SKILLS

13. Use the map on page 10 to describe the relative location of the following places in North Carolina. Use cardinal and intermediate directions.

a. the location of Charlotte relative to Kentucky.
b. the location of Mount Mitchell relative to Alabama.
c. the location of Wilmington relative to Savannah, Georgia.
d. the location of Morehead City relative to the Piedmont.
e. the location of Raleigh relative to Mount Mitchell.
f. the location of Wilmington relative to Norfolk, Virginia.

14. Use the physical map on pages 12–13 to answer the following questions.
a. What is the Appalachian Mountains' relative location to the Piedmont?
b. What is the Appalachian Mountains' relative location to the Coastal Plain?
c. What is the Piedmont's relative location to the Appalachian Mountains?
d. What is the Piedmont's relative location to the Coastal Plain?
e. What is the Coastal Plain's relative location to the Appalachian Mountains?
f. What is the Coastal Plain's relative location to the Piedmont?
g. What is Grandfather Mountain's relative location to the fall line?

PLACE LOCATION

Use the letters on the map below to locate the following places:

15. North Carolina.
16. Georgia.
17. the Atlantic Ocean.
18. South Carolina.
19. Washington, D.C.
20. Tennessee.
21. Virginia.

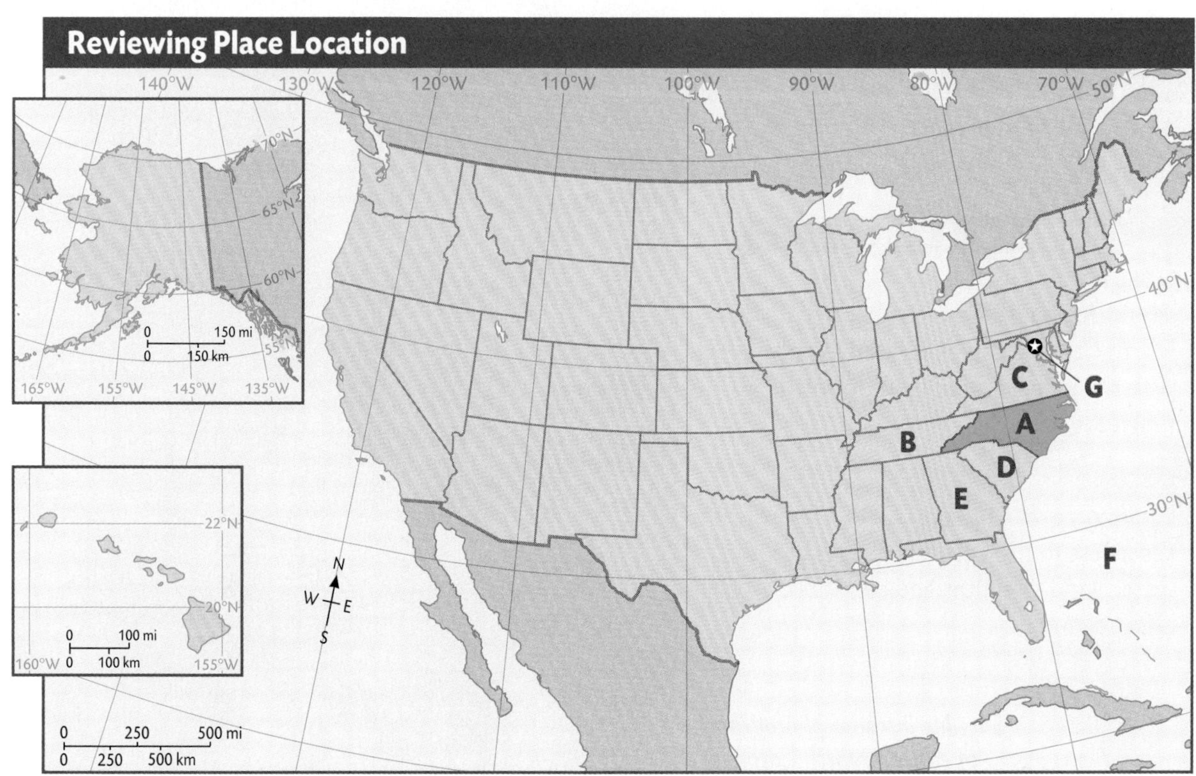

CHAPTER 2

North Carolina in the World

Earth looked like a big blue marble to astronauts flying to the moon. Astronauts and satellites flying closer to Earth can photograph the shapes of the continents. Astronauts can see the shape of North America. They do not see borders or state lines. Even so, they can easily pick out North Carolina when clouds do not cover it. What landforms make it easy for them to recognize North Carolina?

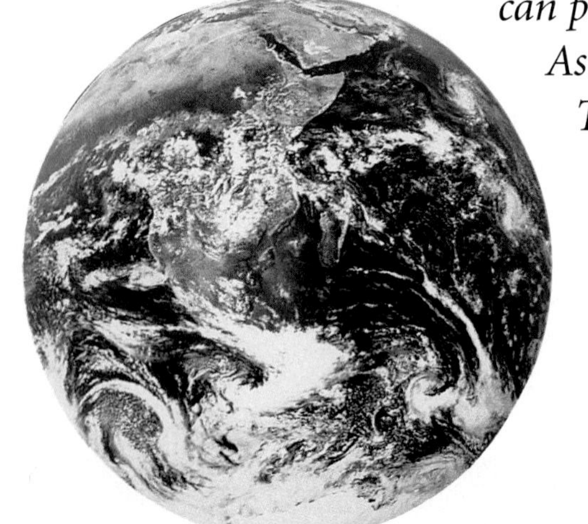

Earth from space.

CHAPTER PREVIEW

LESSON 1
Absolute Location
North Carolina can be located exactly with the global grid of latitude and longitude lines.

LESSON 2
Location and Climate
Closeness to the Equator, nearness to water, wind direction, and elevation affect climate.

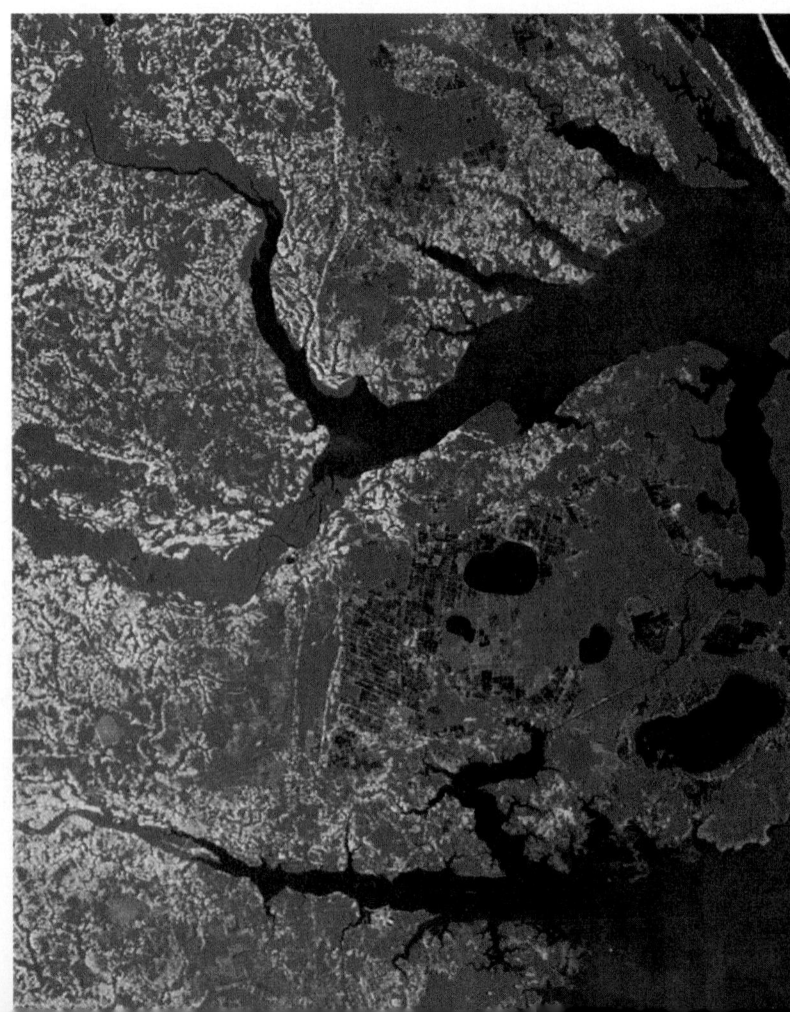

Satellite infrared photograph of eastern North Carolina.

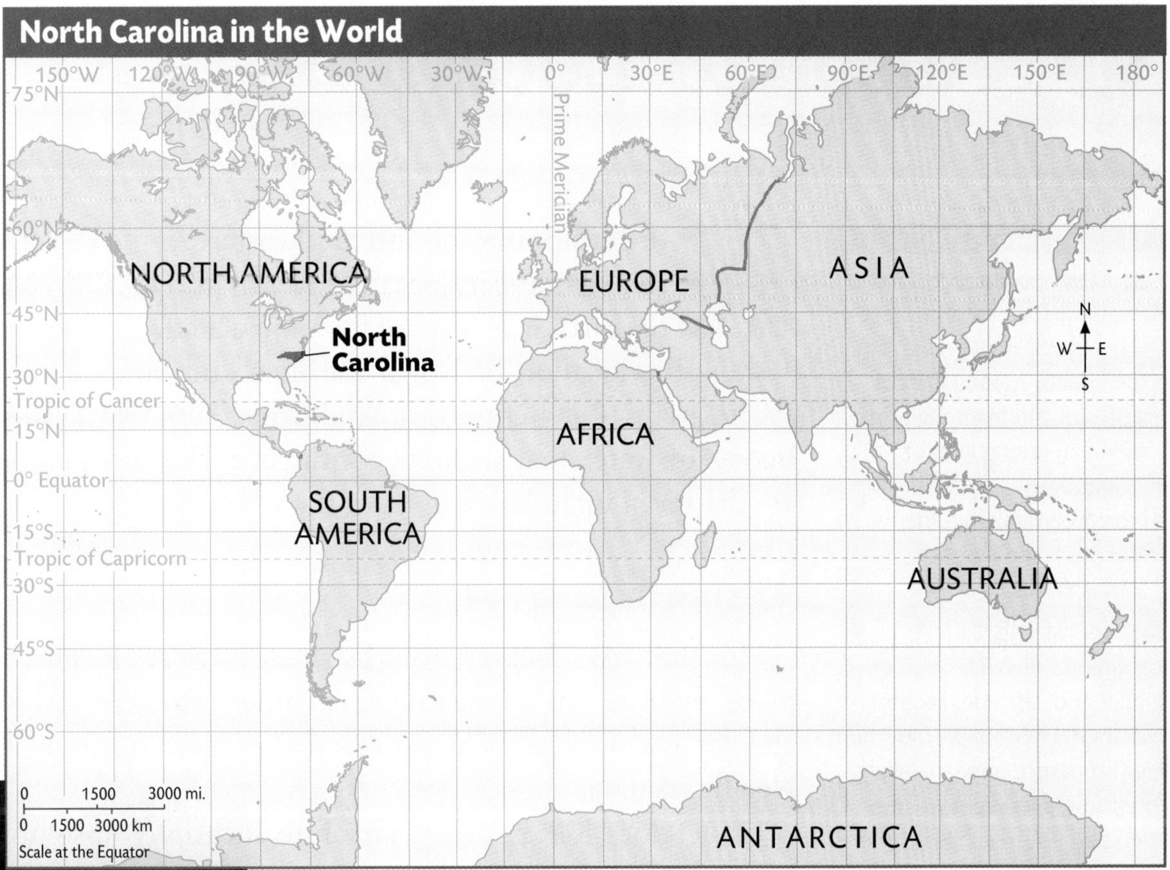

North Carolina in the World

NORTH AMERICA
North Carolina
SOUTH AMERICA
EUROPE
AFRICA
ASIA
AUSTRALIA
ANTARCTICA
Prime Meridian
Tropic of Cancer
0° Equator
Tropic of Capricorn
0 1500 3000 mi.
0 1500 3000 km
Scale at the Equator

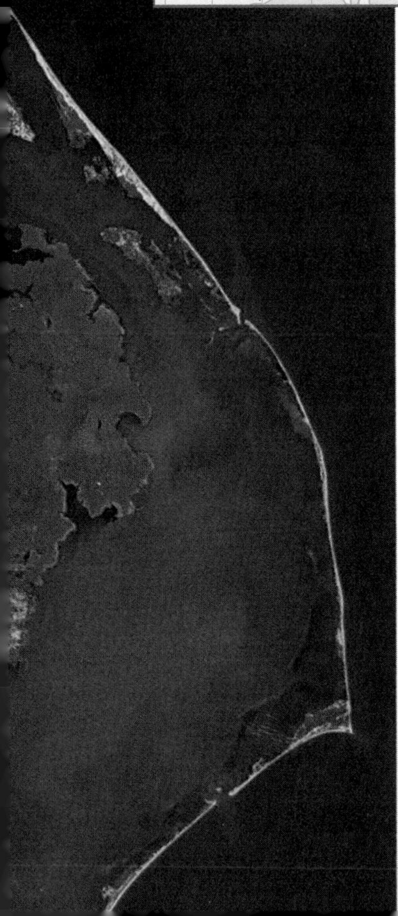

Rachel Carson

Rachel Carson loved the sea. She wrote many books about the sea and nature. Rachel Carson helped Americans understand the importance of the sea and seacoast environment.

In her book *Life at the Edge of the Sea,* Carson tells about a North Carolina experience. In Beaufort, she waded over to Bird Shoal at low tide. She found two defined grooves in the sand. Between those grooves was a faint line.

Carson followed the track carefully. She came upon a young horseshoe crab making its way out to sea.

Rachel Carson traveled the world to understand the sea. She found some of her understanding along the North Carolina coast.

Absolute Location

LESSON PREVIEW

Key Ideas

- Absolute location of a place is measured in degrees from the Equator (along lines of latitude) and from the prime meridian (along lines of longitude).
- North Carolina is in the Northern and Western Hemispheres.

Key Terms

continents, absolute location, global grid, latitude, Equator, Northern Hemisphere, Southern Hemisphere, degree, parallels, longitude, meridians, prime meridian, Western Hemisphere, Eastern Hemisphere.

North Carolina and the southeastern United States share landforms because they share a location on the earth. The maps of the United States in Chapter 1 show the location of North Carolina and other states. World maps show countries, landforms, continents, and bodies of water that separate continents. The **continents** are the seven main landmasses of the world.

Absolute Location

In the last chapter you learned how to locate a place because of its nearness to other places. In this chapter you will learn how to find the exact location of North Carolina.

Exact location is called **absolute location**. Absolute location helps people locate any place on earth exactly.

To find the absolute location of places, mapmakers use a **global grid**. The grid is made up of imaginary lines running north and south and east and west on the earth. The global grid helps you find the absolute location of any place, including North Carolina. The maps below and on page 19 show the global grid and the location of the continents.

The continents of the world are shown below. The global grid is drawn on the map. *Through which continents does the Equator cross?*

Lines of Latitude

Global grid lines drawn east and west around the globe are lines of **latitude.** The **Equator** is the longest line of latitude, ringing the earth at its middle.

The earth is an almost perfect ball or sphere. The Equator

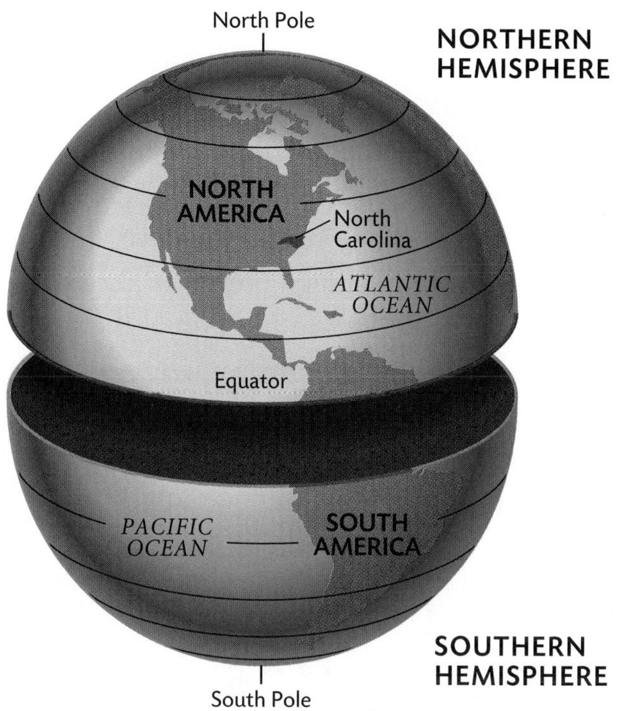

The Equator at 0° latitude divides the sphere of the earth into the Northern Hemisphere and the Southern Hemisphere. *North Carolina lies within which hemisphere?*

divides the earth into two equal parts called hemispheres. Hemisphere means half of a sphere. The area of the earth north of the Equator to the North Pole is the **Northern Hemisphere.** The area of the earth south of the Equator to the South Pole is the **Southern Hemisphere.**

The Equator is given the latitude measurement of 0°. The symbol "°" is used for **degree,** the unit for measuring latitude and longitude. It is written to the right of the measurement. Lines of latitude in the Northern Hemisphere are measured in latitude degrees north. Lines of latitude in the Southern Hemisphere are measured in latitude degrees south.

Because the Equator is 0°, the greater the number of degrees of latitude, the farther a place is away from the Equator. A place 20 degrees north of the Equator is closer to the Equator than a place 35 degrees north of it. There are 90 degrees of latitude between the Equator and the North Pole and 90 degrees of latitude between the Equator and the South Pole.

Lines of latitude are also called **parallels.** This name is used because all points on any line of latitude are parallel,

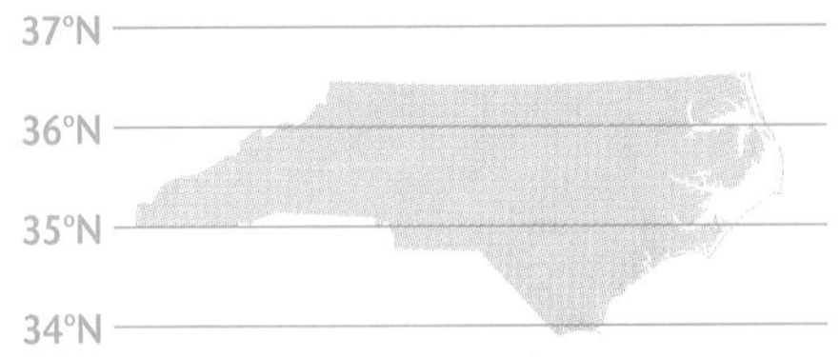

The illustration above shows the lines of latitude that cross North Carolina. *What is another name for lines of latitude?*

or the same distance, from the Equator.

The figure on page 21 shows the earth split in two parts along the Equator. The Equator separates the earth into the Northern Hemisphere and the Southern Hemisphere. Because North Carolina is north of the Equator, it is in the Northern Hemisphere.

North Carolina's northern border is almost 37 degrees north of the Equator. The southern tip of the state, near the city of Wilmington, is about 34 degrees north of the Equator. Therefore, North Carolina is located between latitudes 34°N and 37°N. The capital "N" shows that the latitudes are north of the Equator.

EYEWITNESS TO HISTORY

Mapping North Carolina: 1526–Present

Mapmakers show the location and features of a place on maps. Through the years, mapmakers of North Carolina have improved the tools of mapmaking to help people better understand the features and location of North Carolina.

North Carolina first appeared on a map in 1526. Spanish mapmaker Juan Vespucci drew a world map (right) with a direction symbol. The lines on the map were navigation aids. They did not give absolute location.

John White's map of coastal Carolina (left) includes a direction symbol. It shows a surprisingly accurate map of the Outer Banks. Compare it to the satellite image (page 23) of the same region.

Edward Moseley drew maps of North Carolina in 1733. His map of Ocracoke Inlet shows the latitude. The scale gives accurate distances within the colony.

OCACOCK INLET. Latitude 34°. 55'N°

Meridians of Longitude

Knowing how far north or south a place is from the Equator gives us only half the information we need to find its absolute location. Lines of **longitude** give us the rest of the information—a place's east or west location.

Lines of longitude are also measured in degrees. But instead of being drawn parallel to the Equator, each line runs north to south from the North Pole to the South Pole. These north-south lines of longitude are called **meridians**.

The **prime meridian** is the starting point for measuring longitude. It is given the longitude of 0°.

Like the Equator, the prime meridian also splits the

Vespucci's map

In 1884, the meridian of the Royal Greenwich Observatory in England was chosen throughout the world as the prime meridian of 0°. The 1896 railroad map (above) gives correct longitude measurements for North Carolina and South Carolina.

Today, mapmakers (inset) use tools of high technology to make maps that show more than the state's location. Satellite images help mapmakers draw maps of North Carolina climate, vegetation, use of the environment, and movement of people.

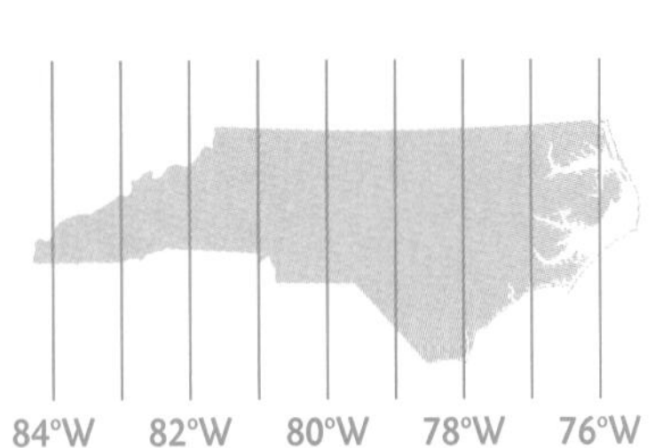

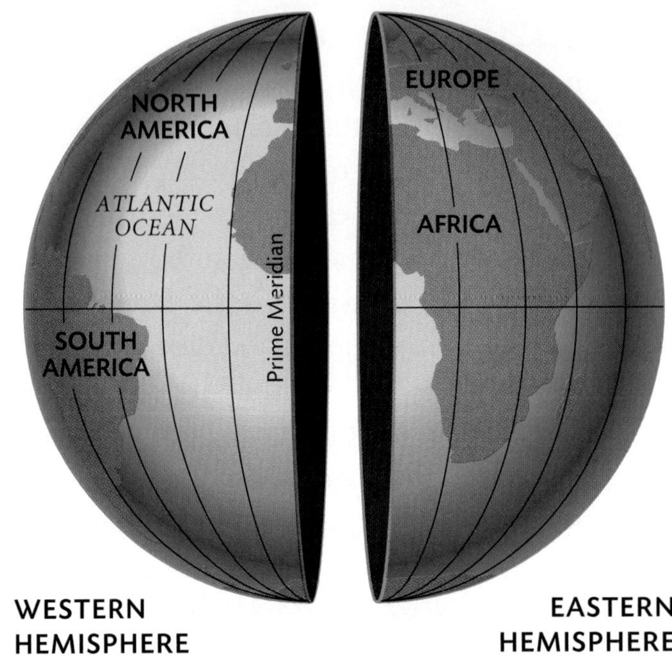

The prime meridian splits the earth into the Western Hemisphere and the Eastern Hemisphere. *In which hemisphere is North Carolina? The state lies within which meridians of longitude?*

earth in half. The prime meridian cuts through England, France, Spain, and Africa. The area of the earth west of the prime meridian is the **Western Hemisphere**. The area of the earth east of the prime meridian is the **Eastern Hemisphere**, as the globe above shows.

The other meridian lines around the globe give longitude measurements. These tell us the distance from the prime meridian in west or east degrees. Meridian lines to the west of the prime meridian are measured in longitude degrees west. Lines to the east of the prime meridian are measured in longitude degrees east.

Longitude in eastern North Carolina is halfway between the 75th and 76th meridians. That is written as 75°30′W. This means the Outer Banks is 75 and a half degrees west of the prime meridian. The western border is at 84°18′W, more than 84 degrees west of the prime meridian.

Time Zones

Longitudinal lines are important in determining time zones around the globe. For every 15 degrees of longitude, time changes by one hour. When it is 8:00 A.M. in North Carolina, it is 7:00 A.M. in Chicago, Illinois. Moving farther west, it is 6:00 A.M. in Denver, Colorado, and 5:00 A.M. in San Francisco.

North Carolina's Absolute Location

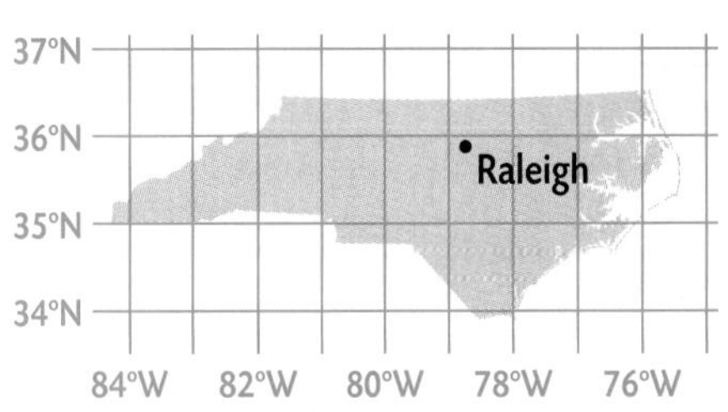

Look at the lines of latitude and longitude above. Raleigh is south of the 36°N latitude. *What is its location on a meridian of longitude?*

Together, the parallels of latitude and the meridians of longitude create the global grid on the earth's surface. With this grid of imaginary lines on maps and globes, North Carolina can be exactly located.

Lines of latitude and longitude give North Carolina's absolute location. You have learned that North Carolina is north of the Equator in the Northern Hemisphere, between 33°N and 37°N. North Carolina is west of the prime meridian in the Western Hemisphere, between 75°W and 85°W.

Where Do You Live?

Absolute and relative location show you exactly where North Carolina is located. If you want to know where a place is in North Carolina, you can find its closest latitude and longitude on a map.

To write absolute location, write the latitude measurement first, then the longitude measurement. Raleigh's absolute location would be written as 36°N, 79°W, because it is closest to those measurements on the global grid.

LESSON 1 REVIEW

Fact Follow-Up

1. What do mapmakers use to find the absolute location of places?
2. What are lines of latitude? What is the longest one called?
3. What are lines of longitude? What is the one at 0° called?
4. In which hemispheres is North Carolina located?

Think These Through

5. Why is a grid system useful in describing the absolute location of places?
6. Would you choose absolute or relative location to give directions to your home? Why?

Location and Climate

LESSON PREVIEW

Key Ideas

- North Carolina's climate is affected by its distance from the Equator.
- North Carolina's climate is affected also by its nearness to water, wind currents, and elevation.

Key Terms

climate, axis, temperate, humid subtropical, ocean current, precipitation, rain shadow effect

Imagine that you have a sled. Where in North Carolina would you be most likely to use it? In Wilmington? In Burlington? Or in Boone?

To answer these questions you need to know two things—the location and climate of each place. **Climate** describes the patterns of weather in a place over many years.

Climate and the Earth's Tilt

Every year North Carolina goes through a change of seasons—summer, autumn, winter, and spring. The seasons change as the earth rotates around the sun. The **axis** of the earth, an imaginary straight line that passes through both poles, is tilted. As the earth orbits, or goes around, the sun in one year, the earth's surface is tilted away from and then back toward the sun.

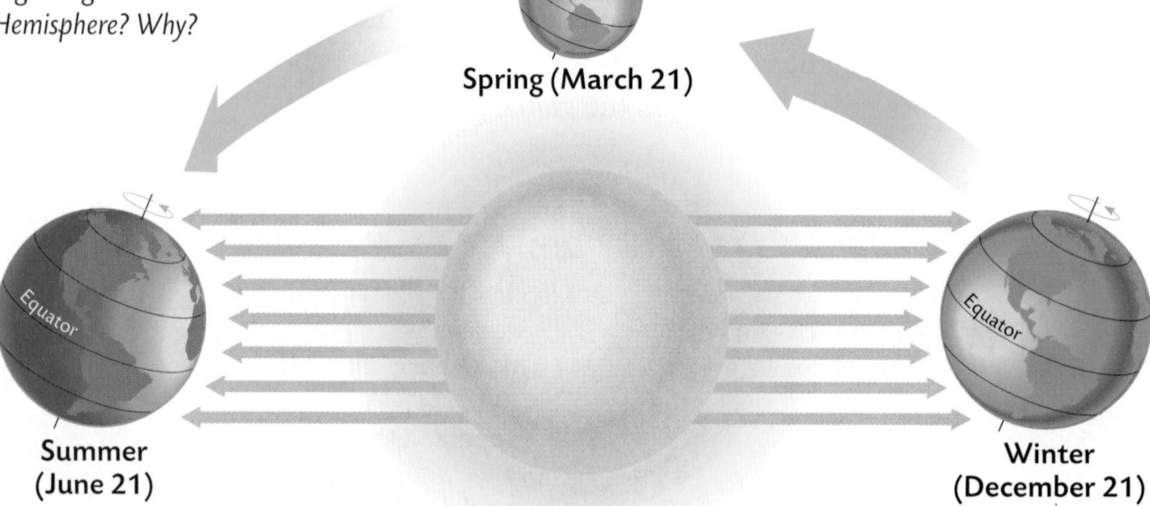

The Northern Hemisphere receives direct sunlight in the summer, beginning on June 21. *When winter begins on December 21 in the Northern Hemisphere, what season is beginning in the Southern Hemisphere? Why?*

Because of the earth's tilt, sunlight falls unevenly across the earth. Areas of the earth's surface along the Equator get more direct sunlight, as shown in the diagram on page 26. Because the sunlight hits the Equator directly all year long, the climate there is always hot and usually rainy.

In other places, the sun's rays do not beat down from directly overhead. Rather, they strike the earth at an angle, spreading the rays out, and lessening the heat. These places have cooler climates. The farther away a place is from the Equator, the cooler its climate.

Over a year's time, the orbit of the earth changes the temperature of the earth. We see these changes through the seasons: summer, autumn, winter, and spring.

On June 21, the Northern Hemisphere is tilted toward the sun and receives direct sun rays. That date is the beginning of summer in North Carolina and the rest of the Northern Hemisphere. By December 21, the Southern Hemisphere is tilted toward the sun and the Northern Hemisphere is tilted away from the sun. That date is the beginning of summer in the Southern Hemisphere and the beginning of winter in the Northern Hemisphere.

Late afternoon sunlight is not as hot on the beach in North Carolina as it is at noon because the sun is not directly overhead. *How is this similar to places located away from the Equator?*

North Carolina's Climate

North Carolina is located midway between the Equator and the Arctic in the middle latitudes. The middle latitudes—from 23.5° to 66.5° in the Northern and Southern Hemispheres—have a **temperate** climate. Temperate climates are mild. They are not as hot as the Equator, nor as cold as the poles. The climates have a variety of temperature and rainfall. There are several types of temperate climates within the middle latitudes (see map, page 28).

North Carolina has the humid subtropical type of temperate climate. The **humid subtropical** climate brings mild and rainy winters, humid springs, and hot summers. Sometimes it snows in this type of climate. Where might that happen in North Carolina?

GAMES People Play

Kite Flying What does it take to fly a kite? Wind, of course. If you go to the coast, you can fly a kite all day. The constant wind makes kite flying easy. In the mountains, if you go high enough you'll find strong winds. In the Piedmont, you will have a harder time flying your kite. You have to wait for brisk winds in fall and spring.

Some people like to be part of the kite. That's when they hang glide off Jockey's Ridge or Grandfather Mountain.

Place **The Western Hemisphere contains every type of climate because of differing elevations, wind currents, and differing distances from the Equator and from water.** *The map shows North Carolina located within which climate region?*

Other Influences on Our Climate Climate is mostly influenced by nearness to the Equator. Other aspects of location also affect the climate of a place. Nearness to large bodies of water, the direction of winds, and the elevation of the land also affect North Carolina's climate.

Nearness to Water North Carolina's climate is affected by two large bodies of water. The Atlantic Ocean borders the eastern part of the state. A few miles off the coast a large, warm current called the Gulf Stream flows through the ocean. An **ocean current** is a strong stream of water running through the ocean. The warm current of the Gulf Stream helps provide North Carolina with mild winters and humid, hot summers.

The Gulf of Mexico south of the United States (see map, page 28) also influences North Carolina's climate. Winds blowing from the Gulf bring the state much of its precipitation. **Precipitation** is moisture that falls from the sky as rain, snow, sleet, or hail.

Wind Currents Which way does the wind blow at your house? Have you noticed that wind and rain come from the same direction?

On the coast, winds may blow from the Northeast or Southwest. Winds from the West and Northwest also blow over the mountains. Winds affecting most of the state blow from the Southwest, from the Gulf of Mexico. Summer storms occur when these winds meet those coming from the West.

In winter, snow forms if two or more air currents meet. The state's largest snowfalls occur when warm air from the Gulf of Mexico collides with winds from the West carrying "polar air" from the northern states and Canada. This cold air chills the wet air, and North Carolina gets snow.

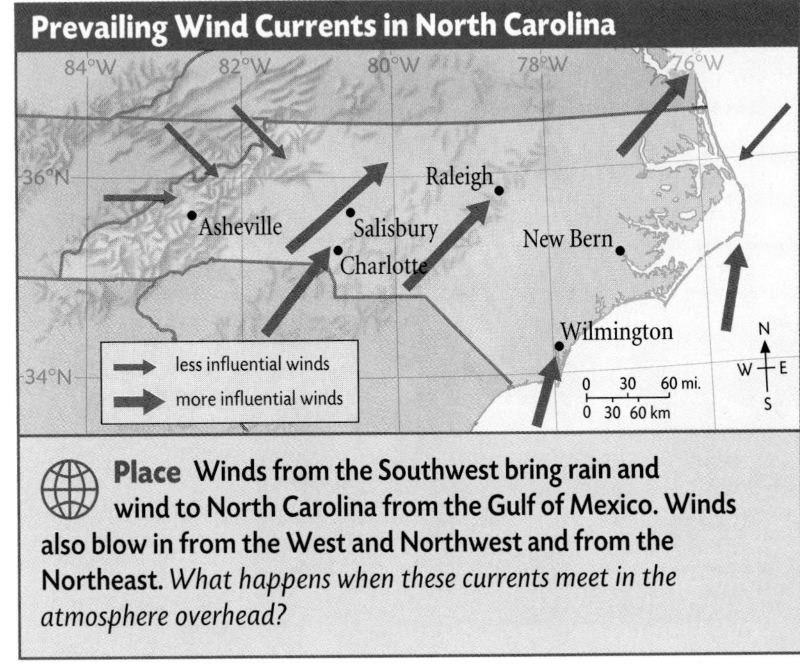

Place Winds from the Southwest bring rain and wind to North Carolina from the Gulf of Mexico. Winds also blow in from the West and Northwest and from the Northeast. *What happens when these currents meet in the atmosphere overhead?*

WORD ORIGINS

High Point does not have the highest elevation in North Carolina. Yet it deserves its name. The Guilford County town was planned as a station on the railroad close to Salem, in Forsyth County. High Point's elevation of 940 feet (282 m) made it the highest point on the North Carolina Railroad.

Elevation and Climate All climates change by elevation, no matter what the latitude is. Temperature drops in higher elevations. In the summer, many people like to travel to the higher elevations of the mountains for cooler temperatures. In winter, people go to the mountains to ski.

The largest annual snows fall above 5,000 feet (1,500 m). For example, Mount Mitchell, the highest point in the state at 6,648 feet (1,994 m), averages about 60 inches (152 cm) of snow a year.

The mountains receive precipitation when moist air

LIVING IN HIGHLANDS

The Wettest Spot in North Carolina

The North Carolina mountains attract people all year long because of their climate. The autumn leaves draw many tourists, and the winter snows bring in skiers. Some people think summer is the best time to visit because of the cooler weather.

Many people do go to the mountains in June, July, and August to be cool and to see beautiful waterfalls. Highlands, North Carolina, is a favorite spot for mountain visitors.

Besides shops, hotels, restaurants, and hiking trails, Highlands, in Macon County, boasts something special. It has the highest rainfall in North Carolina. Some say it has the highest rainfall in the eastern United States. About 80 inches (203 cm) of rain a year fall on Highlands.

The elevation and the moist southerly winds forced up the mountain are the cause of much of this rain.

In the 1800s, many sick people from different parts of the United States traveled to Highlands to get well. They wanted to breathe the cool, clean air. Highlands was advertised as the "greatest health and pleasure resort in the United States."

Some plants of the forests near Highlands were thought to make good medicine. Beebalm, a type of mint, blooms in August. Some believed joe-pye weed cured typhoid fever.

Because of the high rainfall, animals and plants usually found in more tropical spots inhabit this special place in the North Carolina mountains.

A British scientist regularly comes to Highlands to film and study its salamanders. Fungi, ferns, and lichens flourish in the wet woods and boggy marshes.

The mountains of North Carolina receive rain from wind carrying warm, moist air from the Gulf of Mexico. *If the warm, moist air collides with cold, dry air from the North, what can happen?*

from the Gulf of Mexico pushes up their sides. In the summer, rain results. In the winter, snow and rain fall.

The eastern sides of the mountains and the nearby Piedmont receive slightly less precipitation than the western sides. As the illustration above shows, higher peaks block some winds carrying precipitation across the mountains. This is called the **rain shadow effect**.

The Piedmont and Coastal Plain still receive plenty of rain. Winds off the Gulf of Mexico push moisture northeast through the Coastal Plain. Sometimes the rain in the Piedmont and Coastal Plain comes from hurricanes or tropical storms in the Atlantic Ocean. These storms can hit the coast and move inland, carrying plenty of moisture and high wind, even far from the coast.

What would YOU do?

Suppose you want to take a summer vacation. Should you think about elevation and temperature in North Carolina?

Some higher parts of the mountains are cool and rainy. Others are cool and dry.

Beaches are hot and windy. The Piedmont has hot summers with afternoon thunderstorms.

Where would you be comfortable in North Carolina in the summer?

LESSON 2 REVIEW

Fact Follow-Up

1. What is climate?
2. Is climate cooler or warmer close to the Equator?
3. In which climate region is North Carolina?

Think These Through

4. What influences North Carolina's climate?
5. How does the earth's tilt affect the seasons?
6. Where would you use that sled mentioned in the beginning of the lesson?

The Five Themes of Geography: Location

Using Geography's Themes: Absolute Location

Imagine that you are riding with your parents from the grocery store and suddenly your car breaks down. You walk to the nearest telephone and call for help. Relative location will help you describe where you are and where your car is.

Imagine that you are on a big fishing boat so far out in the Atlantic Ocean that you can't see the land. The engine fails and you use the radio to call the Coast Guard for help. Absolute location will describe your location.

Relative location, as you know, describes the location of one place in relation to other places. Absolute location describes where a place is located exactly on the global grid. Both kinds of location describe where places are, but are used in different ways. The use of absolute location to describe exact location of a place requires practice.

Look at the diagrams of the globe on pages 21 and 24. The pictures show the earth's hemispheres. In which hemispheres is North Carolina located?

California is located on the West Coast of the United States. Use the globes to describe the two hemispheres in which California is located. What other states in the United States do you know? Can you describe the hemispheres in which these states are located?

Now look at the map on page 33 to practice using absolute location. Use the map to describe the absolute location of the capitals of the states in the Southeast region of the United States. Remember that the United States is in the Northern and Western Hemispheres.

When writing the location, write the line of latitude first, then the line of longitude. Abbreviate North as N and West as W. For example, Raleigh's location is written as 36°N, 79°W. Compare your answers with a classmate's.

Next, choose a place on the map from North Carolina. Write the absolute location of that place on a piece of paper and give the paper to a classmate. Can the classmate locate the place? See if your classmate can find other places using absolute locations.

Use the absolute locations given below to find places on the map on page 33. Include the state where these places are located.

a. 35°N, 90°W
b. 30°N, 90°W
c. 35°N, 81°W
d. 33°N, 80°W
e. 34°N, 84°W
f. 37°N, 76°W
g. 38°N, 85°W
h. 34°N, 78°W

Finally, practice using the grid system to estimate distance. Each degree of latitude on the global grid is equal to about 69 miles (111 km). About how many miles apart are Charlotte, North Carolina, and Savannah, Georgia?

Distances of degrees of longitude change. At the Equator, the distance between 85°W and 86°W, for example, is about 69 miles. At the poles, the distance measures 0 miles.

You can still figure distances between places by using the map scale. Maps show areas as much smaller than they really are. A **map scale** is a divided line showing the length used to represent the real measurements of the area on the map.

On the map scale above, one inch equals 250 miles. How far is New Orleans, Louisiana, from Tallahassee, Florida? Montgomery, Alabama, from Richmond, Virginia?

Chapter 2 Review

LESSONS LEARNED

LESSON 1 Absolute location gives the exact location of a place. Imaginary lines of the global grid called latitude and longitude help us pinpoint the exact locations of any place on the earth's surface. Degrees of latitude are measured north and south of the Equator. Degrees of longitude are measured east and west of the prime meridian. North Carolina is north of the Equator in the Northern Hemisphere and west of the prime meridian in the Western Hemisphere.

LESSON 2 Location affects climate. A place's nearness to the Equator, to large bodies of water, and to wind currents influence its climate. Elevation also affects climate. North Carolina has a humid subtropical climate. Its climate is influenced by the Gulf of Mexico and Atlantic Ocean, wind currents from the West and Southwest, and the presence of the mountains.

TIME FOR TERMS

continents	absolute location
global grid	latitude
Equator	Northern Hemisphere
Southern Hemisphere	degree
parallels	longitude
meridians	prime meridian
Western Hemisphere	Eastern Hemisphere
climate	axis
temperate	humid subtropical
ocean current	precipitation
rain shadow effect	map scale

FACT FOLLOW-UP

1. How are the Equator and prime meridian alike? How are they different?
2. What is the global grid?
3. How are parallels and meridians alike and different?
4. How many degrees of latitude are there between the North and South Poles?
5. Which—latitude or longitude—is used in determining time zones?
6. Why does sunlight fall unevenly across the earth?
7. What causes changes in the temperature of the earth?
8. Describe the climate of North Carolina.
9. What, other than nearness to the Equator, influences the climate of North Carolina?

THINK THESE THROUGH

10. Is absolute or relative location more important in locating places within North Carolina? Explain why.
11. Describe the absolute and relative locations of North Carolina.
12. Which areas in North Carolina would you expect to receive the most and the least rainfall? Explain why.
13. What is the relationship between elevation and climate?

SHARPENING SKILLS

14. On a short trip around town, would you be more likely to use absolute or relative location? Explain why.

15. If you are traveling from Charlotte to Raleigh, would you be more likely to use absolute or relative location? Explain why.
16. If you were traveling to northern Canada, how would knowing about absolute location be helpful?
17. Why do airplane pilots need absolute location when flying to their destinations?
18. Who else uses absolute location? Why?

PLACE LOCATION

Use the letters on the map below to locate the following places:

19. North America.
20. South America.
21. Australia.
22. Asia.
23. Europe.
24. North Carolina.
25. Antarctica.
26. Name the continents through which the prime meridian runs.
27. Name the continent in the Western Hemisphere through which the Equator runs.

Use the degrees of latitude and longitude on the map to answer the following questions:

28. What degree of longitude is given to the prime meridian?
29. What meridian of longitude runs closest to North Carolina?
30. What parallel of latitude runs closest to North Carolina?

Reviewing Place Location

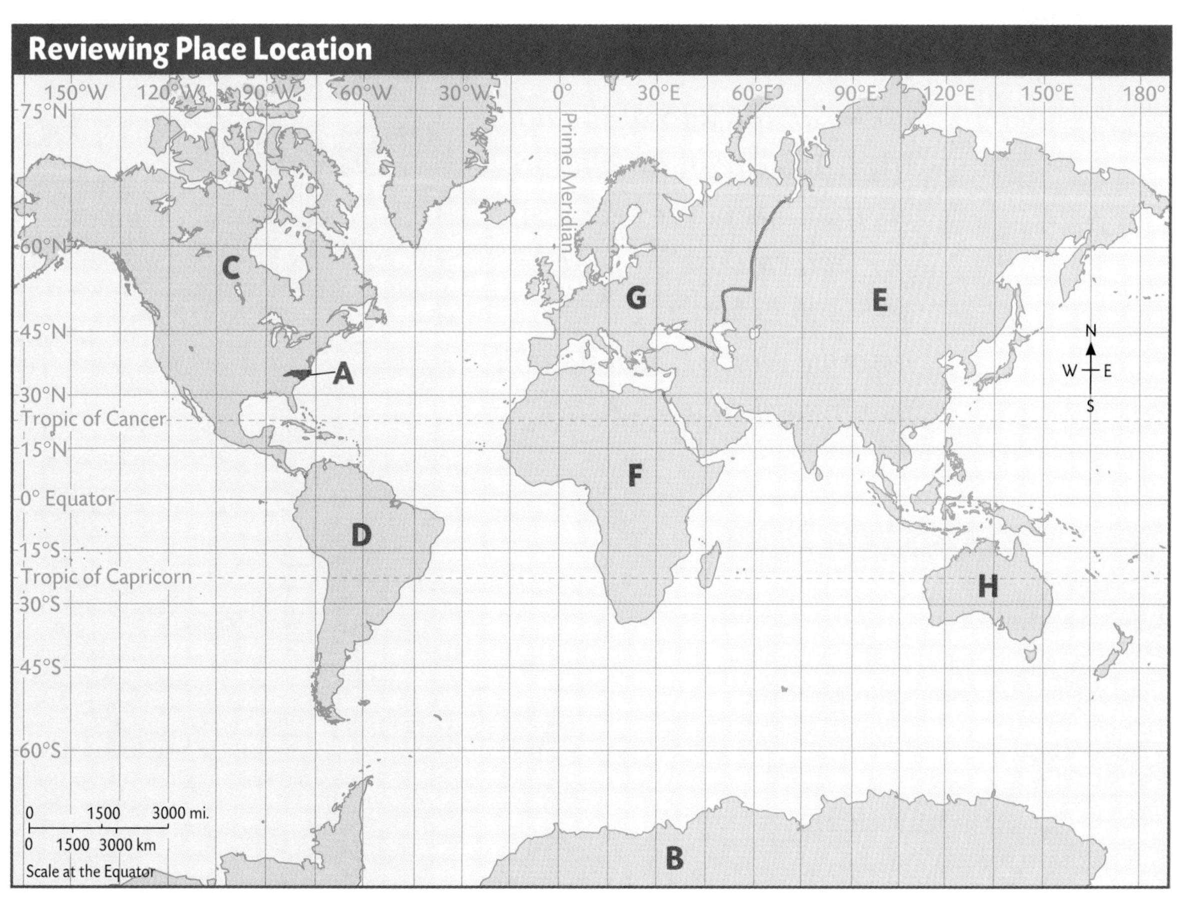

CHAPTER 3

North Carolina's Physical Characteristics

The cardinal, the state bird of North Carolina

Walk softly and slowly when you go to Joyce Kilmer Memorial Forest in the Appalachian Mountains in southwestern North Carolina.

Use all your senses. You might hear the wind rush through the trees. Beneath your feet, the forest floor feels soft where poplar leaves have fallen and become part of the soil. Smell the sap of the tall pine trees. Look up to see the tops of the tall trees. You are in an old forest that has never been cut.

You can use all your senses to experience and describe North Carolina and its physical characteristics.

CHAPTER PREVIEW

LESSON 1
Vegetation
Physical characteristics of North Carolina include its forests and other plant life.

LESSON 2
Natural Resources
North Carolina has an abundance of natural resources.

North Carolina–Mineral and Water Resources

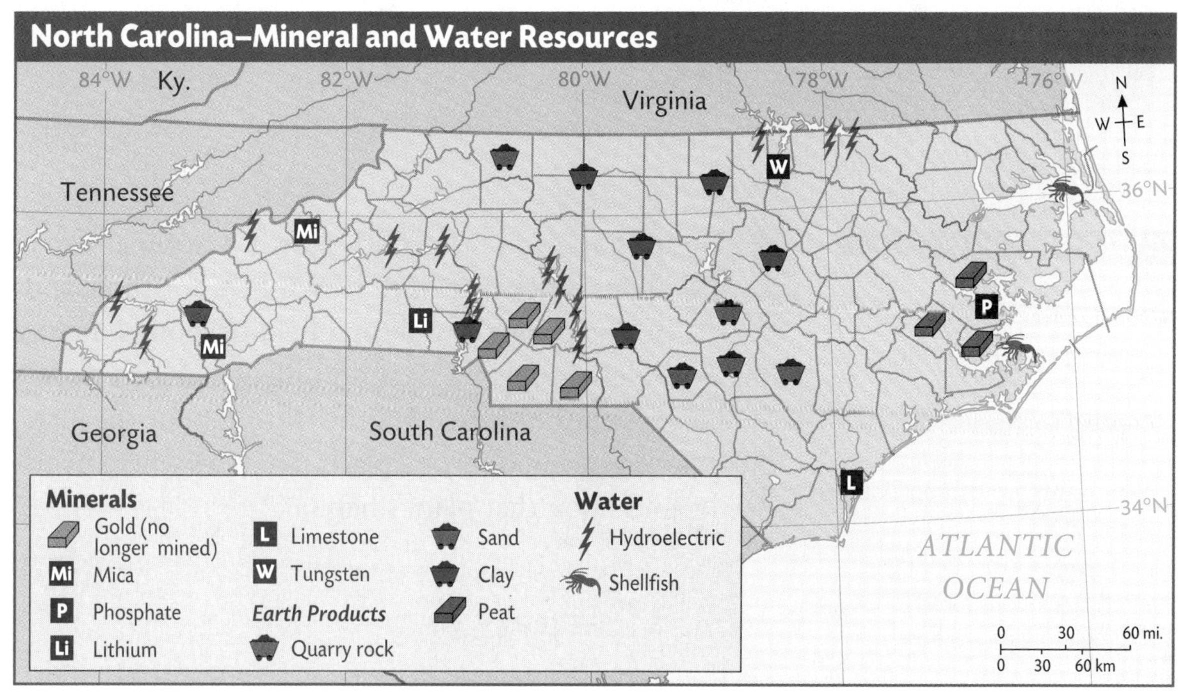

Joyce Kilmer Memorial Forest

CAROLINA CONNECTION

Christmas Trees

A Christmas tree from North Carolina towered over the White House lawn in 1971. Foresters chose the 60-foot-tall Fraser fir from the Pisgah National Forest. A flatbed truck hauled the tree to Washington, D.C. Park Service employees worked for days just to make sure the tree stood straight. Then they spent more time carefully stringing thousands of lights on the soft branches.

The president and his family decorated a North Carolina Christmas tree inside the White House in 1995 (right). The tree in the White House living room grew on a Christmas tree farm in Ashe County.

Lesson 1 Vegetation

LESSON PREVIEW

Key Ideas

- Forests cover much of North Carolina, especially in the Coastal Plain and deep Appalachian Mountains.
- A wide variety of habitats helps plants grow throughout the state.

Key Terms

habitat, deciduous forests, evergreen forests, conifers, canopy

Outdoors you can find North Carolina native plants, ones that have grown here for thousands of years. Take a walk in a field or along a nature path. You might see some common plants. Queen Anne's lace, daisies, and broomsedge grow throughout the state. Other plants grow in only one place. The sites where plants grow depend upon that plant's habitat.

Carolina Habitats

A **habitat** is a place where a plant or an animal naturally lives. In a favorable habitat a plant or animal survives because it receives shelter and nourishment. North Carolina has a mild climate and a variety of soils, so plants of all sorts grow well.

North Carolina has a favorable habitat for trees. Only a few places in North Carolina are treeless. You can find flat grasslands on the coast and bare rocks called balds in the high mountains. In most other places, you will find forests.

Young people explore the parts of a tree at the Cradle of Forestry in Pisgah National Forest. *Why does North Carolina have a favorable habitat for trees?*

Deciduous forests in temperate climates shed their leaves once a year during autumn. Maple, birch, and oak trees are deciduous. Many North Carolina deciduous trees have been cut to make room for homes and farms.

Evergreen forests of pine, fir, and spruce keep their needlelike leaves all year. These forests grow well in the temperate latitudes. We use them as a source of lumber and paper. The forests of North Carolina contain many **conifers**, which are cone-bearing trees.

North Carolina still has a mixture of deciduous and evergreen forests. Pine trees are easily seen all year, especially during the winter after the deciduous trees have lost their golden and scarlet leaves.

A Carolina Forest

Here is how a forest grows. A thunderstorm produces lightning. Lightning strikes a tree and causes a fire. Hundreds of trees burn. Only charred trunks are left. Instead of shade, sunlight reaches the forest floor.

Soon the wind and birds carry hundreds of types of seed to the forest floor. Some seeds fall on the ground and sprout. The ashes of the old forest and rain help the new plants grow.

Some of North Carolina's forests have deciduous trees. Deciduous means the leaves change color before falling from the trees. *When do the leaves fall?*

At first, grasses such as crabgrass and broomsedge cover the once burned area. Pine and cedar seedlings begin to sprout. Within ten years or so, pine and cedar trees emerge from the grass.

The evergreen trees grow fast. They create the first canopy. A **canopy** is the uppermost covering of taller trees.

The Weymouth Woods Preserve contains longleaf pines and other pine trees that grow well in the Sandhills of the Coastal Plain. *How do pines create a canopy in a forest?*

Their branches spread above smaller trees growing underneath. Our state flowering tree, the dogwood, thrives in the shade of tall pines.

Hardwood trees, often oak, hickory, and maple, also grow in the shade of pines. By the time the hardwoods get big, the pines are old and blow over in the wind. Meanwhile, bushes and shrubs sprout beneath the trees, providing a good habitat for wildlife.

The Joyce Kilmer Memorial Forest in the Appalachian Mountains and Weymouth Woods Sandhills Nature Preserve in the Coastal Plain are two of North Carolina's oldest forests. Their canopy provides so much shade that there is little undergrowth.

The location of a forest or field changes the type of vegetation. Scrub oaks are found under pines on the coastal tidelands. The longleaf pine, the state tree, was once the most common pine in the southeastern section of the state. When many longleaf pines were cut, other types of pine took their place.

In the Piedmont and Appalachian Mountains, deciduous forests of hickory, oak, and maple grow. Once the

WORD ORIGINS

Weymouth Woods, a preserve of hardwood swamp trees and longleaf pines near Southern Pines, was given to the state in 1963 by Mrs. Katherine Boyd. The 425-acre (170-square hectometer) forest had been the Boyds' estate.

The Boyds had named their home for Weymouth, England, where they had seen trees that reminded them of eastern North Carolina. The pines there might have been taken back to England by early explorers of North Carolina.

elevation reaches about 5,000 feet (1,500 m) above sea level, hardwoods give way to evergreen forests. In these high places, such evergreen trees as the fir and the spruce take up much of the forests.

North Carolina is sometimes called "the land of the longleaf pine." *Why aren't there as many longleaf pines today as there were in the past?*

Plant Life

Native North Carolina plants might be growing right outside your classroom. A few native plants might thrive only in a swamp or on a mountaintop. You can find other

CONNECTIONS

Geography & the Arts

Quilts and Quilting

There are many ways to show the vegetation and other resources of North Carolina. Some people take pictures. Other people write books. Some draw maps.

Quilters can make beautiful pictures of the trees and plants of North Carolina. The Southern Highland Craft Guild's Folk Art Center displays a quilt sewn by women from the Mountains.

Bright and colorful, the "Land of the Sky" quilt (right) shows tumbling waterfalls and trees decorated with autumn colors.

The quilters also sewed native plants and animals into the design. People square-dance across the quilt. Cherokee baskets are arranged on a table. One woman on the quilt is sewing a quilt!

You can see the quilt at the Folk Art Center near Asheville, where it is on permanent display. You can look at the resources shown on the quilt. You could patch together a quilt. Which trees and plants would you sew into your quilt? What other resources would you include?

The Venus flytrap grows only in southeastern North Carolina. *How does it get its food?*

common plants, such as honeysuckle and holly, in most places. Wildflowers grow across the state. Asters, goldenrods, sunflowers, and lilies thrive everywhere.

The rare Venus flytrap grows only in a few places in southeastern North Carolina. The Cape Fear River valley swamps are its best habitat. The plant leaves look like an open seashell. Inside the shell are sensitive hairs that signal the plant to snap shut when an insect lands. The plant then "eats" the insect. It is against the law to dig up the Venus flytrap.

On the western side of the state, you can find ginseng. Ginseng grows only in mountain habitats. People have used this plant for medicine. Now ginseng also is protected. Harvesting ginseng requires permission.

LESSON 1 REVIEW

Fact Follow-Up

1. What is a habitat?
2. What is the canopy of a forest, and why is it important?
3. What are some rare plants found in North Carolina? What are some common trees and plants found in North Carolina?

Think These Through

4. If a disease killed all the pine trees in North Carolina, how would the forests change?
5. How is lightning helpful and harmful to forests?
6. Why are plants, such as the Venus flytrap and ginseng, protected?

LESSON 2 Natural Resources

Every state has resources. Resources provide wealth to a state or country. North Carolina's resources include its people and the riches of nature, such as land, trees, minerals, wildlife, and water.

LESSON PREVIEW

Key Ideas

- The land yields a bounty of natural products.
- Wood from the forests and minerals from the earth enrich our lives.
- Wildlife provides an important resource that we cherish and enjoy.

Key Terms

peat, mint, hiddenite, panning, quarry, reservoirs, hydroelectricity

Forest Products

From its earliest days, North Carolina has supplied wood products to the world. Tall pine trees held up the great sails of wooden ships. Tar from pine trees helped make the ships watertight.

Today, mills turn timber into lumber, furniture, and paper. Large companies manage huge forests, of mostly pine trees, throughout the state. The companies replace the trees they cut with new seedlings to grow more trees. North Carolina is a leading producer of lumber.

Plants produce another resource near the Pamlico Sound. **Peat** consists of ancient plants that are decayed and pressed into thick layers. Peat is dug up and sold to gardening suppliers. Gardeners use peat to help soil absorb water.

In the Appalachian Mountains, Christmas tree farmers grow spruce, pine, and firs. Trees are planted and harvested like any other crop. Christmas trees, unlike most farm products, take years to grow. Avery and Watauga Counties are centers of Christmas tree production.

Pine straw is raked and baled before being sold to gardening stores for mulch. *What other forest products come from North Carolina?*

Minerals

Gold discoveries in the 1830s made North Carolina the leading gold producer in the United States at the time. The United States treasury opened a mint in Charlotte. A **mint** is where gold and silver are weighed and pressed into coins.

The largest emerald ever found in North America came out of an Alexander County mine in 1974. It weighed several pounds. Green emeralds, named **hiddenite**, honor the discoverer, William Hidden. You will find hiddenite only in North Carolina.

North Carolinians have found other valuable minerals.

EYEWITNESS TO HISTORY

North Carolina Gold

In 1799, Conrad Reed, a Cabarrus County farm boy, was shooting arrows at fish in the Little Meadow Creek near his house. He found a big shiny rock in the stream. He took the heavy rock home. It weighed 17 pounds (7.7 kilograms), perfect for use as a doorstop.

Gold eagle coins

Conrad's father, John Reed, learned the rock was gold and sold it. He and his partners found more gold nuggets in Little Meadow Creek. They began the Reed Gold Mine. The discovery started the first gold rush in the United States. Many people moved to North Carolina to try to strike it rich.

Gold rushers panned and dug for gold in the streams and ground. They carried mud by wheelbarrow to the rocker, a hollowed out log filled with water (right). As the log was rocked, the water and mud washed out, leaving gravel, sand, and—if they were lucky—gold.

At one time, copper, coal, and iron were mined here. Today mines still produce important minerals from the North Carolina earth.

Vance County mines produced tungsten for many years. Tungsten mixed with steel makes steel stronger.

Soft rock called mica is dug from mines north of Asheville. Mica's thin layers are used in the manufacturing of electric generators and other products.

Bessemer City and Kings Mountain areas contain lithium, which is the lightest metal known on earth. Lithium is used in medicine and in the production of batteries.

What would YOU do?

Imagine you are Conrad Reed or William Hidden. How do you think you would feel if you found a big gold nugget or an immense emerald? Would you want to tell anybody? Would you be scared? Would you be proud? What would you do with the money you would get for your find?

North of the Reed Mine, eastern Rowan County began to attract people seeking their fortune. These miners looked for gold in shafts dug deep under ground. Miners (left) wore hats with candles attached to see while they bored holes in rock.

The first gold dollar minted in the country was pressed by a settler from Germany, Christopher Bechtler, who opened a private mint in Rutherfordton.

The United States Congress opened branch mints throughout the South to make coins. For 20 years, all gold coins came from North Carolina. The Charlotte Mint (below) began making gold eagle coins in 1837. The mint closed during the Civil War.

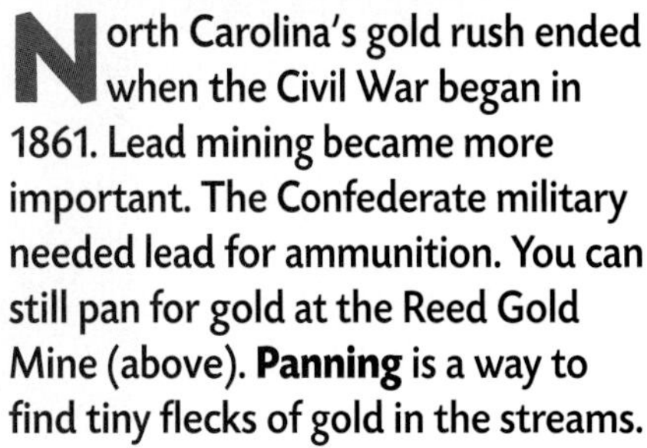

North Carolina's gold rush ended when the Civil War began in 1861. Lead mining became more important. The Confederate military needed lead for ammunition. You can still pan for gold at the Reed Gold Mine (above). Panning is a way to find tiny flecks of gold in the streams.

Other Products from the Earth

The abundant clay of North Carolina makes good bricks. Companies in the Piedmont make more than a billion bricks a year. The bricks in houses and buildings in your community probably came from North Carolina clay.

Kaolin, a white clay used in making china dishes, is mined in the Appalachian Mountains near Kings Mountain. Limestone that is added to cement comes from the Coastal Plain in New Hanover County.

A large mining company in Beaufort County, on the coast, digs phosphate from a huge open pit. Phosphate is a key ingredient in making fertilizers.

Gravel and rocks also provide wealth to North Carolina. Many counties in the Coastal Plain supply sand and gravel to the construction industry.

More than 100 quarries operate in the state, many in the Appalachian Mountains. A **quarry** is an open site where stone is dug. Granite is the most valued quarry stone. The largest granite quarry in the United States is at Mount Airy in Surry County. Buildings in Raleigh and Washington, D.C., contain North Carolina granite.

GAMES People Play

Fun with Rocks The rocks of North Carolina also promote fun. Small stones can be pieces in board games. Hopscotchers use rocks as markers and for drawing lines. Flat rocks are perfect for skipping on the water. Contestants in Highland Games hurl huge stones.

Homemade turkey calls require rocks. Callers rub slate against a cherry or maple box to make the right sound.

Pretty quartz and smooth mica are among the many rocks collected in North Carolina.

Granite is dug from the North Carolina Granite Corporation quarry at Mount Airy in Surry County. Granite was named the state rock. *What is granite used for?*

Water Resources

Fontana Dam controls the water of Fontana Lake to produce electricity for North Carolina and nearby states. *What is special about Fontana Dam?*

Water is our most important natural resource. It comes easily to us from streams and rivers. **Reservoirs**, artificial lakes that collect and hold water, save water for use in cities, towns, and farms. Farm reservoirs are used for irrigation and to water livestock.

Water treatment plants treat the water to make it safe to drink. Many families use water pumped from wells. That water also must be checked to be sure it is clean and disease-free.

North Carolina water produces electricity. Dams across streams store water in reservoirs. The water flows through generators to make electric power. Electricity created through water power is called **hydroelectricity**.

The Yadkin and Catawba Rivers in the Piedmont are two of many rivers that produce hydroelectricity. Mountain dams provide hydroelectricity. Fontana Dam, located on the border of Graham and Swain Counties, is the tallest dam in the state.

Wildlife

As more people move to North Carolina, the state's wild animals are often pushed out of their habitats. Sometimes you will hear of a bear or an alligator wandering into a town. More common sights are deer and raccoons.

Sometimes homes are built on the edge of forests. People and wild animals are trying to live in the same places.

Wild animals still live in North Carolina. Migrating flocks of geese, swans, and ducks swoop down on the lakes of Tyrrell and Hyde Counties. Wildlife officials returned the red wolf to the swamps of the Coastal Plain. Black bears live in remote parts of the state, particularly in the Great Smoky Mountains.

Shrimpers unload their catch at a dock in Carteret County. *What other fish are caught in North Carolina waters?*

Four major kinds of poisonous snakes exist in the state: the copperhead, the most common; the cottonmouth, which lives mostly in the East; the rattlesnake, seen in every region; and the coral snake, which lives mainly in the southeastern Coastal Plain.

Beavers, raccoons, opossums, foxes, squirrels, and rabbits can be found in almost every county. They live where the habitat supports them. Sometimes that means finding food in your family's garbage can or bird feeder.

Fish

North Carolina rivers and coastal waters contain fish and shellfish. Trout, bass, perch, and bream swim in Piedmont lakes and Appalachian streams.

North Carolina fish farms produce freshwater fish, such as trout, bass, and catfish. These fish are sold to restaurants and grocery stores.

In the North Carolina coastal waters, commercial and sport fishermen catch a variety of fish and shellfish. Some fish in deep water far offshore. Others pull in fish and shellfish in shallow waters. Many people drop their lines from fishing piers all along the coast. Surf fishermen cast their lines from the beaches of North Carolina.

LESSON 2 REVIEW

Fact Follow-Up

1. What are some forest resources of North Carolina?
2. What are some mineral resources of North Carolina?
3. What are some other resources from the earth found in North Carolina?

Think These Through

4. Describe the importance of gold to North Carolina.
5. What do you think is the most important natural resource in North Carolina? Why?
6. Why do wild animals often search for food near people's homes?

The Five Themes of Geography: Place

Using Geography's Themes: Physical Characteristics of Place

The geographic theme of **Place** organizes information about any spot on earth by describing its physical and human characteristics. This skill lesson focuses on the physical characteristics of Place.

In the first three chapters, you have already learned about the most important kinds of physical characteristics of North Carolina. They are landforms, climate, vegetation, and natural resources.

You recall from Chapter 1 that the major landforms of North Carolina are the Coastal Plain, the Piedmont, and the Appalachian Mountains.

In Chapter 2 you learned North Carolina has a humid subtropical climate because of its location.

In this chapter you read about the state's natural resources of forests, minerals, water, and wildlife.

To help you remember these characteristics, you need a way of making notes about them. Look at the drawing to the right. It can be called a web chart or spider graph because it looks like a spider's web with the spider in the middle. The web chart is useful for making notes on the physical characteristics of place.

Take a sheet of paper and copy the web chart on it. Next, think about the place where you live. What are some of its physical characteristics?

Describe the landforms of the place where you live. What about the climate? Is there much snow in the winter?

As you complete the web chart for the place where you live, you will want to reread the lesson on climate in Chapter 2 and the lessons in this chapter on vegetation and natural resources to help you describe the physical characteristics of the place where you live.

When you have completed your own web chart, compare it with a classmate's. How are they alike? Comparing your work with a classmate can help both of you become more skillful in using web charts.

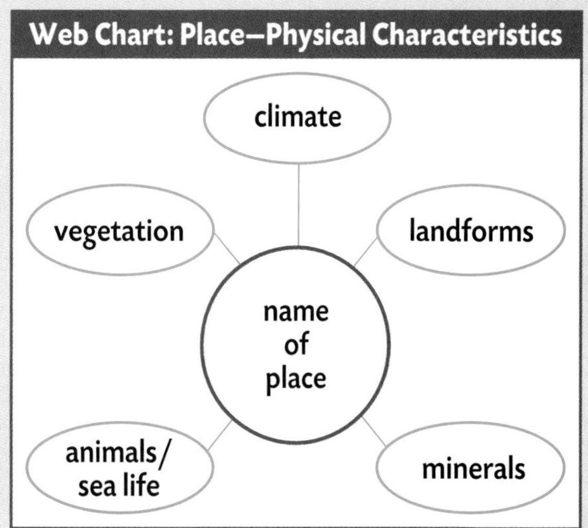

Chapter 3 Review

LESSONS LEARNED

LESSON 1 Deciduous and evergreen trees grow throughout the state. Forests of North Carolina are important as habitats for a variety of plant and animal life. Other plants include wildflowers, honeysuckle, and holly as well as rare plants, such as the Venus flytrap and ginseng.

LESSON 2 North Carolina contains an abundance of natural resources. Trees provide lumber and other wood products. Mineral wealth includes gold, emeralds, quarry rocks, and lithium. Other resources of the earth are clay, phosphate, limestone, and kaolin. Water might be North Carolina's most important natural resource. Animals and fish thrive in North Carolina.

TIME FOR TERMS

habitat	deciduous forests
evergreen forests	conifers
canopy	peat
mint	hiddenite
panning	quarry
reservoirs	hydroelectricity
Place	

FACT FOLLOW-UP

1. Describe the forest resources of North Carolina.
2. How are North Carolina's forests used?
3. What is the relative location of North Carolina's two oldest forests?
4. What are some uses for peat?
5. What precious metals and gems are found in North Carolina?
6. Describe the importance of gold in North Carolina's history.
7. What minerals are found in North Carolina? How are they used?
8. What earth products are found in North Carolina? How are they used?
9. What are some uses of water in North Carolina?
10. What are some animals and sea life found in North Carolina?

THINK THESE THROUGH

11. Why does North Carolina have a good habitat for trees?
12. What would North Carolina be like if there were no forests?
13. Which forest resource of North Carolina do you think is most important? Explain.
14. Which North Carolina mineral resource do you think is most important? Explain.
15. Why is gold mining not as important in North Carolina now as it was before the Civil War?
16. How do North Carolina's earth products help the construction industry?
17. How does an abundance of water resources help North Carolina?
18. Why is it important for wild animals

to survive in North Carolina? Why are some animals losing their habitats?

19. Choose one place in North Carolina that you know well. Describe the physical characteristics of that place.

20. Why are animals included in the physical characteristics of place?

SHARPENING SKILLS

21. Which of the physical characteristics of place do you think is easiest to describe? Why?

22. Which of the physical characteristics of place do you think is hardest to describe? Why?

23. Are there any physical characteristics of place more important than others? What are they? Give reasons for your answer.

24. How would your web chart change if you completed one that showed the physical characteristics of another place in the state? What characteristics would change the most? What characteristics would hardly change at all?

PLACE LOCATION

Using a resource map requires understanding the symbols in the map key. Use the key to locate the state's resources. Use cardinal and intermediate directions to describe their location within the state.

25. gold discovery and mining.

26. sand.

27. shellfish.

28. dams that generate hydroelectric power.

29. tungsten.

30. peat.

31. rock quarries.

32. mica.

33. lithium.

34 phosphate.

35. clay.

36. limestone.

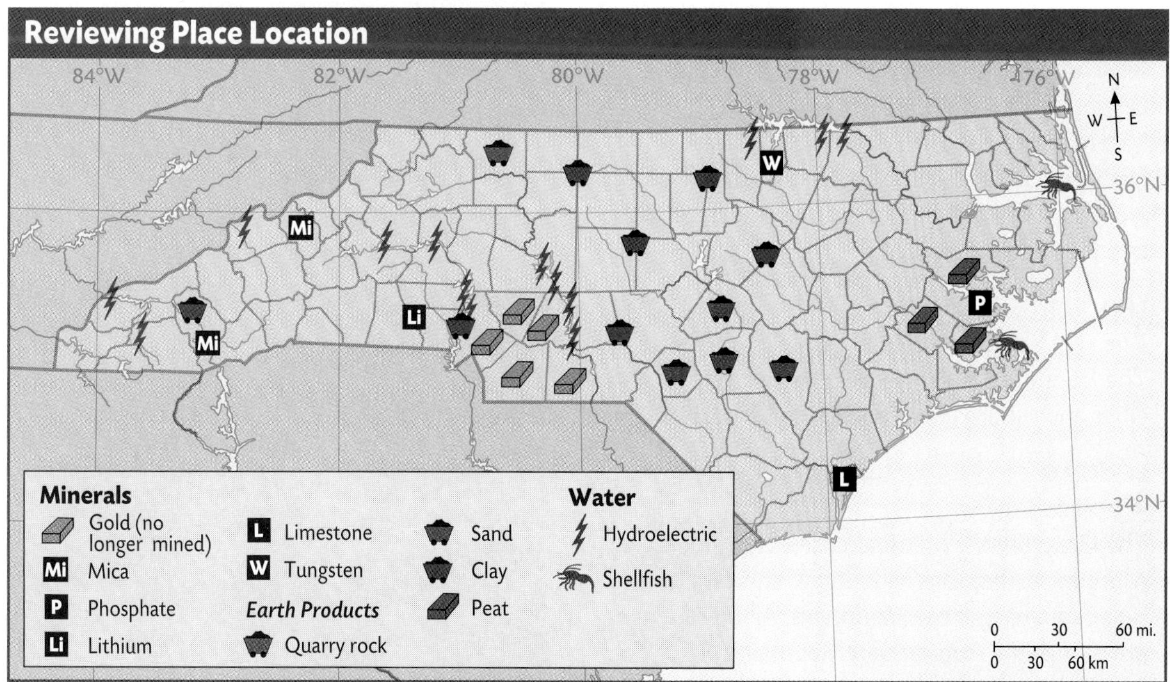

North Carolina's Regions

A journey across North Carolina would go through all three regions of the state. Start at Manteo (bottom), a town on Roanoke Island in the East. End in the West at Murphy (inset), the county seat of Cherokee County.

The 543 miles (874 km) from Manteo to Murphy stretches through the Coastal Plain, the Piedmont, and the Mountains—the three regions of North Carolina. The names of the regions match the landforms of the state.

CHAPTER PREVIEW

LESSON 1
The Tidewater
The Outer Banks, sounds, and swamps of the Tidewater make up the Outer Coastal Plain.

LESSON 2
The Inner Coastal Plain
Flat land continues into the Inner Coastal Plain, an agricultural region that includes the Sandhills and the Carolina bays.

LESSON 3
The Piedmont
The Piedmont's rolling hills are the setting for cities and suburbs from Raleigh to Charlotte.

LESSON 4
The Mountains
The Great Smoky Mountains, the Blue Ridge Mountains, the Black Mountains, and other ranges are part of the Mountains. All these ranges are part of the Appalachian Mountains.

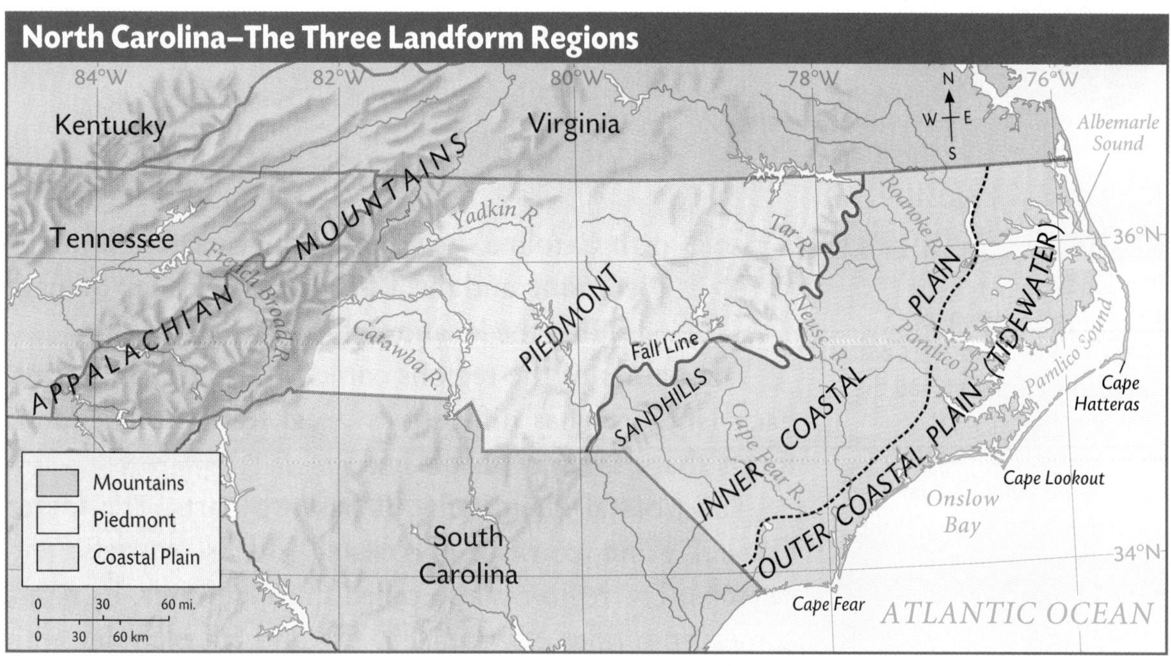

Travel from Murphy to Manteo to see the regions of North Carolina.

Windmills on the Coast

At one time, North Carolina was famous for its windmills. More than 155 windmills sat on the windy coast of North Carolina before the Civil War. A soldier from the North said that he saw more windmills than he "supposed were in existence in the whole country."

A windmill snared the wind in its big blades. The blades turned, which powered machinery to grind grain or pump water inside the windmill. English settlers built the windmills in the North Carolina colony. Colonists received extra land if they agreed to build a windmill.

Cheap electrical power put an end to windmills. Fierce winds often tore down the fragile wooden windmills. Windmills are still used in the western United States.

LESSON 1 The Tidewater

LESSON PREVIEW

Key Ideas

- The physical regions of North Carolina are the Coastal Plain, the Piedmont, and the Mountains.
- The Coastal Plain has two parts—the Inner Coastal Plain and the Outer Coastal Plain, called the Tidewater.
- The Tidewater of islands, sounds, and swamps is washed by ocean tides.

Key Terms

Coastal Plain, Piedmont, Mountains, Outer Coastal Plain, Tidewater, Inner Coastal Plain, Outer Banks, barrier islands, sound, brackish, swamp, pocosin

North Carolina's regions are the **Coastal Plain**, the **Piedmont**, and the **Mountains**. The map on page 53 shows the location of the regions.

The names of the regions come from their landforms. Each landform has different physical features. The landforms shape the way people live.

The Coastal Plain is flat. It has two parts. The **Outer Coastal Plain** consists of coastal islands, sounds, and swamps. The region is also called the **Tidewater.** Its name comes from tides of water that rise and fall each day with the ocean. The Tidewater begins where the sun comes up first in North Carolina: the Outer Banks.

Several rivers flow through the Inner Coastal Plain. The **Inner Coastal Plain** contains more fertile soil than the Tidewater. It is a productive farming area.

The Tidewater includes coastal islands called the Outer Banks. *What else does the Tidewater include?*

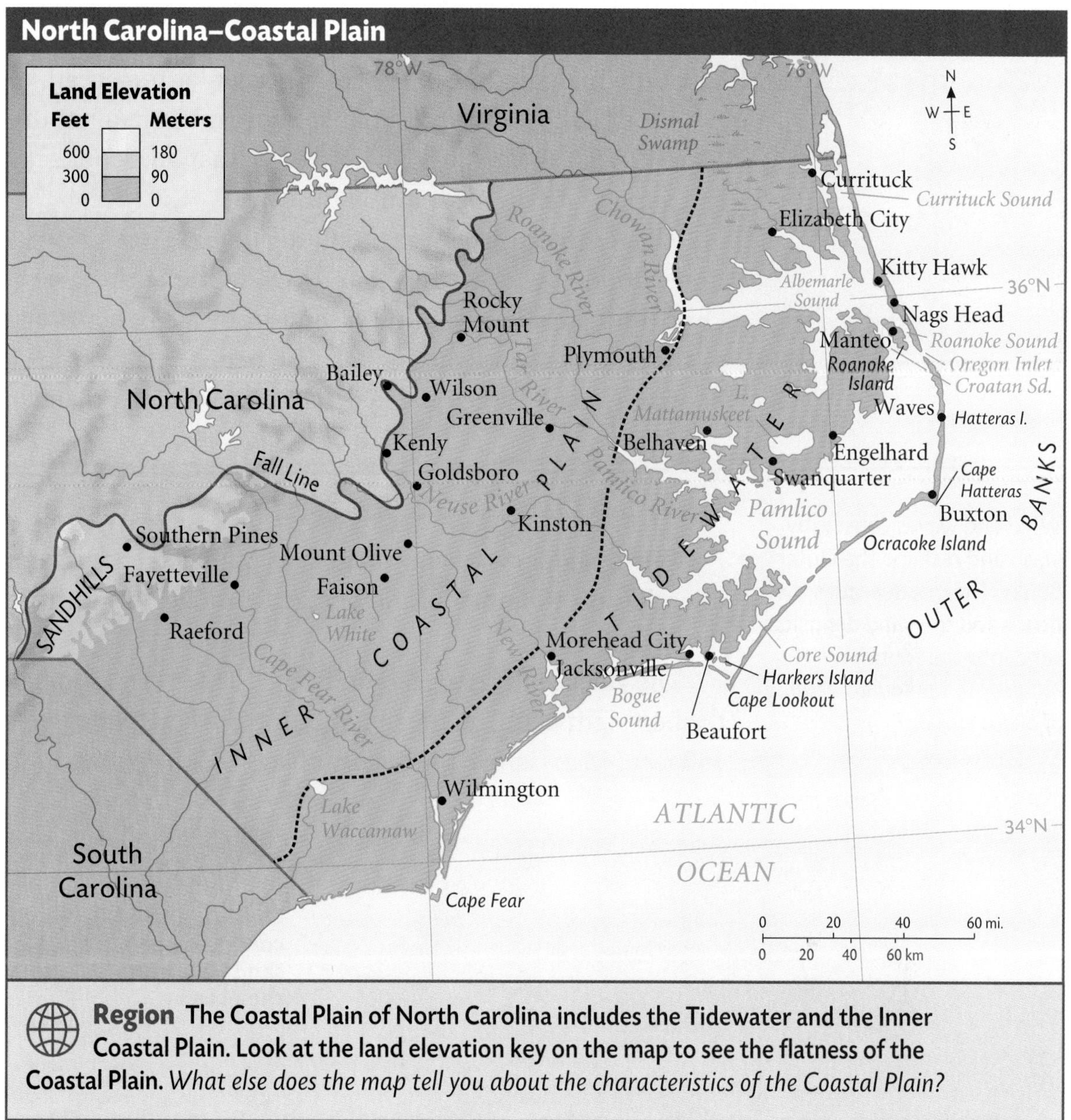

Region The Coastal Plain of North Carolina includes the Tidewater and the Inner Coastal Plain. Look at the land elevation key on the map to see the flatness of the Coastal Plain. *What else does the map tell you about the characteristics of the Coastal Plain?*

The Outer Banks

The **Outer Banks** are huge sand ridges out in the ocean, miles from the North Carolina mainland. You only see the ridge tops. Sand goes deep into the earth, below the ocean's surface.

The Outer Banks are part of the barrier islands that extend along the coast of North Carolina from the Virginia border to the South Carolina border. **Barrier islands** stand between the mainland's shore and the ocean. Barrier islands block the mainland from the rough waves of the ocean.

About half of the Outer Banks shoreline is in a national park. That means it is protected, so that all people can enjoy the Outer Banks' natural beauty.

When large storms hit the Outer Banks, water sometimes floods over the dunes and covers the entire beach. Over time, storms have moved sand from the ocean beach to the sound side of the islands (see below). A **sound** is a body of water between barrier islands and the mainland.

Towns of the Outer Banks

Our imaginary journey begins at Manteo. The eastern town lies on Roanoke Island across Roanoke Sound from Bodie Island.

The village of Nags Head on Bodie Island offers some of the best sightseeing on the Outer Banks. Jockey's Ridge rises 140 feet (42 m) above the sea near Nags Head. People climb

Wind and waves constantly wash and reshape the Outer Banks. The ocean erodes the beach and the wind deposits sand into the sound. *What happens to the sounds because of beach erosion?*

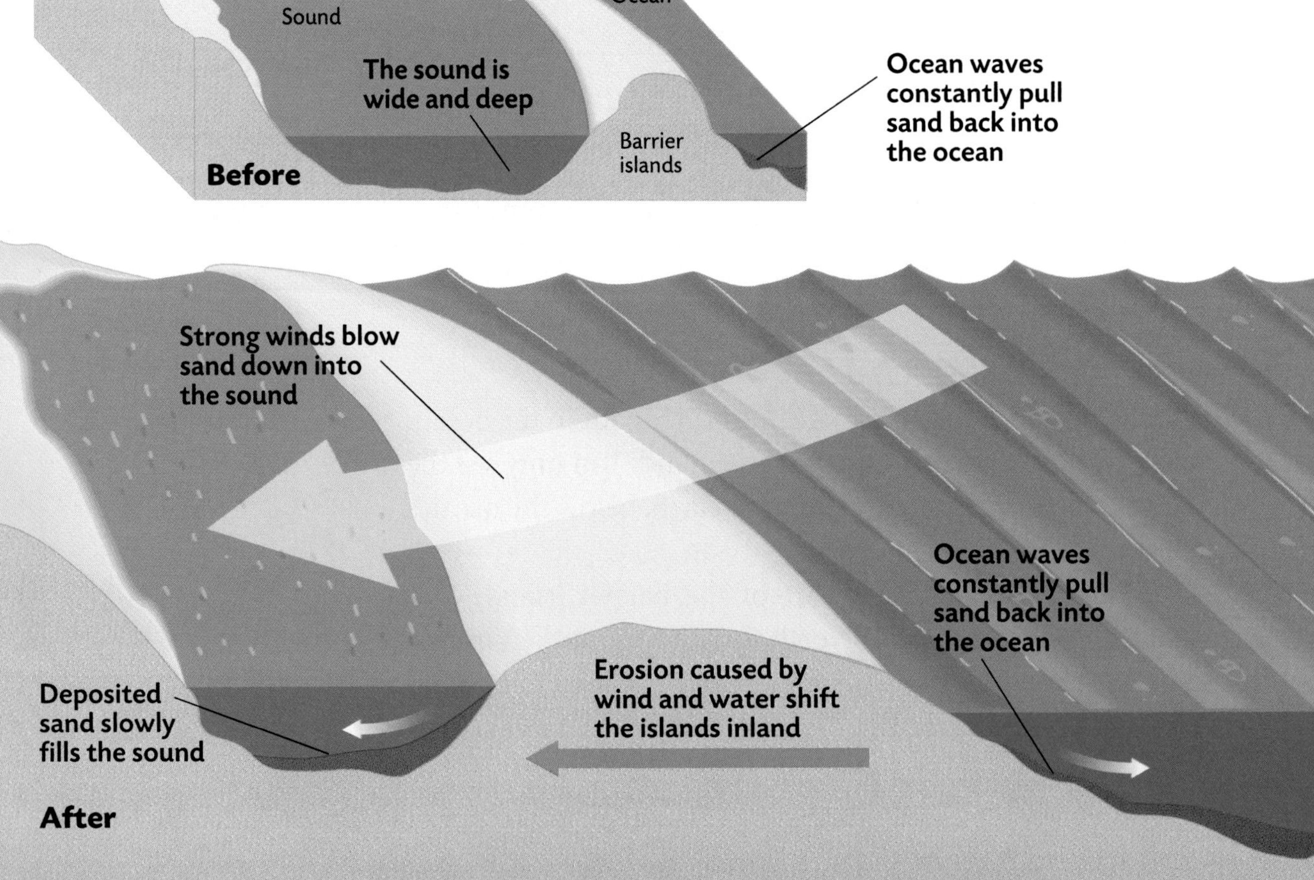

the sand mound every day.

You might notice the hang gliders at Jockey's Ridge. A few miles north, in 1903, the Wright Brothers flew the first airplane at Kitty Hawk.

South of Nags Head you will cross Oregon Inlet to Hatteras Island. You will pass through old villages—Waves, Salvo, and Buxton—where people have lived for centuries. Windmills, like the ones in The Netherlands, once lined the island between the villages.

Harbors and boats dot the coastline of Pamlico Sound at Oriental. *What rivers drain into the Pamlico Sound?*

The ocean off Hatteras Island is known as the Graveyard of the Atlantic because of the shifting sandbars. Ships often ran aground and sank. The Cape Hatteras Lighthouse was built to warn ships to steer away.

State-owned ferries can take you from Hatteras Island to Ocracoke Island or to Cedar Island. After landing on Cedar Island, you can visit Beaufort and the North Carolina Maritime Museum there. The museum displays information about the people, animals, and customs of the coast. Seafood restaurants in Beaufort or Morehead City offer delicious meals.

What would YOU do?

North Carolina has three major regions. If you had to choose one as a place to live, where would you go?

As you read this chapter, think about each region. Think about the fun things to do in each place. Think about the jobs your parents would like. Consider the weather. Would you stay in the region where you live now? Would you move?

Sounds

The barrier islands create some of the unique treasures of North Carolina: its sounds. These bodies of water lie between the mainland and barrier islands. The water in a sound is **brackish**, a mixture of salt and fresh water. Sounds are fed saltwater from rising ocean tides. Freshwater from rivers drains into the sounds.

The Roanoke and Chowan Rivers flow into the Albemarle

Harkers Island fishing village shelters boats, including the shad boat. *Why do you think the shad boat became the official state boat?*

Sound in the northeastern Tidewater. The Pamlico and Neuse Rivers empty into the huge Pamlico Sound in the central Tidewater.

The Cape Fear and New Rivers drain the southern Tidewater and flow through inlets straight into the Atlantic Ocean.

The city of Wilmington grew on the Cape Fear River near the Atlantic Ocean. Its location has made it North Carolina's most important port and largest coastal city.

Residents in the smaller towns along the sounds often fish for a living. Such towns as Currituck, Englehard, Belhaven, Swan Quarter, Oriental, and Harkers Island harbor the traditional shad boats, the official state boat. Shrimp boats chug through the sounds and the ocean to catch seafood enjoyed by people across the country.

You might see dolphins leaping in the sound if you are lucky. Pelicans and sea gulls swoop down along the water's surface in search of food. The sounds of North Carolina feed a large population of people and creatures.

The Pamlico and Albemarle are the major sounds of North Carolina. There are five other sounds that separate barrier islands from the mainland. Look at the map on page 55 to find the names of the other sounds.

Swamps

Some of North Carolina's Tidewater is forested and full of swamps. A **swamp** is a low, wet area. Large pines, scrub oaks, and cypress grow in swamps. The Great Dismal Swamp, north of the Roanoke River, contains a variety of plant and wildlife. It is the largest swamp in the state.

Lake Mattamuskeet, in Hyde County between the Pamlico and Albemarle Sounds, is the largest natural lake in North Carolina. Thousands of geese, swans, and other migratory birds (birds that fly South for the winter) nest there every winter. Pine trees growing north of the lake are harvested for lumber.

A special Tidewater swamp is the **pocosin** (POW · cuh · sin). A pocosin is often described as "a swamp upon a hill." It looks like a saucer turned upside down. Trees cover the rims, and peat soil supports scrub evergreen trees on the outside. Inside the rim are shallow pools of water.

The Great Dismal Swamp in the northern Tidewater is one of several swamps in North Carolina. The swamp canal connected early settlers with the colony of Virginia. *What kinds of plants grow in swamps?*

Fact Follow-Up

1. What is the Tidewater?
2. What are the Outer Banks? How do they change?
3. What are sounds? Where are they found?
4. What are swamps and pocosins? Where are they located?
5. How has Wilmington's location helped make it an important city?

Think These Through

6. Should people living in western North Carolina care about the environment of the Tidewater? Give reasons for your answer.

The Inner Coastal Plain

LESSON PREVIEW

Key Ideas

- The Inner Coastal Plain is flat, but it is more fertile than the Tidewater.
- The Inner Coastal Plain is a major farming center.
- The Inner Coastal Plain includes the Sandhills and Carolina bays.

Key Terms

agriculture, Sandhills, Carolina bays

The Inner Coastal Plain is flat like the Tidewater, but the elevation is higher. It is a vital part of the state because it contains rich farm lands that are the center of agriculture. **Agriculture** is the science of farming.

Forty percent of North Carolina lies in the Inner Coastal Plain. About one third of North Carolina residents live there.

Tobacco Farming

The Inner Coastal Plain is the heart of tobacco farming in North Carolina. Farmers here raise more tobacco than farmers in any other state. The leaves become cigarettes, chewing tobacco, and pipe tobacco in Piedmont factories.

Depending on the time of the year, you may see tobacco in the fields, smell tobacco curing in bulk barns, or hear the rumble of trucks transporting tobacco to warehouses in nearby towns.

Long rows of tobacco gleam in the Coastal Plains's summer sun. *What other crops grow well in the Coastal Plain?*

Bulk barns cure, or dry out, the tobacco with heat. Today's bulk barns are gas heated. Some farmers have as many as a dozen bulk barns in a row.

Once tobacco is ready for sale, farmers take it to the closest town. Wilson, Rocky Mount, Goldsboro, Greenville, and Kinston are some of the cities that have tobacco warehouses where the leaves are sold.

Other Crops

Farmers on the Coastal Plain grow other crops in the fertile soil. Corn and soybeans occupy more acreage than tobacco. Cotton, peanuts, and sweet potatoes are other important crops.

Peanuts do well in the sandy soils near the Roanoke River. Farms there grow more peanuts than any place in North Carolina. Farmers raise sweet potatoes in fields near Smithfield and Clayton. North Carolina grows more sweet potatoes than any other state.

South of Goldsboro, around the towns of Mount Olive and Faison, are large cucumber farms. They sell their cucumbers to pickle companies in the two towns. The pickles are sold all across the United States.

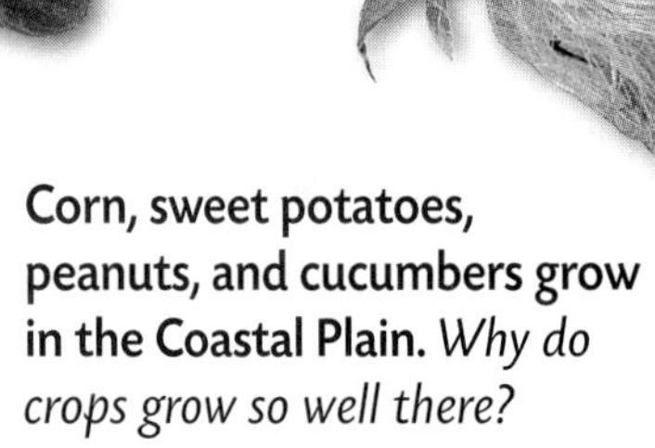

Corn, sweet potatoes, peanuts, and cucumbers grow in the Coastal Plain. *Why do crops grow so well there?*

The Sandhills

Get ready to see one of North Carolina's most unusual landforms. The **Sandhills**, rolling ridges of sand nowhere near the ocean, cover parts of Richmond, Scotland, Cumberland, Moore, Hoke, and Harnett Counties. The hills of sand are remnants of beach sand from a time when the ocean covered most of what is now the Coastal Plain. When the ocean level fell during an ice age, the sand remained.

The long, rolling hills of sand quickly soak up rainwater. The Sandhills are noted for tall longleaf pines, which grow best in well-drained sand. The trees have large, fragrant cones and pine needles about 1 foot (30 cm) long.

The longleaf pine once thrived throughout the Coastal Plain. The pines produced the tar that some say gives the state its Tar Heel nickname. Farmers cut down the forests for lumber and to clear fields for crops. Now the longleaf pine is mostly found in the Sandhills.

The Sandhills have sandy soil that drains well and supports tall pine trees. *What kind of pine tree grows best there?*

Towns in the Sandhills, such as Southern Pines and Raeford, are often the hottest places in the state during the summer. They are also a degree or two warmer during the winter.

Carolina Bays

Southeast of the Sandhills you will come upon another unusual North Carolina feature. Bladen and Columbus Counties contain the **Carolina bays**. The bays are oval-shaped shallow lakes. They often have peat underneath and bay trees growing around them. Bayberries are harvested for the sweet smell they give candles and soap.

At least 1,000 Carolina bays exist on the southern Coastal Plain. Lake Waccamaw, in Columbus County, covers an area 5 miles (8 km) long and 3 miles (5 km) wide. White Lake is a Carolina bay as well. Some Carolina bays are only several feet wide.

The pattern made by the Carolina bays puzzles many scientists. Each bay extends in a southeasterly direction. Some scientists believe that a meteor shower might have struck the earth, digging shallow holes that filled with water.

LESSON 2 REVIEW

Fact Follow-Up

1. Describe the Inner Coastal Plain.
2. What are some agricultural crops grown in the Inner Coastal Plain?
3. What are the Sandhills, and what is their relative location?

Think These Through

4. How are the Carolina bays different from other areas of the Inner Coastal Plain?
5. In what ways do you think the Inner Coastal Plain is important to all of North Carolina?
6. How are the Tidewater and Inner Coastal Plain regions alike? How are they different?
7. Which crop grown on the Inner Coastal Plain is most useful? Explain.

LESSON 3 The Piedmont

Where does the Piedmont begin? It is hard to see from the road, but geographers place the boundary between the Coastal Plain and the Piedmont along the fall line.

LESSON PREVIEW

Key Ideas

- The eastern border of the Piedmont is the fall line.
- The Piedmont is a plateau.
- The Piedmont is filled with suburbs and cities.
- The Piedmont includes the Uwharries, high hills near Asheboro.

Key Terms

fall line, plateau, Triangle, Triad, urban, suburb, Piedmont Crescent, rural

The Fall Line

The **fall line** is the area where the streams come down from the hillier areas of their origin onto the Coastal Plain. Below the fall line, a stream is usually sluggish and smooth, and you can boat on it. Above the fall line, the streams are rocky and shallow, making boating difficult.

The fall line runs roughly in a north-south direction through the eastern United States. You can see on the map on page 64 where the fall line crosses North Carolina, separating the Coastal Plain from the Piedmont.

The Piedmont is a region of hills. *How does the land affect how people build their homes?*

The Piedmont Plateau

Geographers refer to the Piedmont as a plateau. A **plateau** is a mostly level landform that is higher than nearby areas. Although the Piedmont is hilly, the size and shape of most hills do not vary much. The hills extend west to the Mountains Region.

On the eastern side of Raleigh, our state capital, you still see pines and sandy soil. As you head toward Durham and Chapel Hill, the land changes. The hills are higher. Along with pines, you see more hardwood trees.

North Carolina–Piedmont

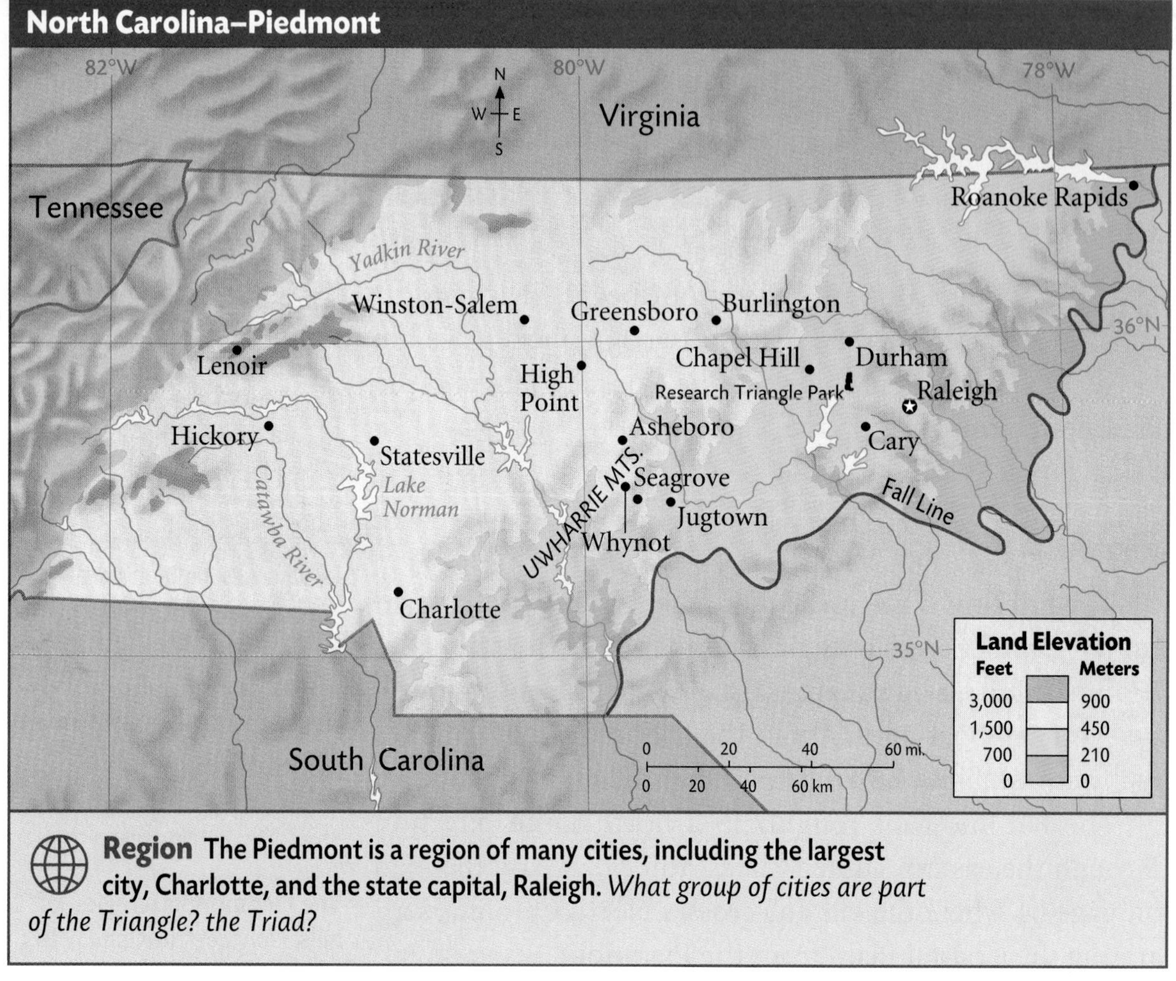

Region The Piedmont is a region of many cities, including the largest city, Charlotte, and the state capital, Raleigh. *What group of cities are part of the Triangle? the Triad?*

The Piedmont is a region of many cities. As you can see on the map, Raleigh, Durham, and Chapel Hill form a triangle. These three cities are called the **Triangle**. In the center of the Triangle is Research Triangle Park.

Farther west, the cities of Greensboro, High Point, and Winston-Salem form an area called the **Triad**. "Triad" means a group of three. These three cities are located in the western Piedmont.

Interstates 40 and 85 take you from the Triangle west to the Triad. Interstate 85 continues southwest to Charlotte.

Charlotte sprawls over much of Mecklenburg County. It is the largest city in the state. Its population of 450,000 is more than double that of Raleigh, the second largest city in the state. Nearly 2 million people live within an hour's drive of Charlotte.

These three city areas make the Piedmont an urban region. **Urban** means city.

Near the cities, suburbs crowd onto former farm fields. A **suburb** is a residential area on the edge of a city. Trees and fields have been replaced by thousands of houses and businesses for the people who live and work in the Piedmont.

The Piedmont Crescent

The North Carolina Railroad laid tracks from Raleigh to Charlotte in the 1800s. The company callcd thc train the Piedmont Crescent after the shape of its route. The crescent-shaped curve of Interstate 85 and Interstate 40 from Raleigh to Charlotte still earns the entire area its name: the **Piedmont Crescent.** The many people who live within a short drive of Interstates 85 and 40 are residents of the crescent.

The railroad and the interstates encouraged families to live nearby. Now, fewer farms dot the Piedmont. Houses and businesses now take up land once used for farming.

Remaining farms might be dairies, tobacco farms, or "pick your own" farms. These "pick your own" farms produce vegetables and fruits. Pickers especially enjoy harvesting blueberries and strawberries.

These Piedmont farmers live in rural areas. **Rural** is another word for the countryside away from cities and suburbs.

Piedmont Crescent

Place The Piedmont Crescent was named for a railroad that traveled through the towns on the map. Compare this map to the one on page 64. *Why did the railroad follow this curved route?*

The Uwharries

South of the Piedmont Crescent are high hills that look like mountains. The Uwharries are the last of the ancient mountain chain that once covered the Piedmont.

The Uwharries have a rocky, thin soil that has made them less suitable for farming. People in the area work in lumbering. They harvest such hardwoods as oak and hickory.

You can hike, picnic, fish, and enjoy nature in the Uwharries. Best of all, you can go to the state zoo.

LIVING IN THE PIEDMONT

The North Carolina Zoological Park

Planners of the North Carolina Zoo wanted to place the zoo where most people in North Carolina could easily visit. The site near Asheboro is near the center of the state and within 90 miles (145 km) of more than one third of the state population.

The zoo's 1,400 acres (560 sq hm) include a variety of landforms that the planners knew would support many kinds of animals. The zoo animals live on hilly and flat land similar to many of the animals' natural habitats.

Purgatory Mountain of the Uwharrie chain dominates the land, which includes rolling hills, valleys, and streams.

The zoo site contains deciduous chestnut, oak, and hickory trees, some evergreen pine trees, as well as grassland.

Besides landforms and vegetation, climate makes the North Carolina Zoo a good place to protect many different species of animals. Because of North Carolina's temperate climate, many animals live outdoors all year. Some animals from tropical areas cannot survive cold weather. They are sheltered during the winter months.

Ridges within the zoo create cool areas during summer months that are well suited for animals from temperate or continental climate regions. Bison and elk live in the cooler ridge valleys.

Humid marshes and grasslands that receive a lot of sunlight are home to animals from warm regions of the earth. Antelope, elephants, and giraffes from Africa live in the grassland habitats. Wildlife native to marshes, such as alligators and herons, live in that part of the zoo.

Even animals that cannot easily survive in North Carolina can be seen in climate-controlled buildings. The most exciting time at the North Carolina Zoo is when visitors see animals out in the open living in a variety of habitats.

People come from around the world to watch North Carolina potters (left) make Seagrove pottery (above) and to buy pots, jugs, and crocks. *What is pottery made from?*

North Carolina established one of the first state zoos in the nation south of Asheboro years ago. The central location makes it easy for people to visit. The North Carolina animal section displays animals from our state.

Near the zoo is Jugtown. It is just down the road from Whynot, not far from Seagrove. These funny names are small towns. They are in the center of an area where famous potters practice their craft.

Early in the state's history, settlers found the clay in part of the eastern Piedmont and the Sandhills to be perfect for pots, jugs, and crocks. Today, potters use the clay to create Seagrove area pottery.

LESSON 3 REVIEW

Fact Follow-Up

1. What is the fall line? How is it important?
2. What are the Triangle and the Triad?
3. How would you describe the Piedmont to someone who has never visited the region?
4. What are some sights you would see if you visited the Uwharries?

Think These Through

5. How are the Piedmont and the Inner Coastal Plain alike and different?
6. How do the land and resources of the Piedmont help people living there contribute to all of North Carolina?

LESSON 4 The Mountains

LESSON PREVIEW

Key Ideas

- The Appalachian Mountains make up the Mountains Region in North Carolina. They include the Blue Ridge Mountains, Brushy Mountains, Black Mountains, and Great Smoky Mountains.
- The mountains are mostly forested, except on rocky balds.
- The Mountains Region is popular for its scenic views, waterfalls, hiking trails, and ski resorts.

Key Terms

Blue Ridge Parkway, forestry, balds

The Blue Ridge Mountains were named for their shades of blue. *What other mountains have names that reflect how they look?*

Long before you reach the Blue Ridge, you will see why that part of the Appalachian Mountains bears its name. On a clear day, the Blue Ridge Mountains look blue from far away. The Brushy Mountains, a range just to the east of the Blue Ridge, get their name because they seem to brush up against the bigger mountains.

The Mountains Region includes these ranges plus the Black Mountains. The best way to see this region of western North Carolina is on North Carolina's most scenic road, the Blue Ridge Parkway.

The Blue Ridge Parkway

Slow down. This is not an interstate. The curves and twists make it unsafe to go fast. The view is different from the interstate. Nowhere else in the state can you see so far.

The **Blue Ridge Parkway** is part of a two-lane road running nearly the entire length of the Blue Ridge. The road begins in Virginia (where it is called Skyline Drive), continues through western North Carolina, and ends in the

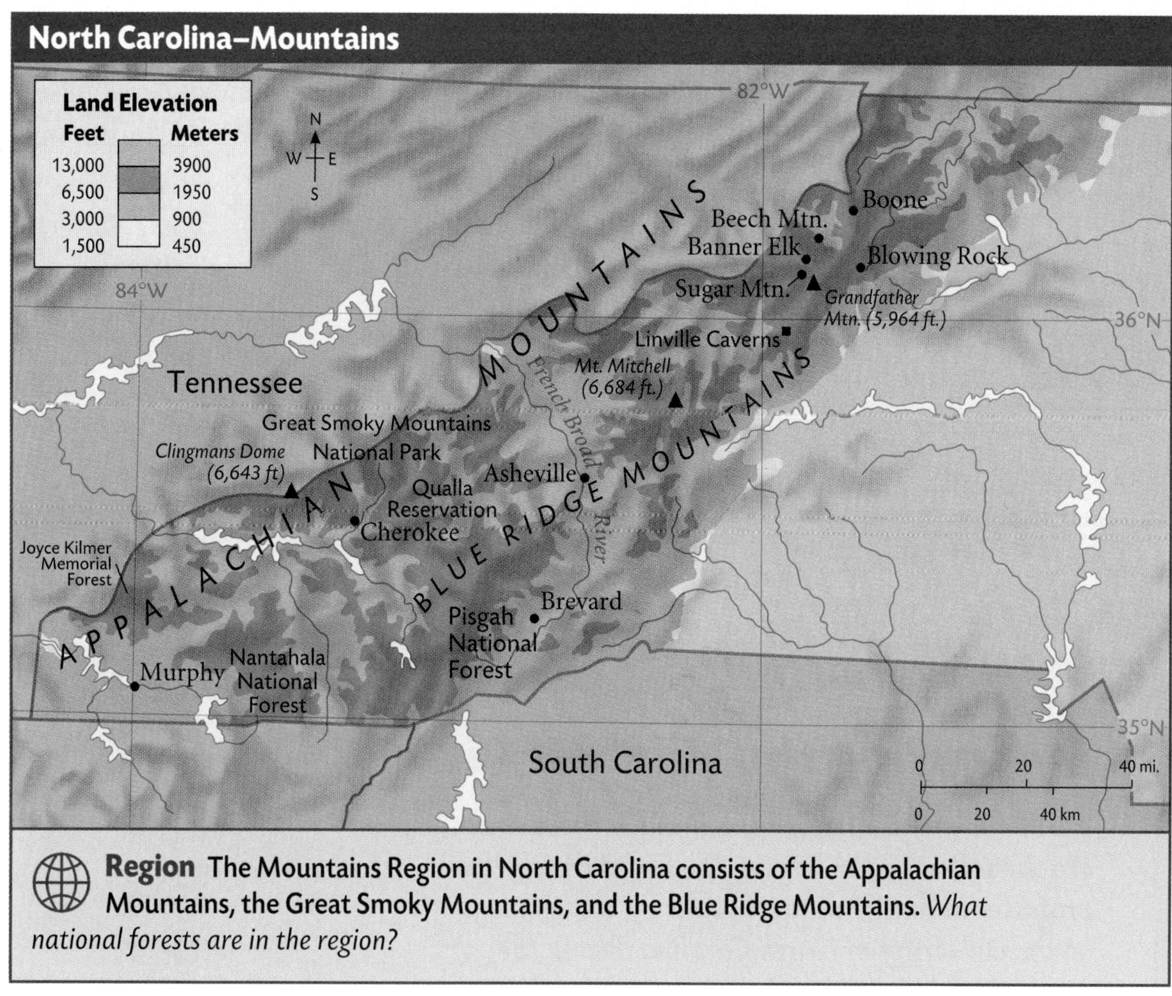

Region **The Mountains Region in North Carolina consists of the Appalachian Mountains, the Great Smoky Mountains, and the Blue Ridge Mountains.** *What national forests are in the region?*

Great Smoky Mountains National Park in Tennessee. It is 469 miles (755 km) long.

North of Blowing Rock you can stop at several state parks near the parkway. Visit the Brinegar family log cabin near Doughton Park. The cabin shows how mountain families lived more than 100 years ago.

Heading south from Blowing Rock, you can visit Grandfather Mountain. You will see mountain animals and cross the mile-high swinging bridge, if you dare. Grandfather Mountain has some of the biggest curves on the parkway. Linville Gorge, where you can hike above the Linville River, is also nearby.

Winter ski resorts can be found to the west of the parkway. Near Grandfather Mountain, the towns of Sugar Mountain, Banner Elk, and Beech Mountain attract skiers. When snow doesn't fall, machines might make the snow.

WORD ORIGINS

Grandfather Mountain looms high over nearby peaks where Avery, Caldwell, and Watauga Counties meet. When seen against the sky, the mountain looks like a profile of an old man. The mountain is near Grandmother Gap and Grandmother Mountain. But it is a long way from Childsburgh (present-day Hillsborough). Cherokees called the peak *Tanawha,* which means "a fabulous hawk or eagle."

Farther south on the parkway towers Mount Mitchell. Its altitude of 6,684 feet (2,005 m) makes it the highest peak east of the Mississippi River.

Mount Mitchell is named for Professor Elisha Mitchell, one of the first scientists to teach at the University of North Carolina in Chapel Hill. Professor Mitchell fell to his death in 1857 while exploring the area around the mountain. Mount Mitchell towers above the Black Mountains, which range north of Asheville.

If you head south on the Blue Ridge Parkway, you will go around Asheville and the Biltmore House. Farther west, Pisgah National Forest offers more curved roads and

EYEWITNESS TO HISTORY

Measuring the Highest Peak

We like to name landforms, especially those that are the tallest or the largest. Dr. Elisha Mitchell, a professor of mathematics, chemistry, and geology at the University of North Carolina during the 1800s, thought scientists should measure landforms.

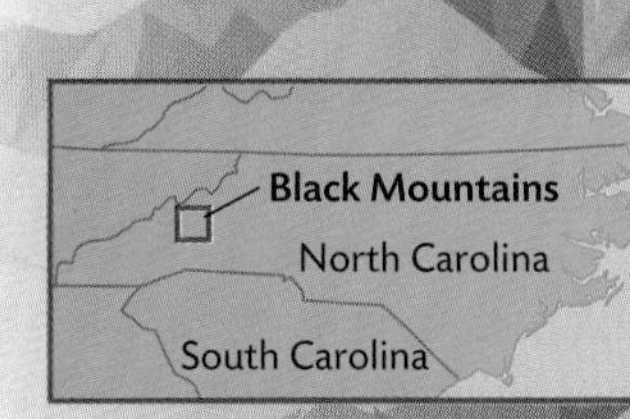

Dr. Elisha Mitchell

Mitchell spent his vacations measuring North Carolina's Black Mountains (below). The Black Mountains are a ridge of mountains, but people thought of them as one mountain because their elevations are so similar. Six of the mountains in that range are among the ten highest peaks in the eastern United States.

There wasn't an easy way to measure a mountain. The most common method then was to read barometric pressure at different heights. Then a math formula was used to figure the heights.

dramatic views. Here, Americans first practiced **forestry**, the science of caring for the resources in forests. Stop at the Cradle of Forestry in America exhibit northwest of Brevard. You might watch a film and take a nature walk.

The Great Smoky Mountains

The Blue Ridge Parkway ends in the Great Smoky Mountains National Park. The park receives the most visitors of all national parks. Half of it lies in Tennessee.

The Great Smokies, as they are usually called, appear to have a smoky haze over the peaks. This bluish appearance,

Congressman Thomas L. Clingman of North Carolina believed that Mitchell had not measured the tallest peak. Clingman believed that he himself had. Mitchell wanted to prove he had measured correctly. He decided to measure with a new method, leveling. Mitchell used a level, string, and a great deal of patience to compare the barometric pressure readings and his level readings.

Mitchell Falls

On a mid-June evening, Dr. Mitchell went walking up a trail. He was found 10 days later at the bottom of a waterfall. He had fallen to his death while exploring. The waterfall is now called Mitchell Falls. The mountain that Elisha Mitchell measured was bought by the state in 1915. North Carolina made it the first state park and named it for the persistent Dr. Mitchell. Mount Mitchell is the tallest mountain in the eastern United States.

much like the Blue Ridge, developed long before today's pollution. It results from air drafts and plant decay.

The Smokies have more than 800 miles (1,288 km) of trails to explore. The park is larger in area than the state of Rhode Island.

Some forests, such as the Joyce Kilmer Memorial Forest, contain trees that might be more than 200 years old. More types of trees grow here than in all of the continent of Europe. The highest peak in the Great Smokies, Clingmans Dome, stands only 41 feet (12 m) lower than Mount Mitchell.

High on the peaks of the Great Smokies are mysterious, treeless fields called **balds**. No one is completely sure how balds started. Cold winds keep trees from successfully sprouting. Laurel and rhododendron, two mountain bushes, do grow on balds.

GAMES People Play

Travel Game "Going on a Picnic" is a fun travel game. The first player says, "I'm going on a picnic, and I will bring an apple (or any food that begins with an *a*)." The next player repeats the first word, then calls out a food that starts with a *b*. Each player has to start from the letter *a*. The game continues through the letter *z*.

Cherokee and Murphy

The Blue Ridge Parkway cuts through the middle of the Qualla Reservation, home to more than 6,000 Cherokees. You can learn about Cherokee culture at the reservation museum. You can also see how the Cherokee lived

The Great Smoky Mountains have trees that are more than 200 years old. *Why is it important to preserve these forests?*

through the centuries at the Oconaluftee Village and in the town of Cherokee.

The signs at Cherokee point southeast toward Highlands and southwest toward Murphy. In Highlands you can see where beautiful waterfalls almost splash onto the road. You can even drive the car under one of them, Bridal Veil Falls. When you cross the Nantahala River, stop and look for rafts filled with people floating by on the white water.

Whiteside Mountain is one of the many striking features of Highlands, North Carolina. The lack of vegetation on its side gives the mountain its name. *What are the parts of mountains called that lack vegetation?*

On the way to Murphy from Highlands, you cross the Appalachian Trail. The walking trail stretches almost 2,000 miles (3,220 km) from Maine to Georgia.

In Murphy, you have gone almost as far west as you can go within North Carolina. If your home is in Elizabeth City, Plymouth, or Belhaven, you have a long trip back.

You have also traveled through North Carolina's three regions. As you learned about the regions, you may have thought about all the people who lived here before your time. The next chapter looks at the state before European settlers came.

LESSON 4 REVIEW

Fact Follow-Up

1. What are some sights you can see in the Blue Ridge Mountains?
2. What is the Blue Ridge Parkway?
3. Where do the Brushy, Blue Ridge, and Great Smoky Mountains get their names?

Think These Through

4. What is important about Mount Mitchell?
5. In what ways are the Mountains Region and the Tidewater alike and different?
6. If you could visit only one place in the Mountains, what would it be? Why?

The Five Themes of Geography: Region

Using Geography's Themes: Region

In Chapter 4 you learned about the three regions of North Carolina. Region is one of the Five Themes of Geography. A **Region** is an area that shares one or more characteristics. Those characteristics make it different from other places surrounding it.

A region may be defined by its physical characteristics. A physical region has a climate, vegetation, landforms, resources, and plant and animal life that are different from surrounding areas.

Look at the two charts below. Both show circles and x-marks. Does one have a region of x-marks? Which one? Where is the region of x-marks located?

If you noted that Chart A has a region of x-marks located in the center of Chart A, you were right!

The charts show that a region has one or more characteristics that the areas around it do not have. You can use this theme of geography to help you think about areas in North Carolina and other places.

Chart A

Chart B

Do you remember making a web chart about the physical characteristics of one of North Carolina's regions? Making the chart was an activity in the skill lesson in Chapter 3. The web chart you made described the physical characteristics of one of the regions of North Carolina. A sketch of the web chart is shown below.

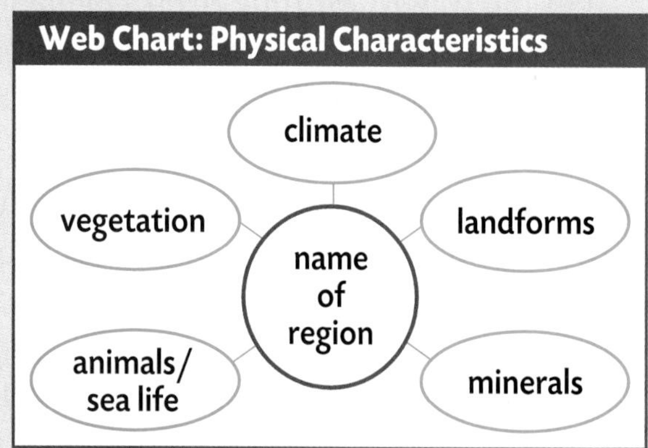

Web Chart: Physical Characteristics

Suppose you wanted to compare the physical characteristics of two regions in North Carolina. You could make two web charts. Or you might make a diagram like the one on page 75. This diagram, called a data retrieval chart, will help you compare the physical characteristics of North Carolina's regions.

If you had chosen to describe the physical characteristics of the Tidewater

(Outer Coastal Plain), your data retrieval chart would include the information given in the column on the left. It is labeled "Tidewater."

On a blank sheet of paper, copy the data retrieval chart. Then, skim Chapter 4 for information about the Inner Coastal Plain in North Carolina and complete the part of the chart labeled "Inner Coastal Plain."

Next, choose the Piedmont Region and complete that part of the chart.

Finally, complete the chart with information about the Mountains Region.

With your finished chart, you will find it easy to compare physical characteristics of any of the regions.

How are the landforms of the two regions on your chart alike and how are they different? By looking at the part of the chart labeled "Landforms," you can easily find the answer to the questions.

Which characteristics change the least from region to region? Why?

Which characteristics change the most? These characteristics are what make a region unique.

What other questions about North Carolina's regions can you answer by reading your date retrieval chart?

Data Retrieval Chart–Physical Characteristics by Region

	Tidewater	Inner Coastal Plain	Piedmont	Mountains
Climate	four seasons; long, hot summers and mild winters; a lot of rain			
Landforms	huge sand ridges, islands, swampy lowlands, swamps, pocosins, sounds			
Minerals	sand, phosphates, peat			
Vegetation	pine, scrub oaks, cypress, blueberries			
Animals and sea life	marine life (shrimp, fish, oysters, clams), geese, swans, migratory birds.			

Chapter 4 Review

LESSONS LEARNED

LESSON 1 North Carolina's three landform regions are the Coastal Plain, Piedmont, and Mountains. The Coastal Plain consists of the Outer Coastal Plain, or Tidewater, and the Inner Coastal Plain. The Tidewater is an area of islands, sounds, and swamps washed by ocean tides.

LESSON 2 The Inner Coastal Plain is a flat region of fertile farmland. The Sandhills are also part of the Inner Coastal Plain. The Carolina bays are shallow lakes of the Inner Coastal Plain.

LESSON 3 The Piedmont Region begins in the East at the fall line. The Piedmont plateau extends to the Appalachian Mountains. It includes three major urban areas. The Piedmont also includes the Uwharries, high hills near Asheboro, home of the North Carolina Zoological Park.

LESSON 4 The Mountains Region extends from the southwestern corner of the state in a northeasterly direction. The Appalachian Mountains in North Carolina include the Blue Ridge Mountains, the Brushy Mountains, the Great Smoky Mountains, and the Black Mountains.

TIME FOR TERMS

Coastal Plain
Mountains
Tidewater
Piedmont
Outer Coastal Plain
Inner Coastal Plain
Outer Banks
sound
swamp
agriculture
Carolina bays
plateau
Triad
suburb
rural
forestry
Region
barrier islands
brackish
pocosin
Sandhills
fall line
Triangle
urban
Piedmont Crescent
Blue Ridge Parkway
balds

FACT FOLLOW-UP

1. Name the regions of North Carolina from east to west.
2. Which region has the largest population?
3. Which region has the largest water areas?
4. Which region has the most industry?
5. In which region are the Uwharries located?
6. What separates the Piedmont from the Inner Coastal Plain?
7. How are the Uwharries and the Blue Ridge Mountains alike and different?
8. In which region are the Carolina bays found?
9. Why do geographers refer to the Piedmont region as a plateau?
10. Which region has the most cities?

THINK THESE THROUGH

11. Suppose you could plan a vacation trip to one of North Carolina's regions. Which would you choose? Explain why.
12. What do you think is the most interesting natural feature found in

North Carolina? Explain why.

13. There are rivers throughout North Carolina. How do you think rivers in the Mountains are different from Tidewater rivers?
14. Which region do you think offers the most recreation opportunities? Explain.
15. North Carolina has often been called a "Variety Vacationland." Do you agree with this description of North Carolina? Why? Why not?

SHARPENING SKILLS

16. A region is an area that shares one or more characteristics and is different from other areas around it. Name as many regions as you can.
17. Think about the county in which you live. What are some regions inside your county? Which characteristics would you use to outline those regions?
18. Is it difficult to tell in which region of North Carolina your county is located? Why?
19. Looking at your chart, you can see the physical characteristics of North Carolina. How do these characteristics make North Carolina part of the larger region of the southeast United States?

PLACE LOCATION

Use the letters on the map to locate the following places in North Carolina:

20. the Piedmont.
21. the Outer Coastal Plain (Tidewater).
22. the Mountains.
23. the Inner Coastal Plain.
24. the fall line.
25. The fall line forms the boundary between which two regions?
26. The dotted line shows a rough boundary between two parts of which region?
27. Which region borders the Atlantic Ocean?
28. Which region borders Tennessee?
29. Which is the westernmost region?
30. Which is the easternmost region?
31. In which region is your county?
32. In which region is the Triangle?
33. In which region are pocosins?

Reviewing Place Location

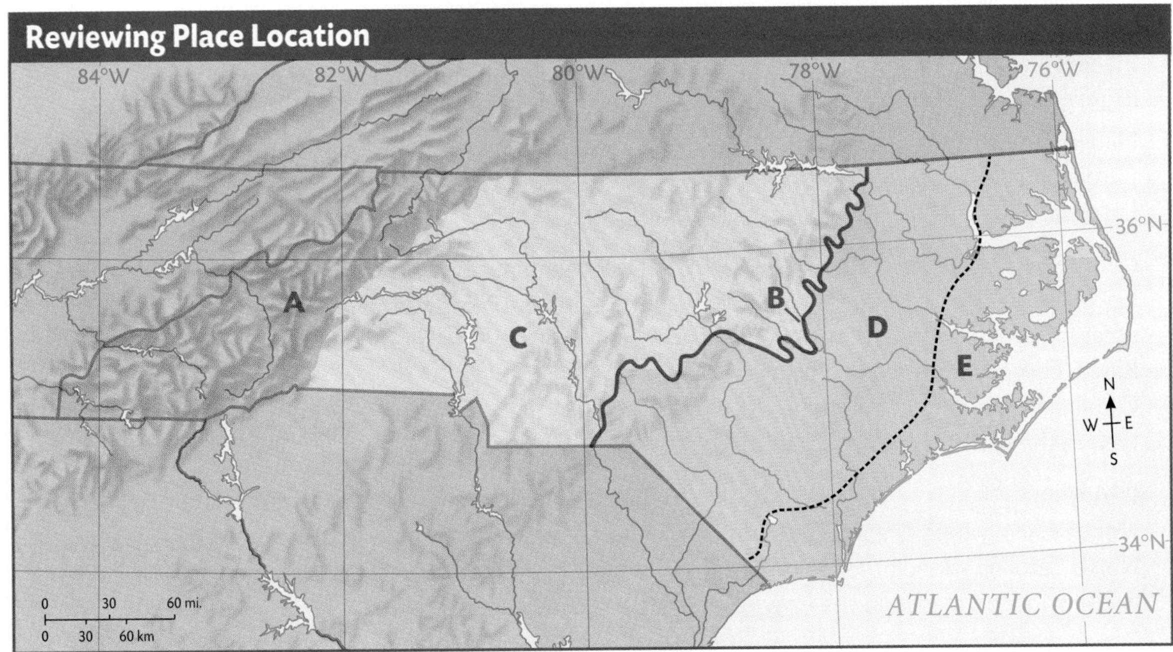

Linking the Past to the Present

A new land! A new country! We must cross the Atlantic Ocean. Sail for 50 days and nights over 4,000 miles and we start a new life.

Sails billow to catch the wind. We wave good-bye to loved ones. The Atlantic Ocean seems so great against such a small ship. Storms, pirates, and illness might chase us across the sea. Yet we will make our way to the shores of a beautiful, bountiful land—the land you know as North Carolina.

UNIT PREVIEW

CHAPTER 5
The First People Come to the Land
Native Americans lived in North Carolina for thousands of years before Europeans settled here.

CHAPTER 6
Europeans Colonize North Carolina
After trying to start a colony on Roanoke Island, Europeans settled in North Carolina in the 1600s along the coast, then in the backcountry.

CHAPTER 7
North Carolinians Create Their State
North Carolina joined other colonies in winning independence. In the early 1800s, most North Carolinians farmed. One third of the state's population were slaves.

CHAPTER 8
The Civil War and North Carolina
Disagreements over slavery divided the state, but North Carolina decided to fight the Civil War on the Confederate side.

CHAPTER 9
North Carolina Grows, 1865-1910
North Carolina grew as tobacco, cotton and textiles, and railroads became more important. Towns grew larger as more people found work there.

Elizabeth II, a replica of early ships that brought settlers to North Carolina

CHAPTER 5

The First People Come to the Land

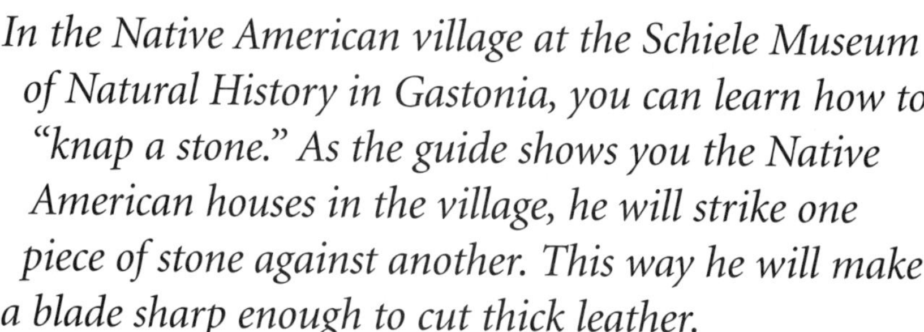

In the Native American village at the Schiele Museum of Natural History in Gastonia, you can learn how to "knap a stone." As the guide shows you the Native American houses in the village, he will strike one piece of stone against another. This way he will make a blade sharp enough to cut thick leather.

Native Americans knapped stones and made other tools to help them in their daily life in what became North Carolina. In this chapter you will see other ways Native Americans shaped their lives to fit the land of our state.

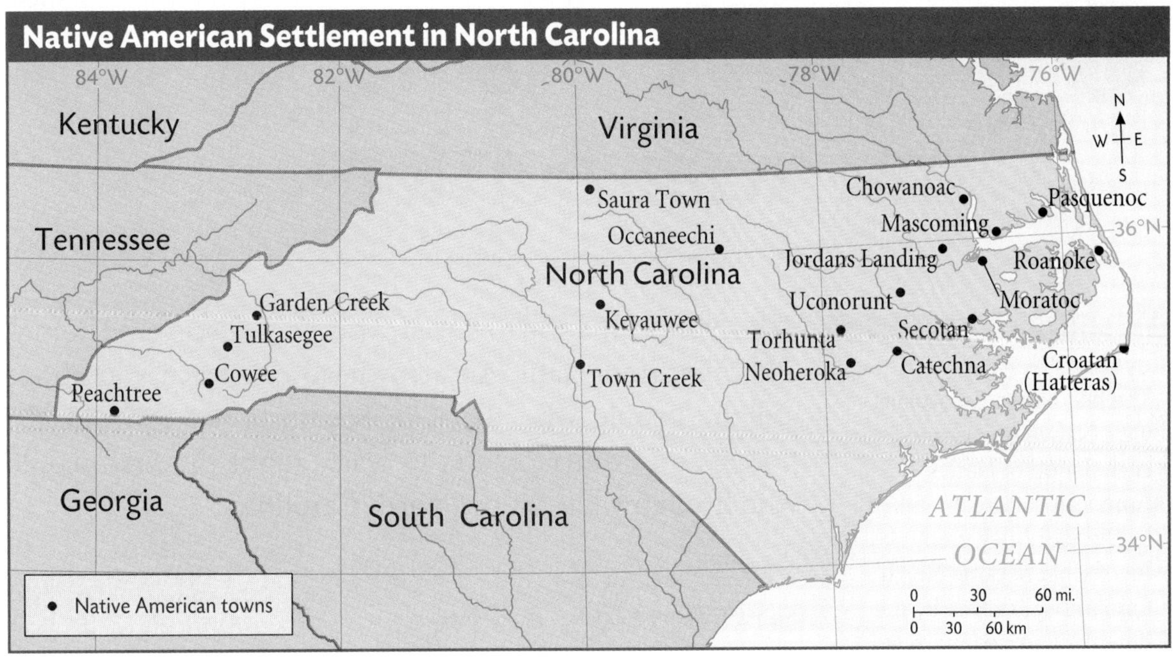

Native American Cousins

Native Americans in North Carolina had ties to other Native Americans. The Cherokee, Tuscarora, and Meherrin traded with relatives in what is now New York State. Native Americans in both places lived on land with forests, streams, and lakes. Both grew some food, hunted, and fished. Their lives were alike.

Other Native Americans in North Carolina—the Catawba, Waccamaw, Tutelo, and Occaneechi—had relatives called the Sioux living on the Great Plains of the West. These western plains had few forests, streams, or lakes. The Sioux used horses to hunt buffalo. They lived in teepees, which could be moved. Native Americans in what became North Carolina lived differently from their western cousins.

Sequoyah, inventor of the Cherokee alphabet

Periods of Native American Settlement

LESSON PREVIEW

Key Ideas

- The first North Carolinians were Native Americans.
- Each period of Native American culture is marked by the tools they used.
- All of what became North Carolina was settled by the time the Europeans arrived.

Key Terms

archaeologists, artifacts, prehistoric, Paleo-Indian people, Archaic people, atlatl, Woodland people, Iroquoian, Algonkian, Siouan, Historic Period

If you find an arrowhead, you have discovered something important. An arrowhead can teach you about the people who made it. Scientists use arrowheads, pottery, and other objects to learn about the first people who lived in what is now North Carolina.

First Settlers Arrive

Scientists believe North Carolina's first settlers arrived more than 12,000 years ago. Their ancestors had come from Asia to North America long before that time. They walked across land joining Asia and North America (see map below). The land connected today's Siberia and Alaska.

Gradually, these first settlers, called Native Americans, moved throughout the continent and into North Carolina. The map shows the route they probably took.

The scientists who dig up arrowheads, spear points, pottery, and other objects of the past are called **archaeologists** (ar·kay·AH·loh·jists). Their discoveries, called **artifacts**, give us clues about the first people and how they lived. They also teach archaeologists when new tools began to be used. This shows how the lives of a group of people changed over time.

Native Americans moved to North America thousands of years ago. *How did they get to North Carolina?*

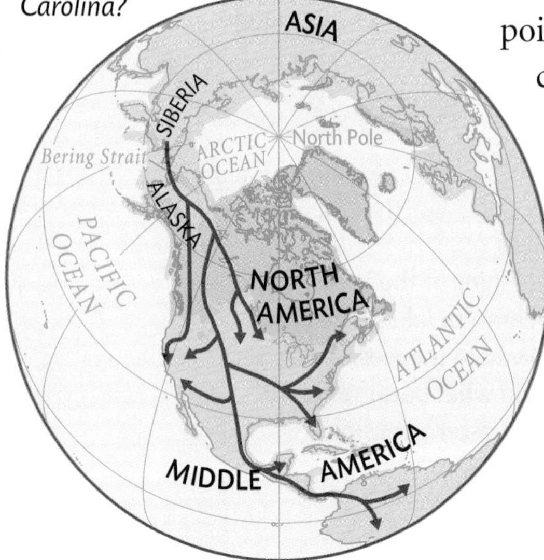

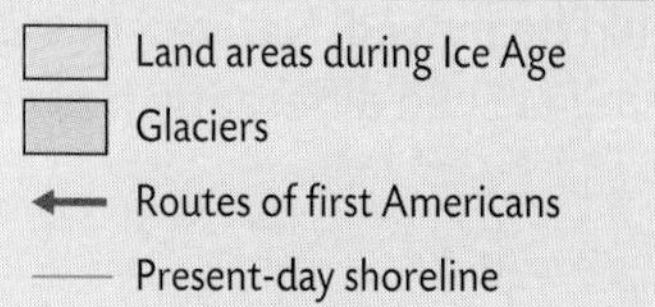

Archaeologists look for artifacts, such as spear points, at a Tuscarora village site. *How do their discoveries teach us about Native Americans?*

The story of Native Americans in North America can be told in four parts. These four periods of time are called Paleo-Indian, Archaic, Woodland, and Historic. The Paleo-Indian, Archaic, and Woodland Periods are prehistoric. **Prehistoric** is the time before history was written. The tools used by Native Americans in each period tell us when and how they lived.

Paleo-Indian People

Archaeologists call the very first settlers **Paleo-Indian** (PAY·lee·oh) **people.** *Paleo* means "very old."

Paleo-Indian people were hunters who lived in small groups. They moved often to find food. They used stone weapons to kill large animals, such as woolly mammoths, giant bison, and musk oxen. Mounds of animal and fish bones tell scientists what Paleo-Indian people ate. These are the only clues we have to tell us their story.

WORD ORIGINS

Knap sounds like nap, but this word isn't about sleeping. It comes from an English word that means "to shape by breaking off pieces." Native Americans knapped quartz, slate, and jasper stone to make sharp spear points, knives, drill bits, and arrowheads.

Archaic People

The group that followed the Paleo-Indian people are called the **Archaic** (ar·KAY·ik) **people.** *Archaic* means "old." The Archaic people had learned how to make better tools,

Native Americans of the Archaic Period used the atlatl to hunt small animals for food. *What other tools did they use to survive?*

and more of them, than the Paleo-Indian people.

Beneath layers of North Carolina soil, archaeologists found a clue that the Archaic people hunted smaller game. That clue? An **atlatl** (aht·LAH·tal), a wooden stick about 18 inches (46 cm) long, with a hook on one end and a hand grip on the other end. An atlatl helped the hunters throw their spears forcefully and accurately.

Other clues, such as grinding stones, bone fishhooks, and the skeletons of the people, showed archaeologists that the Archaic people had better ways to find and prepare food. This means they probably lived longer than the Paleo-Indian people.

EYEWITNESS TO HISTORY

From Pottery to Pouches

People can speak to us from the past through their diaries, letters, or photography. But how can we learn about the distant past before people wrote or before photography was invented?

Archaeologists look at prehistoric pieces of pottery to understand the everyday life of Native Americans. Even a piece of broken pottery (right) can teach us how the pottery was made and if it was used for storage or cooking. It might give us a clue about its maker. Sometimes, its markings reveal glimpses of the artist's desire to make a beautiful object.

What about a leather pouch (left) found buried in a Native American Tuscarora fort? It had been stored in 1713 by a Tuscarora man who was going to fight the colonists. We know more about him than the fact that he was a soldier.

Instead of moving all of the time to find food, the Archaic people moved only as the seasons changed. They collected berries and roots and followed migrating birds, fish, and mammals.

Woodland People

Native Americans lived in all parts of what became North Carolina (see map, page 81). Archaeologists call the groups of people who began farming and making pottery the **Woodland people.** They lived in eastern North America for about 1,500 years.

We also know he was a farmer and a trader because of glass beads, two copper bracelets, buckshot, and squash seeds found in the pouch. The glass beads were made in Europe. So we know the Tuscarora man had traded for them. Native American artists made the bracelets from copper received in trade.

Glass beads

The owner of the pouch carried 200 pieces of lead buckshot. Buckshot meant the Native American carried a long gun. He probably traded with Europeans for the gun and the buckshot. He used the buckshot for hunting. He shot lead musket balls in war.

Buckshot

Along with the buckshot was a supply of squash seeds to be planted for his next crop. Also in the pouch were two pipes and a small pair of pliers used to pull coals from a fire to light tobacco. From these simple objects we know the man farmed tobacco and squash. These artifacts tell us about a man who went to fight and didn't come back. What do they tell you?

Squash seeds

Native Americans of the Woodland Period learned how to make pottery. *How did this help them improve their diet?*

The Woodland people learned to grow food by replanting seeds of squash and gourds. They also grew corn, sunflowers, and beans.

The Woodland people began farming by replanting seeds where they found them. Each year they became better farmers and learned to plant on fertile lands. They began to farm by season, planting in the spring and harvesting in the fall.

Before Native Americans invented pottery, they cooked by dropping heated stones into water contained in animal skins. They added meat to the hot water to cook.

By making bowls and jars of clay, sand, and bits of shell, Woodland people could cook food more easily. With pottery, they could bake bread and boil vegetables and meat. They could store cooked food and carry it.

Woodland people continued to hunt game with bows and arrows. **Game** is a name for wild animals and fish used for food. A favorite game animal was the deer. Woodland people built permanent villages along streams and on the coast near woods filled with game.

Farming, pottery making, and village life allowed Native Americans to settle into communities throughout the Coastal Plain, Piedmont, and Mountains.

Individuals belonged to one of at least 34 different communities, each speaking a different language. People in one community could often speak with neighbors in

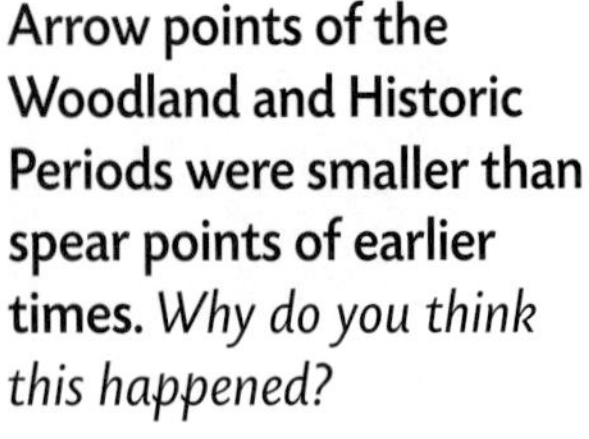

Arrow points of the Woodland and Historic Periods were smaller than spear points of earlier times. *Why do you think this happened?*

another because their languages were similar. The map below shows the communities that shared similar languages. The three major language groups were **Iroquoian**, **Algonkian**, and **Siouan**. The Pee Dee and other Native Americans who lived along the Pee Dee River in today's South Carolina spoke Muskogean languages.

Historic Period

The **Historic Period** began when Europeans arrived in North America. Changes for the Native Americans started shortly after the new settlers arrived. Native Americans became sick and died from diseases caught from European settlers. Native Americans also lost hunting and farming land when settlers took it for their own farms.

These new settlers wrote down their first impressions of the people and the land they saw. These new settlers wrote

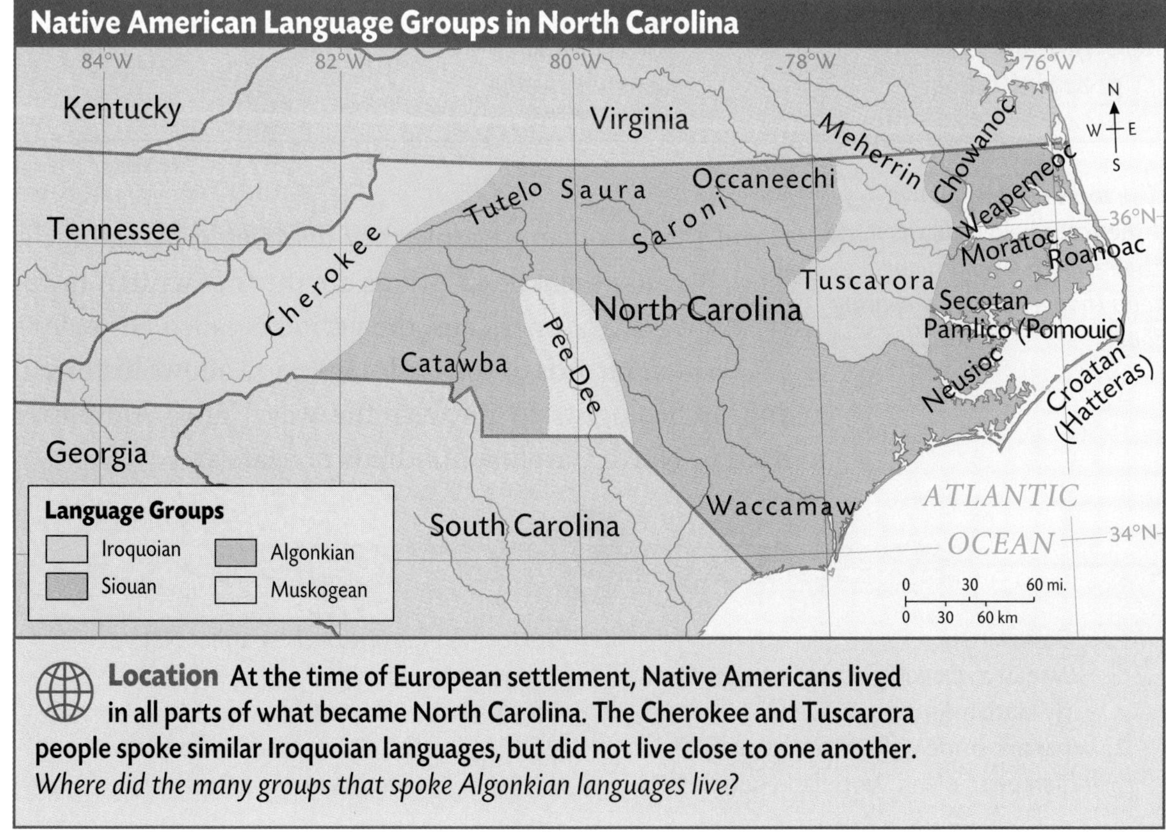

Native American Language Groups in North Carolina

Location At the time of European settlement, Native Americans lived in all parts of what became North Carolina. The Cherokee and Tuscarora people spoke similar Iroquoian languages, but did not live close to one another. *Where did the many groups that spoke Algonkian languages live?*

Native Americans in North Carolina

	Paleo-Indian*	Archaic*	Woodland*	Historic
Time	10,000 B.C. – 8,000 B.C.	8,000 B.C. – 1,000 B.C.	1,000 B.C. – A.D. 1650	1650
Tools	Stone spear points	Atlatl	Bow and arrow, pottery	Bow and arrow, pottery
Way of life	Followed animals constantly; small camp sites	Followed animals by season	Settled in villages along streams; farmed, hunted, and fished	Settled in villages; farmed; lost land as Europeans settled
Food sources	Big game (wooly mammoths, bison, musk ox) and fish	Small game (deer, beaver) and fish; wild berries and roots	Small game; crops of corn, squash, and beans	Small game; crops of corn, squash, beans, and other food
Methods of food preparation	Roasting	Heated stone placed in animal skins with water and food	Water boiled in clay pottery	Water boiled in clay pottery

*prehistoric period

The tools used by Native Americans help us understand their lives. *How did changing tools change ways of preparing food?*

about the Woodland People they discovered living on the land. Because these descriptions are the first written history about Native Americans, the period is called Historic.

Written records of the Historic Period allows historians and archeologists to uncover the way Native Americans lived in North Carolina hundreds of years ago.

LESSON 1 REVIEW

Fact Follow-Up

1. How can archaeologists tell us about how early Native Americans lived?
2. What are some differences between Paleo-Indian people and Woodland people?
3. How did Europeans first affect Native American people?

Think These Through

4. Why was the development of pottery making so important?

LESSON 2 Living Off Nature

Can you recognize most of the plants in the woods? Native Americans could. They knew which plants would help them and which might hurt them.

Food and medicine came from the animals and plants of the forest, ocean, and streams. Native Americans lived close to nature and knew how to get food, clothing, and shelter from the land and sea.

Europeans learned these skills from the Native Americans they met when they settled in North America.

LESSON PREVIEW

Key Ideas

- Native Americans first fed themselves by hunting, fishing, and gathering.
- Most Native Americans began to farm in addition to hunting and gathering.

Key Terms

pemmican, weirs, tonic, ginseng root

Hunting Game

Archaeologists think Paleo-Indian people ate a lot of meat. These first settlers also gathered seeds, nuts, and berries they tasted or saw animals eat.

The Paleo-Indian people probably hunted in small groups. Often the hunters ran their prey off a cliff or hillside. Once the animal fell, the hunters leaped upon it and killed it with their stone spears.

The hunters roasted the meat. After eating some, they saved the rest of the meat, keeping it so it would not spoil. They used the bones for tools and the hides for clothing and bags.

Later Native Americans, the Archaic people, hunted smaller animals with their spear-throwers (atlatles). Fewer people were needed to hunt such game. Others could gather seeds and berries.

Still later, Woodland people hunted with bows and arrows. Sometimes they burned forests to chase

Before Native Americans learned to make pottery, they gathered nuts and berries and roasted fish and game over fire. *How did pottery help them settle in one place?*

the animals into a clearing. The game was easier to kill there, and fewer hunters got hurt. Burning forests also cleared the land for farming.

What would YOU do?

Children in prehistoric times became hungry just as you do. When you want a snack, you can usually find one at home or at a store. If you were an early Woodland child, where might you find a snack?

If you like berries, in the summer you could find blackberries or wild strawberries. In the winter you could eat the berries of summer that your family had dried and stored in a pottery jar.

Farming

Native Americans discovered that the seeds they dropped on the ground sometimes sprouted. They planted these seeds in open spaces by poking holes in the ground with sticks.

They farmed the upland soils and also the areas near rivers where floods left silt that made rich soil. The Woodland people learned to grow corn, beans, squash, pumpkins, and sunflower seeds.

As time passed, the Woodland people became better

This engraving of a farming village shows the kinds of crops grown by Native Americans. *Can you name three of the crops?*

farmers. They grew healthier kinds of beans, corn, and squash. The protein contained in beans and corn improved their diets.

The Woodland people learned how to measure the seasons. They knew when to plant and harvest. They celebrated each season with ceremonies.

The river's edge and deep pits elsewhere gave Native Americans clay. They learned which clays, when heated in a fire, stayed rigid and watertight. Their baked clay became pottery. The clay pots and jars made good cooking and storage vessels.

Woodland people also preserved food to last through the winter. They learned to dry meat and fruit to last a long time without spoiling.

They picked fruit, such as persimmons and wild strawberries, and dried them in the sun. They boiled the fat off meat, kept the grease, and let the meat dry. They mixed grease, dried meat, and dried persimmon into **pemmican**. They could eat this mix on the trails while walking to trade or hunt.

In most communities, men hunted and fished. Women stayed close to the villages to rear small children, so they also helped men care for the nearby farmland.

Native Americans caught fish with spears, nets, and weirs. *What is a weir? Where is one in the painting?*

Fishing

Fishing was always important to Native Americans living near the ocean. Coastal communities, such as Secotan on Pamlico Sound, stretched **weirs**, or fish traps, across the sounds.

Native Americans who lived near rivers learned to fish. Piedmont settlers, such as the Saponi people, built V-shaped rock dams across the Yadkin River. The fish swam into a narrow opening of the dam and were trapped in a woven basket or net. Then the fish were covered in grease, put over a fire, and broiled.

Natural Remedies

Native Americans faced many hardships. Their hunts could last for several days. Harsh cold in winter or drought in summer could mean less food. People grew weak and became ill.

The Native Americans knew that some plants helped them stay healthy. The Algonkian made yaupon tea from a small holly bush that grows on the coast. They also traded this plant to their inland neighbors. A mild form of the tea provided a **tonic**. A tonic is a drink that gives energy.

CONNECTIONS

Geography & Science

Plants and Healing

How does your family treat a cold or a fever? If you were a Native American living hundreds of years ago, you might have used a dogwood tree instead of a drug store.

Why? Plants and herbs were used by Native Americans as their medicine. The bark of the dogwood tree was boiled and made into a tea. Bark tea was thought to bring down a high fever.

Native Americans used other plants for medicine. The Cherokee chewed liverwort root to cure a cough. The Catawba used pipsissewa for heart and stomach problems. Wild garlic might have been used as a chest salve.

Native Americans used plants as medicine. Today, companies that make medicine study plants to see which ones cure illnesses. The companies create new medicines from plant roots, seeds, or leaves.

The scientists also use manufactured ingredients to make it easier for people to take the medicine in a pill or liquid form.

If you were sick, you might not want to search for wild garlic, liverwort root, or pipsissewa. Native Americans knew it was the only way to get medicine.

Dogwood

The Cherokee chewed **ginseng root** each spring. Ginseng roots are shaped like the stick people you drew when you were younger. The Cherokee believed that the shape meant ginseng helped all parts of the body.

Archaeologists examine burned peach pits at the Neoheroka village site. Native Americans learned about orchard crops from Europeans. *What other ideas did the two groups share?*

Europeans and Native Americans

As Native Americans met Europeans, they borrowed ideas from one another. Europeans learned to survive in a land they had never seen. Native Americans learned about new crops and animals to raise.

Native Americans taught Europeans how to build canoes, follow trading paths through the woods, and grow corn, beans, and squash. Europeans also learned methods of warfare from the Native Americans.

Almost all the Native American societies began to grow peaches after the Spanish brought them in the 1500s. The Cherokee and Tuscarora soon became noted for their large orchards. The Tuscarora and Catawba raised cattle and hogs after Europeans brought them.

Yet conflict grew between Native Americans and European settlers. Both wanted the same land for themselves.

LESSON 2 REVIEW

Fact Follow-Up

1. Describe the farming life of Woodland people.
2. What natural remedies were used by Native Americans?
3. What ideas were exchanged between Europeans and Native Americans?

Think These Through

4. Why is it said that Native Americans lived off nature?
5. Which natural resource do you think was most important to Woodland people? Explain why.

LESSON 3 Native American Villages

LESSON PREVIEW

Key Ideas

- Native North Carolinians were villagers.
- They lived together in families and clans.
- Native Americans formed communities to grow food and to provide protection.

Key Terms

stockades, wigwams, council houses, clans, council

By the time the Europeans came, the Native Carolinians had a way of life that was centuries old. The Chowanoac village in today's Bertie County was at least 500 years old when Europeans moved here.

Almost all Native Americans lived in villages. Nausau, the Catawba's main town south of today's Charlotte, had a population of between 100 and 200 people. Town Creek attracted many more Native Americans. The Pee Dee people built a lodge overlooking the Little River. Ceremonies held around a sacred fire happened several times a year. More than 100 Native American villages dotted the landscape (see map, page 81).

Building on Waterways and Trails

Native Americans made canoes from trees. They hollowed the logs with fire, then carved the insides. *What other tools do you see?*

The natives planned where to build their settlements. They often looked near waterways. Waterways provided fish and attracted animals that the natives hunted. Rivers and sounds along the ocean gave them easy ways to travel. Tidewater people lived on the sounds. They had many canoes, carved out of large cypress trees.

Piedmont residents preferred to build villages on hills not far from where creeks emptied into rivers. High hills protected them from floods and roving enemies. They could quickly paddle their canoes to the main channel of the river.

Native Americans celebrated the change of seasons at special places built for ceremonies. At Town

Creek on the Pee Dee River in today's Montgomery County, the Pee Dee built their ceremonial lodge atop a large mound. On the field below it, the people danced or played a game with a ball and long-handled nets, similar to lacrosse.

Some villages had **stockades** around them. Stockades are fences of pointed posts set in the ground. The stockades protected the villages from enemies and wandering wild animals.

The Cherokee lived in the mountains and did not use the canoe as often because mountain streams were usually too shallow and swift. Instead, the Cherokee lived along trails in mountain gaps. The Cherokee also built villages in the wide mountain valleys, where they could farm.

GAMES People Play

Lacrosse is a fast-moving sport played with long-handled sticks and a small rubber ball. The sticks are crooked and covered with a net at one end. Teams score by whipping the ball into the other team's goal.

Native Americans of North America invented the sport, using balls of hide and nets of deer hide.

Housing

Native Americans built two types of houses in North Carolina.

In eastern North Carolina, Native Americans built **wigwams**. They cut down small pine or cedar trees, stripped the bark, and put them in a fire to toughen and make them bend easily. They placed the trees into the ground in a circular pattern and bent the tops together to make a round frame. They covered the wigwam with mud, bark, moss, and grass.

The wigwams of Native American villages were made of bent poles covered by bark, grass, and mud. *How did these materials protect the villagers living there?*

Families put matted reeds or animal skins on the roof. They left a smoke hole in the roof's center because they built fires in the middle of the earth floor. Up to 12 people lived in one wigwam.

In the mountains, the Cherokee built rectangular or square houses large enough for one family. They also bent trees to form the frame, which they covered with bark and wood. They plastered the outside with clay to protect against the cold and rain.

The European settlers brought iron tools for cutting wood. When the Cherokee got some of these, they began

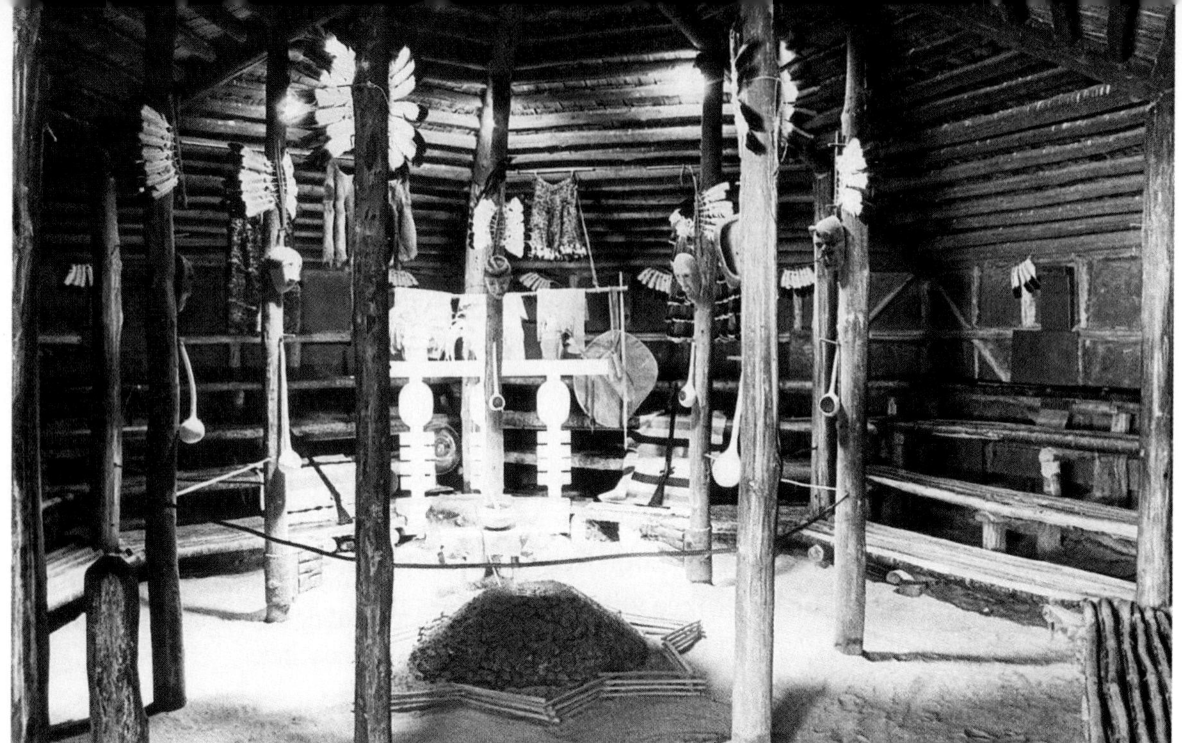

Cherokee leaders made decisions about village life during ceremonies in large council houses. *What do you see that might have been used in ceremonies?*

building log cabins of notched tree trunks and shingled roofs. They plastered the walls inside and out with clay to keep rain and cold wind out of their homes.

Cherokee villagers erected **council houses**, large buildings where they held ceremonies or invited guests to sleep. They built the houses atop mounds of earth in the same manner as wigwams, except the roofs were covered with thatch (woven grass or leaves) instead of bark. An English army officer wrote that one council house was large enough to hold 500 people.

Native American Names

Each Native American community named itself to show respect for the environment. No one called the Catawba by that name before the Europeans arrived. They called themselves *ye is`wa,* Siouan words that mean "the people by the river." They were also known by *e`saw,* or "people of the water."

Cherokee means "the people of the caves" in one Iroquoian language. It describes the hollows of the mountains where they made their first homes. Some scientists believe the word means "people of a different speech."

Hatteras is an Algonkian word meaning "there is less vegetation." The word well describes Cape Hatteras and Roanoke Island, where the Hatteras people lived.

Machapunga, another Algonkian name, also describes unfertile land. The word means "bad dust" or "much dirt," a description of the coast's sandy soil.

Native American names live on in North Carolina in the names of many counties and towns. Ten of North Carolina's 100 counties bear Native American names. Can you name them? See the county listing on page 389.

Family Life

Related families gathered into larger groups called **clans.** Clans elected village leaders to a council. The **council** led the entire community. The leaders met in the council house, a special building where they decided about going to war, moving to better land, or helping someone in need.

Native American leaders in North Carolina did not call themselves "chiefs" or "kings." The Catawba called their leader "man superior," which is a way of saying they chose the best man to lead.

Women also had a strong hand in the shaping of clan life. Most communities traced their name and kinship through women. A man wishing to marry a woman asked permission of her parents. After marriage, the man moved in with the wife's family. If there was a divorce, the husband left, but the children stayed with the mother. The mother's family helped rear her children.

A Cherokee family of the late 1800s sits on the porch of their log cabin. *How were families the center of clan and community life?*

LESSON 3 REVIEW

Fact Follow-Up

1. Why did most Native Americans live on or near waterways?
2. Describe a wigwam.
3. What were clans?

Think These Through

4. Why do you think Native Americans named their towns after natural features?
5. In what ways were women important in Native American society?

Native American Ways of Life

LESSON PREVIEW

Key Ideas

- Nature influenced ways Native Americans thought about the world.
- Native American ideas about sharing and community were different from Europeans.

Key Terms

anthropologists, sacred, Green Corn ceremony, husquenaw

When the Cherokee saw an eclipse of the moon, they believed a giant frog was swallowing it. They danced and made noise to scare the frog away. It always seemed to work. Why do you think that happened?

Native Americans believed that people, animals, and the sun, moon, and stars worked together as parts of nature. In nature, frogs in nearby streams hopped away when they heard noise. So Native Americans believed that they could frighten away a frog swallowing the moon.

Native American Beliefs

We learn about such beliefs from anthropologists. **Anthropologists** (an·throw·PAH·lo·jists) are scientists who study how people live together. As they have examined Native American life, anthropologists have discovered the importance of stories, such as the one you just read.

Deer antlers were part of a headdress used by Tuscarora in ceremonies. *Why was nature an important part of the beliefs of Native Americans?*

In Native American communities, storytellers were highly respected. Because people could not write, the community's traditions were passed along by storytellers. Many Native American stories were hundreds of years old. All of them taught lessons.

As you read about Native American stories, you will be working like an anthropologist. You will discover what Native Americans thought and why they did many things.

Stories

Native American stories are similar in many languages and communities. Both the Cherokee and the Catawba told stories about their ancestors coming across the great mountains of the West and North. By talking about their ancestors' movement across the land, the storytellers passed on knowledge about the past. They kept alive the stories of where Native Americans settled.

Native Americans gathered around fires for religious ceremonies, storytelling, and celebrations. *How do their stories tell us about the way they lived?*

Stories also taught the listeners how their people had always been connected to the land. Many stories told about forces of nature. Animals were often the main characters of the stories. Birds were important because they flew high above the world.

Native Americans believed parts of ordinary life were **sacred**, or holy. For example, the Cherokee believed the four cardinal directions had special meaning. Because the four cardinal directions were important, the number 4 became sacred.

The Cherokee gave special colors to each direction. East was red. It represented life, since the sun was red when it rose in the morning. West was black, symbolizing death, because the day "died" when the sun set. North was blue, representing the wind and snow of winter. South was white for the bright light of day coming from that direction.

Ceremonies

Native Americans marked new seasons with ceremonies, much the way many North Carolinians today celebrate such holidays as Thanksgiving.

The **Green Corn ceremony** was common to all Native Americans in North Carolina. The purpose of the annual ceremony was for people to clean their bodies, houses, and minds. The ceremony came in late summer, when the corn crop was ripening.

The men drank a strong, black drink made from toasted leaves. This drink helped cleanse their digestive systems after not eating food for a few days.

Everyone cleaned out their homes. Trash was burned. Hearth fires were extinguished. Even the ceremonial temple fire was extinguished.

The fires were extinguished so the year's wrongs could be forgotten. Villagers asked each other for forgiveness of wrongs done to one another.

Every village began a feast. They might have used some of the newly harvested corn. Perhaps pumpkins were gathered from the fields and apples and nuts were taken from the trees in the woods. During this feast time, the fires were restarted. Embers were taken from the ceremonial fire and carried to each village. Every village shared the fire from the one burning at the ceremonial temple.

A Native American religious leader dances with a bird attached to his head. *What other things does the painting show him carrying?*

Native American teenagers in eastern North Carolina underwent a time of discipline called the **husquenaw** (HUH·skwe·naw). The village elders put all young people through trials that measured strength of mind and body. The elders believed such experiences helped the community. These young people would be ready to hunt, go to war, and help the community survive difficult times.

Beliefs About Property

Native Americans believed the land was for all the people to use. They did not think the land should be owned by individuals. Whoever happened to be on the land had the right to use it, they thought.

At first, Native Americans shared the land with the Europeans. They did not understand why the land was not given back when the person living there died. The European practice of passing family property to the next generation was puzzling to the Native Americans.

They also thought things they owned should be shared. Native Americans thought it kindly to give away what they had. In turn, Native Americans took what they needed, because they assumed the person who owned those items would not care. Europeans did not share these beliefs.

Tuscarora and other Native Americans in North Carolina still perform ceremonies. *How do such ceremonies help their communities?*

Customs Collide

Thousands of years of living in North Carolina had produced Native American beliefs and customs. Those ways of life worked well as long as Native Americans were the only people living in North America.

People from Europe would come as settlers. European beliefs and customs were different from those of Native Americans. The differences soon led to war. Native Americans would lose these wars. Most would be killed or driven away. Others would die of disease.

LESSON 4 REVIEW

Fact Follow-Up

1. What do anthropologists do?
2. What was the Green Corn ceremony? Why was it important?

Think These Through

3. How did ceremonies and beliefs show Native Americans' respect for nature?
4. Is there anything in the ceremonies of today that is similar to those of Native Americans? Explain your answer.
5. Why did Europeans' and Native Americans' differing views of property cause conflicts?

The Five Themes of Geography: Human-Environmental Interaction

Using Geography's Themes: Human-Environmental Interaction

Natural Environments

Pretend that you are walking around outside your house. What natural features—trees, bodies of water, hills, or mountains—would you see? Take a sheet of paper and label it "Graphic Organizer: Natural Environments." Make a list of these natural features on the left side of the page. Label that list "Natural Environment of My Home."

To practice "reading" the natural environment, look at the photograph of the Cheoah River below. What natural features can you find? List them on a separate sheet of paper and compare your list with a classmate's.

Graphic Organizer: Natural Environments

Natural Environment of My Home	Natural Features Long Ago

After "reading" the natural environment in the photograph, you might want to add more items to your list, "Natural Environment of My Home."

Next, skim through Chapter 4 and make a list of all the natural resources that Native Americans living in North Carolina might have seen. Place this list on the right side of the graphic organizer (see the example below) and label the list "Natural Features Long Ago."

Compare the lists you made of the natural environment of your home and of long ago. What natural features are on both lists? What are some differences? Why do you think there are differences?

Human Environments

One reason for differences in your two lists is that people over the years have changed the natural environment by building homes and other structures,

cutting trees, plowing fields, and building roads and bridges. What are some other things people have done to change the natural environment?

Study the photograph of Charlotte on the right. What human changes to the natural environment can you find? Make a list of these human changes and compare your list with a classmate's.

Think about the area around your home. How many human changes to the environment can you see there? Take a sheet of paper and title it "Graphic Organizer: Environmental Change." Make a list of the human changes along the left side of the page. Label the list "Humans Change the Environment Today."

Now, skim Chapter 5 and look for ways Native Americans changed the natural environment long ago. Make a list of these changes along the right side of the page. Label the list "Native Americans Changed the Environment." Your paper should look like the graphic organizer above.

Compare the two lists. Are any of the changes to the environment the same? What are some differences in the lists? Have people today changed the natural environment more or less than the long-ago Native Americans?

Graphic Organizer: Environmental Change

Humans Change the Environment Today	Native Americans Changed the Environment

Human-Environmental Interaction

Geographers have a term to describe the ways people change (or interact with) the environment. The term is **Human-Environmental Interaction**. Human-Environmental Interaction is one of the Five Themes of Geography. You have already learned about the themes of Location, Place, and Region. Now you will be able to see how human-environmental interaction works anytime you look out a window or take a walk or ride—even, perhaps, as you watch television or read a story or a book.

Chapter 5 Review

LESSONS LEARNED

LESSON 1 Archaeologists divide Native American life into periods, based on the tools they used. Paleo-Indian people used stone spear points; Archaic people used the atlatl; Woodland people used the bow and arrow and made pottery. Historic people used the bow and arrow, also. They are put in a different period because their lives were described in writing.

LESSON 2 To survive, the first Native Americans hunted and gathered. Most Native Americans later learned to fish and farm, which allowed them to settle in one spot.

LESSON 3 Native Americans built villages near waterways. Village houses were wigwams built in a round or square frame. Village life was organized around groups of related families called clans.

LESSON 4 The beliefs of Native Americans were closely related to the natural world. Anthropologists are scientists who study how people live in groups. They look at Native American stories and ceremonies to learn about Native American beliefs. The Green Corn ceremony was a way for a village to clean its homes and villagers to cleanse their bodies and minds. Native American beliefs differed from Europeans.

TIME FOR TERMS

archaeologists
prehistoric
artifacts
Paleo-Indian people
Archaic people
Woodland people
Iroquoian
Siouan
pemmican
ginseng root
wigwams
clans
anthropologists
Green Corn ceremony
Human-Environmental Interaction
atlatl
game
Algonkian
Historic Period
weirs
stockades
council houses
council
sacred
husquenaw

FACT FOLLOW-UP

1. What were the four periods of Native American settlement in North Carolina?
2. How do archaeologists know what these periods were?
3. How did Native Americans' ways of hunting change? Why did they change?
4. How did the development of agriculture change the settlement patterns of Native Americans?
5. What languages were spoken in North Carolina when Europeans first came?
6. How did the eating habits of Native American people change over time?
7. How did Native Americans change in the ways they interacted with the environment?
8. What did Native American groups learn from one another? How did they learn from one another?
9. How did the coming of Europeans change Native Americans' ways of living?
10. Describe village life at the time of the coming of Europeans.

11. Describe how families and clans were important to Native Americans at the time Europeans came.

THINK THESE THROUGH

12. How did the lives of Native Americans illustrate human-environmental interaction?
13. Was the position of women in Native American society the same as the position of women today? Explain your answer.
14. How did their beliefs reflect how Native Americans used the natural resources around them?
15. Why did Native Americans show so much respect for nature?
16. Was the coming of the Europeans a benefit to Native Americans? Explain.
17. What do you think North Carolina would be like today if the Europeans had not come? Why?
18. What do you think North Carolina would be like today if there had been no Native American people? Why?

SHARPENING SKILLS

19. Explain to one of your classmates what human-environmental interaction means.
20. How do humans change the environment today?
21. How do you think humans might change the environment in the future?
22. What are some positive, or good, ways humans change the environment?
23. What are some negative, or bad, ways humans change the environment?
24. What are some things *you* can do to change the environment in positive ways?

PLACE LOCATION

Use the the map key to name the language group of these Native Americans:

25. Tuscarora.
26. Cherokee.
27. Pee Dee.
28. Catawba.
29. Croatan.

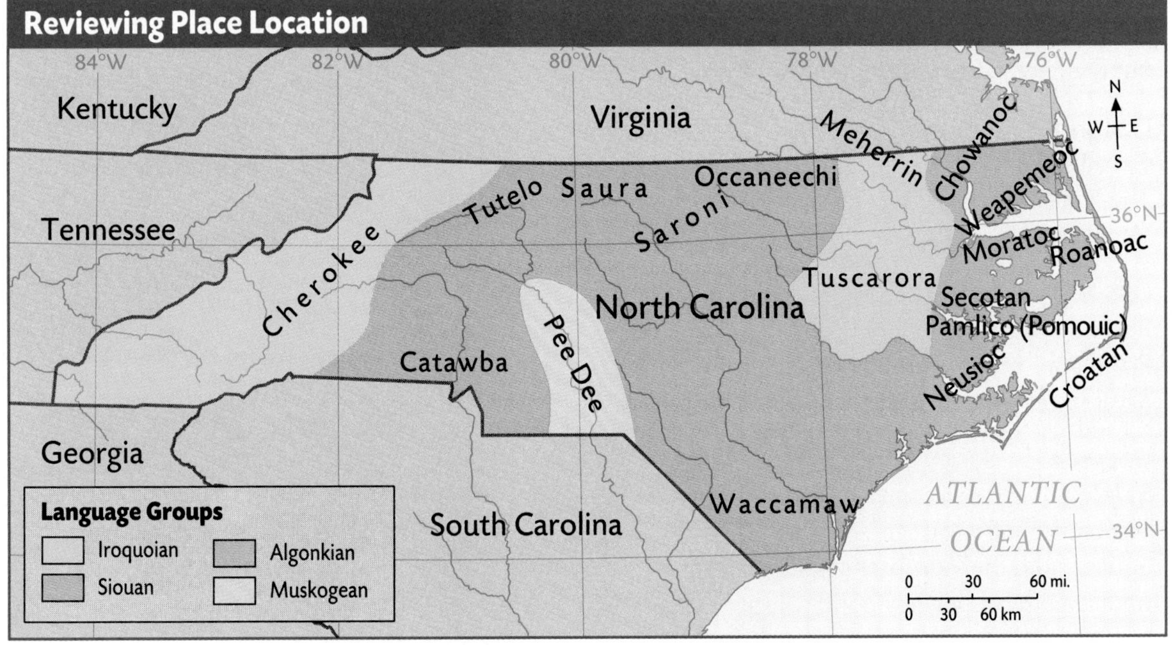

CHAPTER 6

Europeans Colonize North Carolina

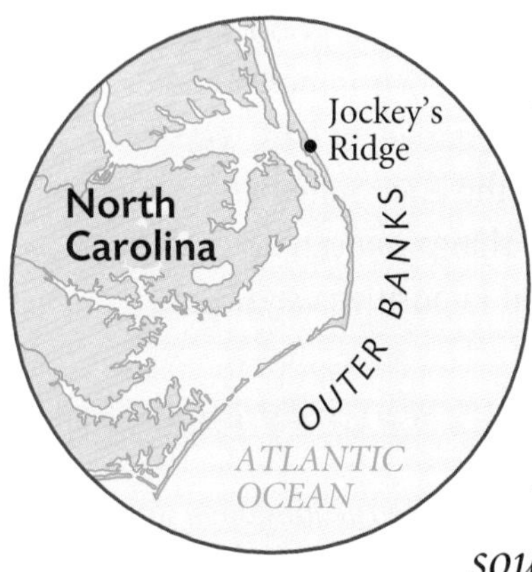

Jockey's Ridge near Nags Head, North Carolina, rises 148 feet (44 m) above the beach.

From the top of the great sand dune you can see where Europeans first came to North Carolina. To the southwest on Roanoke Island, the English built their first colony. Look northward, where English settlers came from Virginia. To the south and east, past the Outer Banks, lies the vast Atlantic Ocean. So many ships sank there, sailors called the Outer Banks the Graveyard of the Atlantic.

CHAPTER PREVIEW

LESSON 1
Europeans Look for a New Home
Early attempts to settle North Carolina failed, but the English learned from the experience.

LESSON 2
Carolina Settled
The first colonists of Carolina came from Virginia in the 1600s.

LESSON 3
Early Successes
Plantations of tobacco and rice and profit from naval stores were the first successes of the colony.

LESSON 4
Settling the Backcountry
The backcountry was settled in the 1700s upriver from the Tidewater sounds and along trading paths of the Piedmont.

Jockey's Ridge

Early English Settlements in Eastern North Carolina

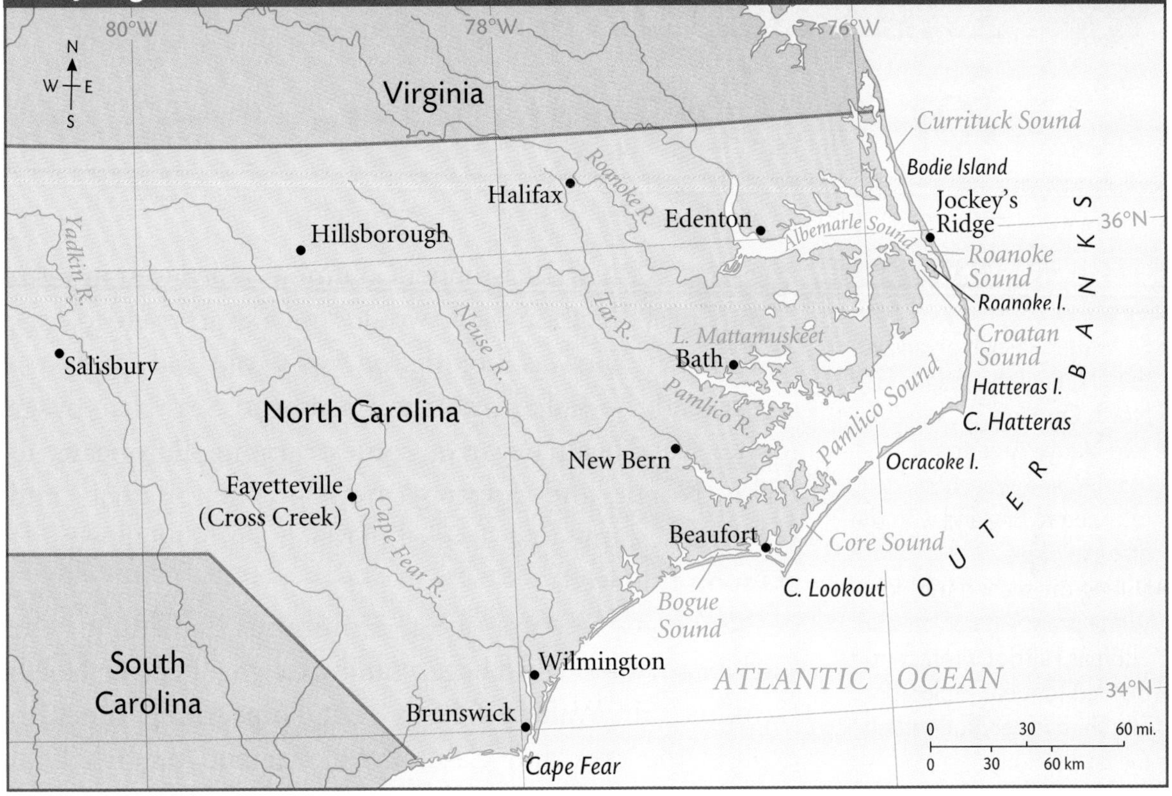

80°W
78°W
76°W
36°N
34°N
N
W
E
S
Virginia
North Carolina
South Carolina
Currituck Sound
Bodie Island
Jockey's Ridge
Roanoke Sound
Roanoke I.
Croatan Sound
Hatteras I.
C. Hatteras
Ocracoke I.
OUTER BANKS
Halifax
Edenton
Albemarle Sound
Hillsborough
Roanoke R.
Tar R.
Neuse R.
Yadkin R.
Salisbury
L. Mattamuskeet
Bath
Pamlico R.
Pamlico Sound
New Bern
Fayetteville (Cross Creek)
Cape Fear R.
Beaufort
Core Sound
C. Lookout
Bogue Sound
Wilmington
Brunswick
Cape Fear
ATLANTIC OCEAN
0 30 60 mi.
0 30 60 km

Blackbeard

Edward Teach, an Englishman, raided Spanish ships in the Caribbean. He took Spanish gold for England. Some of the treasure he kept for himself as Blackbeard the pirate.

Teach's nickname came from the way he scared sailors. He would light paper and rope tied to his long hair and tangled beard. The smoke blackened his beard and made him appear to be on fire.

Carolina's coast gave Blackbeard good hideouts between raids. His piracy hurt trade. Some officials protected him, but Virginia's governor wanted him arrested. Blackbeard died in a sword fight near Ocracoke Inlet during the attempted capture. In 1997, divers discovered a shipwreck that appeared to be his.

Europeans Look for a New Home

LESSON PREVIEW

Key Ideas

- Sir Walter Raleigh organized the first English voyages to North Carolina.
- Two Native Americans, Manteo and Wanchese, returned to England with the first explorers.
- During the second trip, John White drew watercolors and Thomas Harriot wrote reports that led to more exploration.
- The third expedition settled the Lost Colony.

Key Terms

colony, colonists, Lost Colony

When Christopher Columbus sailed west in 1492, he thought he would find a short route to Asia. He was looking for Asia's gold and spices.

Instead, he sailed into the Caribbean Sea. His voyage to the Caribbean began a contest among Europeans to reach North and South America. The Spanish and Portuguese came first. English, French, and Dutch explorers soon followed.

Ninety-two years after Columbus sailed to the Caribbean, the English began sailing to what became North Carolina. Sir Walter Raleigh sent ships three times to explore the area and claim it for England on behalf of Queen Elizabeth I.

Manteo and Wanchese

The first English explorers in 1584 met two Native Americans, Manteo and Wanchese, on the Outer Banks. The English had never seen people dressed like Manteo and Wanchese. They had not heard the language that the two men spoke.

Manteo and Wanchese sailed back to England with the explorers that same year. They probably thought the English looked and sounded strange, too. Yet they willingly went to England. Manteo and Wanchese's visit helped encourage Queen Elizabeth to support Raleigh's plan for exploration. Their visit became a first step in building an English colony in what became North Carolina.

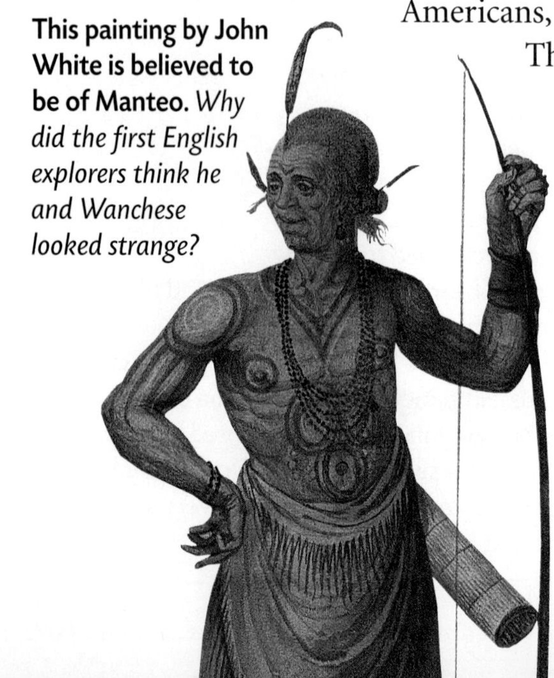

This painting by John White is believed to be of Manteo. *Why did the first English explorers think he and Wanchese looked strange?*

John White's map of Roanoke Island includes names of Native American villages. *What does he show people doing?*

A **colony** is an area settled by people from another country. These settlers, called **colonists**, remain connected to their home country through government, economy, and ways of life.

GAMES People Play

Sailor's Knots If you were a sailor aboard a ship that brought settlers, you would know how to tie lines. A square knot ties back part of a sail. The fisherman's knot ties rope to a buoy or an anchor ring. You may know how to tie these knots. You can use them in a string game called cat's cradle.

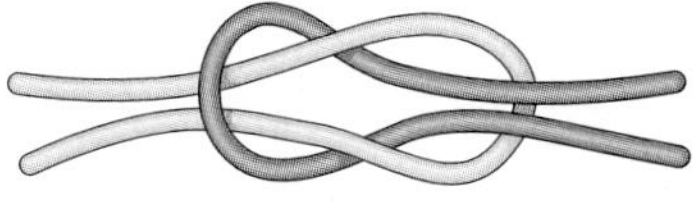

First English Colony

Manteo and Wanchese returned to the Outer Banks aboard a second ship from England in 1585. John White returned to paint pictures of the Native Americans and the land. Scientist Thomas Harriot came to write about the area.

Ralph Lane commanded the colony. The colony did not last. The colonists left it after one year. They had arrived too late in the year to plant crops, and the Native Americans did not have enough food to share.

Records of the Failed Colony

Lane's colony taught the English about the eastern coast of North Carolina. Harriot wrote about the area. White painted watercolors and drew maps. Their work helps us understand Native American ceremonies, clothing, housing, and food.

White's maps are so detailed, you can see schools of fish swimming in the water. Some of White's paintings and maps are shown in these chapters.

Harriot published a book containing White's paintings. Harriot hoped people would settle in North America. He listed resources colonists would find near Roanoke Island: iron, copper, and other minerals; animal skins and furs; cedar, oak, walnut, and cypress trees; and such crops as

LIVING IN PAMLICO SOUND

John White's Pamlico

John White came to the new land eager to explore it. He found many things to draw that would interest the people back in England. Pamlico Sound was one of the places John White explored.

What did he see? Birds and fish unlike any he had seen before. People who had a brownish red skin. He saw the people catch fish with nets. He saw them smoke the fish to save for winter. He watched the people paddle their canoes.

If John White came to Pamlico Sound today, what would he see?

More people than he saw in 1587. People with skins of all colors. People who are fishing with lines and hooks.

Would clothing be different? Few people wear clothing made from animal skins as the Native Americans did.

We do not know if White's drawings show the everyday wear of the Native Americans. Perhaps they show what people wore when they worked and played on the beach. Americans today dress differently at the beach.

Transport ships, pleasure craft, and fishing boats now crowd the water. John White would be surprised by how quickly they move.

White would see some birds and fish, but perhaps not the same kinds or as many.

He would see restaurants serving many different kinds of food, not just what could be caught in a day's fishing or hunting. What would John White think of a fast-food restaurant?

beans, corn, wheat, peas, melons, pumpkins, grapes, and strawberries.

Harriot's book about Roanoke inspired Queen Elizabeth to help Raleigh send a third voyage to North America in 1587.

English explorers landed where people were already living, such as these Native Americans painted by John White. *How do you think they felt about the English moving to their home?*

The Lost Colony

John White led 117 men and women, including his daughter and son-in-law, on the expedition. Raleigh wanted the colony built near deep water, so the group sailed for the Chesapeake Bay.

White's ship stopped first along the Carolina coast to drop off Manteo. He was returning home after a second trip to England.

The captain refused to carry the colonists beyond Roanoke Island north to the Chesapeake Bay. Without transportation the colonists were stuck. John White and the others would have to begin their colony on Roanoke.

Soon after they arrived, John White became a grandfather. Virginia Dare, the first English baby in North America, was born August 18, 1587. Shortly after her birth, White returned to England for supplies.

White came back in 1590. His entire colony was gone. He found the words *CRO* and *CROATOAN* carved on a tree and a wooden post. White knew the words referred to Manteo's village, south of Roanoke on Ocracoke Island. Bad weather and fearful sailors kept him from going there.

White returned to England without seeing his family. None of the English organizers of the colony ever saw the Roanoke colonists again. The settlement became known as the **Lost Colony**.

People still wonder what happened to the Roanoke settlers. Some think that descendants of the lost colonists are Lumbees, a Native American group. Another idea is that the colonists may have walked to the Chesapeake Bay.

Sir Walter Raleigh planned the first three English voyages to what became North Carolina, but he never came here himself. *Why should our state capital be named for him?*

Legacy of the Lost Colony

In 1607, English colonists started the Jamestown Colony in Virginia, the first permanent English colony in North America. The Roanoke colony had failed, but Jamestown succeeded on the Chesapeake, where Raleigh had wanted John White to settle. The Jamestown colonists had learned lessons from the failures on Roanoke Island.

We keep the mystery of the lost colonists alive today through an outdoor drama performed each year in Manteo, a town on Roanoke Island named for the Native American friend of the English. Thousands of people see *The Lost Colony* performed. They learn about North Carolina's earliest European settlers in this drama by Paul Green.

A scene from *The Lost Colony* shows Native Americans meeting the English. *Have you ever seen a performance of it? Where does the play take place?*

LESSON 1 REVIEW

Fact Follow-Up

1. What was the Lost Colony? Why was it "lost"?
2. How did Manteo and Wanchese help the European settlement of Carolina?
3. Who were John White, Ralph Lane, and Thomas Harriot? What did they do?
4. Who was Virginia Dare?

Think These Through

5. Suppose you had been one of the first Europeans to visit Carolina. What would you have liked most about the place? Why?
6. Would you call Sir Walter Raleigh a success or a failure? Why?

LESSON 2 Carolina Settled

Fifty years after the Roanoke colony disappeared, the English again settled in the land that became North Carolina. In the 1630s, families moved from Virginia and New England. They were looking for farmland near the coast. England encouraged settlement along the Atlantic coast. English colonies on the coasts of New England and Virginia had succeeded. Land near water was important. Boats were the easiest way to move people and goods.

LESSON PREVIEW

Key Ideas

- Settlers from Virginia settled the Albemarle Sound.
- Early settlers had conflicts with the Lords Proprietors, the owners of the new colony of Carolina.
- The colony grew slowly because of these conflicts, plus conflicts over religious issues and with Native Americans and pirates.

Key Terms

Lords Proprietors, assembly

Settling the Albemarle Sound

At first, the settlers came to the Outer Banks east of Albemarle Sound (see map, page 107). The shifting sands of the islands made travel difficult. For the people who did land on the islands, there were no real roads. The first English settlers found it difficult to travel or ship goods.

Finally, the English settlers decided to live on the mainland, close to the sounds. Land was cheap and food available. The settlers found timothy grass, well suited for grazing cattle. The pine forests had wood for shelter. The sounds were filled with fish and attracted wildlife. These families wanted to remain near the water mainly because transportation was faster and cheaper.

Good roads were impossible to build through the large swamp north of the Albemarle Sound. The colonists called it the Great Dismal Swamp. They used boats to transport forest products, tobacco, and wheat to Chesapeake Bay for trade in Virginia.

WORD ORIGINS

Discovered in 1585, **Lake Mattamuskeet** appears on John White's map as Paquippe, a Native American word meaning a shallow lake. Also known as Paquike Lake, it was called Mattamuskeet on a 1733 map. Mattamuskeet is from the Native American word ***Mata-mackya-t-ui***, meaning "It is a moving swamp" or "quaky bog." The lake is 3 feet (0.9 m) below sea level, and its maximum depth is 5 feet (1.5 m). Today the lake is a wildlife preserve.

Lords Proprietors

Then, in 1663, people on the Albemarle Sound learned that they no longer were part of the Virginia colony. They had been made part of a new English colony called Carolina. The royal colony was named for the English King, Charles I.

King Charles II gave the colony to eight wealthy men. They had supported him during an English civil war. They belonged to the richest and most important families in England. The new rulers of Carolina were called the **Lords Proprietors.**

They were the first governing body of an English colony south of Virginia. The proprietors governed until 1729. Then the King of England took over the governing of the colonies. By that time North and South Carolina were separated.

The proprietors promoted the land to the English as a place to come and live. The more land the proprietors granted to settlers, the more money they made. The proprietors could charge an annual tax on the land. When more people settled, tax collections for the proprietors increased. Until the king took over the government, the proprietors had the right to sell all the land from present-day Virginia to Florida and from the Atlantic to the Pacific Oceans.

Unhappy Settlers

Many of the original settlers on the Albemarle Sound were not happy with the

King Charles II is shown as a boy and on the charter giving his Carolina colony to the Lords Proprietors. *Why did he award the colony to them?*

proprietors. They did not want to pay taxes. They did not want to give land to newcomers arriving after the Lords Proprietors took control.

New laws passed by the English Parliament required Carolina settlers to pay taxes on tobacco traded with Virginia. The settlers' most important trading took place with Virginia through the Albemarle Sound area. The barrier islands made trade with England difficult. It was easier for Carolina's coastal settlers to trade within the colonies. Albemarle Sound settlers refused to pay the tax because it would increase the cost of trading with Virginia.

When the proprietors sent representatives to collect the tax, the settlers arrested them and elected their own representatives to run the colony. These local representatives met as an assembly. An **assembly** is a group of citizens elected to pass laws.

Christoph von Graffenried of Switzerland founded New Bern. He was held captive for a short time by the Tuscarora. *Why did the Tuscarora oppose European settlement?*

In the middle of these trade and tax problems, the Tuscarora attacked the colony. They fought colonists along the Neuse and Pamlico Rivers. The Tuscarora wanted to remove the colonists from the area. They thought too many people were coming to live on their land. The Tuscarora and other Native Americans did not want to lose hunting and farming land to the new settlers.

Pirates also caused problems for the settlers in the coastal area. Pirates captured ships and stole the money and products on board. They knew when ships carried valuable cargo. They skillfully sailed through the dangerous waters of the Outer Banks.

Pirates kept crops from reaching markets by attacking ships full of tobacco or lumber. Pirates also captured goods coming from England that the colonists needed. Yet some colonists wanted to buy what the pirates had to sell.

Besides Blackbeard, other pirates robbed from colonists.

Pirates such as Blackbeard could sell their stolen goods to colonists eager for supplies. *How did pirate activities keep Carolina from growing?*

Two famous pirates were women—Anne Bonney and Mary Read.

Creating North Carolina

Finally, the proprietors decided to split the colony. They appointed two governors in 1712, creating two separate colonies, North Carolina and South Carolina.

Most people were still settled on the coast and along the rivers. Slowly colonists began moving inland. England encouraged colonists to move. The country sent soldiers to build forts to protect settlers moving westward. As the assembly solved the problems of trade, the population on the coast grew. Demand for land led to more westward movement. When the Tuscarora opposed the English settlement, a series of battles against them began. Soldiers came to the colonies to help fight the Native Americans. The Tuscarora were defeated by 1715, opening more land to settlement.

Conflicts over taxes, settlement, and religion slowed the development of North Carolina. The land was good, but pirates and conflicts with Native Americans also kept settlers away.

LESSON 2 REVIEW

Fact Follow-Up

1. What were some problems faced by early European settlers in Carolina?
2. Who were the Lords Proprietors? How did they come to govern Carolina?
3. Why did settlers sometimes not get along with the Lords Proprietors?

Think These Through

4. Why did few European settlers come to Carolina? Do you think you would have come? Why?
5. Do you think Carolina should have been separated into North and South Carolina? Why or why not?

LESSON 3 Early Successes

On Albemarle Sound's northwestern shore, a village became a town. Virginians and other colonists had settled on the shores of the sound at Queen Anne's Town. Before that it was a Roanoke village. Can you guess what modern day town this is? It was named for Proprietor and Governor Charles Eden in 1722.

The Lords Proprietors began to earn money from North Carolina, especially from those who began plantations along the Albemarle Sound and farther south, near Cape Fear.

LESSON PREVIEW

Key Ideas

- Settlers began building plantations of rice and tobacco and earned money from timber products.
- Slaves did the hard work of planting and harvesting crops on plantations and the difficult work of processing naval stores from trees.
- Towns grew along the sounds as plantations grew.

Key Terms

plantation, naval stores, slaves, the Tar Heel State, the Pine State

Plantations

At first, the part of their colony that made the most money for the proprietors was south of Cape Fear in what became South Carolina. Some settlers built large plantations on the rivers there. A **plantation** is a large farm specializing in growing and marketing a profitable crop.

Planters grew rice and raised cattle. They paid taxes on these first products and shipped their goods from Charles Town (today's Charleston, South Carolina) to England. Charles Town was located where the Ashley and Cooper Rivers flow into the ocean, a good site for a port.

Settlers of the Cape Fear also grew rice. Planters in the Albemarle area earned money from tobacco. Families harvested and packed tobacco in 1,000-pound (450-kg) stacks, and moved it in huge barrels to market.

Rice and tobacco made plantation owners wealthy in the Carolina colonies. Soon after settlement, colonists found another moneymaking product.

This engraving of a tobacco plantation shows the huge barrels used to store the crop after harvest. *Who is shown doing the work? Why?*

This engraving shows tar draining from a brick building where pine logs burned. *Why was North Carolina a good place to make tar and other naval stores?*

Naval Stores

England's shipyards were busy building hundreds of wooden ships. Shipbuilders paid high prices for timber and ship supplies. North Carolina's forests could supply both.

Tall trees became the masts that held sails aloft. Huge pine forests provided **naval stores**, the tar and pitch used to waterproof wooden ships.

Cape Fear settlers started producing naval stores. Slaves did the hard work of producing naval stores in the pine forests. **Slaves** were captured Africans who were forced to come to North and South America by slave traders. North Carolina's settlers purchased some of these slaves. Slaves were considered property and worked without pay.

Slaves cut slashes in trees to allow the sticky sap to run down into buckets. This sap, called pitch, could seal leaks in ships' hulls. Pine trees were cut and burned in clay pits. Tar drained from the burning logs. Tar helped waterproof ships and ship supplies, such as ropes.

Collecting the tar was a hot, smelly job. The slaves got tar on their feet. One story claims that the tarred heels of the naval store workers gave North Carolina its nickname, **the Tar Heel State**. Naval stores gave rise to another nickname. Naval stores came from pine trees. Sometimes people call North Carolina **the Pine State**.

Slavery on Plantations

Tobacco planters from the Albemarle area and rice planters from the Cape Fear Valley and South Carolina also depended on slaves to do most of their work. Slaves in South Carolina had experience farming rice. They had grown rice in Africa and helped increase rice production.

Good crops earned money for the planters. The plantations earned so much money, the planters began to farm more land. More land required more workers.

How Slavery Grew in the Colony

Many of the workers were slaves. Slave traders shipped thousands of slaves from western Africa every year to the Americas. Most of the men and women taken off the slave ships were sold for work on sugar plantations in the Caribbean Sea or South America. English settlers purchased many slaves for work in North America, especially for hard labor on southern plantations.

The need for slave labor was so great that the Cape Fear region had more African American residents than white. Charles Town became a slave trading center. As the plantations in the Albemarle area grew, wealthy planters bought slaves at auctions held in the squares of Charles Town.

Life for these new residents of the colony was difficult. The slave workers lived on plantations and small farms. The slaves on plantations worked in large groups. On small farms one or two slaves would work in the fields with the owners.

Some planters treated the slaves well. Others treated slaves as if they were farm animals. No matter how the people were treated, they did not have freedom.

Orton Plantation and other colonial plantations were built by slaves. *How does the house show a plantation owner's wealth?*

Early Towns

The work of slaves and the success of plantations helped towns grow. Early plantations sold their goods along the water's edge of North Carolina. These ports and marketplaces became towns (see map, below). These towns attracted merchants who bought and sold local products and fine goods made in England. Lawyers and other newcomers also wanted to work in the Tidewater area.

Bath and New Bern were the chief cities of the Pamlico Sound, located on rivers flowing into the sound. Bath grew on the Pamlico River. New Bern arose where the Trent and Neuse Rivers come together and drain into the Pamlico Sound.

Bath had become the first town of the colony after English settlers built a settlement there in March 1706. Bath became the colony's first official port of entry, where a customs office collected taxes on trade goods.

New Bern, named for a large city in Switzerland, was settled by colonists from Switzerland and Germany a few years later. New Bern started well because of strong leadership and a town design that left room for future growth.

Edenton served the people of Albemarle Sound. It grew on Queen Anne's Creek southeast of where the Chowan River emptied into the sound. Edenton had the advantage of becoming

Early Towns of the North Carolina Colony

Location The early towns of North Carolina were located in the Tidewater. *Why were the first towns of the colony located on bodies of water? How did they help the colony grow?*

an early capital of the colony.

Beaufort was settled farther south as a fishing village. Originally called Fishtown, Beaufort became an official colonial port on Bogue Sound in 1722, the same year Edenton was incorporated.

Although the barrier islands were still a problem to shipping, sea captains began marking channels through the inlets from the sea. With safer transportation, the cities grew in importance as ports.

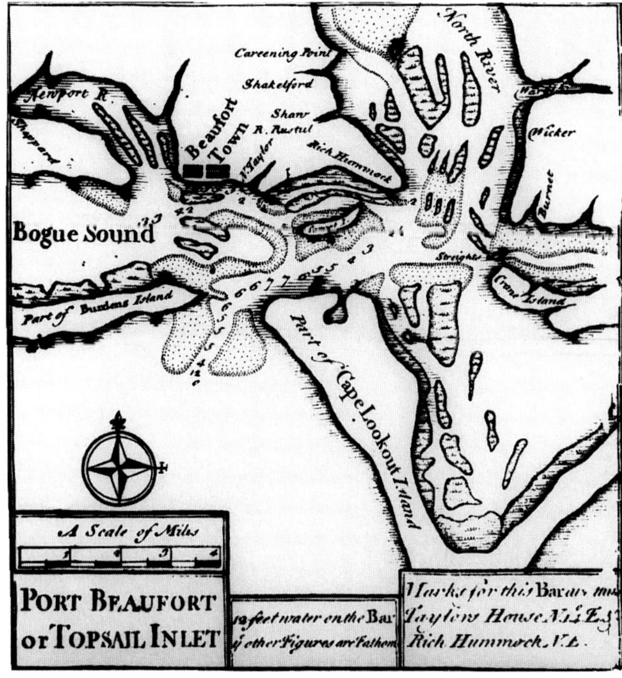

This early map of Beaufort shows the depth of Beaufort Inlet. *How did this kind of knowledge help the early towns of the colony?*

Settling Cape Fear

The Cape Fear River valley had attracted settlers soon after a 100-mile (161-km) road from New Bern to the Cape Fear River was completed. Settlers from Albemarle, Charles Town, the Caribbean islands, and England settled the Cape Fear River basin in the 1720s.

They built the town of Brunswick. Because Brunswick lacked a good harbor, some residents moved 16 miles (26 km) up the Cape Fear River. There they founded Wilmington in 1733. The town had a deep harbor and provided the colony with a deepwater route to the Atlantic Ocean.

LESSON 3 REVIEW

Fact Follow-Up

1. What was a plantation? What were some early plantation crops?
2. What were some early North Carolina towns?
3. Why were enslaved people brought to North Carolina? How did they live in the colony?
4. What are naval stores? Why were they important in early North Carolina?

Think These Through

5. In which of the early towns would you have most liked to live? Why?
6. Should enslaved people have been brought to North Carolina? Give reasons for your answer.

Settling the Backcountry

LESSON PREVIEW

Key Ideas

- About a century after the first English came to North Carolina, Scotch-Irish, Germans, and other people moved to the backcountry.
- Europeans who settled the backcountry occupied lands where Native Americans hunted, causing conflict and some cooperation.
- The Catawba and the Cherokee took different sides in a war fought between the English and French. The Catawba helped the English settlers. The Cherokee sided with the French.

Key Terms

backcountry, Great Trading Path, Great Wagon Road

Many new colonists could not afford to begin plantations. They began moving west and upriver from Wilmington and Edenton. By the 1730s, a century after the settlement of the Albemarle Sound, North Carolinians had moved into the Piedmont.

To eleven-year-old William Few, Jr., the Piedmont seemed empty when his family moved to Hillsborough in 1758. "There were no schools, no churches or parsons, or doctors or lawyers, no stores, groceries or taverns."

Backcountry Communities: Coastal Plain

Cross Creek, later named Fayetteville, was started upriver from Wilmington. The town began on the Cape Fear River at a good place to dock boats. Cross Creek's location helped the farmers and traders of the Cape Fear River valley.

Cross Creek, the Sandhills, and other areas away from the coast were called the **backcountry**. The backcountry was so far from the coast that communication and trade were not easy. River boats were the only way to travel in the backcountry of the Coastal Plain.

Halifax became a center of trade for settlers in the Roanoke River valley. It contained the richest farm lands in the colony. It soon rivaled the Cape Fear River area as a place where planters could make money. Halifax sent its tobacco and wheat downriver to the Albemarle Sound and Edenton, then out to sea (see map, page 123).

Backcountry Communities: Piedmont

Hillsborough and Salisbury grew in the Piedmont along land routes that linked the mountains to settlements

Transportation in North Carolina, 1775

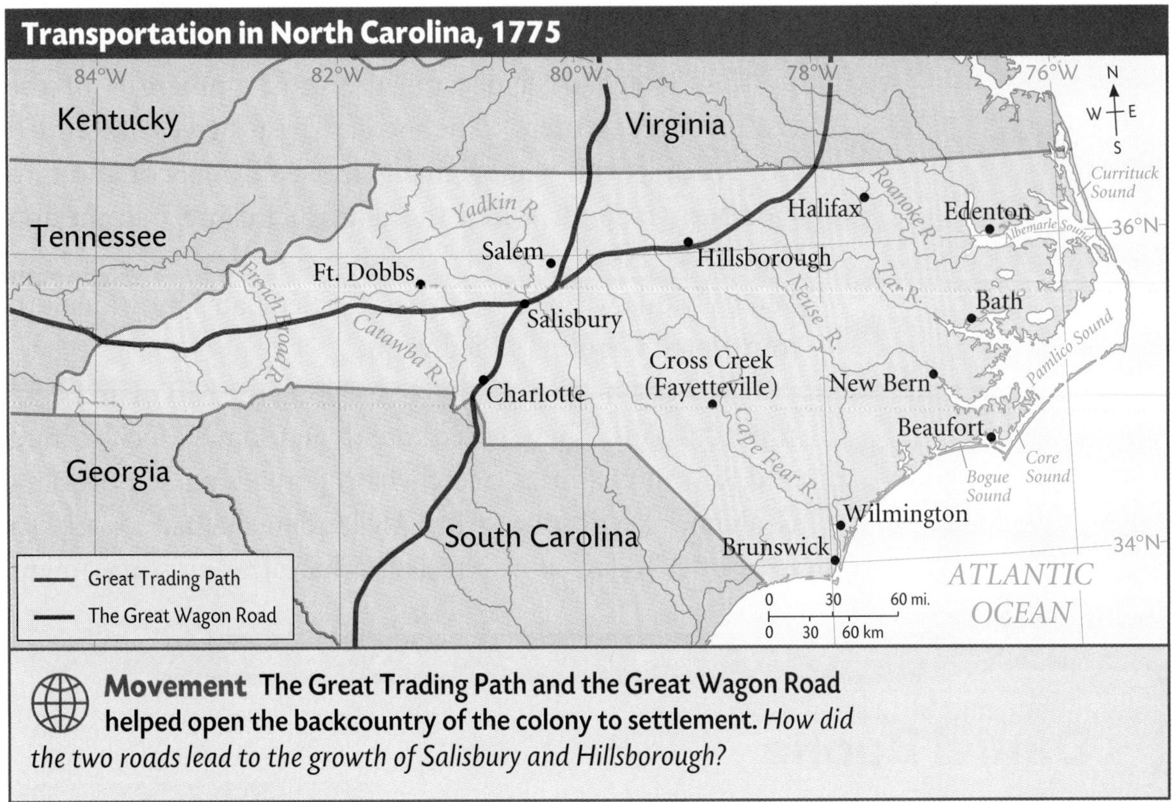

Movement **The Great Trading Path and the Great Wagon Road helped open the backcountry of the colony to settlement.** *How did the two roads lead to the growth of Salisbury and Hillsborough?*

in Virginia. These routes followed trails used by Native Americans. These trails were called the **Great Trading Path** and the **Great Wagon Road.**

Halfway along the Great Trading Path, traders established Hillsborough. The town quickly became a center for government in the backcountry.

West of the intersection of the Great Trading Path and the Great Wagon Road, settlers founded Salisbury. The village became a stopping place for settlers heading west and south. Daniel Boone stopped in Salisbury to buy supplies for his trips into the wilderness.

Hillsborough and Salisbury grew as settlers moved still farther into the backcountry.

What would YOU do?

Your family has made a long journey across the ocean to your new home in North Carolina. You know your family is not staying on the coast but rather is traveling farther inland. What would you need to pack?

Tools are important. Clothes are necessary. What about a sewing needle? thread? seeds? furniture? weapons? pots and jars? What would be left behind?

Scotch-Irish and Scottish Highlanders

English settlers moved from the Tidewater into the backcountry to raise families and plant crops. People from England, Europe, and other colonies in the new land also came to live in the backcountry.

The Scotch-Irish became the most numerous of the backcountry settlers. The Scotch-Irish were descended from people who had originally moved from Scotland into Northern Ireland. When the land in Ireland became too crowded, some Scotch-Irish families moved to Pennsylvania. Children of these settlers later moved south into North Carolina's Piedmont.

The Scotch-Irish set up farms along the two main backcountry roads. They settled mainly in today's Mecklenburg and Rowan Counties. Scotch-Irish families named Brevard, Graham, Davidson, and Alexander helped establish Charlotte. Today, some streets in Charlotte and some towns

EYEWITNESS TO HISTORY

Daniel Boone

On a tree in Watauga County, Daniel Boone wrote: D BOON CILLED A BAR ON THIS TREE 1760. Boone left his mark on other trees (right) in other wilderness areas. He explored the backcountry and brought settlers across the mountains.

Daniel Boone's family moved to the backcountry of the Yadkin River valley of North Carolina in 1750. At sixteen, Daniel was a skilled hunter who loved the freedom of outdoor life.

in North Carolina are named after these families.

Other people originally from Scotland moved to Wilmington, then moved to Cross Creek. They settled on the pine-tree-covered ridges of the Sandhills. These settlers were Scottish Highlanders. They spoke the Gaelic (gay·lik) language. For years their churches held services in that language.

Germans Settle the Backcountry

Germans also came south from Pennsylvania. They were called "Dutch" by their "Irish" friends because the German language is called Deutsch (doytsch) in German.

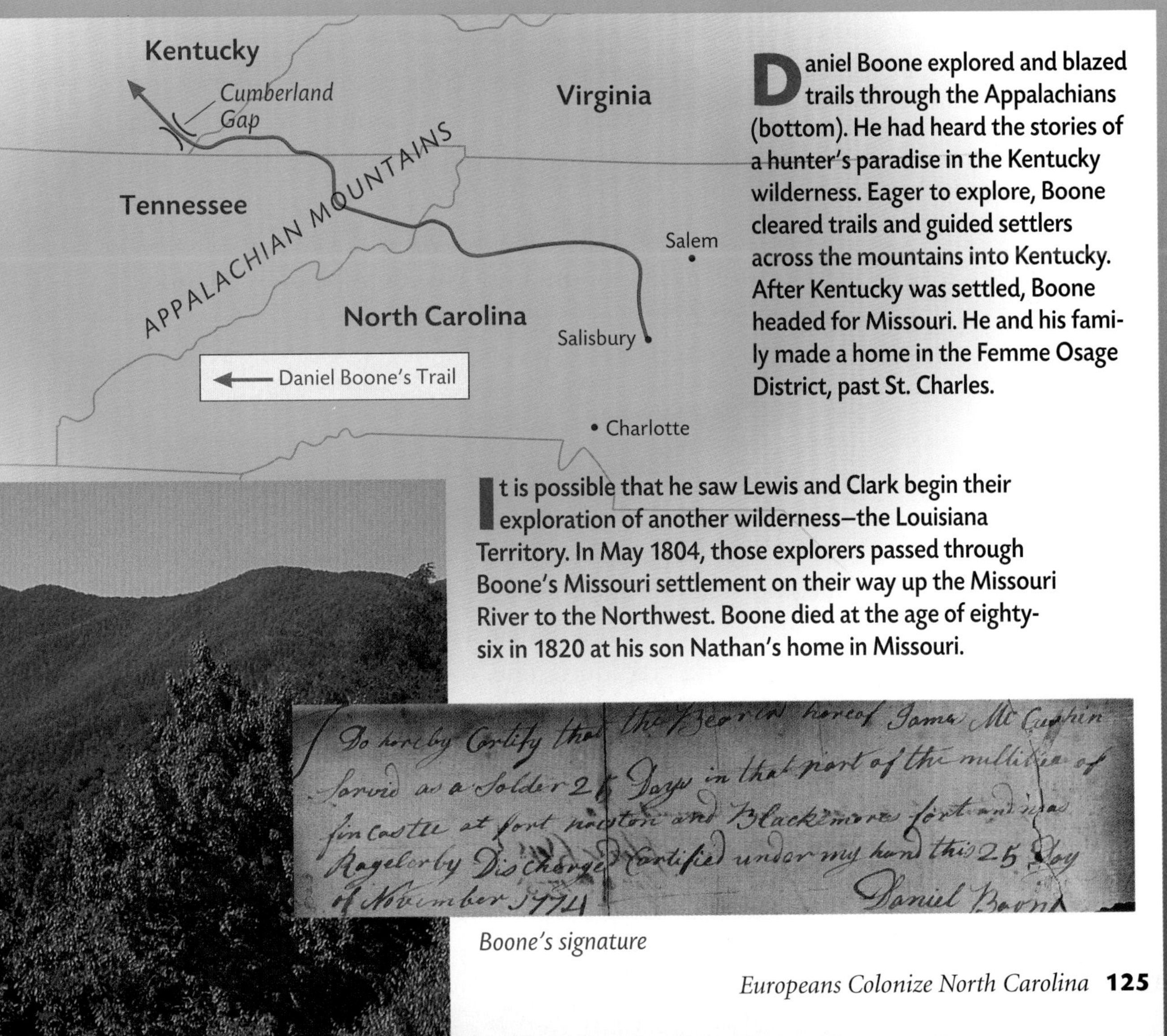

Daniel Boone explored and blazed trails through the Appalachians (bottom). He had heard the stories of a hunter's paradise in the Kentucky wilderness. Eager to explore, Boone cleared trails and guided settlers across the mountains into Kentucky. After Kentucky was settled, Boone headed for Missouri. He and his family made a home in the Femme Osage District, past St. Charles.

It is possible that he saw Lewis and Clark begin their exploration of another wilderness—the Louisiana Territory. In May 1804, those explorers passed through Boone's Missouri settlement on their way up the Missouri River to the Northwest. Boone died at the age of eighty-six in 1820 at his son Nathan's home in Missouri.

I Do hereby Certify that the Bearer hereof James McCuchin Servid as a Solder 2[illegible] Days in that part of the millitia of fincastle at fort [illegible] and Blackmores fort and was Regelerly Discharge Certified under my hand this 25 Day of November 1774
Daniel Boone

Boone's signature

In Old Salem today you can learn how Piedmont settlers lived during colonial times. *What religious group founded Salem? Where were they from?*

Most Germans kept to themselves in their own neighborhoods. Most spoke their native language even after they settled in North Carolina. The Germans built farms mostly to the south of Salisbury and west of the Catawba River along the South Fork River.

The closest-knit group of Germans were the Moravians. They were a religious community that settled on a special tract of land called Wachovia, where Winston-Salem later grew. The Moravians lived apart from other Piedmont pioneers. Winston-Salem began as the Moravian town of Salem.

By 1760, one century after King Charles II gave Carolina to the Lords Proprietors, settlers had moved all the way west to the Catawba River. In fact, by that time, there were more backcountry settlers than people on the coast or Native Americans in the mountains. This population growth led to conflicts.

Conflicts in the Backcountry

As Europeans moved into the backcountry, Native Americans there died from diseases that had killed Native Americans on the coast. Many people of the Catawba tribe died of smallpox and measles.

Native Americans and backcountry settlers also misunderstood the traditions and daily lives of one another. Native Americans let livestock roam in the woods and claimed what they needed. They didn't understand how settlers claimed ownership of animals by branding and fencing them.

The Catawba and Cherokee had walked trading paths to the coast, where they traded peacefully with the new settlers for many years. They got along well until more families settled. Then they fought for land, just as the Tuscarora had fought on the coast.

War in the Backcountry

Both France and England had wanted the land where Native Americans lived. For several years the English fought in the French and Indian War against the French.

The Cherokee sided with the French to protect their lands from the backcountry settlers. The Catawba, already surrounded by settlers, sided with the English. The Cherokee attacked settlements on the Catawba River in 1759, killing many English. The survivors retreated to a backcountry English fort called Fort Dobbs (see map, page 123).

When the war ended with English victory, settlers could enter land all the way to the Blue Ridge, although the Cherokee did not like it. The Catawba, who had helped the settlers, received land from the English near Sugar Creek, close to the boundary separating North Carolina and South Carolina.

The Cherokee kept their mountain towns and lands. They would fight the backcountry settlers again during the American Revolution.

English settlers fled to Fort Dobbs (now a state historic site) after an attack by the Cherokee. *Why did the Cherokee fight the settlers?*

LESSON 4 REVIEW

Fact Follow-Up

1. What Europeans settled the backcountry?
2. What were some important backcountry towns? Where were they located?
3. What were some challenges faced by European settlers in the backcountry?
4. How did European settlement affect Native Americans in the backcountry?

Think These Through

5. How did differing ideas about property cause trouble between Native Americans and Europeans ?
6. Imagine that you lived in colonial North Carolina. Where would you prefer to live—along the coast or in the backcountry? Give reasons for your answer.

The Five Themes of Geography: Movement

Using Geography's Themes: Movement

Movement of People

Have you ever moved from one house to another? Or from one town to another? Or even from another state into North Carolina? Talk with other members of your class to learn whether they have moved, how many times they have moved, and how far they have moved.

Make a chart showing this movement. Think about recording information on a chart like this one:

Movement of Classmates

Never Moved	Moved 1–5 Times	Moved 6–10 Times
John	Lisa	Brittany
Sarah	Lakeisha	David
Mark	Javier	Freddie

Now that you have charted the movement of members of your class, show that movement on a map. To map the movement of your class, you will need to know the names of cities, towns, or states that class members left to come to your town. Then, by finding those places on a map, you can link those places with your town. (You will need to have a map of North Carolina or the United States.)

Your map of movement might look something like the one below.

Now, skim Chapter 6 for examples of the movement of people. Make a list of movement inside North Carolina and movement from other places into North Carolina. Take a sheet of paper and copy the chart shown at the top of page 129. (Note: pay attention to the map of North

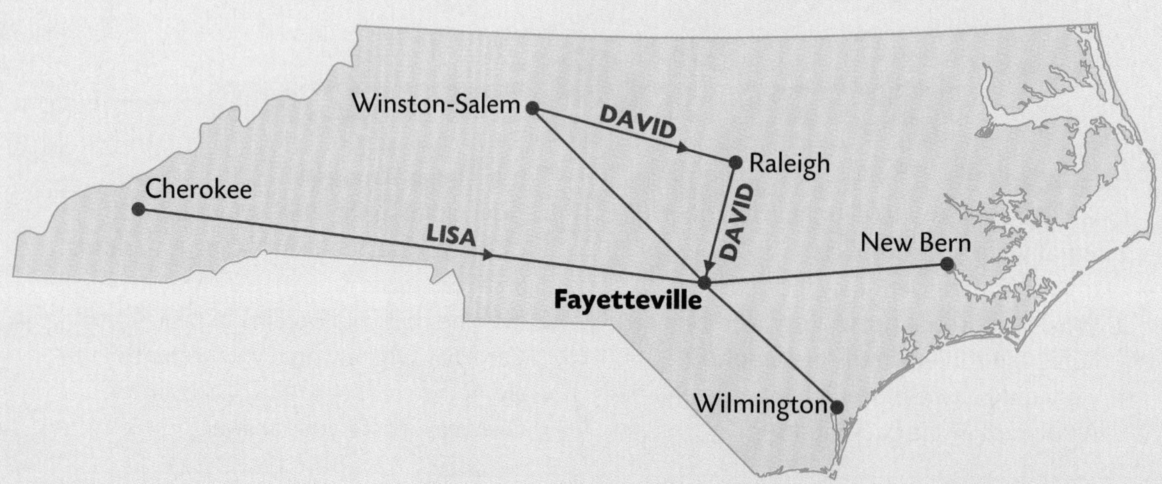

Movement of People			
Movement in North Carolina		Movement to North Carolina	
From	To	From	To

Carolina on page 107 and to the map showing early towns and waterways on page 120.)

Finally, think about the ways you and your classmates have moved and how people moved in early North Carolina. How is moving different now?

Movement of Goods

A second kind of movement is the movement of goods. To begin thinking about the movement of goods, recall what you ate for your last meal. Where did the food you ate come from?

Or look at the labels in a piece of your clothing. Where was it made, and how do you think it moved here?

The next time you go to a supermarket, check the labels on some of your favorite foods. Where are they made, and how do you think they are brought to North Carolina?

Next, skim Chapter 6 to find information about goods that moved into North Carolina, inside North Carolina, and between North Carolina and other places. On a sheet of paper, make notes about the movement of goods in early North Carolina. Organize your notes like the example below:

Movement of Goods		
Product	From (Origin)	To (Destination)

Think about how the movement of goods has changed over time. How did goods move in early North Carolina? How do they move today? The map at the beginning of the chapter will help you answer the questions.

Movement of Ideas

A third kind of movement is the movement of ideas or information. In early North Carolina, ideas and information in letters and newspapers moved by horseback or by boat. Other ideas came into the colony with the settlers. What ideas moved into North Carolina? How do ideas move today? You get information by mail, of course, but ideas also move electronically—by radio, TV, and computer.

The **Movement** of people, goods, and ideas is the fifth theme of geography. Now, you know about the Five Themes of Geography: Location, Place, Region, Human-Environmental Interaction, and Movement. These themes are tools you will use again and again as you learn about North Carolina.

Chapter 6 Review

LESSONS LEARNED

LESSON 1 Early attempts to settle in North Carolina by the English failed. The experience of the Lost Colony taught English explorers about the region and its natives.

LESSON 2 The first permanent settlers in Carolina came from Virginia and settled in the Albemarle region. They had conflicts with the new owners of the colony, the Lords Proprietors. Those conflicts, plus conflicts with Native Americans and pirates, made the colony grow slowly.

LESSON 3 Some settlers built plantations of rice and tobacco and earned money from timber products. African slaves worked on the plantations and processed naval stores from trees. Towns grew along the sounds as plantations grew.

LESSON 4 New settlers began communities in the backcountry—up the Roanoke River at Halifax and up the Cape Fear River at Cross Creek (Fayetteville). Hillsborough and Salisbury grew along trading paths. Native Americans of the backcountry did not want the new settlers in the region.

TIME FOR TERMS

colony
colonists
Lost Colony
Lords Proprietors
assembly
plantation
naval stores
slaves
the Tar Heel State
the Pine State
backcountry
Great Trading Path
Great Wagon Road
Movement

FACT FOLLOW-UP

1. How did the barrier islands affect the early history of North Carolina?
2. What areas of North Carolina were the first to be settled by Europeans?
3. Who were the Lords Proprietors? Why did the Albemarle region settlers rebel against them?
4. Why were Africans brought into the Carolina colony? Describe their lives here.
5. What were naval stores? How did they earn money for the Carolina colony?
6. What was the backcountry? What were some early settlements there?
7. Why did people move into the backcountry?
8. What groups of Europeans moved into the backcountry? Where did they settle?
9. Why were there troubles with Native Americans in the Carolina backcountry?
10. Describe relations between European settlers and the Cherokee people.

THINK THESE THROUGH

11. Carolina once covered a much larger area than North Carolina does today. Why is North Carolina smaller?
12. Could conflicts between Native Americans and Europeans have been prevented? Explain.
13. Someone has said that the real builders of Carolina were African slaves. Is this an accurate statement? Why or why not?

14. North Carolina was the least successful of the English colonies in North America. Why?
15. If you could have been a member of any European group to settle in the Carolina backcountry, which would you choose? Why?
16. If North Carolina had contained a good port, how would its history have been different?
17. How can the geographic theme of Movement be applied to the early history of North Carolina?

SHARPENING SKILLS

18. How does an interstate highway show the theme of Movement?
19. How has movement helped North Carolina develop?
20. How can a map show movement? What kinds of movement can a map show?
21. Do you think there was more movement in early North Carolina history, or is there more movement today? Give reasons for your answer.
22. In what ways does the story of Daniel Boone show movement?

PLACE LOCATION

Use the letters on the map to locate the following places:

23. Roanoke Island.
24. Wilmington.
25. Cross Creek.
26. Cape Fear River.
27. Beaufort.
28. Pamlico Sound.
29. New Bern.
30. Bath.
31. Albemarle Sound.
32. Edenton.
33. Roanoke River.
34. Halifax.
35. Hillsborough.
36. Salisbury.
37. Atlantic Ocean.

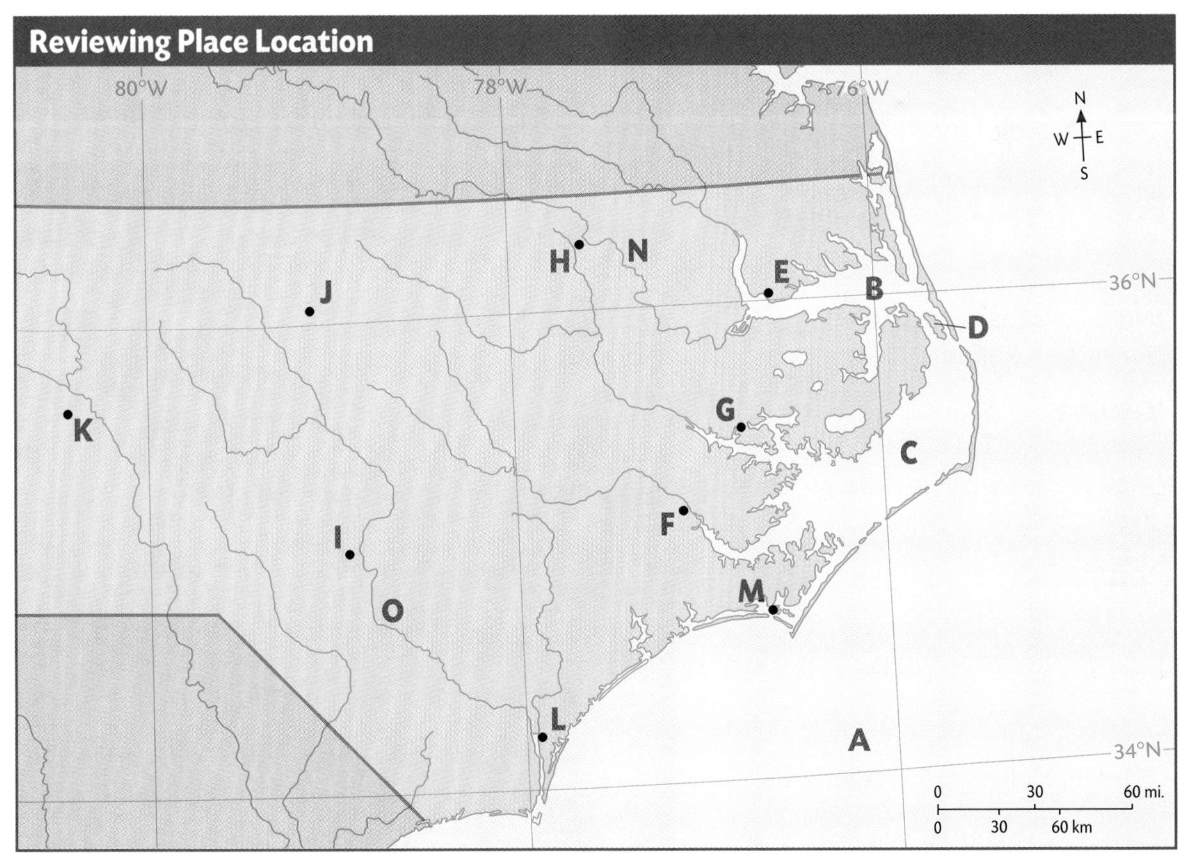

CHAPTER 7 North Carolinians Create Their State

General Charles Cornwallis

The Charlotte Hornets of the National Basketball Association have a story about their name from the American Revolution.

British General Charles Cornwallis captured Charles Town, South Carolina, in May 1780. He thought he would easily take North Carolina next. But the North Carolina state militia fought hard for independence, especially near Charlotte. Cornwallis called Charlotte the "hornet's nest" of the Revolution.

CHAPTER PREVIEW

LESSON 1
A Colony Becomes a State
North Carolina fought in the American Revolution.

LESSON 2
Farming as a Way of Life
Most North Carolinians lived on farms in the 1800s.

LESSON 3
Masters and Slaves
Slaveowners controlled the lives of slave workers.

LESSON 4
The Old North State Wakes Up
Progress came to North Carolina.

General Nathanael Greene leads troops against the British.

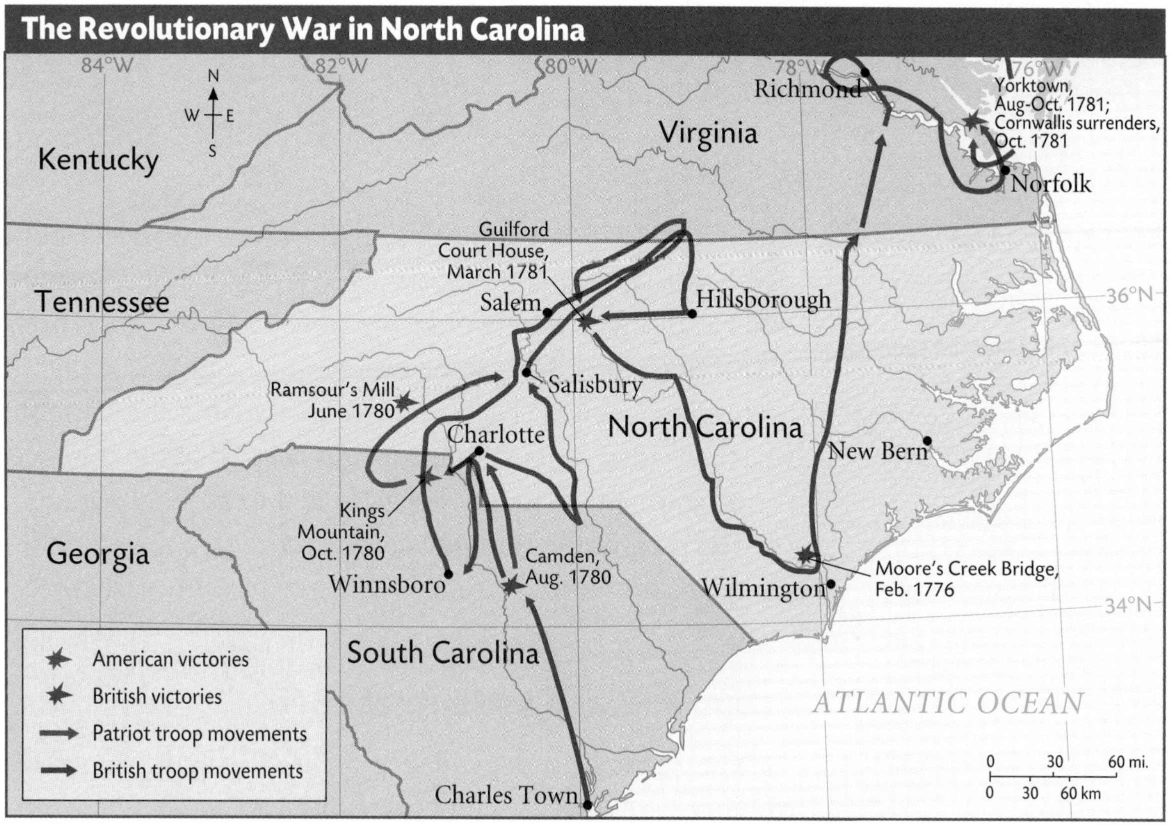

The Revolutionary War in North Carolina

The Gathering of the Clans

Would you expect to find a gathering of Scots on a mountaintop in North Carolina? If you go the second weekend in July, you will find hundreds of Scots or people of Scottish descent on top of Grandfather Mountain.

Descendants of early colonial Scottish settlers and people from all over the United States come to the Highland Games and Gathering of the Clan. Games, music, and parades are a part of the fun. It is a way for people to remember the homeland of some North Carolina settlers.

Lesson 1 A Colony Becomes a State

LESSON PREVIEW

Key Ideas

- Conflict between the backcountry and the colonial government came before, and were similar to, conflicts between the colonies and England.
- North Carolinians took a lead in declaring the 13 American colonies independent of England.
- Residents fought against English troops, although some residents sided with England in the Revolutionary War.

Key Terms

Regulators, militia, Committees of Correspondence, Loyalists, Patriots, delegates, Halifax Resolves, Parliament, Edenton Tea Party

In May 1775, Governor Josiah Martin was worried about North Carolina colonists who favored independence. He thought they would try to capture the governor's mansion in New Bern, so he ordered that cannon be placed around the house. The colonists carried off the cannon. Martin headed for Fort Johnson, but heard that the colonists would soon attack the fort. Martin fled to an English ship.

The theft of the cannon was one more step toward independence for North Carolina. Other steps came earlier.

Steps Toward Independence

The spirit of independence grew quickly in England's original 13 American colonies. American settlers had supported the British in a war against France. Yet soon after the war ended in 1763, some colonial leaders began to oppose British rule. By 1776, popular American leaders were ready to lead the colonies in a war against the British.

Some backcountry settlers in North Carolina were ready to fight the British as early as 1771. These settlers believed that the British governor, William Tryon, and his colonial government treated them badly.

Governor Tryon had built a "palace" in New Bern. News of what the governor had done angered these backcountry settlers. They did not like paying for the palace with their taxes. Also, it was too far away from the backcountry for settlers to receive services from the colonial governments.

These settlers demanded that the backcountry have more representatives in the colonial legislature. They also wanted better treatment from government officials. Because these settlers wanted to regulate, or fix, these troubles, they were called **Regulators**.

Battle of Alamance

Governor William Tryon talks to a group of back-country farmers during the Regulators' protest. *Why did the Regulators fight the governor?*

The Regulators did not trust the British colonial government in New Bern. The Regulators closed courts in Hillsborough as a way of demanding better treatment. They kept officials from collecting taxes.

In 1771, Governor Tryon led eastern militia to arrest the Regulators. A **militia** included citizens who served when they were needed. The Regulators attacked Tryon's militia at Alamance Creek. Tryon easily defeated the Regulators.

The Regulators had opposed the English government by fighting the royal governor's militia. Most colonists were not yet ready to oppose the royal government with force. But after the Regulators' defeat, protests against taxation spread throughout North Carolina.

Path to the Revolution

North Carolinians formed **Committees of Correspondence** to keep in touch with other colonies. England's government had passed laws putting taxes on tea, paper, glass, and lead. The committees collected information about laws passed in England that affected the colonies.

The laws passed in England were written for all the people of Great Britain. England, Scotland, and Wales were part of Great Britain. That is why the English are also called the British.

The lawmaking body of Great Britain, called **Parliament**, believed laws passed in Great Britain should be obeyed in the colonies.

In 1773, people in Boston, Massachusetts, refused to pay a tax on tea. They showed their anger by tossing tea chests into Boston Harbor. This Boston Tea Party showed how angry colonists were about Parliament's taxes on the colonies.

After the British Parliament declared Massachusetts was unlawfully resisting the King, Massachusetts and Virginia called for all the colonies to send representatives to a meeting to protest Parliament's actions.

In August 1774, a colonywide assembly met in New Bern. The assembly agreed to stop buying British goods and elected three delegates to the First Continental Congress. This Congress met in Philadelphia the next month and voted to stop all trade with Britain.

In Edenton, North Carolina, 50 women joined Penelope Barker to support the assembly's actions with a

EYEWITNESS TO HISTORY

Margaret Tryon: Life in a Palace

Life for young Margaret Tryon in the colony of North Carolina was not like the life of a farm child. The reason? Her father was the royal governor and her family lived in Tryon Palace in New Bern.

Margaret had her own room. She had toys to keep her company. A doll in a beautiful dress had its own special bed. Margaret's family had the best that money could buy. Lovely gardens surrounded the house. Visitors came from the new colonies and from Britain to see her father.

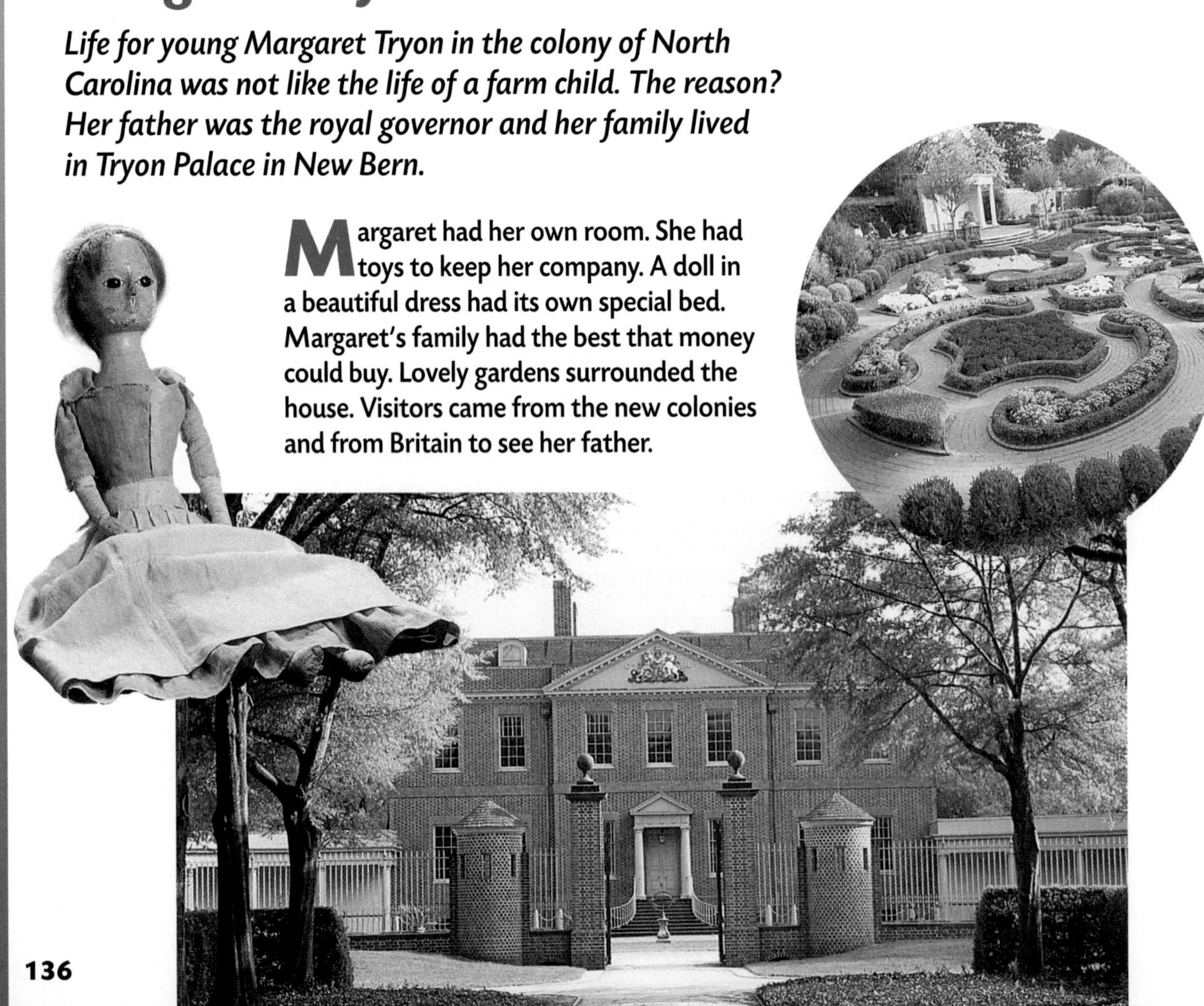

petition. The meeting in October 1774 was called the **Edenton Tea Party**.

Fighting for Independence

The American colonies' war for independence began when British troops and local militia fought in April 1775 at Lexington and Concord in Massachusetts. The war came to North Carolina in February 1776.

A battle broke out at Moore's Creek Bridge in Pender County. An army of **Loyalists** (people loyal to the British king) from the Sandhills fought an army of **Patriots** (people

Margaret might have studied Latin, reading, and mathematics at home. She might have taken lessons playing the spinet. This was an instrument like a piano. Margaret's mother played the spinet. Her mother might also have wanted Margaret to learn needlework, or fine sewing.

Margaret's bed covers had colorful designs of birds on them. A fireplace heated her room. A warming pan, a long-handled closed pan of metal filled with warm coals, warmed her sheets before she got into bed.

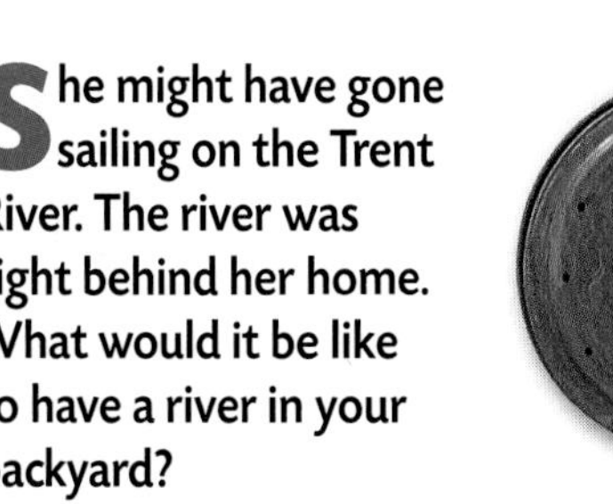

She might have gone sailing on the Trent River. The river was right behind her home. What would it be like to have a river in your backyard?

People dressed as Scottish Highlanders reenact the Battle of Moore's Creek. *Why were the Highlanders called Loyalists?*

demanding independence) from Wilmington.

The Loyalists at Moore's Creek Bridge were settlers from the Highlands of Scotland. Before they came to North Carolina, the British government had made them sign pledges never to oppose the king. The British government used the Highlanders to stop the independence movement in North Carolina, but the Patriots won the battle.

In April 1776, Patriots sent delegates from all over the colony to meet in Halifax to discuss how to oppose the British. **Delegates** are leaders who represent the people in making important decisions at a meeting. The delegates passed the **Halifax Resolves**. The resolves urged the other 12 colonies to declare independence.

Three delegates from North Carolina—Joseph Hewes, John Penn, and William Hooper—read the resolves to the Second Continental Congress in Philadelphia. This Congress ran the war for independence.

On July 4, 1776, the three delegates joined delegates from the other colonies to sign the Declaration of Independence. All the colonies declared freedom from Great Britain.

WORD ORIGINS

Do you know a town called Cross Creek? Have you heard of Campbellton?

Cross Creek was a trading center founded about 1730. It later joined the nearby town of Campbellton.

After the Revolutionary War, the people of the towns decided to join together into one town named for the Marquis de Lafayette. He was a French general who helped defeat the British.

The town? If you said **Fayetteville**, you are right.

North Carolina in the War

North Carolina soldiers joined the newly formed Continental Army commanded by George Washington. They fought the British in New Jersey, Pennsylvania, and the southern colonies (see map, page 133).

A British army under Lord Charles Cornwallis invaded the state in 1780. Although outnumbered, backcountry militia defeated Cornwallis at Ramsour's Mill and then again at Kings Mountain, South Carolina.

George Washington named Nathanael Greene as the commander of the Southern Department of the Continental Army. He wanted Greene to take advantage of Cornwallis's losses.

Greene and Cornwallis met in battle at Guilford Courthouse, where Greensboro is today. Cornwallis claimed victory because his soldiers remained on the battleground. But Greene's troops hurt the British army. When Cornwallis later invaded Virginia, his weakened army lost the Battle of Yorktown. The British surrendered to the Americans. The war was over. The colonies had won independence.

General Nathanael Greene commanded the southern troops in the Revolutionary War against the British. *How did his army help the colonies win independence?*

Joining a New Country

After the war, most North Carolinians began to unite. Some Loyalists moved to the mountains and helped establish such communities as Mills River in Henderson County. Other Loyalists, such as the Highlanders, moved to Nova Scotia in Canada to live with others who had remained loyal to Britain throughout the revolution.

In 1787, North Carolina sent delegates to the Constitutional Convention in Philadelphia to help write a document organizing the new national government. William Blount of Bertie County, Richard Dobbs Spaight of New Bern, and Hugh Williamson of Edenton signed the document on behalf of North Carolina and worked for its acceptance in the state.

At first, the people of North Carolina refused to accept the Constitution. They wanted it to include a Bill of Rights that guaranteed certain freedoms for individuals. After the Bill of Rights was proposed, North Carolina became the 12th state to accept the Constitution.

LESSON 1 REVIEW

Fact Follow-Up

1. Who were the Regulators? What did they want to do?
2. What Revolutionary War battles were fought in North Carolina?
3. Why did North Carolina not approve of the United States Constitution at first?

Think These Through

4. Imagine that you are an advisor to Governor Tryon. What advice would you give him about the Regulators? Why?
5. Suppose you had lived during this time. Would you have been on the side of the Loyalists or the Patriots? Why?

LESSON 2

Farming as a Way of Life

LESSON PREVIEW

Key Ideas

- Almost all North Carolinians farmed in the early 1800s.
- Most families worked hard to provide enough for themselves and their animals.
- Neighbors worked together to be sure everyone had enough to live.

Key Terms

drovers, barter, fibers, raising, clubbing, camp meeting

Today, pigs ride to market in big trailer trucks. Back in the early 1800s, people called **drovers** herded pigs and cows along country roads. Neighbors worked together to herd the animals down the main roads to market.

In 1852, a Concord woman reported that 1,000 pigs passed by her front door. Owners of a toll bridge near Hickory charged for each pig that crossed the bridge.

Farming Life

Farmers had settled North Carolina since the colony began. Now that North Carolina had become a state in a new nation, farming continued to be the way most people made a living. During the 1800s, most North Carolinians lived on farms. There were some large plantations in eastern North Carolina, but most farms were small.

Most farm families grew what they needed to feed themselves and their livestock. Farmers sold extra crops

North Carolina farm families after the Revolution cooked meals on wood stoves. *Where did they get most of their food?*

and cattle to buy items they could not produce, such as nails, molasses, or salt.

Farms varied in size, but few families could plant more than 100 acres (40 sq hm) during a season. Every family grew corn and wheat.

Farmers in the early 1800s needed cattle for plowing, transportation, and for food. *These oxen are well suited for which tasks on the farm?*

The wheat was planted on the hillsides in the fall and became ready for harvest the following spring. Corn was planted in the bottomlands along streams and harvested each fall.

Families also planted gardens near their houses. They raised cabbages, potatoes, peas, and other vegetables. Some farmers grew orchards of apples or peaches.

Families needed their livestock. Most farm animals ran loose in the woods. The milk cow stayed in the barn or shed at night. Farmers fenced in crops to protect them from the roaming livestock.

Each family had a brand or mark to identify its animals. This custom allowed even poor families to have large numbers of animals. Families didn't need to own large amounts of land to graze their animals.

The appearance of farmhouses varied. Most families on the Coastal Plain lived in houses of wooden boards. In the Tidewater, where rock was scarce, some houses were built on foundations of cedar or cypress logs.

In the Piedmont and Mountains, people built one-story or two-story log houses. These homes were never more than one room wide and about 30 feet (9 m) long.

If they could afford it, families weatherproofed the logs. They put up boards that lapped over at the edges. This kept out the rain and wind. Most families also built their barns out of logs.

Farm Communities

North Carolinians sometimes lived out of sight of one another, but never out of reach. Everyone was part of a small rural neighborhood. A typical neighborhood extended about 8 miles (13 km) in any direction. This is the distance neighbors could walk in a day.

Neighbors cooperated with one another. They often got what they needed by bartering with one another. To **barter** means to exchange goods without paying money.

For example, every family kept sheep and grew flax or cotton. Family members spun the **fibers**—strands of cotton, flax, or sheep's wool—into yarn on the spinning wheel.

Not every family could afford a loom to weave the yarn into cloth. So families who owned a loom could weave cloth in exchange for a product they did not have and could not make. A weaver could make cloth for a shoemaker, who, in turn, could provide a pair of shoes for the weaver.

What would YOU do?

Most nine-year-olds in North Carolina did not go to school during the early 1800s. With schools in only the largest towns, parents in rural areas would hire a teacher to live with the family and teach the children at home. What would life be like with a teacher living in your house? What would be different? the same?

Farm Recreation

Farm folk did not separate work from recreation. Many houses and barns were built by a **raising**. People got together and raised the walls and roof of a building in less than a day.

Farmers camp outside Fayetteville during a trip to market. Farmers traveling together to market was called clubbing. *How else did farmers mix work and fun?*

When they completed the work, all celebrated with a large meal. If someone brought a fiddle, there might be dancing. Later, older folks told stories. A barn raising was also a time when young people could meet and play.

Hog slaughters, corn shuckings, and quiltings also brought neighbors together. They enjoyed the times work could be made easier by sharing it with friends.

Neighbors also traveled together to take their harvested crops or animals to distant markets. Such a journey was called **clubbing**. Eastern farmers drove wagons to Fayetteville, New Bern, or Tarboro. Piedmont and mountain farmers clubbed to South Carolina, since Camden and Charleston were more easily reached than Wilmington.

If they took animals to market, the men, boys, and animals camped out near cow pens and "hog hotels." The animals slept in pens, and the drovers slept in the sheds nearby. One hog hotel near Asheville could hold 3,000 hogs a night.

Girls demonstrate hoop rolling at House in the Horseshoe in Moore County. *What games of today do you think kids of the early 1800s played?*

Schools and Churches

There were no public schools for children to attend in the early days of North Carolina. Sometimes teachers lived in a farm community with different families. They taught the children reading, writing, and mathematics.

In the early 1800s, most villages and towns contained churches. About half the people of North Carolina belonged to a church. Many churches were not large enough to pay for a full-time minister. Members pooled their money to pay a traveling minister to lead church services once a month.

Several different Christian churches were popular among North Carolinians. Every community had Baptist and Methodist churches. Presbyterian and Lutheran churches were found most often in Piedmont counties.

GAMES People Play

Rolling a Hoop Children at the edge of town created a cloud of dust as they played. Running and yelling, each child rolled a large hoop. Short sticks clicked against the ash hoops, making cricketlike noises.

Keeping the hoop up and rolling longer than anyone else made you the champion.

All you needed for the game was a road, a hoop, and a stick—and a boy or girl willing to run like the wind.

Bath Methodist Church is one of the oldest Methodist churches in North Carolina. *What other churches existed in North Carolina in the early 1800s?*

After independence, churches belonging to the Church of England were called Episcopalian. Moravian churches were located around Salem in the Piedmont.

An important part of worship for many North Carolinians was the **camp meeting**. Each summer, when crops were ripening in the fields, neighbors set aside work for a long weekend together. At the campground they prayed, listened to preachers, and visited with friends. The meeting caused a revival of religious faith. Revival means bringing back an old interest.

LESSON 2 REVIEW

Fact Follow-Up

1. How were farm jobs different in spring, summer, autumn, and winter? Who did the work in farm families?
2. How were houses different in different parts of North Carolina? Why?
3. How did farm families make entertainment out of work that had to be done?

Think These Through

4. How did the lives of farm families show human-environmental interaction?
5. How did the lives of farm families show the movement of people, goods, and ideas?
6. Would you rather have been a child in early North Carolina or today? Give reasons for your answer.

LESSON 3 Masters and Slaves

In the early 1800s, the richest family in North Carolina was the Camerons of Orange County. Paul Cameron owned six plantations side by side. He lived on the largest one, called Fairntosh. Cameron raised tobacco, cotton, grain, and livestock. His 400 slaves raised most of the food the family ate and all the fiber they needed for clothing. Cameron also owned a town house in Raleigh and another plantation in Alabama.

LESSON PREVIEW

Key Ideas

- One out of four North Carolinians owned slaves.
- One third of all people in North Carolina were slaves. About half the slaves lived on big plantations. The other half worked on small farms.
- Despite the hard work and lack of freedom, slaves forged a strong community.

Key Terms

quarters, free people of color.

Different Ways of Life

Most North Carolinians in the early 1800s did not live on plantations. They worked on small farms. Three out of four North Carolina families did not own slaves. They earned their wealth from what they alone produced.

The Camerons were unique. Few state residents owned more than 20 slaves. The wealthy white families who did owned plantations. These families had wealth enough to purchase slaves. Those slaves added to the families' wealth. One fourth of North Carolina families owned from one to hundreds of slaves after the Revolutionary War.

Planters owned large homes. Their wealth allowed them to buy new furniture, art, and fine clothes. Their homes were quite different from the smaller farms where most people lived.

The richest man on the coast, Josiah Collins of Somerset, lived in Tyrrell County. Slaves dug a six-mile long

African American slaves built Josiah Collins' plantation house at Somerset. *How did they help make the plantation owner wealthy?*

canal to connect the plantation to a river. They grew large amounts of rice and corn on the rich soil, which he shipped to Norfolk, Virginia.

Peter Hairston, a rich planter in the Piedmont, lived in the fork of the Yadkin and South Yadkin Rivers in Davie County. His Cooleemee plantation was about half the size of Paul Cameron's.

Areas with the richest soil had the greatest concentration of plantations. More planters lived in the Roanoke River valley than anywhere else. They raised tobacco, cotton, and wheat. Other planters raised cotton in the counties along the South Carolina border, and a few grew rice near Wilmington.

Few planters lived in the hillier sections of the state, in the Uwharries, or west of the Catawba River.

Slave Life

After the Revolution, slavery spread across the state. By the 1800s, one third of all North Carolinians were African Americans held in slavery.

When slaveowning families had only two or three slaves, the slaves worked side by side with the members of the family. Planting, hoeing, and harvesting were done together. The treatment of slaves changed from family to family. Some were well treated. Other families treated slaves no better than livestock.

Slaves on larger plantations sometimes lived in better conditions

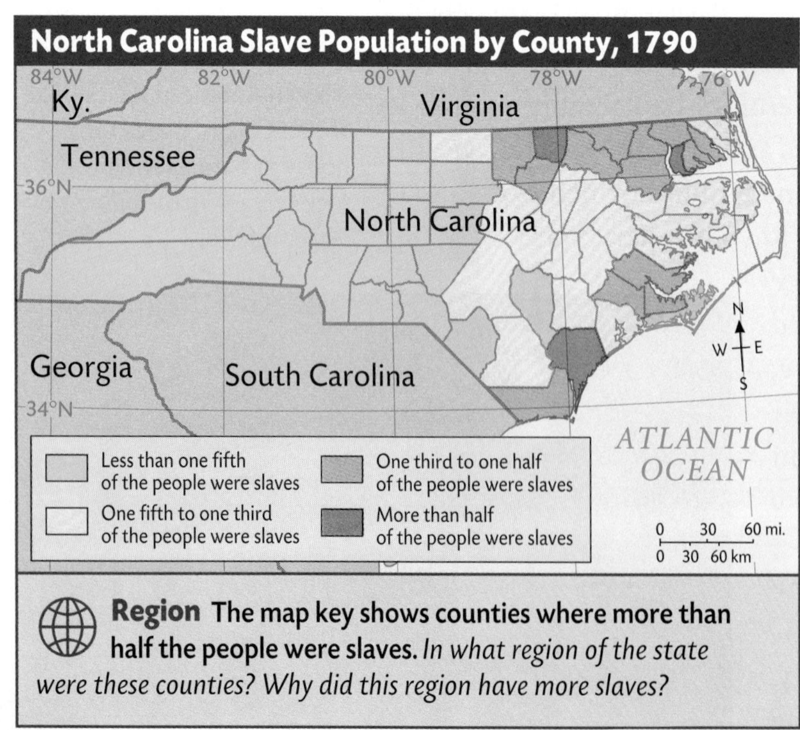

Region **The map key shows counties where more than half the people were slaves.** *In what region of the state were these counties? Why did this region have more slaves?*

Some African Americans tried to escape slavery by running away. But because slaves were treated like property, as this poster from Stokes County shows, owners punished runaway slaves. *How else was slave life hard?*

because the owners had more wealth. The planters could give them more food and better shelter.

On plantations, slaves often worked in groups to get work done. As many as 10 or 12 men and women might hoe or harvest together. Most plantation slaves planted, weeded, and harvested crops.

Skilled slaves cooked in the houses, raised the livestock, or did other tasks in the shops and houses. On the Cameron plantations, Cyrus Cameron ran the mill, Ben Sears operated the grain thresher, and Virgil Bennehen was the doctor to his fellow slaves.

Almost all slaves lived together in a group of cabins known as the **quarters**. These were often crude one-room log cabins. The typical farm home, on the other hand, had two or three rooms.

Many slaves planted gardens to supplement the corn meal and bacon the planters provided. Planters also gave slaves a small amount of clothing. Slaves got only one outfit each spring and another after harvest.

By law, slaves were not allowed to be married. Still, many slave couples married anyway, declaring their faithfulness to each other within their slave community. Learning to read and write was also against the law. Sometimes slaves were taught by their owners. Many slaves had to teach themselves.

The Cruelty of Slavery

When a plantation owner died, slaves were often sold to pay the bills. African American families were painfully reminded that they were another person's property every time a family member was sold. The rest of the family could not go with a slave who was sold.

Slave life was a cruel life of hard work. A man, woman, or child could always be punished for breaking equipment or disobeying a command. Slavery was a constant contest between owners and slaves. The slaves worked hard but tried to resist the slaveowner. A slave might break a hoe on purpose. This was a way to resist or control work.

CONNECTIONS

Geography & Language Arts

The Poetry of George Moses Horton

As a slave, George Moses Horton wasn't supposed to be able to read or write, but he did. Horton was a poet and believed he was the only "poet of color" in the South.

Horton lived near Chapel Hill before the Civil War. Young men attending the University of Chapel Hill asked him to write poetry for them. Those young men, born to freedom, saw nothing strange in asking for a love poem written by a man who could never attend that university.

Horton would ask for the young woman's name and compose a poem using a letter of her name to begin each line. See how he wrote a poem about a woman named Julia? The first line starts with the letter *j*, the second with *u*, the third with *l*, the fourth with *i*, and the next line with the letter *a*. Can you write a poem like this using your name?

Horton wanted to live a life of freedom. He found freedom when he joined the Union Army in Raleigh in 1865. The army, commanded by General William Sherman, was marching toward Virginia as the war ended.

Horton continued to write poetry and published three books of poems. He later moved to Philadelphia, where he died in 1887.

The slaveowner tried to get as much work out of a slave as possible. Slaveowners tried to encourage slaves to work harder by using punishments or rewards.

Charles Pettigrew, a neighbor of Josiah Collins, ran a plantation store where slaves could buy things with points they had earned working the fields. Other planters used punishment. A slave's few privileges would be taken away. Often a slave was punished with a whipping.

No matter how they were treated, slaves could almost never have the one thing they most wanted—freedom.

Thomas Day, a free person of color, carved beautiful furniture that he sold to wealthy planters. *What skills did he need to make this washstand?*

Free People of Color

A few African Americans were not slaves. These **free people of color** were often skilled workers who had bought their freedom or been granted it by their former owners. In North Carolina, more free people of color lived in Halifax and New Bern than any other place.

Several of these African Americans became well known in the state. John Chavis was one of the best private-school teachers in Raleigh. Some of his pupils became state leaders. Thomas Day of Milton in Caswell County was the master furniture maker of North Carolina.

LESSON 3 REVIEW

Fact Follow-Up

1. What was a slave? What kind of work did most slaves do?
2. How were the lives of slaves different from the lives of small farmers? In what ways were their lives alike?
3. Who were some famous free people of color living in North Carolina? Why were they famous?

Think These Through

4. Why did so few people in North Carolina own slaves?
5. Why were there very few slaves west of the Catawba River?
6. In what region of North Carolina were there the most slaves? In what region were there the fewest? See the map on page 146.

The Old North State Wakes Up

LESSON PREVIEW

Key Ideas

- During the 1830s, North Carolina began to change.
- The coming of the railroad encouraged growth of towns and mills and helped farmers.
- The state began paying attention to public education during the 1840s.

Key Terms

convention, Convention of 1835, Wilmington and Weldon Railroad, North Carolina Railroad

In 1856, North Carolina Governor John W. Ellis proclaimed the importance of railroads at the opening of the North Carolina Railroad. "Here we are today, more than 200 miles from the ocean…to celebrate an event which brings that ocean to our very doors."

Ellis and other leaders believed railroads would solve the state's problems. Canal and river connections had been limited to eastern North Carolina. Lack of transportation had slowed North Carolina's growth.

Slow to Change

North Carolina was not growing in the early 1800s. Many people lived in poverty. Most worked on small farms and grew only enough to feed themselves.

Other problems grew from poor transportation. There wasn't a large port close to where most people lived. Rivers west of the fall line were not navigable. Rivers east of the fall line served the plantations well but were far from where many farmers lived.

People needed transportation to move goods to market. Roads were little more than trails through woods and passable only in dry weather. Canals would have improved transportation. None were built in the Piedmont.

The Dismal Swamp Canal connected the Albemarle Sound with Virginia. *In the early 1800s, water routes served which region? What regions needed transportation?*

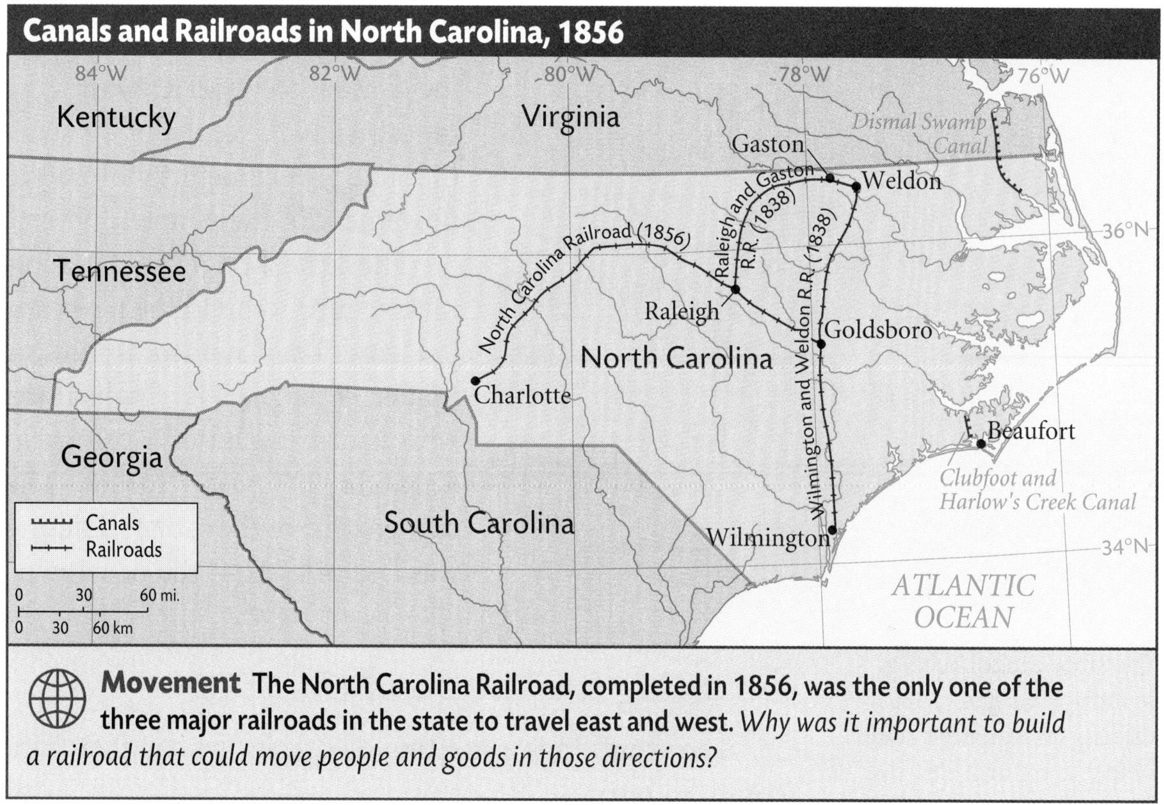

Canals and Railroads in North Carolina, 1856

Movement The North Carolina Railroad, completed in 1856, was the only one of the three major railroads in the state to travel east and west. *Why was it important to build a railroad that could move people and goods in those directions?*

Disagreements between the eastern and western parts of the state did not help improve transportation. Eastern leaders thought they had all the transportation they needed. They prospered from their rivers, sounds, and canals (see map above).

Roads were expensive to build. People in the Coastal Plain did not want to pay taxes to build roads or canals in the Piedmont or the Mountains. People in those regions could not convince state leaders to build roads they needed to get goods to market. Some showed their displeasure by moving to settle in the western states. North Carolina's population almost stopped growing. Making a living became difficult for many.

A New State Capital

Eastern and western political leaders had agreed on one thing. In 1791, they decided that Wake County was the best site for the state capital. The colonial capital had been on

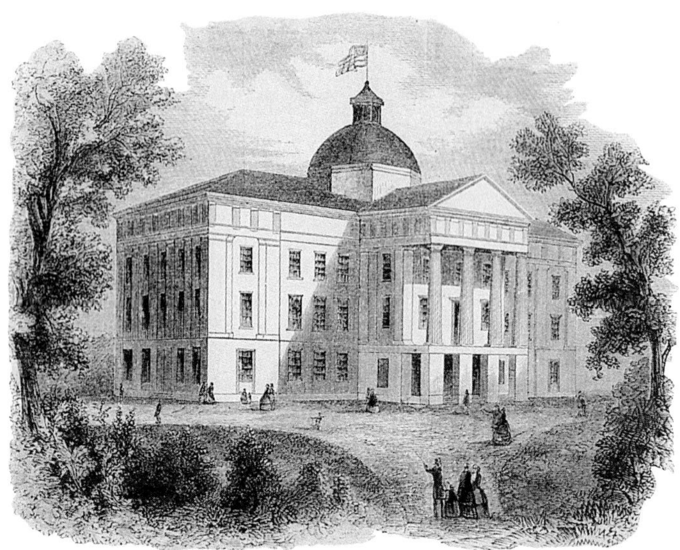

the coast at New Bern. By moving the capital to the center of the state, the state government followed the movement of the people.

The state bought 1,000 acres (400 sq hm) to build the new capital city. They named it for Sir Walter Raleigh, the Englishman who had dreamed of a colony in Carolina 207 years earlier. The cornerstone of the capitol building was laid in 1792 in the new town.

The state capitol building in Raleigh burned in 1831, causing an argument about where to rebuild. *How did the Convention of 1835 settle similar disagreements between regions of the state?*

Debating the Future of the State

A **convention** is a meeting of citizens who gather for a common purpose. People in the western section of North Carolina decided they wanted a convention. They wanted changes to help North Carolina make progress.

Delegates from the Piedmont and the Mountains wanted fair representation in the state legislature. At the **Convention of 1835** they decided to write a new state constitution.

The new constitution gave the legislature the ability to do more for citizens. Most important, the new constitution made representation between east and west equal. More people had moved to the Piedmont and the Mountains. The delegates recognized the patterns of settlement and gave more representation to those regions.

Railroads Help Movement

North Carolina also invested in a new form of transportation: the railroad. The railway era had begun in the United States in the early 1830s. State leaders planned to build three railroads through the state.

The **Wilmington and Weldon Railroad** and the Raleigh and Gaston Company ran trains north and south through the Coastal Plain beginning in 1838. The Wilmington and Weldon helped Coastal Plain farmers move their goods to Wilmington. With the Raleigh and Gaston Railroad, farmers close to the Roanoke River valley could ship goods to Virginia.

The third railroad was an east-west line. With more people serving in the legislature from the Piedmont and the Mountains, the state was ready to pay for a railroad that headed west. Governor Ellis opened the **North Carolina Railroad** in 1856. The state gave money to build the railway from Goldsboro to Charlotte. It had to be built to go around the Uwharrie Mountains. Because more people lived north of the mountains, the train went through Raleigh, Greensboro, and Salisbury on its way to Charlotte.

The North Carolina Railroad led to the growth of towns along the line. Wilson, Raleigh, Durham, Greensboro, and Salisbury became important farm markets and factory locations. The two towns at either end of the line—Goldsboro and Charlotte—also expanded. Towns bypassed by the railroad, such as Fayetteville, grew more slowly.

The officers of the Raleigh and Gaston Railroad stand on a locomotive of the line. *How did railroad construction (left) help North Carolina grow?*

St. Mary's College in Raleigh, shown in the 1850s, was one of several colleges begun by church groups in the 1830s and 1840s. *How did these colleges help the state?*

Education

In 1793, a cornerstone was laid for the first building of the University of North Carolina, the nation's first publicly supported college. The university opened in 1793 south of Hillsborough at New Hope Chapel, which became known as Chapel Hill.

In the 1830s and 1840s, the state began spending money on a public-school system. By the 1840s, every county in the state had at least one school. Girls and boys could go to school for free. Slave children were not allowed to attend these schools.

In the 1850s, the state hired its first superintendent of education. Calvin H. Wiley trained teachers, organized school libraries, and wrote useful textbooks. In Raleigh the state opened the School for the Deaf and Dorothea Dix Hospital for mentally ill people.

Several church groups opened new colleges during the 1830s and 1840s. The Baptists began Wake Forest. The Presbyterians started Davidson. The Quakers or Friends opened a school that became Guilford College. The Methodists planned Trinity (now Duke) and Greensboro Female College. The Episcopalians opened St. Mary's School in Raleigh.

When the Civil War came in 1861, the state had never had a brighter future. Why would North Carolinians have wanted to go to war?

LESSON 4 REVIEW

Fact Follow-Up

1. Westerners and easterners in North Carolina often disagreed. What were some of their disagreements?
2. Where were the first railroads in North Carolina built? Why?
3. What were some advances in education during this period?

Think These Through

4. If you had lived in North Carolina during this time, which change would have been most important to you? Why?
5. Did African Americans benefit from the changes described in this chapter? Explain your answer.
6. How did railways help the state?

Demonstrating Skills in Constructive Interpersonal Relationships and Social Participation

Understanding Perspectives

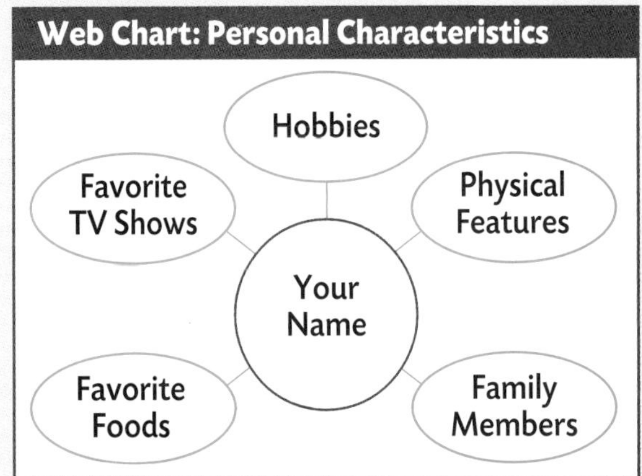
Web Chart: Personal Characteristics

Have you ever seen pictures like the two below? They are two pictures of the same building, but they were taken from different points of view, one from in front (left), the other from above.

Point of view, or perspective, can make two pictures of the same thing look different. Just like pictures, people can have different points of view, different perspectives.

Have you ever had an argument with someone? Has anyone ever said to you, "You need to look at things from another point of view"?

Seeing the world through someone else's eyes is a skill you can learn. You begin by thinking about your own life and making some notes about it. The web chart above will help you. Copy it on a sheet of paper and fill it in. Then show it to someone who knows you well. Does that person think the notes describe you well?

Now try making notes about one of your classmates. Use a copy of the same chart you used to describe yourself. Ask the classmate some questions as you fill in the chart.

Next, try using a chart to describe Margaret Tryon, the daughter of the royal governor who built the palace in New Bern. There is information about Margaret on pages 136-137. What do you think she believed about the Revolution?

Different people have different points of view, or perspectives. Understanding their points of view helps us understand their actions.

Chapter 7 Review

LESSONS LEARNED

LESSON 1 Early disagreements between colonists and the colonial government grew into the Regulator conflict, which ended with the Battle of Alamance. North Carolinians protested laws passed by the British and supported rebellion in other colonies. North Carolina took a lead in declaring the 13 American colonies independent of Britain. Some North Carolinians wanted to remain colonists of the British.

LESSON 2 Almost all North Carolinians farmed in the early 1800s. Families worked to provide enough for themselves. Neighbors cooperated with one another in their work and play.

LESSON 3 Most white people in North Carolina did not own slaves. Still, slaves made up one third of the population. About half of the slaves lived on big plantations. The rest worked on small farms. Slaves lived a difficult life. Despite any privileges given them by their owners, they lacked the one thing they wanted most—freedom.

LESSON 4 During the 1830s, North Carolina began to improve because of the Convention of 1835 and the coming of the railroad. The convention made representation equal between the eastern and western parts of the state. Railroads improved connections for farmers who needed to get their crops sold. The state also began a public-school system.

TIME FOR TERMS

Regulators
Committees of Correspondence
Loyalists
delegates
drovers
fibers
clubbing
quarters
convention
Wilmington and Weldon Railroad
militia
Parliament
Edenton Tea Party
Patriots
Halifax Resolves
barter
raising
camp meeting
free people of color
Convention of 1835
North Carolina Railroad

FACT FOLLOW-UP

1. Why did the building of Tryon's Palace make some people angry?
2. What were some reasons why the Regulators acted as they did?
3. Why did Patriots and Loyalists disagree?
4. Where in North Carolina were Revolutionary War battles fought?
5. Who were some of the political leaders of North Carolina during this period, and what did they do?
6. What were some of the problems faced by small farmers? How did they solve them?
7. On what kind of farms did most slaves live? Why?
8. Describe the lives of slaves who worked in fields and those who worked in other jobs.
9. Why did North Carolina need to build railroads?
10. What were some regional disagreements in the early 1800s?

THINK THESE THROUGH

11. Which was the most important Revolutionary War battle fought in North Carolina? Explain why.
12. Who had the better life—a slave on a plantation or a poor farmer? Explain your answer.
13. North Carolina was a "backward" state in the early 1800s. Why?
14. How did the Convention of 1835 change North Carolina?
15. How could the theme of Movement be applied to North Carolina during the Revolutionary War period?

SHARPENING SKILLS

16. Imagine that you were one of the Regulators. Describe yourself. Explain your actions.
17. Imagine that you were a plantation owner in the Roanoke River valley. Describe yourself and your beliefs. Would you have supported the Convention of 1835? Explain.
18. Imagine that you were a white farm child or the child of a slave laborer in the early 1800s. Describe yourself.
19. Imagine that you were an African American slave in the early 1800s. Describe your life.

PLACE LOCATION

Use the letters on the map to locate the following places involved in the Revolution:

20. Charlotte.
21. Guilford County Courthouse.
22. Kings Mountain.
23. Charles Town.
24. Moore's Creek Bridge.
25. Yorktown.

Reviewing Place Location

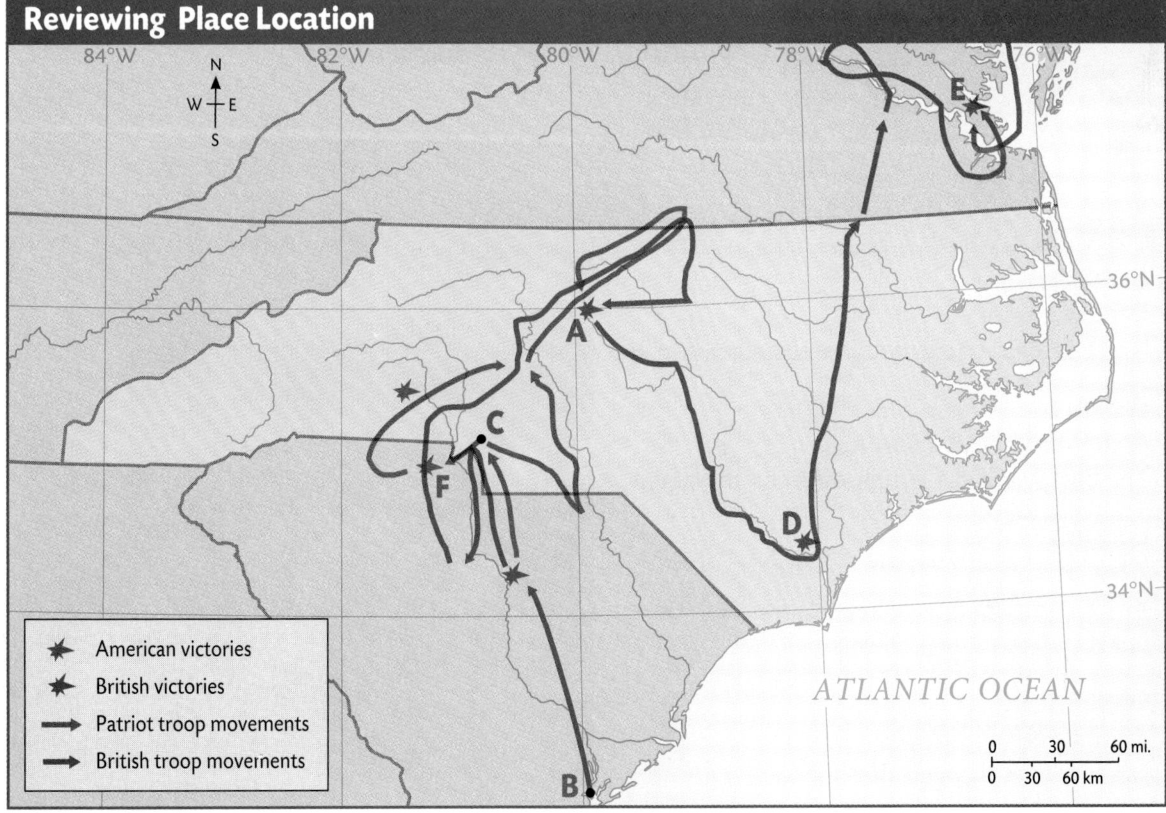

CHAPTER 8 The Civil War and North Carolina

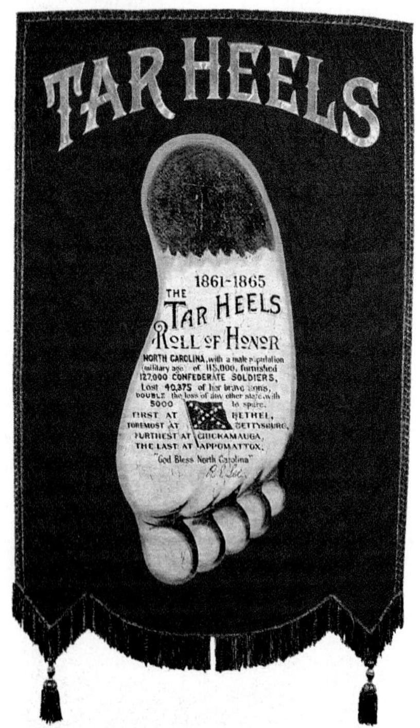

North Carolina and ten other southern states formed the Confederate States of America and declared their independence from the United States. The Confederacy fought against northern states of the United States in the Civil War.

The Tar Heel State provided more troops for the Confederacy than any other state. The soldiers earned fame as tough fighters.

This red Tar Heel banner was probably made for a gathering of Civil War veterans that honored them for their bravery.

CHAPTER PREVIEW

The Civil War in North Carolina

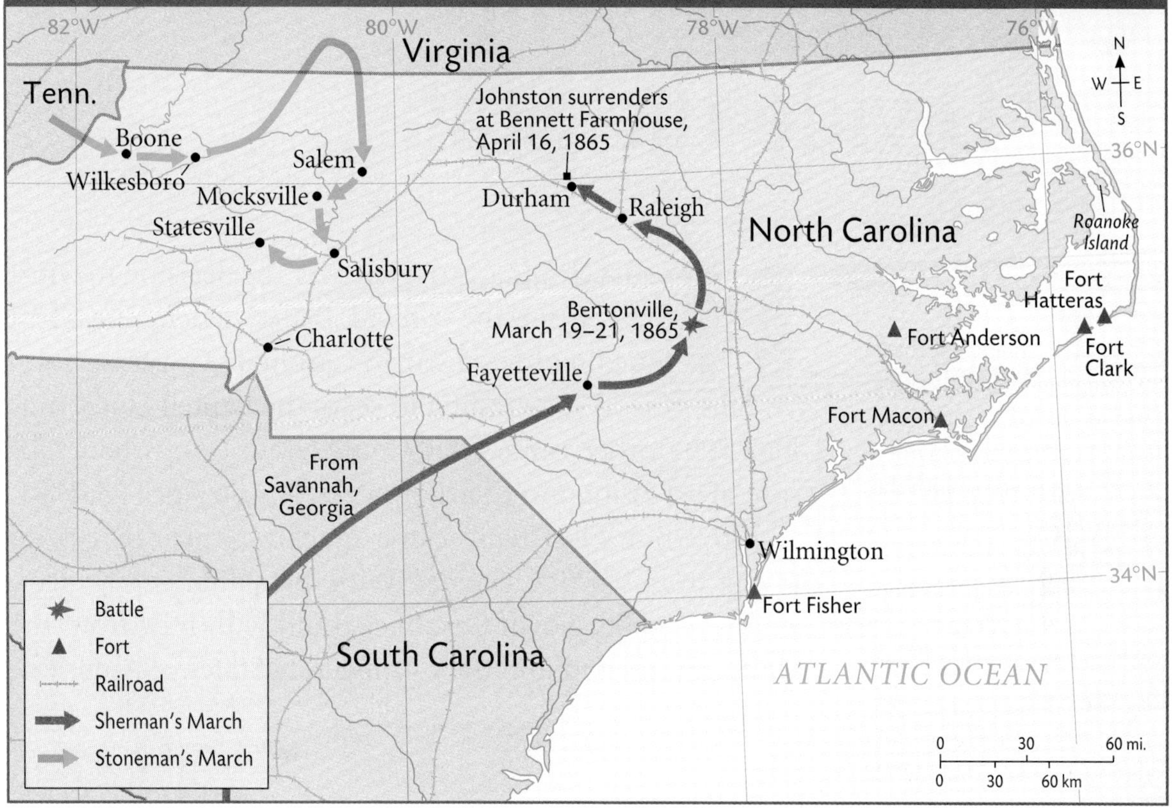

82°W 80°W 78°W 76°W
36°N 34°N

Virginia
Tenn.
North Carolina
South Carolina
ATLANTIC OCEAN

Boone
Wilkesboro
Salem
Mocksville
Statesville
Salisbury
Charlotte
Johnston surrenders at Bennett Farmhouse, April 16, 1865
Durham
Raleigh
Bentonville, March 19–21, 1865
Fayetteville
From Savannah, Georgia
Wilmington
Fort Fisher
Fort Macon
Fort Anderson
Fort Hatteras
Fort Clark
Roanoke Island

Battle
Fort
Railroad
Sherman's March
Stoneman's March

0 30 60 mi.
0 30 60 km

Confederate troops from North Carolina

Harriet Jacobs

Born into slavery in 1813, Harriet Ann Jacobs' heart "burned for freedom." Her life in Edenton changed in 1835 when she went into hiding to escape slavery. Jacobs lived for seven years above her grand-mother's kitchen. Her determination was to free her children and herself.

Jacobs achieved her freedom. She wrote a book, *Incidents in the Life of a Slave Girl,* describing her hidden life. Most of her family, including her children, thought she was dead. Harriet Jacobs managed to free herself and then protected her children.

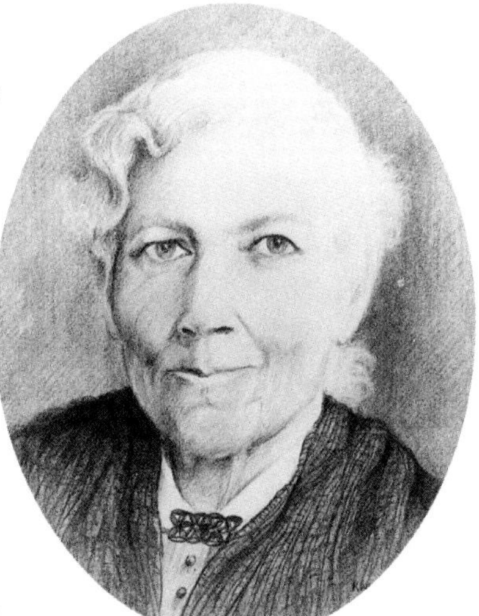

Disagreements Divide the State

LESSON PREVIEW

Key Ideas

- The northern and southern states argued about slavery and its spread.
- North Carolinians did not agree about siding with the Confederacy, but the state finally did join.
- The Underground Railroad was a way for African Americans to escape slavery.

Key Terms

abolitionists, Underground Railroad, secede, Confederate States of America (Confederacy), Union

North Carolina struggled over the decision to withdraw from the United States. Then, President Lincoln ordered North Carolina's Governor John W. Ellis to send state militia to serve the United States military. The order came after Confederate troops had captured Fort Sumter in Charleston Harbor on April 13, 1861.

Governor Ellis' reply came quickly. "You can get no troops from North Carolina." With this statement the decision was made. North Carolina would withdraw from the United States and join the Confederate States of America.

Slavery

Slaves raised the cotton grown on the large plantations of North Carolina. Southerners wanted to continue slavery and expand it into new territories.

Many northerners did not want slavery in the new territories of the United States. Others, known as **abolitionists**, wanted all slaves freed.

The North grew in population and gained more representatives in Congress during the early 1800s. They could pass laws that kept slavery out of western territories. Southerners were against these laws.

Naturally, slaves wanted to be free. Hundreds of African Americans escaped by fleeing to the North on the **Underground Railroad**. On the way North, slaves hid in barns and homes of people opposed to slavery. The Underground Railroad was not a real railroad. It was an escape route for slaves heading to freedom.

Levi Coffin, a founder of the Underground Railroad,

was a slave of a Randolph County family that had moved to Ohio. Coffin helped slaves escape by taking them to safe hiding places. A favored hiding place was a hat shop in Jamestown, in Guilford County.

When African Americans from North Carolina got to the North, they spoke out against slavery. David Walker, a free person of color from Wilmington, wrote an *Appeal* for the nation to stop slavery. Harriet Jacobs wrote about hiding seven years and then escaping slavery.

By 1860, the North had developed more industries than the South, where most people lived on farms. *How did these different ways of life lead to fighting the Civil War?*

Opposite Ways of Life

There were other problems between the North and the South. The two regions had different ways of life.

The northern states' populations were growing quickly. More people lived there, nearly 23 million. Europeans arrived daily in northern cities. Canals and railroads helped industry grow. Rich farmland produced grain and livestock.

In southern states, farming was the way of life. Southerners prided themselves on living close to the land. Small farming communities dotted the southern countryside. Only about 9 million people lived in the South.

They felt they were better off than northerners, who lived in large dirty cities. Northerners thought southern states were slow to make progress. Many believed an economy based on slave labor was wrong. Southern states argued that factory workers were no better off than slaves.

These differences led to angry arguments, especially over slavery. The arguments led to war. Southern states voted to **secede**, or withdraw, from the United States, and form a new nation called the **Confederate States of America**, or **Confederacy**. The southern states of the Confederacy were Virginia, North Carolina, Tennessee, South Carolina, Georgia, Florida, Alabama, Mississippi, Louisiana, Arkansas, and Texas.

Led by the president of the United States, Abraham Lincoln, the northern states fought to preserve the **Union**, the United States. These northern troops fought against the Confederacy in the Civil War from 1861 to 1865.

What would YOU do?

Imagine being a slave thinking about an escape on the Underground Railroad. The danger will be high. Scarce food and little rest will make you weak and slow. You will be leaving family and friends behind.

You won't be able to cry out loud or laugh. Getting caught could mean death or being sold. Yet if you don't go, you will be a slave forever.

The person taking you to freedom will give you a signal at midnight. A soft whistle will mean it is safe for you to go. Run or stay? You have to decide.

Slow to Join

North Carolina did not secede and join the Confederacy right away. The state was divided between landowners with slaves who wanted to leave the Union and others who did not.

North Carolina joined the Confederacy once the Union declared it would fight the Southern states. When forced to choose, North Carolinians felt closer to other Southerners. North Carolina joined the new Confederate nation even though people in the Piedmont and the Mountains were not enthusiastic about fighting.

LESSON  REVIEW

Fact Follow-Up

1. Who were abolitionists?
2. What were some differences between North and South just before the Civil War?
3. What was the Underground Railroad?
4. Which region of North Carolina was most in favor of secession? Why?

Think These Through

5. Why do you think North Carolina joined the Confederacy, even though many opposed secession?
6. If you had been alive in the 1850s, would you have been an abolitionist or in favor of secession? Give reasons for your answer.

LESSON 2

Civil War in North Carolina

One North Carolina leader explained why his soldiers seldom retreated. They had "tar on their heels," which held them to the ground. That story is different than the one about collecting tar from trees during colonial times. Which story sounds more likely as the way the state got its nickname, the Tar Heel State?

LESSON PREVIEW

Key Ideas

- More citizens from North Carolina fought in the Civil War than from any other state.
- Women kept farms running.
- Blockade-runners supplied weapons to the Confederacy.
- Union troops destroyed property in the state.

Key Terms

blockade, blockade-runners, Battle of Bentonville

Four Years of Civil War

Henry Lawson Wyatt of Edgecombe County was the first North Carolinian killed in the war. He died in a battle at Bethel, Virginia. He and other Tar Heels became known for their bravery and persistence.

During the four years of war, North Carolina sent 125,000 men to fight for the Confederacy, more than any other state. Another 15,000 Tar Heels fought for the Union. At least 40,000 of these men died from battle and illnesses.

Charles Stevens Powell of Johnston County was among 125,000 North Carolinians who fought for the Confederacy. *Why did North Carolina decide to fight on that side?*

Divisions over the War

Even after the war began, some North Carolinians opposed the Confederacy. Some residents of the Piedmont and the Mountains did not volunteer to fight for the South. Others joined secret groups to oppose the Confederacy. A red thread stitched into a shirt or coat collar identified them as pro-Union. The Red Strings, as they were called, lived mostly in the Uwharrie and Brushy Mountains. In the Coastal Plain, opponents of the war were called Buffaloes. They fought against local Confederates and attacked plantations.

Slaves also opposed the war. Many on the Coastal Plain escaped to the Northern army. Thousands of former slaves met in towns captured by Union soldiers early in the war. African Americans began communities in New Bern, Plymouth, and Beaufort. Some joined the Union military that occupied Tidewater towns. On plantations farther inland, many enslaved people worked as usual.

Sarah Blalock fought as Private "Sam" Blalock alongside her husband Keith Blalock in the Civil War. *What did most women do during wartime?*

Women Work the Farms

Women, children, and old men had to do all the farm work when young men left to join the army. Women ran the farms to feed their families. Because the war was expensive, the Confederate government raised taxes. There was little money in North Carolina, so families had to pay taxes with food or livestock. There was little left to eat.

In Yanceyville, High Point, and Salisbury, women took part in "bread riots," where they demanded flour to feed their children. Near Newton, women nearly caused a riot. They threatened to beat up a rich man who was cheating a woman whose husband had died in battle.

Many families became poor and hungry. Still, most people stayed loyal to the Confederacy.

War in North Carolina

Soon after the war started, the Union navy sent ships to Southern ports in the Gulf of Mexico and along the Atlantic Coast to set up a **blockade**. A blockade is a string of ships that blocks enemy ships from entering a port. The Union tried to keep the Confederacy from shipping military supplies or trade goods through its ports.

Fort Hatteras and Fort Clark on the Outer Banks fell to Union troops soon after the war began. Edenton, New Bern, and other Tidewater port towns also quickly surrendered to Union troops. Wilmington, however, remained a Confederate port through most of the war.

The Confederacy needed its ships to dock in Wilmington so supplies could reach the Confederate soldiers. Fast, sleek ships called **blockade-runners** sailed in and out with supplies. Fort Fisher, near the mouth of the Cape Fear River, protected the blockade-runners from Union ships once they came into port.

The supplies reached the Confederate army commanded by General Robert E. Lee on the Wilmington and Weldon Railroad. The railroad became known as "the lifeline of the Confederacy."

In December 1864, Union troops attacked Fort Fisher. Bombs burst over the fort, but Confederate forces held. There was a brief stop to fighting during Christmas. In January 1865, Union marines swarmed over the fort. After hand-to-hand combat, Fort Fisher fell to the Union. Blockade-runners no longer had a safe port.

Parker D. Robbins of Bertie County, a free person of color, joined the Union Army. *Why did many African Americans want to fight on the Union side?*

Forts Hatteras and Clark were captured by Union forces in August 1861. Most Tidewater towns, except Wilmington, quickly fell to the Union. *Why was Wilmington important to the Confederacy?*

Sherman's March

Few major Civil War battles were fought in North Carolina. But the state was damaged by war, mostly in 1865.

Union General William T. Sherman brought the horror of war to North Carolina on his march from Savannah, Georgia, toward Richmond, Virginia, the capital of the Confederacy. During his march, troops burned crops and acres of pine trees, destroyed homes and buildings, and stole food and other supplies.

A Confederate force under General Joseph Johnston fought some of Sherman's army in Johnston County. For two

EYEWITNESS TO HISTORY

Blockade-Running

The Cape Fear region offers many ways to and from the sea. Fifty miles (81 km) of shoreline make it hard for Union captains to spot every Confederate ship transporting supplies into Wilmington.

Confederate ammunition

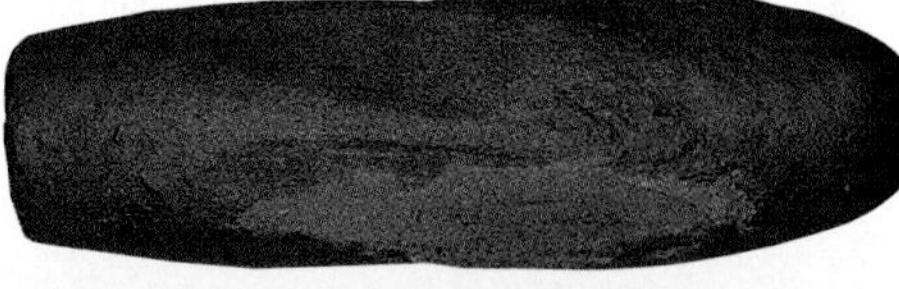

A long, sleek ship approaches port in the dark of night. The captain wants to sail as quietly as possible. Lights are out. The ship is built low to the water and painted the color of water. Her masts resemble thin trees. The captain keeps his ship turned so that the masts might be mistaken for pine trees on shore. Fort Fisher hasn't been captured by the Union army yet, so blockade-runners have protection. A good captain and a fast ship can make it through.

Fort Fisher

days the Union and Confederate forces clashed during the **Battle of Bentonville**, the only major Civil War battle fought in North Carolina. When the remainder of Sherman's army arrived, the Confederates retreated.

Surrender of the Confederates

There were two Southern surrenders to end the Civil War. General Robert E. Lee turned over his Army of Northern Virginia to General Ulysses S. Grant at Appomattox, Virginia. Three weeks later, on April 29, 1865, General Johnston surrendered to Sherman in North

In the darkness Confederate Captain John Newland Maffitt (left) prepares to dash through the Union lines with a cargo of gunpowder. Maffitt slips past the Union ships and reaches port. The gunpowder makes its way by railroad to the Confederate army.

A ship going to England might hold cotton. Cotton sells for high prices in England. Upon its return to Wilmington, the ship will have necessary goods for the Confederate army. Gunpowder and food supplies will help the Confederacy last a little longer in the war.

The Ad Vance *blockade-runner*

The CSS *Shenandoah* sailed around the world fighting Union ships at the end of the war. *Who was the ship's captain?*

Carolina. They met in Durham County at the James Bennett farm. Sherman ordered his troops to return horses and mules to the Confederates so they could begin spring planting.

The last Confederate navy ship to surrender, the *Shenandoah,* was commanded by James Iredell Waddell, from Pittsboro. Captain Waddell sailed past the tip of Africa to Australia. Then he sailed north to the Arctic, back south to San Francisco, and around Cape Horn to the Atlantic Ocean. He robbed any Union ship he could find. He stopped fighting when he boarded a ship and found out the war was over. He sailed to Liverpool, England, and lowered the Confederate flag. Everywhere, finally, the civil war was over.

LESSON 2 REVIEW

Fact Follow-Up

1. What was the blockade, and what were blockade-runners?
2. Describe conditions of the people left behind in North Carolina during the war.
3. Describe battles fought in North Carolina during the war.
4. What was the importance of Fort Fisher?

Think These Through

5. Why do you think North Carolina strongly supported the war as a Confederate state?
6. How did the relative location of North Carolina affect the state in the Civil War?

African Americans Embrace Freedom

"I'm free! I'm free! Shout hosanna!" The shout was heard through the streets of New Bern on New Year's Day, 1863. Escaped slaves, protected by the Northern army, paraded up and down the streets. President Abraham Lincoln's Emancipation Proclamation had set them free.

For years afterward, African Americans in North Carolina celebrated New Year's Day as Emancipation Day. The holiday reminded them of the struggles they had endured during slavery and in the early days of freedom.

LESSON PREVIEW

Key Ideas

- The Emancipation Proclamation and the end of the Civil War freed slaves.
- Most African Americans continued to farm, working as sharecroppers on former plantations.
- African Americans organized churches and schools.
- Many whites resented the gains made by African Americans.

Key Terms

Emancipation Proclamation, sharecropping, Reconstruction, Ku Klux Klan

Emancipation's Effects

The **Emancipation Proclamation**, declared by President Abraham Lincoln in 1863, freed all slaves in the Confederate states under Union control. In 1865, when Northern soldiers occupied much of North Carolina, all slaves in the state were freed. No longer could one person buy, sell, or treat another as property.

After the Civil War, African Americans of all ages began attending schools run by the Freedmen's Bureau. *Why was education important to former slaves?*

Many African Americans immediately left the places they had worked as slaves. They chose to move into towns. Some people stayed near the plantations, but lived in their own communities. Most wanted to work, but they had few choices.

Most African Americans had no education and could not own property. Few had developed skills other than

LIVING IN NEW BERN

Life in an Occupied Town

Feb. 28, 1863

Dear Cousin Pete,

Here in New Bern we're having a hard time. Union troops took over our town in March last year.

The soldiers have dark blue uniforms. The officers have long swords as well as pistols.

They are not as hungry looking as we are. A Union soldier offered me a ration, but I said, "No, thanks." Momma said I should have taken it.

I confess I do go and watch the Union soldiers when they march. It reminds me of when the Confederate soldiers marched off to war.

We can go about like we want in the day. But nobody can go about at night. You have to have a pass in the day, but they don't get checked much.

One other thing is different. Many slaves have come into town. They have heard about freedom.

President Lincoln granted freedom to the slaves last month. There are no more slaves now. We never had slaves anyhow.

Momma says today I have to stay close to the house. There have been riots over food. People who have been hurt in the riots have trouble getting doctors and medicine.

If your Momma hears from Daddy, please write to Momma. She worries. I hope you get this letter. If you do, write back, and tell me how you and your family are doing in Wilmington.

Yr cousin,
James

New Bern in 1864

farming. For a while, they were helped by a United States government agency, the Freedmen's Bureau, which gave them food, clothing, and work.

Plantation life was gone, yet crops of cotton and tobacco offered a living for newly freed people. Former slaves started out with a year-long agreement to work in a field. African Americans disliked the labor contracts. Instead, they offered to rent pieces of farmland. They shared most of the harvest with the landowners. People called this relationship **sharecropping**.

Sharecropping was risky, but the former slaves' risk was greater. They hoped to grow enough food to feed their families after the landowners received their share first. The landowners knew they would get at least enough to eat and hoped the sharecroppers would raise enough additional crops to make money for them. The sharecroppers hoped the rest would pay for their needs for a year.

Thousands of former slaves became sharecroppers. They had the skills to farm but did not have enough money to buy land. Most had to find work raising cotton or tobacco on land they did not own. Even when crops were plentiful, sharecroppers could not make much money. Landowners charged them for seeds, tools, and the use of the land. Sharecroppers often ended the year in debt.

African Americans worked as sharecroppers after the Civil War. *Why did sharecropping make it difficult for them to earn money?*

WORD ORIGINS

The Emancipation Proclamation freed the slaves. The word **emancipation** comes from emancipate. To emancipate means "to release someone from a contract or restraint." The word emancipate comes from the Latin ***mancipare***, which means "slave."

African American Communities

African Americans quickly worked to improve their lives. With the help of northern churches, they built small school houses and sent their children to get the education that they had been denied. More than 100 schools were built within two years.

By 1900, about 2,000 private African American schools had been built. Two schools in North Carolina were the Palmer Institute, which was open until the 1960s, and Laurinburg Institute, which is well known today.

Most African Americans set up their own churches. Churches became centers of African American community life. The church became a place where people could speak their minds without fear.

Neither whites nor African Americans were certain that they wanted to worship together at this time. Both sides were still angry and distrustful.

African American churches in the North helped organize colleges to train young men and women. These young people came to North Carolina to serve as ministers and teachers for the churches and schools.

GAMES People Play

Word Game African American children played a rhyming word game.

"Saa-sa brewa, ode-hye!" cried each child who held a wooden block. The children sat in a circle and took turns holding the block. All sang together the same line as they passed the blocks and hit them on the floor.

If a player failed to pick up a block and keep up, he or she was out. Every time the line was repeated, it was said faster and faster. The winner was the last one keeping time with the blocks.

The Freedmen's School in Pitt County opened in 1866. It was one of hundreds that offered schooling to former slaves. *Who taught in these schools?*

Biddle (now Johnson C. Smith) in Charlotte, Shaw and St. Augustine in Raleigh, and Livingstone in Salisbury were built to give college education to African Americans. Graduates became preachers and educators. Barber-Scotia in Concord began as a school for young African American women.

African Americans Win Rights

After the war, African American men could vote. African Americans became citizens of the United States. Slavery was outlawed.

Former slaves became important members of the Republican party because that party had worked to free them. Former slaves helped write a constitution for the state in 1868. This constitution gave North Carolina better schools and public services.

Some newly freed people became members of the state legislature. John A. Hyman of Warren County became the most famous of these leaders. He served in the state legislature. He was the first African American elected to the United States Congress from North Carolina.

After the end of slavery, African Americans became citizens of the United States and could vote and run for office for the first time. *Why are such rights important?*

White Resentment

Reconstruction followed the Confederate defeat. **Reconstruction** was the method of bringing former Confederate states back into the Union. The United States government controlled the governments of the former Confederate states.

The federal government, led by the Republican party, wanted to punish the South. It required former Confederate soldiers to sign statements swearing their loyalty to the United States. State governments were forced to make the changes to the Constitution called amendments that gave African Americans the same rights as other Americans.

Members of the Ku Klux Klan wore robes and masks to disguise themselves while they did violence to African Americans. *Why did the Ku Klux Klan act this way?*

Some people joined the Republican party, especially those North Carolinians who did not want the state to join the Confederacy. Many lived in the Mountains. Other people who had supported the Union joined the Republican party. Whites who had fought for the Confederacy stayed in the Democratic party. Many former Confederates lost property. Either they could not pay the higher taxes or they were suspected of not being loyal to the Union.

These changes angered many people who had survived the war. They looked for ways to regain their land and take control of their lives.

Some white men joined the **Ku Klux Klan**, a secret organization. These men were angry over Reconstruction. They ignored the new laws protecting the rights of African Americans. They believed whites should stay in control of African Americans.

Members of the Klan wore red or white gowns and masks to terrorize Republicans of all races. The Klan murdered more than 20 people across the state and beat hundreds of individuals who opposed them.

Eventually, the national government stopped the violence. Also, people began to learn ways to live together in this changing state of North Carolina.

Despite resentment and violence, African Americans made progress. African American communities grew. Several African American men served in Congress during Reconstruction.

LESSON 3 REVIEW

Fact Follow-Up

1. Describe the condition of former slaves in the years just after the Civil War.
2. What was sharecropping?
3. How did the federal government treat the South during Reconstruction?
4. What was the Ku Klux Klan? What were its aims?

Think These Through

5. Compare sharecropping and slavery.
6. What do you think was the most important advancement of African Americans in the years just after the Civil War? Explain your answer.

Farming After the War

LESSON PREVIEW

Key Ideas

- Recovery after the Civil War was very difficult for farmers.
- Farmers lost property when prices of cotton and tobacco dropped.
- Leonidas Polk helped farmers through his work.

Key Terms

borrow, cooperatives

A woman and two small children stood out in a field. The woman held onto a plow with the harness wrapped around the children's waists. The three were trying to pull the plow down a row. The mule had died the winter before. Suddenly a voice rang out. "Sally!" The woman stopped. The children dropped the harness and began to run towards the lone figure at the edge of the field.

After four years of war, their father had returned. What was once a prosperous farm had become a place of struggle for survival. It would be years before it would become a thriving farm again.

Changes in Farming

After the war, North Carolina farmers grew cotton or tobacco to make money. These two crops received the highest prices, but by growing them farmers gave up some of their independence. They no longer could rely on just themselves to survive.

This cornfield at Duke Homestead shows how a farm might have looked after the Civil War. *Why were the years after the war tough on farmers in North Carolina?*

Farmers loaded tobacco into their barns for curing (right). Brown Brothers in Winston (left) processed dried tobacco into cigarettes. *Why did more farmers grow tobacco and cotton after the war?*

First, they had to **borrow** money to buy fertilizer and seed. This means the farmer did not have the money to pay for those items, so banks or merchants loaned the farmer money to buy them. The farmer had to pay back the borrowed money.

Second, the number of farms increased. Farmers grew different crops in different parts of the state. Farmers in northern counties grew tobacco. Farmers in the Coastal Plain and Piedmont grew cotton. Even farmers in the Uwharrie Mountains tried to grow cotton. For example, almost no Stanly County families grew cotton before the Civil War. Afterward, almost all of them did. In Franklin County, the number of farms doubled after the Civil War.

Because everyone grew the same crops, factories could set low prices to buy all they needed. Cotton sold for 25 cents a pound in 1867, 12 cents in 1877, and only 5 cents in 1896. Tobacco prices also fell.

When cotton prices fell, farmers could not make enough money to pay back what they owed. They did not have money to buy goods. Many families could not make a living.

Sometimes the families had to sell their land to pay their bills. Since farming was the only way of life they knew, many families stayed on farms as sharecroppers. Others gave up farming and moved to the towns to find work in the factories.

Killing hogs and weaving cloth became less important. Stores in town offered cotton-mill cloth, which was cheaper than cloth made on looms at home. It was cheaper for families to buy bacon than to cure pork themselves.

Farmers in North Carolina still grew corn and wheat to feed their families and livestock. Yet little money could be made from corn or wheat because farmers in the Midwest grew those crops at less cost. Life was hard for most farmers.

Solving Farm Problems

Many North Carolinians wanted to solve farm problems. With long growing seasons and good land, farming was still important. Having better farms was necessary for survival.

Leonidas L. Polk, who served in the Civil War, emerged as a national farm leader. As North Carolina's first commissioner of agriculture, Polk started farmer clubs. Farmers got together and helped one another find better ways to grow crops.

Leonidas L. Polk was North Carolina's first commissioner of agriculture. He began farmer clubs as part of the North Carolina Farmer's Association. *What was the purpose of these clubs?*

To help all farmers, Polk and others founded the North Carolina College of Agriculture and Mechanical Arts (now North Carolina State University). The college opened in October 1889. Its promise was to help North Carolinians become better farmers and better producers.

The farmer clubs, organized as the North Carolina

The Farmer's Alliance sold tobacco and other crops through ads, such as the one above, in its magazine, *Progressive Farmer.* *How did the alliance and the founding of North Carolina College of Agriculture (above) help farmers?*

Farmer's Association, became part of a national organization, the National Farmers' Alliance. Polk became its leader and moved to Washington, D.C.

The efforts of farmers to better themselves only partially succeeded. They tried to grow different crops, but merchants wanted to buy cotton and tobacco before anything else. Farm women took the lead in growing sweet potatoes and raising chickens and eggs for the town merchants. This helped the family income.

Farmers also formed **cooperatives**, which means they bought supplies together and sold their crops as a group. Groups could get better prices and had more to sell. Beginning in 1900, prices for crops improved and farmers began to make more money.

LESSON 4 REVIEW

Fact Follow-Up

1. Describe conditions faced by farmers just after the Civil War.
2. How did falling farm prices affect farm families?
3. Who was Leonidas L. Polk?
4. What was the purpose of founding what is now North Carolina State University?

Think These Through

5. Why did farmers continue to grow cotton and tobacco even when the crops did not make enough money?
6. Suppose you were a farmer's child in the late 1800s. What could you have done to improve your family's life? Explain.
7. How did cooperatives help farmers?

Using Information for Problem Solving, Decision Making, and Planning

Using a Time Line

Have you ever seen a time line? Time lines help you organize information so that important events can be seen clearly. The time line is of a woman who was fifty years old in 1995. Notice how events in her life are organized in ten-year periods.

In making the time line, the woman had to make two decisions: (1) how to divide the periods of her life (she chose to use decades or ten-year periods) and (2) what events to include in the time line (she used personal events and important national events).

Now that you have read her time line, see if you can make a time line of your own life. How will you divide the line into periods? What events will you include in your own time line? Use the example on the right to make your time line. When you have finished your time line, compare it to a classmate's.

Making a time line helps you organize and remember events in history—just as it helped you remember and organize events in your own life. Try making a time line for the Civil War. Will you begin your time line in 1861, when the war began, or will you begin earlier, when the northern and southern states began to argue? When you have completed your time line, compare yours with a classmate's.

Now, skim Chapters 6 and 7. What are some other time lines you can make to organize information in those chapters?

You can use time lines for the rest of this year when you need to organize and remember information about different times in history.

Organizing a Time Line

National Events		Personal Events
World War II ends	1945	born 3-3-45
Korean War begins		starts school
Eisenhower elected	1955	becomes a Brownie Scout
		first dance
President Kennedy dies		graduates from H.S.
Civil Rights activities	1965	
Vietnam War		graduates from college
M.L. King killed		teaches in Greensboro
Nixon resigns		moves to Raleigh
Vietnam falls	1975	
		gets married
		first child born
Reagan is president		moves to Charlotte
	1985	children begin school
fall of communism		visits Europe
		moves to Wilmington
	1995	teaches in Wilmington

Chapter 8 Review

LESSONS LEARNED

LESSON 1 The northern and southern states disagreed about the future of slavery. Most southerners wanted to be able to own slaves wherever they moved. The argument led to war. North Carolina reluctantly fought on the side of the South, called the Confederacy. The Underground Railroad was a way for African Americans to escape slavery.

LESSON 2 Once North Carolina decided to fight for the Confederate side, many citizens fought on that side. Women farmed during the war to keep families fed. Blockade-runners kept North Carolina trade active and supplied weapons to the Confederacy. Union troops under General William T. Sherman destroyed property during a march through the state near the end of the war, which the Confederacy lost.

LESSON 3 The Emancipation Proclamation and the end of the Civil War freed slaves. Most African Americans became sharecroppers and continued to farm. African Americans organized their own churches and schools. Some resentful whites joined the Ku Klux Klan to oppose the gains made by African Americans. African Americans made slow progress.

LESSON 4 Farmers had a tough time after the Civil War. They lost property when prices of cotton and tobacco dropped. Leonidas L. Polk helped farmers through his work.

TIME FOR TERMS

abolitionists
secede
Union
blockade
Battle of Bentonville
sharecropping
Reconstruction
borrow
Underground Railroad
Confederate States of America (Confederacy)
blockade-runners
Emancipation Proclamation
Ku Klux Klan
cooperatives

FACT FOLLOW-UP

1. What were the reasons North Carolina chose to join the Confederacy?
2. Describe differences between North and South just before the Civil War.
3. Describe efforts to save enslaved people before the Civil War.
4. Describe conditions for the average North Carolinian during the Civil War.
5. What were conditions faced by newly freed slaves?
6. What were major events of the Reconstruction period in North Carolina?
7. Describe the sharecropping system and how it differed from slavery.
8. Describe efforts to improve farming in North Carolina. How successful were they?

THINK THESE THROUGH

9. Why did North Carolina contribute as much as it did to the Confederate war effort?

10. How did different regions of the state respond to the Civil War? Why?
11. Suppose you had been a political leader in North Carolina in 1861. Would you have voted for secession? Explain your answer.
12. Think about the lives of average North Carolina farmers in 1850 and in 1900. At which time were they better off? Explain.
13. Think about the lives of African Americans in 1850 and in 1900. At which time were they better off? Explain.

SHARPENING SKILLS

14. Using information from Chapter 6, make a time line for European exploration and settlement in North Carolina.
15. What would you include in a time line of Native Americans in North Carolina before Europeans came? Skim Chapter 5 to find information.
16. How could time lines be used for planning?

PLACE LOCATION

Use the letters on the map to name and locate the following places that were significant during the Civil War in North Carolina:

17. Only significant land battle fought in North Carolina during the Civil War.
18. Site of surrender of Confederate troops under General Joseph Johnston to Union troops commanded by General William Sherman.
19. Fort that guarded the entrance to the Cape Fear River and Wilmington.
20. Fort that guarded the Outer Banks.

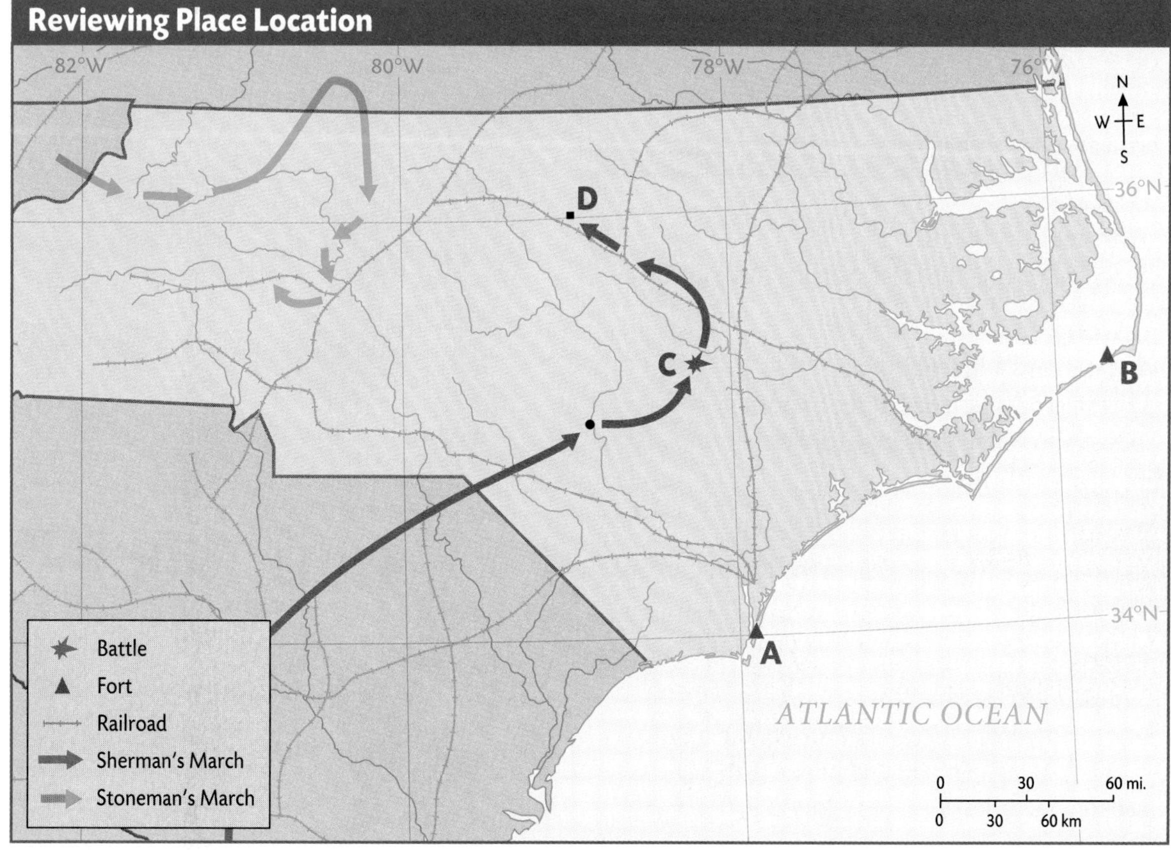

North Carolina Grows, 1865–1910

1880s roller polo

Skating was the latest craze all over the country in the 1880s. The Cross Cut Polo Club of Durham played polo on roller skates. Wherever the club played, its sponsors, W. Duke, Sons and Company, gave away free cigarettes. The Duke family made a fortune by such clever marketing and by carefully advertising its tobacco products. Textile mills also promoted its products by sponsoring athletic teams. Tobacco and textiles helped North Carolina grow after the Civil War.

CHAPTER PREVIEW

LESSON 1
Tobacco and Farms
Tobacco became the chief crop in North Carolina.

LESSON 2
Cotton and Textiles
Cotton production fueled the important first industry in North Carolina—textiles.

LESSON 3
Trains Help North Carolina Recover
Railroads after the war helped the North Carolina economy grow.

LESSON 4
Working After the War
North Carolinians began to find work in towns growing along railroads and beside textile and tobacco factories.

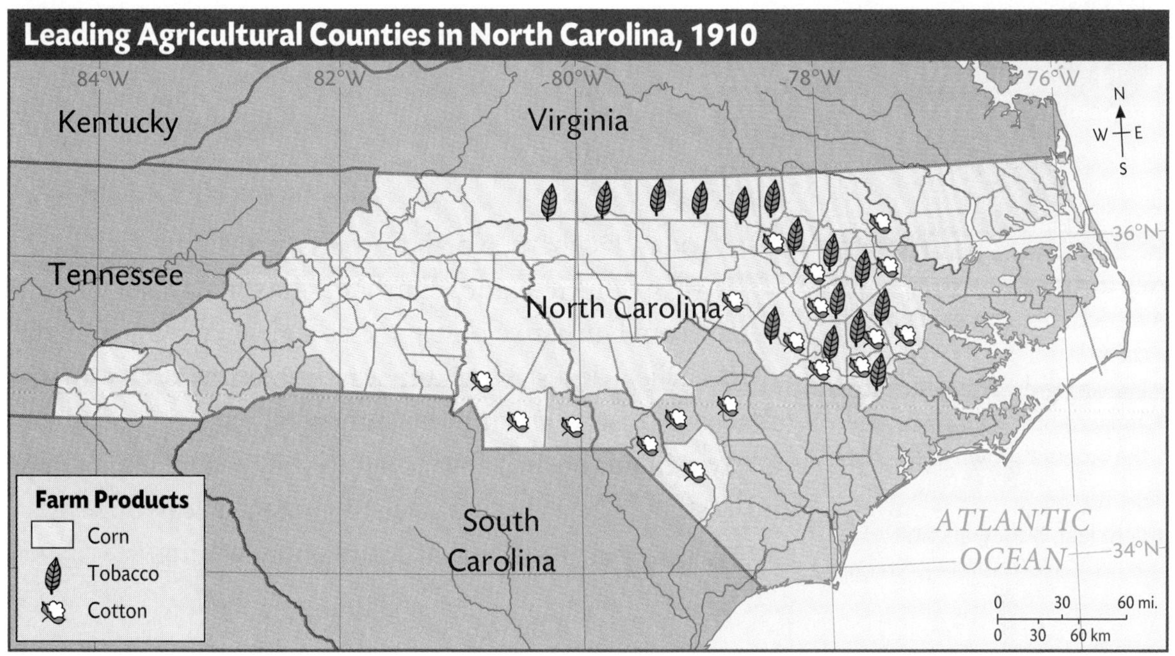

Duke tobacco ads

CAROLINA CONNECTION

Mill Team Basketball

Some North Carolinians are famous worldwide because of basketball. Basketball has a long history in North Carolina. Textile mills organized basketball teams and tournaments to advertise their textile products.

In 1921, textile mill teams from North Carolina and South Carolina met to play at a Weavers Convention in Greenville, South Carolina. Both men's and women's teams (below) played. One team came from the Ivey Mill Company in Hickory, North Carolina. The weavers must have enjoyed cheering for their fellow textile workers on the basketball court.

Tobacco and Farms

LESSON PREVIEW

Key Ideas

- Tobacco became an important crop.
- Industry grew around tobacco.
- Tobacco processing increased the amount grown in the state.

Key Terms

bright leaf, burley, auction

Today, Durham, North Carolina, proclaims itself as the "City of Medicine." Durham's hospitals have patients from Durham County and as far away as Saudi Arabia.

In earlier times, Durham was known as a city of the tobacco industry. During the summers, the smell of tobacco leaves filled the air. Now, tobacco warehouses hold shops and restaurants. Where barrels of tobacco leaf once were stored, shoppers look for antiques and clothing.

Tobacco in North Carolina

After the Civil War, tobacco became the most important crop in North Carolina. Union soldiers fighting here had discovered a special type of tobacco, called bright leaf. They took the habit of smoking it back to the North. The demand for tobacco grew.

Families who grew small amounts of tobacco before the Civil War grew more of it after the war. Washington Duke began processing tobacco soon after the Civil War. W. Duke, Sons and Company grew quickly. It joined other companies to form the American Tobacco Company. The firm bought the Bull Durham Company and other small tobacco processors.

Washington Duke stands in front of his first tobacco production cabin in Durham. *Why did some tobacco farmers such as Duke turn to producing tobacco?*

In 1874, R. J. Reynolds moved to Winston-Salem. He started a company with a few workers who made chewing tobacco. In 25 years, the town grew from 400 to 22,700. Many worked for Reynolds.

Where Tobacco Grew

Tobacco grew throughout the eastern United States before the Civil War. North Carolina was not the largest grower of tobacco until after the 1880s.

North Carolina's farmers first grew bright leaf tobacco along the Virginia border (see map, page 183). The name **bright leaf** came from the color of the cured tobacco leaf.

As demand for bright leaf grew, farmers in other parts of the state began producing the crop. Raising tobacco required a lot of hard labor. Most farm families could raise only a few acres. Even a small crop brought farmers more income than cotton.

Today, machinery has replaced much of the human labor. Bright leaf tobacco is raised on larger farms, especially in the Coastal Plain.

Mountain farmers produced a darker, heavier, air-cured tobacco, called **burley**. That type is still grown there today.

Handling Tobacco

Tobacco had to be handled carefully by many workers. The tobacco shoots grew from a seed bed, then were transplanted to a field. As the plants grew, workers suckered them—removed the small shoots from the stalks. Then the larger leaves could grow bigger and broader.

After the Civil War, demand for tobacco grew. Farmers grew the crop up to their front doors. *What type of tobacco became most popular?*

The leaves were pulled off as they ripened and taken to the curing barn, where they were dried. Farmers built curing barns of pine logs or boards. Workers fed long logs into a brick furnace inside the barn. A large pipe, or flue, ran from the furnace along all four inner walls. The tobacco leaves were dried at temperatures up to about 180 degrees Fahrenheit (82° Centigrade) until all moisture was gone.

Someone had to watch the curing process all night because if the temperature got too hot or the fire went out, the leaves would be ruined.

Selling Tobacco

Farmers stored their cured tobacco on their farms in packhouses until marketing time. Then farmers brought their bales of tobacco to warehouses. The warehouses held the tobacco until auction time.

At an **auction**—a sale of property to the highest bidder—interested buyers from big tobacco companies listened to the auctioneer, the person who ran the sale. He called for prices on the bundles of tobacco leaves. The auctioneer sang out the prices with a loud voice. Buyers walked through the huge building to bid on the musical prices.

Tobacco companies built warehouses in eastern railroad towns. Wilson, Greenville, Rocky Mount, and Goldsboro grew into large tobacco markets. Towns in the Piedmont, such as Durham, Oxford, and Winston-Salem, built warehouses for tobacco storage and sale.

Durham grew as the W. Duke and Sons Tobacco Company grew. *How did railroads built near factories help make Durham and Winston-Salem important tobacco towns?*

Manufacturing Tobacco

Tobacco companies transported the tobacco to their plants in Durham and Winston-Salem. They moved the tobacco by wagon and, later, by train.

In the early days of the industry, workers rolled small squares of paper around tobacco to make a cigarette. A machine invented in Virginia

The Duke tobacco factory at Durham included Washington Duke's big new home. *How did Duke become wealthy making cigarettes?*

caught the attention of James Buchanan Duke, Washington Duke's son. He bought two of the inventions and brought them to Durham. One machine could roll 200 cigarettes a minute.

The machine transformed the tobacco industry. Its efficiency increased the sale of cigarettes and the demand for flue-cured tobacco. Duke also increased sales by advertising. He grew so wealthy that he began to buy other tobacco companies. Duke soon controlled three fourths of the industry.

Under Duke's leadership, North Carolina led the nation in tobacco production. Tobacco remains an important part of the state's economy, but the industry began to change in the 1960s. Concerns in the United States about the health problems caused by tobacco reduced the sale of cigarettes. The number of farmers growing tobacco began to decrease. Other products, such as soybeans, became important.

LESSON 1 REVIEW

Fact Follow-Up

1. How did demand for tobacco products grow after the Civil War?
2. What was the importance of the Duke and Reynolds families?
3. Describe tobacco production.
4. Where were major tobacco factories located?

Think These Through

5. What physical characteristics of place in North Carolina encouraged growing tobacco?
6. Apply the geographic theme of Movement to the development of the tobacco industry.

Cotton and Textiles

LESSON PREVIEW

Key Ideas

- Farmers grew more cotton.
- Textile mills spread throughout North Carolina.
- Cotton prices fell as more farmers grew cotton.
- Textile mills attracted workers from farms and became the biggest industry in North Carolina.

Key Terms

textile, chop cotton, bolls, denim

A young boy wrote to the newspaper in Gastonia. He had a complaint. "Why do the mill village boys and girls have so much more than we who live up town?" He wrote that every mill community in and around Gastonia was "full of playground equipment."

There were other differences between mill villages and farms and towns. Some differences created problems for mill workers.

Cotton Still Growing

Immediately after the Civil War, most farm families grew food crops for survival. They raised corn, sweet potatoes, and hay for their livestock. Because Duke's cigarette machine worked so well, tobacco companies needed more tobacco. Farmers began planting more bright leaf tobacco to sell to cigarette makers.

Small family farms also began raising more cotton after textile mills began producing cloth again after the war. **Textile** means woven or knit cloth and refers to businesses that make cloth. Cotton did not bring as high a price as tobacco did later. Cotton did bring in enough money to keep food on the table for a family.

Cotton Farm Life

Textile mills wanted cotton, and North Carolina farmers wanted to supply them. Growing cotton took up much of the year for North Carolina families. They planted cotton in the spring. When the shoots poked out of the ground as the weather warmed, so did the weeds. All family members chopped cotton. To **chop** cotton is to remove excess cotton plants. In September, students would take a month off from school to pick the crop.

Cotton pickers draped long sacks across their shoulders and walked down each row to pick the cotton **bolls**. Bolls are the white fluffy balls of the cotton plant. Grownups and children picked cotton from dawn to sundown. Picking cotton hurt the back. Pickers had to lean over to pull bolls off the low plants. Cotton husks cut fingers as the picker pulled the boll.

The cotton was rolled into bundles and loaded on wagons. At a nearby gin, seeds were removed from the bolls. Next, a machine pressed the cotton into bales. Ginned bales could weigh as much as 800 pounds.

What would YOU do?

Your father, mother, and sister are to start work in a textile mill in town next week. Your family must move there.

You know the country and like some of your chores, especially milking. In town you might be able to have one cow, but other things will change. You will have to wear shoes every day.

What will life be like in town? You will have free time. How will you spend it?

Spread of Textile Mills

Textile companies bought the seedless cotton. Mills combed the cotton and spun it into thread. Workers wove thread into yarn. On mechanical looms, workers turned the yarn into cloth.

Three scenes show parts of cotton production: harvesting in eastern North Carolina, moving by wagon in Mecklenburg, and pressing into bales in New Hanover. *Where did the cotton go next?*

Textile mills started springing up all over North Carolina. Most at first were located in the Piedmont along fast-flowing streams that powered the mills.

Textile mills had been in the state since 1813 when Michael Schenck built a cotton mill in Lincoln County. Other families opened textile mills before the Civil War. The Battles in Rocky Mount, the Fries of Winston-Salem, the Moreheads of Rockingham County, and the Holts of Alamance County were early leaders in textile manufacturing.

After the Civil War, the textile mills began production again. As orders came from the Northeast for cloth, mills in Piedmont towns needed cotton as a raw material.

Farmers in the Cape Fear Valley and along the South Carolina border provided the most cotton for the mills. Roads from Shelby in the West to Lumberton in the East cut through cotton fields that stretched as far as anyone could see. Cotton grew all the way north to Lexington, Statesville, and Hickory.

Textile mills grew as companies bought more cotton. Many small farmers began selling cotton. With a steady source of cotton, mills could drop prices.

Farm families discovered they could earn more money working at a mill than they could working on their farm. Cotton prices were too low for farmers to make a living.

After the boll weevil attacked cotton crops in the South in the 1890s and again in the 1920s, many farm families in North Carolina moved to get jobs in textile mills. Many workers came from the Piedmont and Mountains. Mills produced cloth from cotton not yet hit by the boll weevil.

Textile production became the biggest industry in the state in the early 1900s. North Carolina and South Carolina led the country in textiles.

Greensboro's Cone Mills became the world's largest maker of **denim**, the dark blue cotton cloth used to make blue jeans. Cannon Mills built the town of Kannapolis

WORD ORIGINS

Kannapolis combines two names. Part of the name comes from a family and part of the name is a Greek word. ***Polis*** means "city," and Kanna comes from a form of the family name of Cannon.

The 600 acres (240 sq hm) that James William Cannon bought beside the Southern Railway tracks became Kannapolis. Cannon bought the land in 1906 and built a mill and houses for the workers to rent.

and became a major manufacturer of towels, curtains, and bedding.

Almost every town in the Piedmont had a textile mill. Gastonia had the largest number of mills.

Tompkins Mill in Charlotte and Cone Mills in Greensboro were two of many textile mills in the Piedmont. *Why did farm families move off the farm to work in the textile mills?*

Textiles and Education

Because of the many textile mills, the North Carolina State College in Raleigh began a textiles department. In 1901, the college opened a mill building with machinery for making yarn and fabrics.

The college began teaching students cotton production—how to card and spin cotton, weave and design cloth, and dye fabric. The college also began courses to teach manufacturers the science of textiles. Today, North Carolina State University leads the world in textiles education.

LESSON 2 REVIEW

Fact Follow-Up

1. Describe how cotton is grown and harvested.
2. What areas of the state were included in the cotton-growing region?
3. How did the boll weevil affect farm life?

Think These Through

4. Why was cotton farming difficult?
5. Why did the Piedmont become the location of most cotton mills?
6. Why was it important to teach about textile production at the college in Raleigh?

LESSON 3 Trains Help North Carolina Recover

LESSON PREVIEW

Key Ideas

- Trains recovered after the war.
- Trains helped industry.
- Trains created new industry.

At the North Carolina Transportation Museum in Spencer, you can walk through the private railroad car of one of the richest men in the United States. James B. Duke traveled in his own railroad car after he became rich from his tobacco business.

Imagine living in a railroad car. Wealthy people spent thousands of dollars to make a train car livable. Restored cars now are housed in the repair shops once used by the Southern Railway. The museum holds gleaming dining cars alongside locomotives that pulled the trains.

North Carolina Railroads, 1860

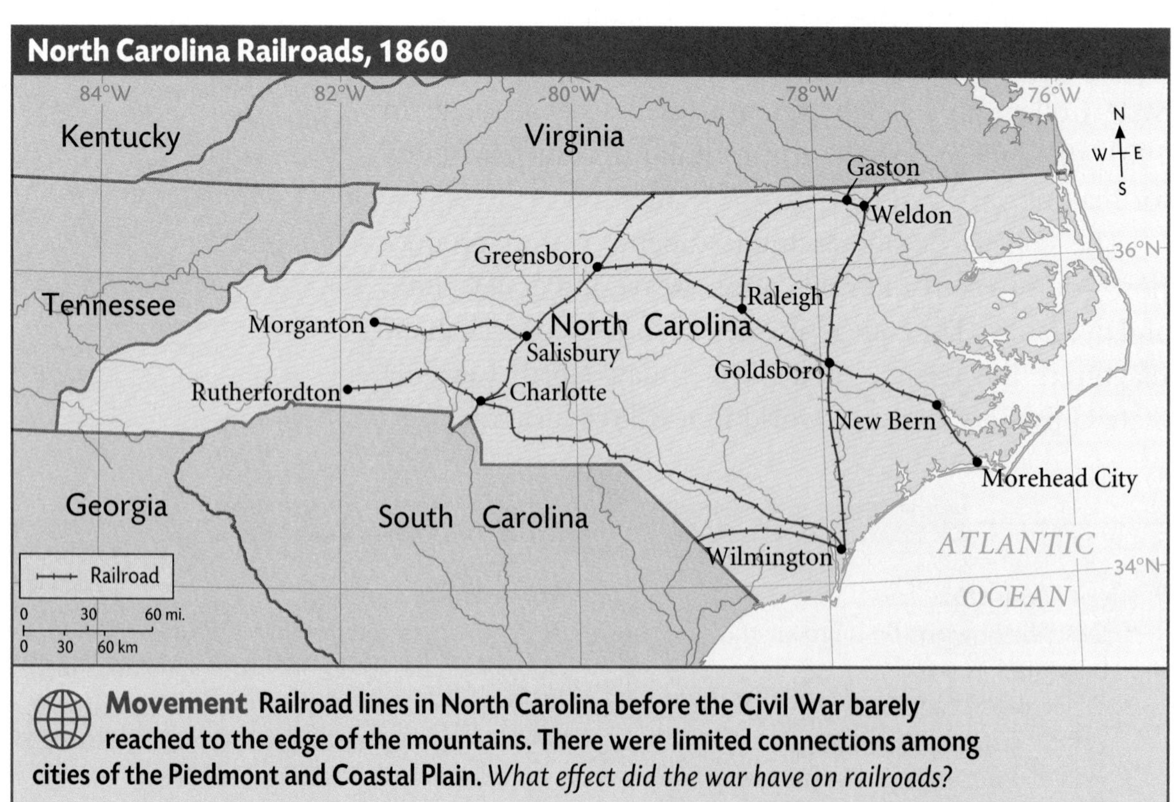

Movement Railroad lines in North Carolina before the Civil War barely reached to the edge of the mountains. There were limited connections among cities of the Piedmont and Coastal Plain. *What effect did the war have on railroads?*

Railroads Rebuild

The trains in North Carolina could not run immediately after the Civil War. Sherman's troops tore up tracks, wrecked trains, and left them in ruin.

A short time later, trains ran again in the state. The problem was that they were not running very far.

The state government and private businesses spent money to build railroads in North Carolina during the 1880s. *Why was it important for the state to do this?*

Short lines linked Raleigh to Goldsboro and Raleigh to Charlotte. The north-south Wilmington to Weldon route was long, but did not connect the Coastal Plain and Piedmont to the Mountains.

After the war, state leaders understood that North Carolina needed railroads to move goods. But North Carolina was poor. Businessmen and the state joined together to pay for more railroads by the 1880s.

North Carolina Railroads, 1900

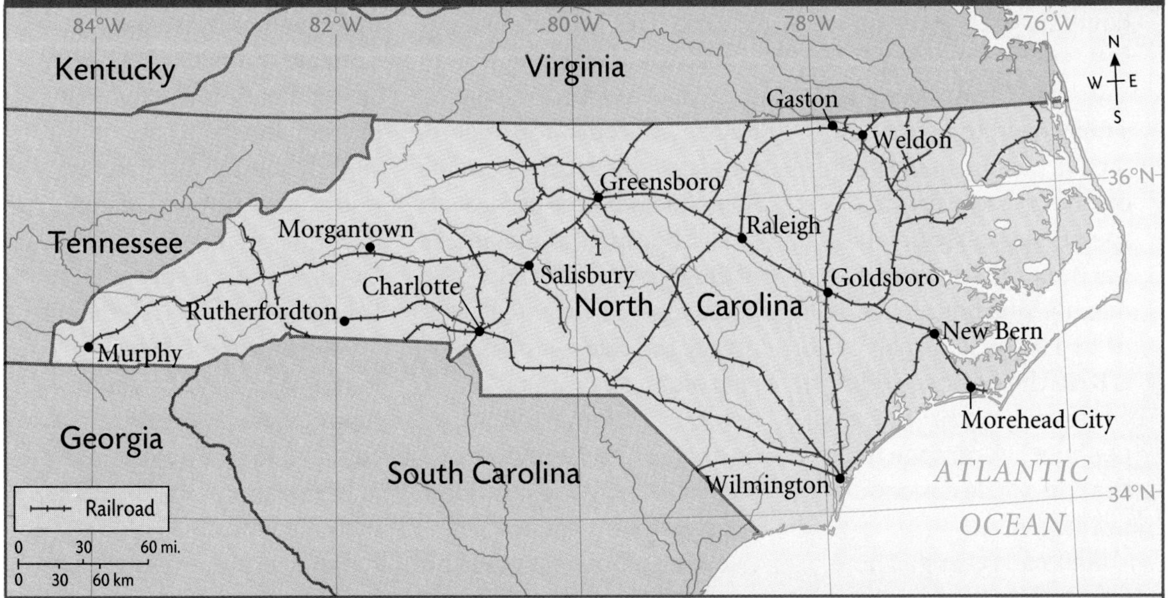

84°W 82°W 80°W 78°W 76°W 36°N 34°N
N S E W
Kentucky
Virginia
Tennessee
Georgia
South Carolina
North Carolina
ATLANTIC OCEAN
Gaston
Weldon
Greensboro
Raleigh
Morgantown
Salisbury
Charlotte
Goldsboro
Rutherfordton
New Bern
Murphy
Morehead City
Wilmington
Railroad
0 30 60 mi.
0 30 60 km

Movement By 1900, railroads crisscrossed North Carolina. They helped new industries, promoted the growth of towns, and united the state. Look at the map on page 192. *Where did railroads go in 1900 that they did not reach in 1860?*

Moving Goods

Because of the lack of rail connections, many farmers brought their products to market by horse and wagon. The trips were slow and difficult. Farmers wanted railroads to get tobacco and cotton to market quickly.

CONNECTIONS

Geography & Math

Railroads Speed Travel

Before railroads, people in North Carolina walked or rode horses and buggies. As the map shows, in two hours you could ride from the center of Raleigh to the edge of Wake County.

If it is 16 miles (25.8 km) from the capitol building to the Chatham County line, and it takes a person two hours to reach there, how fast is he or she riding?

To find the answer, you simply need to figure how far the person would go in one hour, because rate of speed is expressed in miles per hour (abbreviated as m.p.h.). One hour is one half of two hours. One half of 16 is 8, so the person is riding at a rate of 8 m.p.h. (12.9 km per hour). A carriage made the trip a little easier but not faster.

Railroads changed how far a person could travel in two hours. Early railroad travel helped people go farther in a short amount of time. This was news!

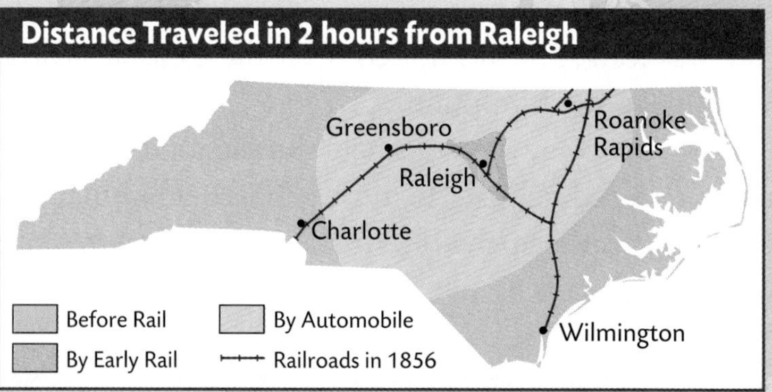

Instead of reaching the edge of Wake County in two hours, you could hop aboard a train on the North Carolina Railroad and reach as far west as Hillsborough, in the middle of Orange County. Taking two hours to go 38 miles (61.2 km) meant the train was chugging along at a rate of 19 m.p.h. (30.6 km/h), which is one half of 38. Because people, mail, and goods could reach different counties in two hours, business could be conducted more quickly.

The automobile put more places within reach. A family could travel from the middle of Raleigh to Salisbury or Concord, both slightly northeast of Charlotte, in two hours by interstate highway.

To reach Salisbury in two hours, how fast would you have to go? You would need to know that the distance to Salisbury is about 120 miles (193 km) from Raleigh. Remember, all you need to figure out is how far you could go in one hour.

Think about how different your life would be if you had to get everywhere by foot or by horse. How long would it take you to get to school from your home? Could you go to the same school?

Textile mills and tobacco companies were eager to sell their products outside of North Carolina. They shipped cigarettes and textiles on railroads to the rest of the country.

As the textile and tobacco industries grew, the need for more railroads grew. During the 1880s, the state completed a line through the mountains to the Tennessee border. By the turn of the century, three major railroads controlled lines through the Coastal Plain, along the fall line, and through the Piedmont and the Mountains. Compare the maps showing railroads in 1860 and 1900 (pages 192 and 193).

Railways carried cotton, passengers, and tobacco across the state. Piedmont textile mills could process cotton grown in eastern North Carolina. Durham and Winston-Salem tobacco factories could ship their goods to other states. People living in Asheville could more easily visit friends in Wilmington or Morehead City.

Towns Along the Railroads

Train tracks transformed the landscape of North Carolina. Before North Carolinians built railroads, only a few people lived in towns.

Carrboro began receiving the benefits of good transportation after the railroad came to town. *How were North Carolina towns and cities changed by the railroad?*

North Carolina had some of the smallest cities in the United States before the Civil War. The only sizable places were Wilmington and Fayetteville. Connected by the Cape Fear River, together they made up the only large port.

Everything changed when the three small railroads were repaired after the war and the state laid more track. Towns built before the railroads grew quickly. Durham, Winston, and Hickory were small crossroads of less than 500 people before their depots drew people to live and work there.

Asheville and Charlotte changed dramatically after the railroad reached those towns. In just ten years, Asheville grew from 2,600 to more than 10,400 people after the Western North Carolina Railroad opened. Charlotte doubled in size, despite the Civil War, after the North Carolina Railroad reached it in 1856. In 40 years—from 1870 to 1910—Charlotte grew from the fifth largest to the largest town in North Carolina.

New towns grew along the railroads. High Point earned its name because it was the highest elevation point on the North Carolina Railroad.

In some cases new towns caused the decline of older ones. In Wilkesboro, tracks ran a mile to the north of town. Thus, North Wilkesboro grew to be a much bigger community than Wilkesboro. Gastonia, instead of Dallas, became the principal town of Gaston County because that is where the railroad cut through the county.

Even small towns such as Hamlet, North Carolina, were changed by the railroad. *How did the railroad change the lives of North Carolinians?*

The goods and people traveling on the railroads helped North Carolina. The small towns along railroad lines were glad to have the loud, smoky Iron Horse, as the locomotive was called. A train meant mail was delivered faster. More goods could be sold. People could catch a ride to another place—if they didn't mind getting covered with coal dust.

The Southern Railway Company built Spencer Shops as a repair yard for its engines and rail cars. *How did the railroad encourage the growth of other towns?*

The railroads themselves were an added industry for the state. Tracks, locomotives, and rail cars had to be kept in good repair. The North Carolina Railroad line, which ran from Charlotte to Goldsboro, needed a repair yard midway between the ends of the line. The railroad built Company Shops in Alamance County as the line's repair site. It grew into the city we know as Burlington, now larger than its older neighbor, Graham.

In 1896, Spencer Shops opened near Salisbury as the repair center for the Southern Railway Company. Thousands of cars and locomotives ran across the country on the Southern Railway. Their machines came to Spencer to be repaired in shops run by hundreds of workers. Today, the Spencer Transportation Museum tells the story of railroads in North Carolina.

LESSON 3 REVIEW

Fact Follow-Up

1. Describe the condition of North Carolina railroads just after the Civil War.
2. Why did farmers want railroads?
3. How did railroads change towns in North Carolina?
4. How were railroads an industry?

Think These Through

5. How would the tobacco and textile industries have been different if railroads had not been built?
6. Why was east-west transportation more of a problem for North Carolinians than north-south transportation?

Working After the War

LESSON PREVIEW

Key Ideas
- After the Civil War, people looked for jobs outside of farming.
- African Americans faced hard times in towns and on farms.
- Mill villages became homes for mill workers.

Key Terms
segregation, mill village

Four years of Civil War brought freedom from slavery for African Americans in the United States. African Americans expected to vote, become educated, and find good jobs.

African American women looked for work in the Piedmont's tobacco industry. They were hired to do hot, sticky stemming work. This meant they pulled the leaves off tobacco plants by hand. African American women opened oysters or picked crabs. They would cut their hands on the sharp shells as they earned a few pennies a pound.

African American men could not find much better jobs in mills, factories, and on farms. They were hired only to do hard, manual labor.

Work in Towns

As you have read, factory towns processed tobacco and cotton into cigarettes and cloth. Other towns grew up around railroad repair shops.

Whites and African Americans looked for jobs in towns. Townspeople found work at a variety of jobs. Some

Cities in the late 1800s offered new attractions, such as this streetcar in Asheville. Coal furnaces, telephones, and electric lights also were available by 1900. *What else drew people to towns?*

were store clerks or owners. Others worked in the new tobacco and textile factories.

Many farm workers were sharecroppers. Farm life might mean a year of hard work and still no money. Bad weather and low crop prices were two of many problems.

Hard Times for African Americans

When African Americans needed jobs after the Civil War, the Freedmen's Bureau tried to make sure African Americans received fair treatment in hiring. After Reconstruction, relations between the races began to worsen again. The bureau closed.

Jobs that had once been available to African Americans became scarce. Whites took most of the jobs available in the growing textile and tobacco towns. African Americans could work as cooks, cleaners of homes and businesses, and laundry workers.

The tobacco industry hired African Americans but did not pay them the wages of the white male workers. They were not offered the same promotions as white male workers.

GAMES People Play

Marbles Children who lived on farms or in towns carried marbles in a bag or handkerchief. They drew a circle up to 36 inches in the dirt. The players placed the same number of marbles inside the circle. They took turns trying to knock other players' marbles out of the circle with a shooter, a slightly larger marble. A player got to keep any marble he or she knocked out.

During segregation, schools for African Americans were not as well equipped as those for white children. *What kinds of laws allowed this unequal treatment?*

This also was true of the textile industry in its early years.

Segregation was a set of laws and social practices which required African Americans and whites to separate. Segregation hurt African Americans almost as much as slavery had. Not only were fewer jobs available, but African Americans had to attend separate schools. The laws told them where they could sit on buses and trains. It told these American citizens where they could drink water.

The hard-won right to vote was lost by the early 1900s. Laws were passed requiring the payment of taxes or proof of the ability to read before voting. These laws were written to keep African Americans from voting. White North

EYEWITNESS TO HISTORY

Working in a Mill

Do you think you would like to get up and go to work everyday? Until 1903, if you lived in a mill village you might go to work even if you were nine or ten years old.

A day in the textile mill might start around 5:00 A.M. and end at 7:00 P.M. That is not much different than work on the farm. The cows needed milking at 4:00 A.M. You and your family worked on the farm until sunset.

Mill recreation

Some mill rooms were freezing cold in winter and blistering hot in summer. The clacking, screaming machines made it hard to hear. Farm work was hard, too. Work outside had to be done in hot or cold weather.

Carolinians did not speak out against the new customs.

Without the right to vote, African Americans could not change the laws. Many African Americans moved out of the state. They sought work in the northeastern United States where large industries offered more opportunity and better wages.

Mill Villages

White workers found the companies more helpful. Those who lived near mills lived together in a group of houses called a **mill village**. The textile mill owned the houses

Hair and clothes became covered in lint (left), but you could wash off at home in a house with running water. On the farm, you had to haul water from the well.

Bare feet (right) picked up splinters from the wooden floor. If you wanted to receive pay, you had to work whether you felt sick or not.

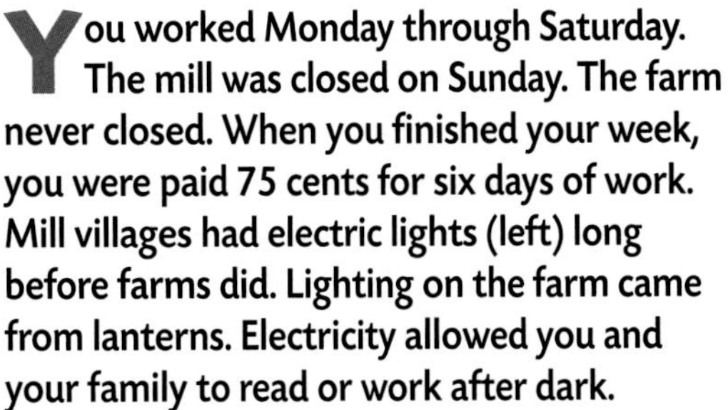

You worked Monday through Saturday. The mill was closed on Sunday. The farm never closed. When you finished your week, you were paid 75 cents for six days of work. Mill villages had electric lights (left) long before farms did. Lighting on the farm came from lanterns. Electricity allowed you and your family to read or work after dark.

Mills in Kannapolis (bottom) and in Concord (top), provided homes for mill workers. *How was mill village life different from farm life?*

and rented them to families. Mill villages also had doctors, churches, and stores for the mill workers.

Every Piedmont town contained mill villages in the early 1900s. Erwin Mills in West Durham, Proximity in Greensboro, Forest Hill in Concord, and Atherton in Charlotte were among the largest. Some large mill villages grew into towns, such as Kannapolis and Bessemer City.

Remember the young boy who wrote to the newspaper about playgrounds and other recreation in mill villages? He did not know life in a mill village was not easy for children who had to work. Tobacco factories also hired children. Children worked because their families needed the extra money.

In 1903, it became against the law for children to work in factories in North Carolina. Children were encouraged to go to school. Mill village owners built schools.

Mill villages were ruled by the owners of the mills. Work conditions depended upon the mill owners.

LESSON 4 REVIEW

Fact Follow-Up

1. Why did people leave farms to work in factories?
2. What was segregation? How did it affect African Americans?
3. Describe life in a mill village. How was it difficult? How did it improve lives?

Think These Through

4. Suppose you had been an educated African American in 1900. Would you have remained in North Carolina or left?
5. Imagine that you are a child working in a textile mill. What would your life be like?

Using Information for Problem Solving, Decision Making, and Planning

Deciding to Move From the Farm to the City

Have you ever had to make a difficult decision? You may have had to choose between two activities you really wanted to do—going to baseball practice or seeing a movie. Before you made your decision, you might have thought of reasons for choosing baseball practice or seeing a movie. Here is how one fourth grader organized his decision making:

Baseball Practice or Movies?
Going to Baseball Practice
1. I am a team member.
2. I want to play baseball better.
3. I like baseball.
Seeing a Movie
1. It is fun.
2. I get tired at practice.
3. My friends want me to go.

Now, for practice, think of a decision you might need to make. Take a piece of paper and draw a chart like the one above. Remember to put the two choices you have on the chart. Then list the best reasons you have for each choice. Does listing reasons help you make your decision?

In North Carolina in the late 1800s, many farm families had to decide whether to stay on the farm or leave and go to work in a textile mill. Some families decided to remain on their farms; others moved into mill villages.

Skim Chapter 9 and notice especially the pictures of life on the farm and life in the mills. Reread any sections of the chapter that will help you understand differences between life on the farm and life in a mill village.

What were the differences? What were the hardships of each way of life? What were the attractions?

Use your answers to draw a chart like the one below. Record reasons for staying on farms and reasons for leaving them.

If you had been a member of a family facing such a decision in the late 1800s, what would your decision have been? Why?

Staying on the Farm or Leaving?
Reasons for Leaving the Farm
1.
2.
3.
Reasons for Staying on the Farm
1.
2.
3.

Chapter 9 Review

LESSONS LEARNED

LESSON 1 Tobacco became the leading crop grown for cash by farmers after the Civil War. Processing of bright leaf tobacco was led by Washington Duke and R. J. Reynolds.

LESSON 2 More farmers planted cotton as textile mills grew after the Civil War. Low cotton prices hurt farmers, many of whom ended up moving their families to mill villages to work in textile mills.

LESSON 3 Railroads helped farmers, encouraged the growth of industry, and led to the development of new towns and the growth of old towns. Some towns were founded as repair sites for railroad companies.

LESSON 4 New industries of tobacco and textile manufacturing drew families off the farm. Mill villages were built by textile companies to house new workers. African Americans found only the lowest paid jobs open to them. They also faced other hardships as segregation laws were passed in North Carolina.

TIME FOR TERMS

bright leaf
auction
chop
denim
mill village
burley
textile
bolls
segregation

FACT FOLLOW-UP

1. How did R. J. Reynolds and the Duke family change Winston-Salem and Durham?
2. Why did eastern farmers become the main North Carolina tobacco growers?
3. How did railroads contribute to the growth of the tobacco industry?
4. How did improved machines affect the tobacco industry?
5. Describe the life of a worker on a cotton farm.
6. What caused some cotton farmers to give up farming to move to a mill village?
7. How did railroads help the growth of the textile industry?
8. What North Carolina towns were important railroad centers?
9. Describe the life of an average African American in segregated North Carolina.
10. How did African Americans lose the right to vote by the 1900s?

THINK THESE THROUGH

11. What were some examples of the geographic theme of Human-Environmental Interaction in the textile and tobacco industries?
12. Many names are associated with the textile industry but only two with the tobacco industry. Why?

13. How did the physical characteristics of place affect the tobacco and textile industries?
14. Was life in a mill village an improvement over farm life? Why or why not?
15. How is the geographic theme of Movement seen in the tobacco, textile, and railroad industries?
16. Look at the map on page 183. Why was corn the leading crop in so many North Carolina counties in 1910?
17. Was life better in 1900 for African Americans in North Carolina than it had been in 1850? Give reasons for your answer.
18. There were more textile mills than tobacco factories, but tobacco was more profitable. Why?

SHARPENING SKILLS

19. Imagine that you are a young African American living in North Carolina in 1900. Make a decision-making diagram to help you decide whether to remain in North Carolina or move to the North.
20. What were some other decisions North Carolinians had to make in the late 1800s? With which of these decisions would a decision-making diagram have been helpful?
21. What are some decisions faced by North Carolina farmers today? Design a decision-making diagram to help make one of these decisions.

PLACE LOCATION

Use the letters on the map key to locate the following places:

22. Area where cotton was the main crop in 1910.
23. Area where tobacco was the main crop in 1910.
24. Area of North Carolina where corn was the main crop in 1910.
25. In what region were most cotton mills?

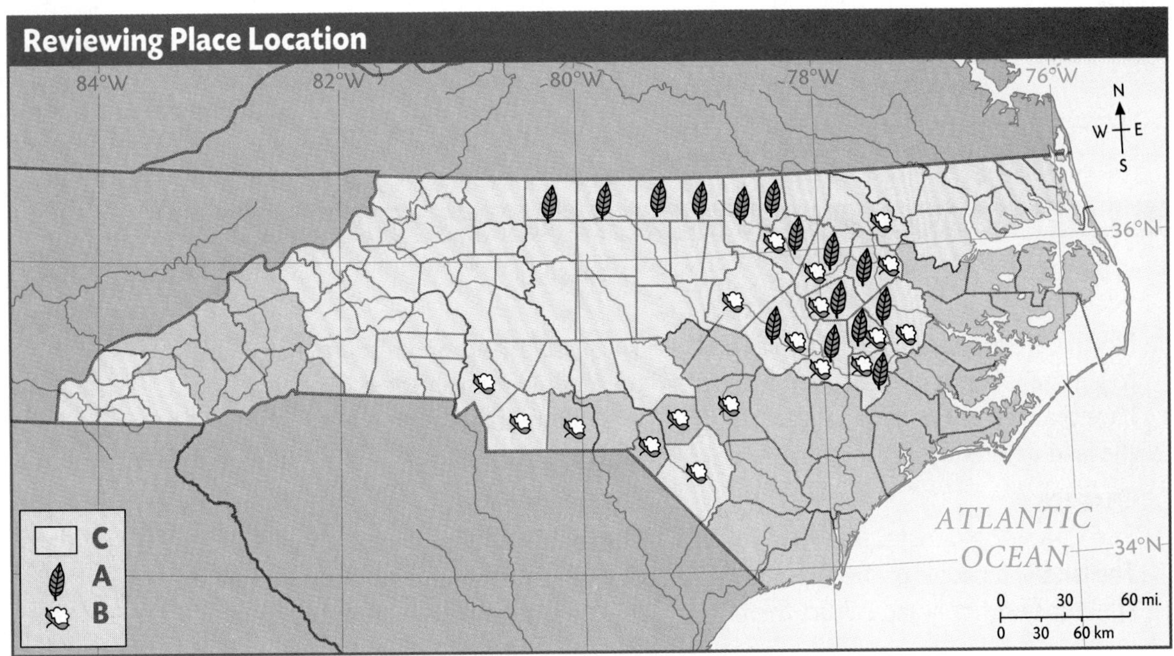

Land and People of North Carolina

Listen to the songs of the people. North Carolina's talented songsters tell the state's story with their voices and words.

Each person and each region has a song to sing, a story to tell. They join in a chorus to sing of the people, places, and events of North Carolina. The song began long ago and changes as new voices gather together. Listen to the song that is North Carolina. It is your song.

UNIT PREVIEW

CHAPTER 10
Twentieth-Century Foundations
North Carolina has changed from a rural to a more urban state. Cities and farms have changed as North Carolinians use the land differently.

CHAPTER 11
The Changing Coastal Plain
The land and people of the Coastal Plain affect the economy and culture there.

CHAPTER 12
The Piedmont
The people, land, and resources of the Piedmont affect the economy and culture there.

CHAPTER 13
Mountain Life Today
The coming of the railroad brought change to the mountains. Ways people use the land still affect life in the region.

The Banjo Lesson,
by Henry Ossawa Tanner

CHAPTER 10

Twentieth-Century Foundations

In 1910, twelve-year-old Paul Morgan rode in a wagon with his father and some neighbor boys to Raleigh. They had left their farm near Zebulon early that morning so they could make the long trip—28 miles (45 km)—before nightfall. Paul was excited. He had never seen a city with telegraph and telephone wires, such large buildings, or so many people. After the wagon reached Raleigh, everyone went to bed right away. They wanted to be ready for a big meeting of young farmers the next day. Paul was tired, but he did not sleep much. At home, nights were quiet. In Raleigh, the metal shoes of horses clicking on the pavement kept him awake.

Telegraph

CHAPTER PREVIEW

LESSON 1
Land and People
In the twentieth century, North Carolina changed from a rural to an urban state.

LESSON 2
Changing Cities and Farmland
The ways North Carolinians used the land changed the cities and farmland of the state.

LESSON 3
Economy of North Carolina
The economy of North Carolina provides a variety of jobs for its people.

Raleigh, circa 1910

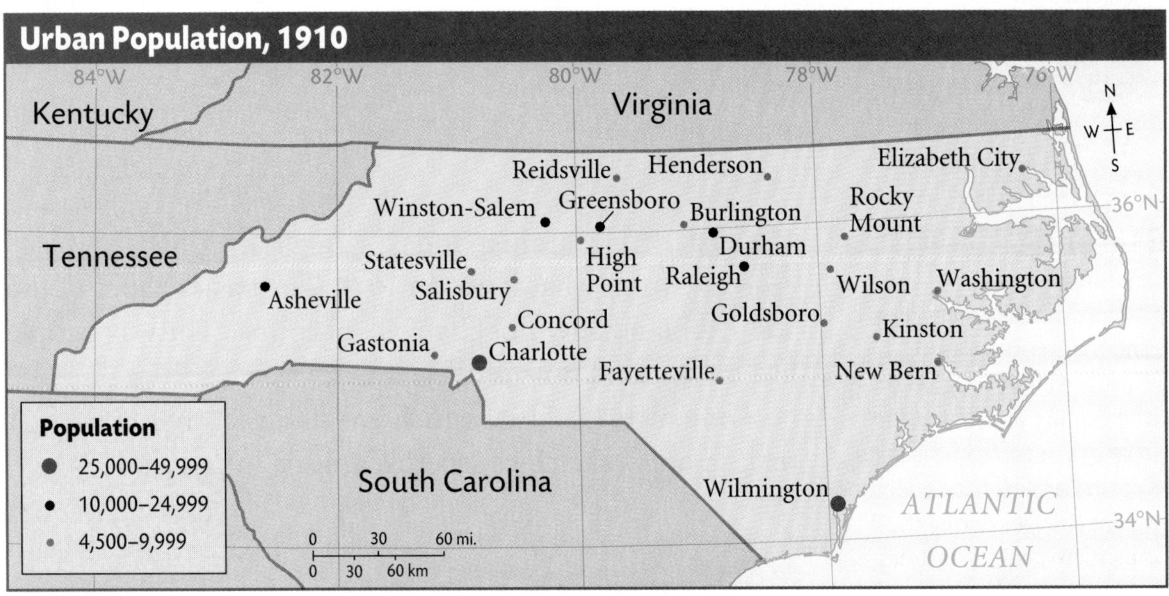

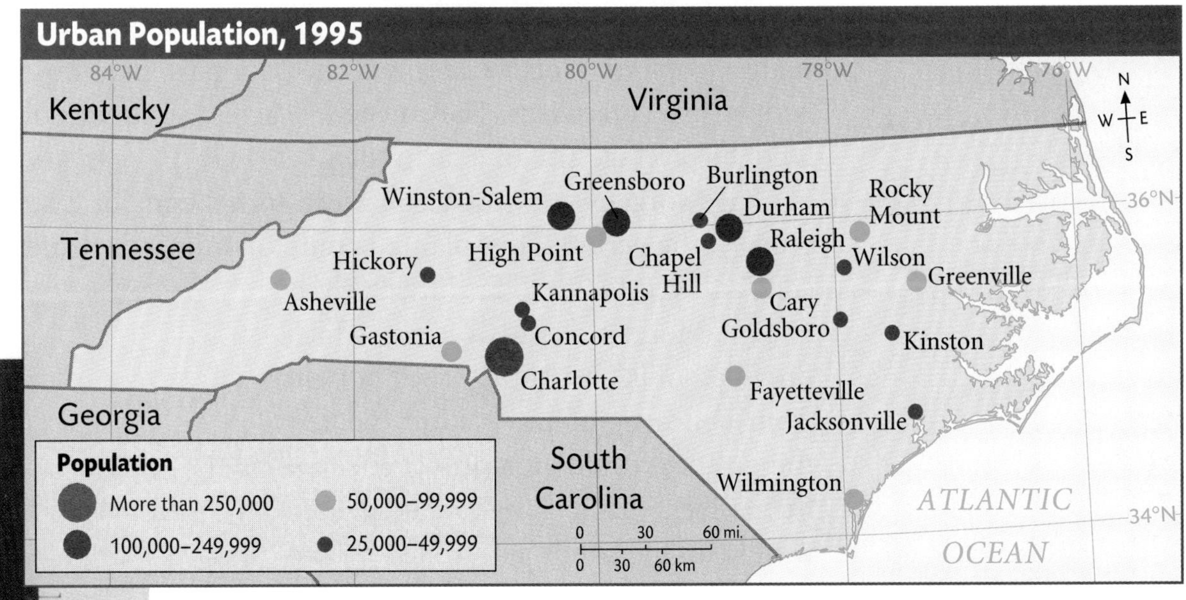

NCSU Textiles Attract International Students

N.C. State University's School of Textiles senior class of 1925 included graduates from outside North Carolina.

One Texan graduated. Four students were from South Carolina. Three men came from China. International students continue to study textiles at N.C. State (right). The North Carolina textile industry now covers the globe because of public education.

Land and People

LESSON PREVIEW

Key Ideas

- A North Carolina farm boy and the census of 1910 illustrate life at the turn of the century and hint at the changes to come in the state.
- North Carolina has undergone major changes during the twentieth century as it has gone from a rural to an urban state.

Key Term

census

North Carolina today is a vastly different place from what it was in 1910. The basic shapes of the land have not changed, of course. The way people live on the land now is different.

For a picture of how much has changed, we should first make a quick sketch of North Carolina in 1910.

North Carolina in 1910

In 1910, Paul Morgan's life was similar to the lives of many people in North Carolina. The Morgans, like most people, lived on a farm. They owned 90 acres (36 sq hm) of land, the average size of a farm then.

The Morgans grew tobacco and cotton, the major cash crops of the period. They planted grain for animal feed and corn and vegetables to feed themselves.

The Morgans kept two cows, which provided milk and butter. They bought from a nearby country store the few things they could not grow or make themselves. Their house was lighted with kerosene lamps and heated by two fireplaces.

They had no electricity, so they did not have any electrical appliances. Without refrigerators, the family preserved meat by smoking and salting it. They kept milk and butter fresh by lowering them into cool well water.

Most children in 1910 did not attend school beyond the age of twelve. Work was long and hard. Mules, wagons,

single-furrow plows, and hoes for tilling corn or tobacco and chopping cotton were the tools farmers used. Entertainment came from activities for the entire family. Barn raisings, hog killings, harvesting, and church services gave families and neighbors time together.

The Census of 1910

Very few people are alive today who lived in 1910. Paul Morgan's life and the world of 1910 are remembered through stories he told. Historians and geographers study stories like these to understand the past.

Scholars also study the past through the census. A **census** is taken every ten years to record the population of the nation. United States law requires census-takers to count the people living in cities and counties in every state. The census report includes other information about farming, manufacturing, and housing.

The 1910 census shows that North Carolina was still a rural state. Most people lived in the countryside, on farms

The 1910 census (above) found that most people in North Carolina lived on farms then. Farmers used wagons and mules to do chores. This farmer in 1910 hauled tobacco in Nash County. ***How does Paul Morgan represent the farming way of life?***

Wilmington decorated its streets for a visit from United States President William Howard Taft in 1909. In 1910, Wilmington was one of the few cities in North Carolina with more than 10,000 people. *Why were there so few cities?*

and away from cities. Farmland stretched up to the borders of towns and cities. These communities, while growing quickly, were still small. As the map on page 209 shows, only seven cities in North Carolina had populations more than 10,000: Charlotte, Wilmington, Winston-Salem, Raleigh, Asheville, Durham, and Greensboro.

There were more than 250,000 farms in North Carolina in 1910. More than 22 million (8.8 million sq hm) acres of land were planted. Farmers raised mainly tobacco, cotton, wheat, sweet potatoes, peanuts, and corn. North Carolina was first in the country in the production of sweet potatoes and second in burley tobacco. Bright leaf tobacco was still a new crop.

Many farmers were sharecroppers, working land owned by someone else. Many of these sharecroppers were African Americans.

North Carolina had a population of more than 2,200,000. African Americans made up almost one third of that total. The rest of the population, like the Morgans, were descendants of European settlers who had moved to the United States before the Civil War.

Signs of Change in Paul Morgan's life

North Carolina in 1910 was quite different from the state that you live in today. Yet North Carolina was changing. The life of Paul Morgan and his family showed a new North Carolina taking shape.

Although Paul lived his entire life in the house where he was born, a changing North Carolina made his life different from his father's. Even before his trip to Raleigh, Paul had opportunities that his father had never had.

A small school had opened three miles from the farm. He walked there with friends for grades one through six. The school term lasted three to six months, instead of nine months like it is today.

His father wanted Paul to go to school. There had not been a school nearby when Paul's father was young, so he had never learned to read. Soon Paul could read Bible verses to his father.

Paul's father was determined that his children would have all the schooling that was available. After Paul finished sixth grade, he left home for more education. First he went to Bunn, then to Zebulon. After he finished high school, he enrolled at North Carolina State College in Raleigh.

He studied agriculture for a year before leaving in the fall of 1917 to fight for the United States in World War I. The war took him and many North Carolinians to Europe, where they saw other ways of living and a broader world beyond their home state.

Signs of Change in the Census of 1910

Paul Morgan's story shows the quick shift in ways of life in North Carolina. The 1910 census also shows changes were coming to the state.

The Piedmont Region began leading the state in growth. In 1910, Charlotte was listed for the first time as the city in North Carolina with the largest population. Before 1910, Wilmington had led the state in population. Other Piedmont cities were growing rapidly, especially Durham, High Point, and the twin cities of Winston and Salem. The two

The Cape Hatteras High School class of 1910 stands in front of the school. Most people in 1910 did not go to high school. ***Why?***

cities joined in 1913.

The growth of Tidewater towns, such as New Bern and Elizabeth City, had slowed. But Inner Coastal Plain towns, such as Wilson, Fayetteville, and Rocky Mount were growing almost as quickly as Piedmont towns.

Asheville, the leading mountain town, was steadily increasing in population. Asheville had first begun to grow in the 1880s when the railroad reached the town.

Asheville had grown from 9,200 in 1890 to 19,200 people by 1910. *What encouraged the fast growth of the mountain city?*

The census of 1910 showed that city growth was changing the state. For the first time, more than 10 percent of the people lived in an urban area.

North Carolina in 2000

The chart below compares North Carolina in 1910 and in the mid-1990s. *How many cities now have a population over 25,000? Look at the map on page 209 to name those cities.*

The changes first shown in the census of 1910 continued throughout the twentieth century. In the mid-1990s, North Carolina's population had grown to nearly 7 million. The chart below shows other changes between 1910 and 1995. Most North Carolinians now live in a city or suburb. As the map on page 209 shows, five cities have

North Carolina–Then and Now

	1910	mid–1990s
Total population	2,206,287	6,992,300
Percent urban	14.4	52
Number of cities over 25,000	2 (Charlotte and Wilmington)	22
Major crops, agricultural products	cotton, corn, sweet potatoes, and tobacco	tobacco and sweet potatoes livestock (hogs and poultry)
Number of acres farmed	22,000,000	9,300,000
Average farm size	90 acres	160 acres

By 1997, most North Carolinians lived in a city or suburb, such as this suburb of Raleigh. *Do you live in a city, suburb, or in a rural area?*

populations of more than 100,000—Charlotte, Winston-Salem, Greensboro, Durham, and Raleigh. These cities grew as people continued to move from the countryside. Also, people from other parts of the country and the world moved to North Carolina.

North Carolina's population continues to increase. The state's universities, research firms, military bases, and manufacturers bring in thousands of new residents every year. An increasing number of retirees settle in North Carolina. The state's many different features offer something for almost everyone.

GAMES People Play

Roller Blades Skates called roller blades offer city children lots of excitement. The single row of wheels lets you move as quickly as an ice skater.

Wearing knee pads and helmets, children across North Carolina put on their roller blades and go at it. Portable goals, a puck, and sticks give you ice hockey without the ice. Choose up team players and skate.

LESSON 1 REVIEW

Fact Follow-Up

1. What is a census?
2. How did the census describe farming in North Carolina in 1910?
3. What is the difference between urban and rural places?
4. What were leading towns and cities in each of North Carolina's three regions in 1910? What are leading cities today?

Think These Through

5. Compare your life and Paul Morgan's. How are they similar? How are they different?
6. What do you think was the most important change in North Carolina since 1910? Why?

Changing Cities and Farmland

LESSON PREVIEW

Key Ideas

- Agriculture changed as fewer people worked on farms, chores became mechanized, and scientists developed ways to improve production.
- Cities changed as more people moved to them. They became crowded and faced challenges of air pollution, water use, and energy use.
- Crowded city dwellers often moved into suburbs.

Key Terms

livestock

Today, the rooms of Paul Morgan's farmhouse remain empty most of the time. Paul's children and grandchildren live in Raleigh, Greenville, and Rocky Mount. They use the house for weekend getaways. As you will read, none of Paul's children followed him into farming. Just as the Morgans moved away from the farm, thousands of other people from rural North Carolina moved to cities.

New Ways of Farming

If you rode along the road where Paul Morgan lived, you might think people no longer farmed in North Carolina. Many old farmhouses, barns, and sheds are falling down. Trees grow in places where crops were planted or livestock grazed. Rows of houses have replaced rows of corn.

Actually, North Carolina's farmers produce more now than they did years ago. Farming has changed. Farms are larger now.

Family farms, such as this one in Jones County, have been bought by businesses. *Where do the farm families move?*

Many of the farm tools of the past are now found in museums. Mules and wagons are seen only at festivals celebrating the past. Hoes are still used in gardens. They are not used much in big cotton or tobacco fields. No longer do most farmers harvest tobacco, cotton, or corn by hand.

Farmers use new tools that increase the number and quality of their crops. Farm tools of today

North Carolina–Agricultural Products

84°W 82°W 80°W 78°W 76°W 36°N 34°N

Virginia
Tennessee
South Carolina
ATLANTIC OCEAN

Elizabeth City
Greensboro
Winston-Salem
Durham
Raleigh
Asheville
Charlotte
Fayetteville
Wilmington

Agricultural Products

Corn	Fruit
Cotton	Vegetables
Peanuts	Beef cattle
Soybeans	Dairy products
Sweet potatoes	Hogs
Tobacco	Poultry
Wheat	

Region

- Mountains
- Piedmont
- Coastal Plain

0 30 60 mi.
0 30 60 km

N S E W

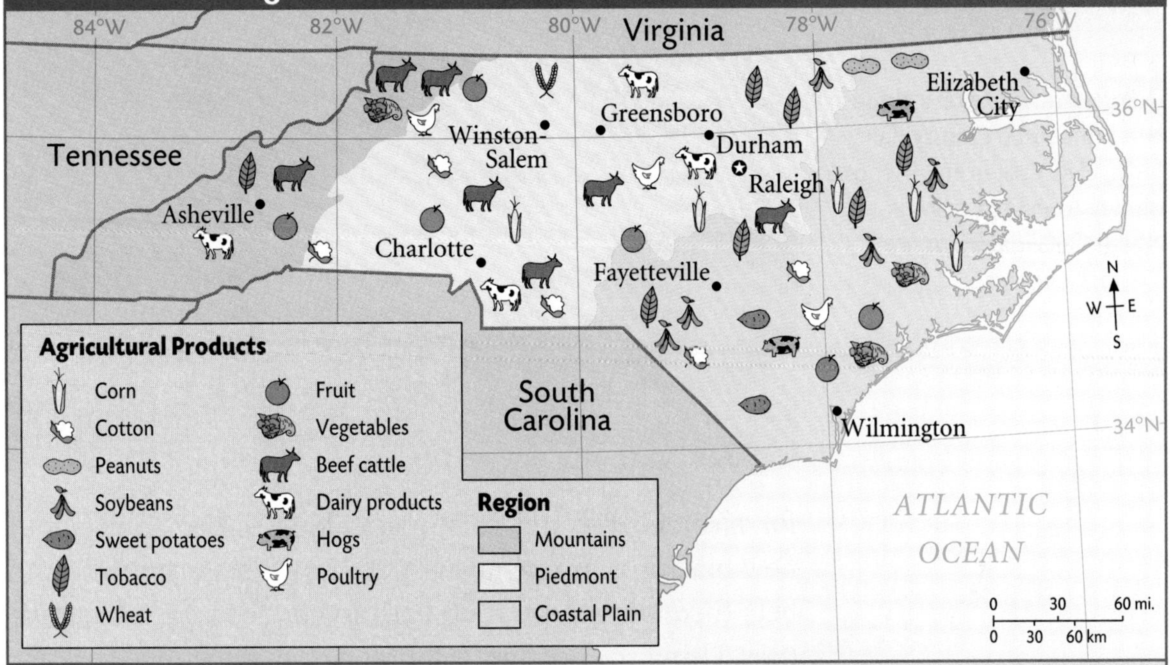

Place North Carolina farmers raise many products. Some products are raised everywhere in the state. Some are produced only in one region. *What products are raised throughout the state?*

would have amazed Paul Morgan. Machines plow fields, plant seeds, irrigate plants, and harvest crops.

Scientists at universities and research companies create chemicals to improve fertilizers, weed and pest killers, and animal medicines. Scientists use powerful microscopes to study plant and animal cells. All this knowledge has given farmers better crops to grow and stronger livestock to raise.

Farmers have many ways of learning about new methods for raising crops and livestock. The government's Cooperative Extension Service teaches farmers how to use scientific discoveries. Magazines

Machines plant, weed, and harvest tobacco and other crops. *What have been other changes in farming since Paul Morgan's time?*

Dairy cattle graze on a slope of a Buncombe County dairy farm. Livestock brings in more money than field crops in North Carolina. *What are livestock animals?*

for farmers, TV, and radio pass along information about new machines. Some farmers are now using computers to help them plan their work. Farming has become a big business. Using science and technology, fewer people work for greater crop production.

New Farm Products

The presence of high-tech equipment is not the only reason farms look different. Agricultural products have changed too. In Paul's old neighborhood and on farms throughout North Carolina, tobacco and cotton are no longer the only cash crops. Farmers are raising more corn and newer crops, such as soybeans.

Livestock production is now big business. **Livestock** is the name for animals raised on farms—beef and dairy cattle, hogs, and poultry (chickens and turkeys). Field crops were once the biggest moneymakers for farmers. Today, livestock brings in the most farm income in the state.

Fields planted years ago in tobacco or cotton are now the sites of huge hog farms in the Coastal Plain. Farms once were planted in corn or tobacco in the mountains and the Piedmont. Now those fields are planted in hay and grain to feed dairy or beef cattle. Other farmland is taken up by turkey and chicken houses. Poultry has become a major source of agricultural income.

These changes in farming have created challenges to the environment. Fertilizers on cropland and animal waste from livestock areas sometimes run into nearby streams. The chemicals and waste can make the water unsafe for fish and humans.

City Growth

North Carolina became a much more urban state in the twentieth century. As you have read, mill and railroad towns, such as Greensboro and Durham, grew into big cities. Other cities, such as Charlotte, Raleigh, and Winston-Salem, grew larger.

Paul Morgan's story tells you how this happened. After Paul returned home from war in France, he married, settled on the farm, and raised three children. Paul and his wife stayed on the farm. Their children moved to cities.

Paul's two boys graduated from the School of Agriculture at North Carolina State, thinking they would follow their father as farmers. Both ended up in banking. One managed farms in the western United States and Mexico for a North Carolina bank. The other son installed computerized banking systems. Paul's daughter graduated from Meredith College in Raleigh and became a librarian at Duke University.

Stories similar to Paul's can be told all over North Carolina. People moved to the cities for all kinds of reasons. Fewer people were needed to farm because of improved machine and farming methods. As factories, mills, and other businesses

Archivists in Duke University's Special Collections Library organize an exhibit. University librarians, bankers, lawyers, and many other workers in North Carolina cities grew up on farms. *Why do most North Carolinians now live in cities?*

What would YOU do?

Someone wants to build a lake and dam. The lake will provide fun and recreation and even food. The dam will provide power for businesses and homes. The problem is that the water will cover your land and home. What would you do?

You have to sell or give up your land. Would you move your house to another place? Would you want new land instead of money?

expanded in cities, people moved there to find jobs.

At first, houses, stores, and businesses were built close together in the cities. People walked or rode horse-drawn wagons. Electric trollies and automobiles were invented. Then people could begin to move out of the cities to suburbs. These suburbs were often built on land once occupied by farms. Suburb construction eliminated a lot of open spaces near cities.

People who moved to suburbs still needed transport to work. Roads were built to connect suburbs to cities. These roads took up land that had been used for farming. Some roads cut through natural environments. Woods and meadows disappeared throughout the state.

LIVING IN LAKE NORMAN

The "Great River" Forms a Large Lake

Once a small stream joined with several streams below Mount Mitchell. It became a river called Eswa Taroa, "The Great River," by the Native Americans. For thousands of years it flowed peacefully or wildly overran its banks.

A need for electricity changed the flow of the "Great River", or the Catawba, as it came to be called. The textile mills up and down the river needed power. By 1928, there were ten dams on the Catawba River providing electric power to the region. The dams created Lake James, Lake Rhodhiss, and Lake Hickory.

There was room for one more dam. This one created the largest lake in the Carolinas. It became a major source of hydroelectric power. An entire valley–more than 33,000 acres–was flooded.

Timber in the valley was cut. Lake Norman was officially dedicated in 1959. Then it took four years to dig the lake and build Cowens Ford Dam. When water filled the valley, Lake Norman was 34 miles (55 km) long and 8 miles (13 km) wide. It took all of 1962 and 1963 to fill it up.

Wildlife lives on the lake and its shore. Parks offer camping spaces. Fishing and sailing are favored sports around the lake. About 520 miles (837 km) of shoreline offer visitors recreation and residents homes to live along the lakeshore.

Challenges of Growth

Growth in cities also brought new challenges to the environment. More people use more resources, such as fuel. Coal, fuel oil, or natural gas is needed to heat buildings. More cars mean more gasoline is used. Sometimes so much fuel is used, North Carolina cities become dangerously polluted.

Cities and towns must have clean water. Water goes into people's homes. Industry uses large amounts of water in manufacturing. As you have read, water flowing through generators also is important in making electricity. During the 1920s, several companies built hydroelectric dams to form lakes. Some of these lakes—Lake Norman near Charlotte or Kerr Lake on the North Carolina and Virginia border—are quite large.

Many dams were built during the 1920s and later, including this dam on the Yadkin River. *How did dams meet the needs of North Carolina?*

These lakes now serve many purposes. They generate electric power. They provide water for millions of people. And people swim, fish, and go boating in them. All of these lakes have to be protected from pollution.

LESSON 2 REVIEW

Fact Follow-Up

1. How has agriculture changed in North Carolina in the twentieth century?
2. What is a suburb? How is it different from a rural or urban area?
3. How does city growth challenge the environment?
4. Why have so many rivers been dammed?

Think These Through

5. What was the most important agricultural change in the twentieth century? Why?
6. Which do you think is more of a challenge to the environment: agriculture or city and suburban growth? Explain why.
7. Why is water one of the most important natural resources?

LESSON 3

Economy of North Carolina

LESSON PREVIEW

Key Ideas

- North Carolinians work in all sorts of occupations: agriculture, manufacturing, and a variety of service jobs.
- A good transportation system helped attract new industry.
- Tourism, education, research, and the military are important parts of the state economy.

Key Terms

service industries, Good Roads Movement, "Scott Roads," hub, research

In 1910, Paul Morgan rode to Raleigh on a dirt road. Back then, most roads between towns and farm country were not paved. Only some streets in towns and cities had hard surfaces. When it rained, farm wagons sometimes got stuck in the mud. Muddy roads made traveling in cars and trucks nearly impossible.

As North Carolina's economy changed, North Carolinians no longer could wait for roads to dry. Farmers needed dependable roads to take their crops and livestock to market in town. City factories needed highways to receive supplies quickly and to transport goods.

A Changing Economy

People today work at a wide variety of jobs in North Carolina. The chart below shows the many categories of jobs where people work. They manufacture textiles, medicine, electronics, and transportation equipment. They process farm crops and seafood. They farm and fish. Many

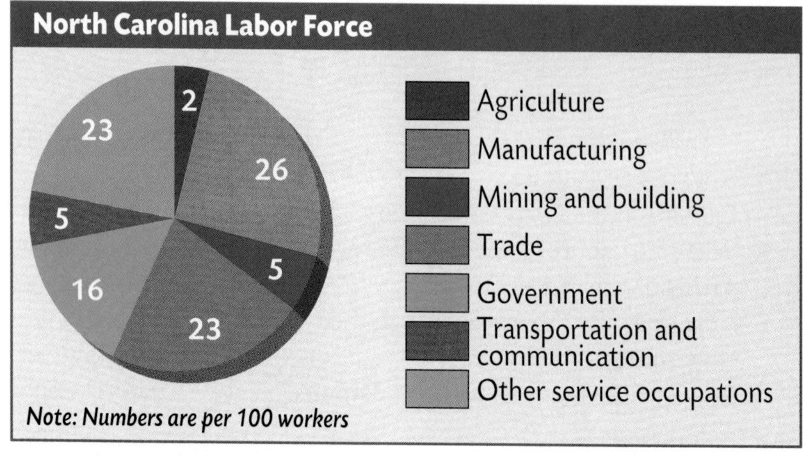

This pie chart shows kinds of jobs North Carolinians do and the percentages of people working in those jobs. *What is the highest percent? lowest?*

Textile mills make cloth on computerized looms. *What other industries that are important to North Carolina's economy use computers?*

North Carolinians work for the state government. Others work in service industry jobs. **Service industries** provide services to people through tourism, the military, law, medicine, research, education, and sales.

Agriculture

There are fewer acres producing field crops or supporting livestock now than there were 90 years ago. Far fewer people make their living farming. Only about two out of every hundred jobs are on the farm now, as the chart on page 222 shows.

Yet farming is still important to North Carolina. The state ranks third in the nation in farm income. Farms are bigger now—they average 160 acres (64 sq hm). As the chart on page 214 shows, average farm size in 1910 was 90 acres (36 sq hm). There are about 50,000 farms across the state.

North Carolina still leads the nation in producing sweet potatoes. The state now ranks first in growing tobacco and in raising turkeys and hogs.

Manufacturing

The basic industries that existed in North Carolina in 1910 are stronger than ever. Textile mills weave cloth and make blue jeans, towels, hosiery, bedspreads, and carpet.

Furniture manufacturers build beds, chairs, tables, and desks. Wood-product companies process trees into paper, pulp, lumber, and chemicals. Tobacco processors roll cigarettes and package pipe and chewing tobacco. All these industries now use high-tech machines and computers to produce their goods.

WORD ORIGINS

The word **pharmaceutical** comes from the Greek word ***pharmakeuticos*** which means "to dispense drugs." Pharmaceutical companies make medicines. A pharmacy is the place where patients buy medicines.

There are many new industries in North Carolina today. The state is a major manufacturer of computers, telecommunications equipment, and appliances. Food processors clean, can or jar, and ship seafood, fruits, and vegetables. Pharmaceutical companies study healthy uses of medicine. They develop new drugs to fight illnesses. Transportation manufacturers build cars, boats, trucks, recreational vehicles, mobile homes, and tires.

North Carolina's government has worked to bring industry to the state. Businesses came because the transportation system was good. Taxes and other costs were low. The state's people were willing to work hard at the new jobs.

Transportation

As you have read, railroads crisscrossed the entire state by 1900 (see map page 193). You could travel from Asheville to Zebulon or Ahoskie to Yadkinville by train. Railroads

The construction of interstates is the most recent improvement in North Carolina roads. *How did the Good Roads Movement and "Scott Roads" improve transportation in the state?*

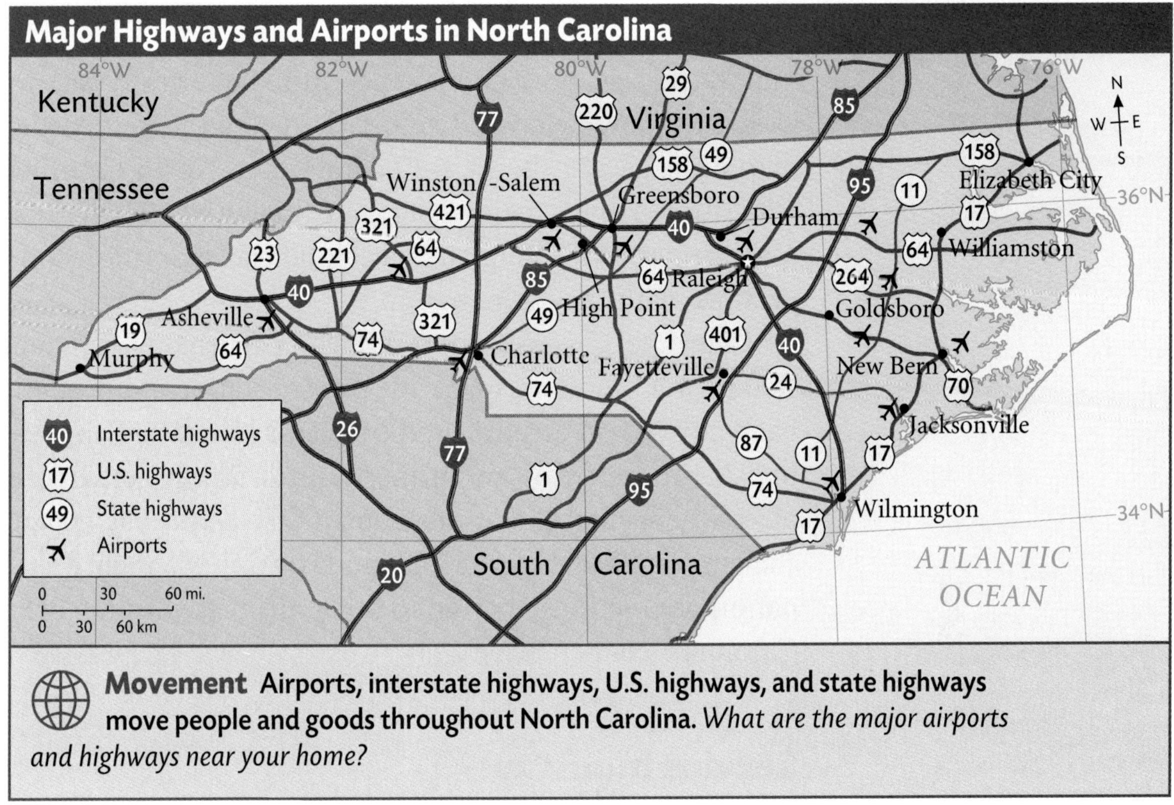

Movement **Airports, interstate highways, U.S. highways, and state highways move people and goods throughout North Carolina.** *What are the major airports and highways near your home?*

helped farmers sell crops outside of North Carolina. Cities grew near factories and train depots. Movement of goods became easier.

The road-building program that North Carolina undertook in the 1920s also transformed the state. Governor Cameron Morrison and the legislature began the **Good Roads Movement**. The state paid for roads connecting every county.

Highways continued to be built after World War II. North Carolina voters approved a road-building program during the term of Governor Kerr Scott in the late 1940s. Almost 15,000 miles (24,150 km) of dirt roads, called "**Scott Roads**," were paved. The roads helped rural people quickly reach towns and cities.

President Dwight Eisenhower proposed a national interstate system to connect cities all over the country. Interstates are still being completed in North Carolina.

In 1990, Interstate 40 was finished to Wilmington, bringing an increase of traffic and people to the southern

Tidewater. I-40 now crosses the entire state from east to west, then runs westward across the United States. As the map on page 225 shows, I-40 connects in North Carolina with three other major interstate highways. These run north and south, giving our state good transportation connections with the entire nation.

Charlotte, Greensboro, and Raleigh-Durham are major centers for another form of transportation—airplanes. Each city has an airport used by major airlines as hubs. A **hub** is the center of an airline transportation network, a place where an airline routes most of its traffic. Passengers change planes at these airports and continue to their destinations. Sometimes they go to other airports within North Carolina (see map, page 225).

Service Industry

Planes, trains, and automobiles bring visitors to North Carolina. They contribute greatly to an important segment of the economy: tourism. Tourism is a service industry. Tourism includes jobs that help visitors to North Carolina enjoy themselves. Millions of people visit North Carolina each year. They spend hundreds of millions of dollars to support our economy.

Tour guides at the Duke Homestead and other North Carolina museums work in tourism, which is a service industry. *What are other service industry jobs?*

Teachers at North Carolina State University and other institutions of higher learning instruct college students. *What do you have to do in school now if you want to attend college in about ten years?*

Education

Your teacher is part of the service economy. Teachers instruct students in public and private schools in every community in North Carolina. Teachers who work in public schools are employed by one of the more than 100 school systems in the state. Each county and a few cities run school systems.

North Carolina has an integrated school system now. Segregated schools that separated African Americans from whites ended with court decisions in the 1950s. Now all children in North Carolina can attend public schools together, regardless of their race.

Most North Carolinians now finish high school. Those who want to continue their education can enroll in state colleges and universities. The University of North Carolina system includes 16 institutions of higher learning. There are many private schools run by church organizations.

State-supported community colleges offer college-level courses within driving distance of most people. Most people go to community colleges to study for jobs in hospitals, offices, or industries. Other classes for adults are taught in the evenings at county schools.

Inventions and Research

North Carolinians have often dreamed of making life easier for everyone through inventions. John Motley Morehead of Eden discovered acetylene, an important chemical used in welding, in his father's small laboratory.

R. F. Butler and Caleb D. Bradham invented a new soft drink at a New Bern drug store. Bradham later called the drink Pepsi-Cola.

Of course, two brothers from Dayton, Ohio, opened the twentieth century with one of the most important inventions in history. Orville and Wilbur Wright proved on the

EYEWITNESS TO HISTORY

A University Grows With North Carolina

In 1899, North Carolina State University, then the North Carolina College of Agriculture and Mechanic Arts, taught the "useful and practical arts to the industrial classes." Aimed at the sons of farmers, mechanics, and merchants, the school wanted the people of North Carolina to know about the technology of the twentieth century.

N.C. State

New technology meant better ways to plant and harvest food. Finding stronger seeds and larger plants meant more food at harvest time.

N.C. State scientists

As the state's population grew and other ways of making a living became important, new technology also meant improving textile production. The state's textile mills received help from textile graduates trained in the college's loom room (below).

dunes of Kitty Hawk that a machine could fly.

All of these inventions were the result of research. **Research** is careful study and experimentation to discover facts. Much research takes place at big universities, such as Wake Forest University in Winston-Salem. North Carolina also has become a place where industries locate their research laboratories. North Carolina is a leader in research.

Duke University in Durham, the University of North Carolina at Chapel Hill, and North Carolina State University in Raleigh also are major research universities. Because their locations formed a triangle, Governor Luther Hodges believed the universities would attract industries

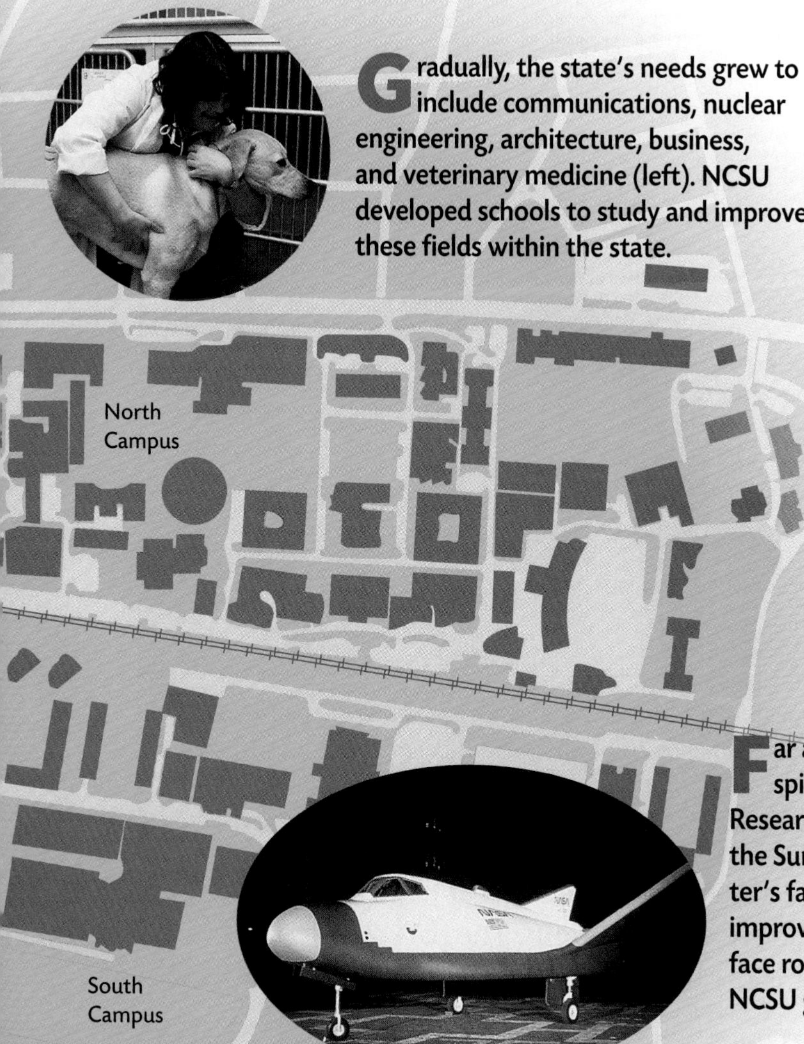

Gradually, the state's needs grew to include communications, nuclear engineering, architecture, business, and veterinary medicine (left). NCSU developed schools to study and improve these fields within the state.

At NCSU, lasers cut fabric and metal (above). Computers send messages and design vehicles. Television studios broadcast classes to your home. Faculty go out into the community to teach. Professors study dinosaur eggs to see how they are alike and different from animals today.

Far away from the fields of North Carolina spins the planet Mars. The Mars Mission Research Center (left) at NCSU contributed to the Summer 1997 space flight to Mars. The center's faculty and students held experiments to improve the spacecraft's heat shield and the surface rover's controls. In the twentieth century, NCSU grew with North Carolina and the world.

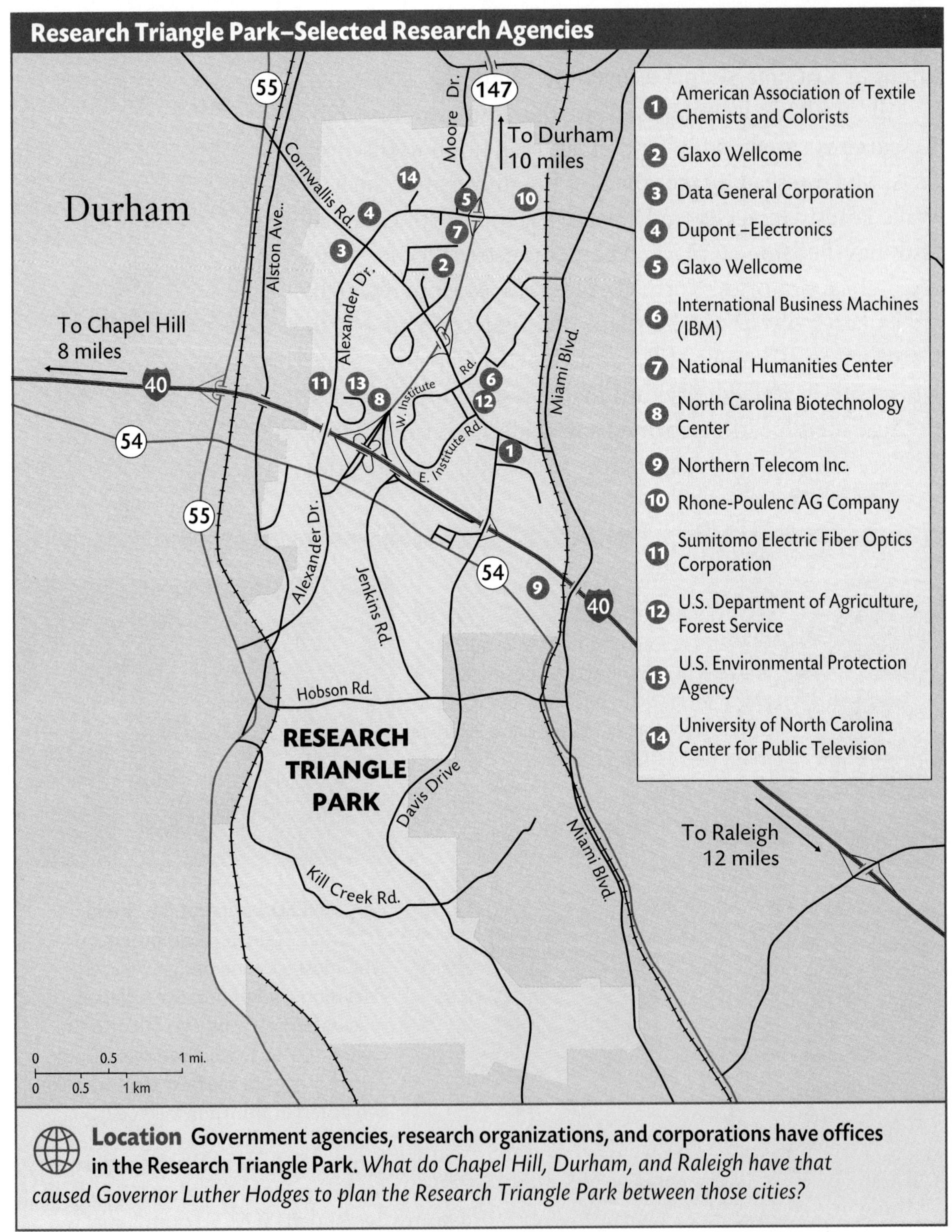

Location **Government agencies, research organizations, and corporations have offices in the Research Triangle Park.** *What do Chapel Hill, Durham, and Raleigh have that caused Governor Luther Hodges to plan the Research Triangle Park between those cities?*

that would open research facilities at Research Triangle Park (see map above). He was right. The park, located near each university, is the headquarters for many research agencies.

Glaxo Wellcome, a drug manufacturer, is one of many corporations with offices in the Research Triangle Park. *How does research help such companies?*

The Research Triangle Park, begun in 1957 with the purchase of 5,000 acres (2,000 sq hm) of land, is now the site of many government agencies and major industries (see map on page 230). More than 50 companies conduct research in the park. Many hire scientists trained by the universities.

Military Installations

World Wars I and II brought many people to North Carolina. A mild climate and the low cost of available land led the government to place several military bases in the state. Today, there are nine major military bases in North Carolina. All nine are in the Coastal Plain. Most of them are in the Tidewater.

Fort Bragg was built near Fayetteville during World War I as an army base. It grew into the largest artillery post in the world during World War II. Artillery is the branch of the army that fires cannon. To provide space for firing cannon, the United States government bought land in Hoke and Harnett Counties. Today, Fort Bragg is as big as some counties. By 1995, Fayetteville had almost 100,000 people.

Fort Bragg in Fayetteville is one of the largest army bases in the United States. *Why do you think all of North Carolina's miltary bases are located in the Coastal Plain?*

Cherry Point Marine Air Base and Camp Lejeune Marine Base train United States Marines. These troops fight on land, sea, and in the air with other armed forces.

Cherry Point, near Havelock, trains pilots and maintains aircraft for the Marine Corps. Camp Lejeune in Jacksonville trains marines to make landings from the sea on the 11 miles (18 km) of beachfront it owns.

These bases have had a major impact on North Carolina. People from all over the United States moved to the state for military training. Many have decided to stay after their service ended. The bases have created new businesses for the cities where they were located.

Jacksonville and Fayetteville have continued to grow in the last 20 years. Part of that growth came from businesses built to support the bases.

Other cities in North Carolina benefit from military bases. Goldsboro is the site of Seymour Johnson Air Force Base. Pope Air Force Base is in Spring Lake, north of Fayetteville. From bases at Elizabeth City and Fort Macon, the Coast Guard patrols the ocean.

LESSON 3 REVIEW

Fact Follow-Up

1. What were the Good Roads Movement and "Scott Roads"?
2. What are the most important manufactured products of North Carolina?
3. What are service industries?

Think These Through

4. How is education in the state today different from education in Paul Morgan's time?
5. Which in your opinion is most important to North Carolina: agriculture, manufacturing, or the service industry? Why?
6. What do you think was the most important transportation change in North Carolina? Explain why.
7. What is research? Why is it so important to North Carolina?

Acquiring Information From a Variety of Sources

Looking at Changes and Their Causes and Effects

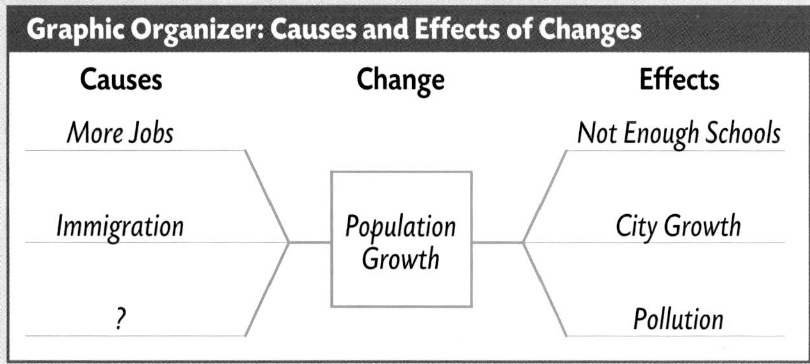

Paul Morgan and his family lived through many changes. If he were alive today, he would be amazed to discover that Raleigh is a busy city with suburbs stretching all the way to Zebulon.

Look at some of the changes during his life and the lives of his children. Take a sheet of paper and read again about Paul Morgan in Chapter 10. When you read about a change Paul and his family lived through, note it on the paper. When you have finished, compare your list with a classmate's.

All changes have **causes**, or reasons, for the change, and all changes have results, or **effects**. Look again at your list of changes. Choose one change the family lived through. Can you find in Chapter 10 information about the **causes and effects** of that change?

(Hint: Causes happen before the change. Effects follow the change. Causes either make or help make the change happen. Effects are the result of change.)

To help you study the changes in the Morgans' lives, take one as an example. Look at the diagram above. This graphic organizer shows the causes and effects of the changes in population.

Can you think of other causes and effects of the changes in population?

If you can, copy the diagram on a sheet of paper. To add to the diagram, simply add more information under "Causes" or "Effects."

Now you are ready to practice with your own cause-and-effect chart. On a sheet of paper, draw a blank diagram like the one above. Choose one of the changes you listed earlier about the Morgans. Write the name of the change on the line in the center of the diagram. Read again about the changes and its causes and effects. Write the causes of the change on the left side of the diagram and the effects on the right side.

When you have finished, compare your graphic organizer with that of a classmate. Did your classmate choose a different change?

Chapter 10 Review

LESSONS LEARNED

LESSON 1 North Carolina has changed since 1910. There were signs of the future in the lives of individual North Carolinians, such as Paul Morgan, and in the information contained in the census of 1910. Those signs included the state's transformation from a rural to an urban state and the improving education of its citizens.

LESSON 2 The lives of North Carolinians changed in the twentieth century as many families moved off farms and into cities. Farm life changed because of technology and science. Cities changed as they became more crowded and threatened with pollution. Many city dwellers moved to suburbs.

LESSON 3 The economy of North Carolina is diverse. The people of North Carolina make a living at many different kinds of jobs in agriculture, manufacturing, education, research, tourism, and the military. Fort Bragg and Research Triangle Park have helped the state's economy. North Carolina's economy also grew because of its good roads, wide variety of work, and large population.

TIME FOR TERMS

census	livestock
service industries	Good Roads Movement
"Scott Roads"	hub
research	

FACT FOLLOW-UP

1. What are rural, urban, and suburban areas?
2. In what ways are North Carolinians today like Paul Morgan? In what ways are they different?
3. How did changes in agriculture affect manufacturing?
4. How did changes in education affect the people of North Carolina?
5. Describe changes in transportation in North Carolina in the twentieth century.
6. How have transportation changes affected the environment?
7. How has the growth of suburbs affected agriculture?
8. How have military installations affected North Carolina?
9. Why is the population of North Carolina growing?

THINK THESE THROUGH

10. Which change described in Chapter 10 affected the most people? Explain your answer.
11. Which change described in Chapter 10 helped people most? Explain why.
12. Why are North Carolina's largest cities located in the Piedmont Region?
13. Which do you think was more important for North Carolina: changes in education or changes in transportation? Explain your answer.

14. If you planned to build a North Carolina Disney World, where would you build it in order to make the most money? Explain why.

20. Review Chapter 9 and choose a change from 1865 to 1910. Make a cause-and-effect diagram to study that change.

SHARPENING SKILLS

15. Choose another change from Lesson 1 and make a cause-and-effect diagram to study that change.
16. Do the changes you have studied have more than one cause? Why do you think so?
17. Are all happenings that come before a change causes of that change? Explain your answer.
18. Look at the maps on page 209. Make a cause-and-effect diagram to study urban population. Read Lesson 2 to list the causes and effects of city growth.
19. Review Lesson 3 and make a cause-and-effect diagram on one economic change.

PLACE LOCATION

Use the map key to identify the region or regions where the following agricultural products are grown or raised:

21. hogs.
22. poultry.
23. tobacco.
24. cotton.
25. sweet potatoes.
26. peanuts.
27. wheat.
28. corn.
29. soybeans.
30. dairy cattle.
31. beef cattle.
32. fruit.
33. vegetables.

Use the key to identify the agricultural products that are grown in the following regions:

34. the Coastal Plain.
35. the Piedmont.
36. the Mountains.

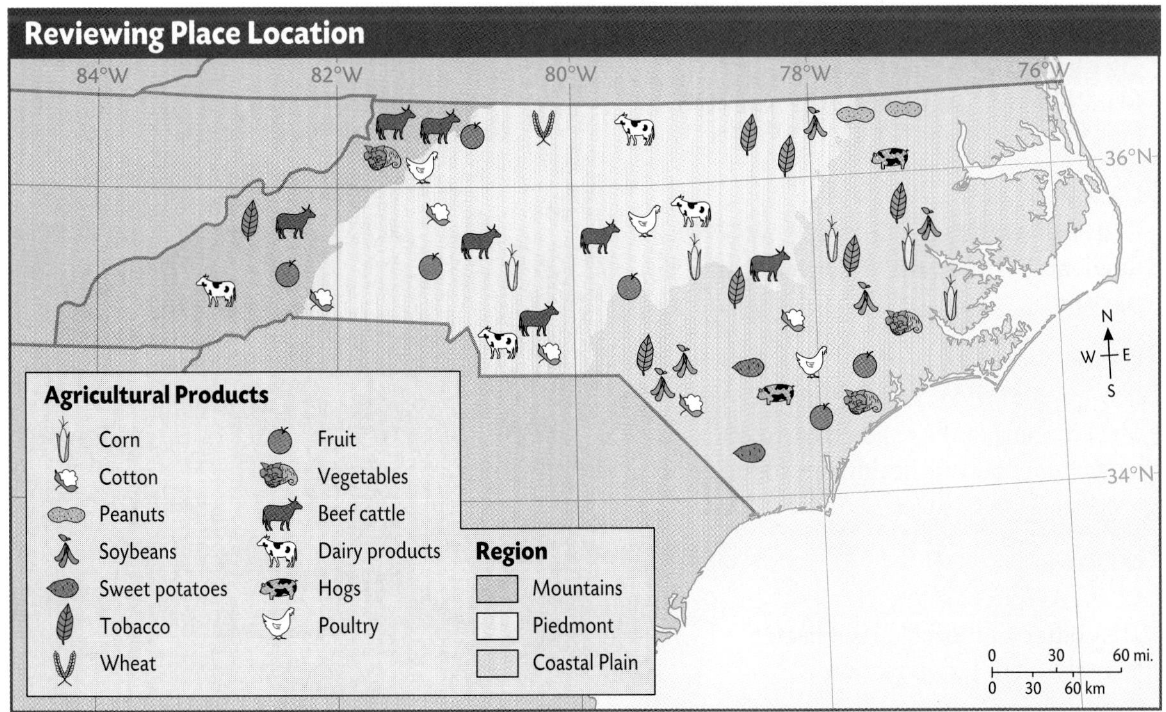

CHAPTER 11

The Changing Coastal Plain

Outer Banks ponies once roamed wild. They are descended from horses brought over from Europe for the southern colonies in the seventeenth century. Near Corolla, now heavily populated by people, ponies and autos do not mix. Fenced areas try to protect ponies from autos.

At a supermarket parking lot in Corolla, the ponies line up for handouts of carrots and apples. The free spirits have found an easy way to graze, but people are discouraged from feeding them.

Outer Banks wild pony

CHAPTER PREVIEW

LESSON 1
Living Together in the Coastal Plain
Many different groups of people have lived in the Coastal Plain.

LESSON 2
Communities of the Coastal Plain
Residents of the Coastal Plain have changed the land.

LESSON 3
Economy of the Coastal Plain
The economy of the region is based on agriculture, tourism, health care, food processing, and textiles.

LESSON 4
Coastal Plain Culture
The culture of the region is reflected in festivals, food, and recreation.

Nags Head

North Carolina–Coastal Plain Region

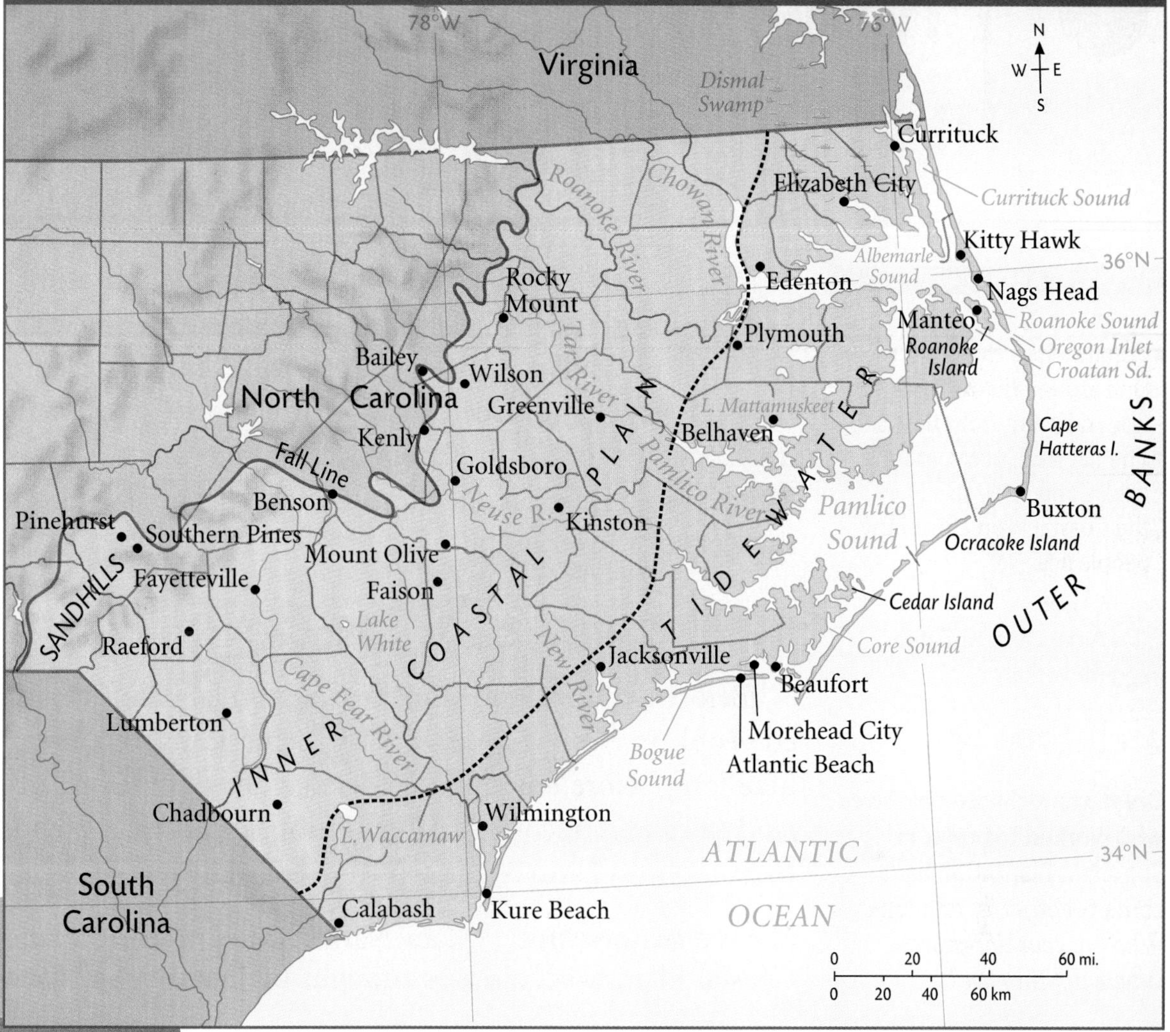

78°W
76°W
N
W
E
S
Virginia
Dismal Swamp
Currituck
Elizabeth City
Currituck Sound
Roanoke River
Chowan River
Kitty Hawk
Albemarle Sound
36°N
Edenton
Nags Head
Rocky Mount
Manteo
Roanoke Sound
Plymouth
Roanoke Island
Oregon Inlet
Croatan Sd.
Tar River
Bailey
Wilson
North Carolina
Greenville
L. Mattamuskeet
Belhaven
Cape Hatteras I.
Kenly
Fall Line
Goldsboro
Pamlico River
Benson
Neuse R.
Kinston
Pamlico Sound
Buxton
Pinehurst
Southern Pines
Ocracoke Island
Mount Olive
Fayetteville
Faison
Cedar Island
Lake White
Raeford
Core Sound
SANDHILLS
INNER COASTAL PLAIN
TIDEWATER
OUTER BANKS
Jacksonville
Beaufort
Cape Fear River
New River
Lumberton
Morehead City
Bogue Sound
Atlantic Beach
Chadbourn
Wilmington
L. Waccamaw
ATLANTIC OCEAN
34°N
South Carolina
Calabash
Kure Beach
0 20 40 60 mi.
0 20 40 60 km

Native Americans from Wales?

There is a legend that connects two groups of settlers in North Carolina—the Native American Madoc tribe and the Welsh, a group of settlers in North Carolina from Great Britain. According to the legend, the son of a Welsh king sailed across the sea in 1100. He returned to Wales and took Native Americans with him.

In the late 1600s, a Welsh preacher, Morgan Jones, was captured by the Madoc while traveling through the Carolinas. He prayed all night. His prayer was in the language of Wales. The chief heard Jones and said, "You speak our language. You shall not die."

Living Together in the Coastal Plain

LESSON PREVIEW

Key Ideas

- Communities change as the land around them is used in ways different from the past.
- The flat land, rivers, sounds, ocean, and open spaces in the Coastal Plain affect how people live.

Key Terms

Latin Americans, Hispanics, migrant workers

As early as 1732 people were buying and selling land in North Carolina. On November 13, 1732, in Halifax County James Milliken sold Henry Dawson some land. Deed Book 1 in Halifax County tells the story of this North Carolina early land sale. It shows Milliken sold Dawson one hundred acres near the banks of the Roanoke River.

Settlers of the Coastal Plain

Before that first land sale, the Coastal Plain had attracted people to North Carolina. Native Americans were living here long before any other settlers came, long before any land sales were recorded. Then, Europeans, Africans, and, most recently, Latin Americans moved to the region.

Native Americans Many Native Americans died in the Coastal Plain from diseases brought by European settlers.

Great-grandchildren of slaves who worked together at Somerset Plantation have come together at reunions. *Who are your ancestors? Where did they live?*

Native American communities remain in the region. You can visit a Native American Festival in Robeson County. You will see ceremonial dress, special crafts, and dancing.

The Lumbee people of Robeson County make up the largest Native American community in North Carolina. They live mainly in the towns of Pembroke and Lumberton.

Saponi and Meherrin live in Halifax and Northampton Counties in the northeast Tidewater. The strong Sampson County community of Native Americans is called the Coharie. The Waccamaw originated in Columbus County.

Members of the Waccamaw meet in a pow-wow—a celebration of their heritage through dancing, storytelling, and traditional dress. *Have you ever been to a pow-wow? What happens?*

Europeans As you learned, the first Europeans who settled North Carolina were English. They moved from Virginia into the Albemarle Sound area of the Coastal Plain. Their descendants still farm and fish in that area.

Later European immigrants moved to North Carolina from Scotland, Ireland, and Germany. Their descendants still live in the Coastal Plain.

Africans Large plantation owners brought Africans to North Carolina. In Tyrrell County, Somerset Plantation is a state historic site that shows how difficult life was for slaves. Somerset creates an opportunity for visitors to learn about the strong African American community that thrived there before and after slavery. Descendants of some of the Somerset slaves now hold family reunions.

Many African American families who came to the region during the slave-holding years stayed on when freedom came. Most farmed by sharecropping land, cultivating tobacco, corn, cotton, and peanuts. Others sought new opportunities in North Carolina towns or outside of the South.

New Residents of the Coastal Plain

The fields of the Coastal Plain have attracted new groups of people. In the last 20 years, a growing number of Latin Americans have settled in the Coastal Plain. **Latin Americans** are people of the Western Hemisphere who live south of the United States and speak Spanish, Portuguese, or French. **Hispanics** are Latin Americans who speak Spanish.

Most Latin Americans in North Carolina are Hispanic. They practice their culture through their faith as Roman Catholics, the language they speak, the foods they eat, and the sports they play.

EYEWITNESS TO HISTORY

Protecting Ships at Sea

The North Carolina lighthouses are signs of the state's seafaring heritage. In the 1870s, each lighthouse was painted in distinctive markings. That way, passing ships could easily figure their location.

The Currituck Beach Lighthouse near Corolla is naturally red from the bricks used to build it in 1875. It illuminates a dark spot between a light in Virginia and the Bodie Island Lighthouse.

Currituck Lighthouse

The oldest lighthouse, Baldhead Light, on Baldhead Island off Cape Fear, was replaced by the Cape Fear Lighthouse in 1903. The Baldhead Light was too far inland to warn ships away from the Frying Pan Shoals.

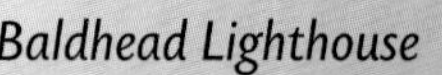

Baldhead Lighthouse

Ocracoke Lighthouse

The Cape Fear Lighthouse was replaced 50 years later by one of the brightest lighthouses in the world, the Oak Island Lighthouse. The beacon can be seen 19 miles (31 km) away.

Oak Island Lighthouse

South Carolina

Many came to the state to work as migrant workers on Coastal Plain farms. **Migrant workers** move through the United States, living in camps near farms to pick ripe crops. Many migrant workers decided to remain in the Coastal Plain. Jobs in construction also have lured Latin Americans to stay and settle in the Coastal Plain.

Many people moved to North Carolina after military bases were built during World War II. Nearby cities grew quickly. People who retired from the military often came back to the town where they were based. They looked for jobs, settled down, and built homes. Jobs and the land's beauty brought many people to the Coastal Plain.

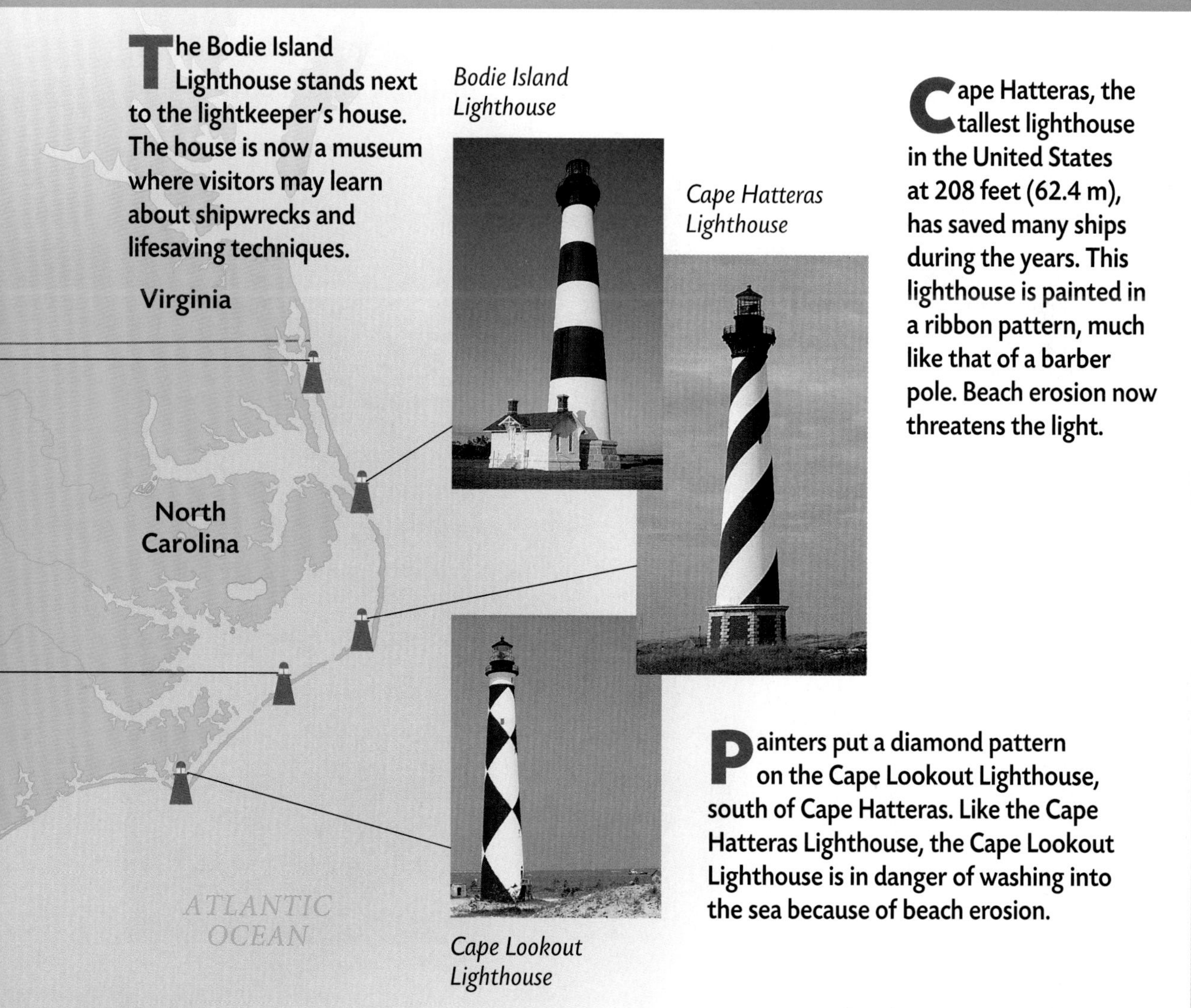

The Bodie Island Lighthouse stands next to the lightkeeper's house. The house is now a museum where visitors may learn about shipwrecks and lifesaving techniques.

Bodie Island Lighthouse

Cape Hatteras Lighthouse

Cape Hatteras, the tallest lighthouse in the United States at 208 feet (62.4 m), has saved many ships during the years. This lighthouse is painted in a ribbon pattern, much like that of a barber pole. Beach erosion now threatens the light.

Cape Lookout Lighthouse

Painters put a diamond pattern on the Cape Lookout Lighthouse, south of Cape Hatteras. Like the Cape Hatteras Lighthouse, the Cape Lookout Lighthouse is in danger of washing into the sea because of beach erosion.

The Land of the Coastal Plain

Several cities dot the the Coastal Plain. Wilson, Greenville, Goldsboro, Kinston, and Rocky Mount are in the heart of the Inner Coastal Plain. These cities have from 30,000 to 60,000 people. Each offers a relaxed atmosphere, jobs, and shopping. Greenville is a medical center and the home of East Carolina University. The cities all are about the same distance apart (see map, page 237).

Fayetteville, Jacksonville, and Wilmington are the largest cities in the region. Fayetteville and Jacksonville grew because of military bases. Wilmington is the state's largest port.

Some Tidewater towns are close to one another. Others are separated by miles of pine trees or swamps of cypress. The closer you move toward the beach, condominiums, beach houses, and hotels occupy more land. Harbors and

Catholic festivals are celebrated by a group of people who are new to the Coastal Plain. *Who celebrates those festivals?*

Elizabeth City and other coastal cities attract tourists. They enjoy visiting museums, fishing, or sailing. *How else can you have fun on the Coastal Plain?*

boat repair shops crowd Wilmington, Beaufort, Morehead City, Elizabeth City, and the once isolated villages of the Outer Banks.

Towns where population growth slowed after colonial days are growing again because of their nearness to the sea. New Bern, Washington, Edenton, and Elizabeth City offer historic sites and access to open water. Lighthouses, once necessary to keep ships safely away from hidden sandbars, now attract tourists.

The Coastal Plain has become a rapidly changing region. People from all over have settled in the region. Isolated fishing villages have become busy towns. Cities have grown.

GAMES People Play

Beach Games What do you do when you go to the beach? People like to play sports on the sandy beaches of North Carolina. Take your Frisbee, your volleyball, or your beach ball.

Beach volleyball tournaments are held behind the large hotels. People throw Frisbees to each other and their dogs. Sometimes the Frisbees sail into the ocean. Nobody seems to mind.

LESSON 1 REVIEW

Fact Follow-Up

1. What groups of people live in the Coastal Plain Region today?
2. What are the cities of the Coastal Plain?
3. Which groups of people have moved to the Coastal Plain most recently?
4. What has attracted people to the Coastal Plain?

Think These Through

5. How do cities of the Tidewater differ from cities in the Inner Coastal Plain? Explain the differences.
6. How does nearness to the sea affect the growth of towns and cities?
7. Why have Latin Americans moved to the Coastal Plain?

Communities of the Coastal Plain

LESSON PREVIEW

Key Ideas

- The shape of the coast and the land of the Coastal Plain affect how its residents live.
- New jobs and new people move to eastern North Carolina.

Key Terms

batik

Do you know the story behind the name Nags Head? On the coast there are several different versions of how the small coastal town got the name.

One story tells of residents who walked a wild pony, with a lantern tied to his neck, up and down the beach. Unsuspecting sailors thought a ship had found safe harbor. They tried to come into that harbor and wrecked upon the beach where the people recovered the ship's cargo. A less exciting story tells of a dune shaped like a horse's head when seen from a fisherman's boat.

The Changing Tidewater

Some old stories about Nags Head tell about life long ago on North Carolina's coast. Today's stories tell us about a changing life. The Tidewater continues to change every day, as it always has.

The road from Atlantic Beach to Salter Path was dirt and gravel 35 years ago. Today, you can drive on the same road. Now you can go 45 miles (72.5 km) per hour on a paved road past shops and restaurants.

Once a few wooden fishing cabins stood against the dunes. Tall condominiums and hotels now face the Atlantic. Fishing is about all that remains from the old life in communities along the Outer Banks.

North Carolina beaches have been among the last to be developed along the eastern coast. Good roads and thousands of people

Beaufort's waterfront runs along Front Street, the location of the Maritime Museum. *What would you want to learn about there?*

looking for vacation spots have caused the old way of life to nearly disappear.

West of the sounds, construction continues. Golf courses, tennis courts, and yacht basins have been built for visitors and the local population. The remains of farmhouses suggests a different way of life. Old landmarks here are hard to find.

Construction of homes, condominiums, and hotels has changed the Outer Banks from the 1930s (above) to today (below). *How did good transportation lead to growth on the islands?*

Marines from Camp Lejeune and their families fill the seafood restaurants near Jacksonville on weekends. Military helicopters sometimes fly low over the beaches as the pilots and crews train. Coast Guard ships dock at their base in Elizabeth City.

In Beaufort at the Maritime Museum, you can learn about ships and sailing. You can see how whalers once worked on the Outer Banks and how shrimp boats gather their harvest. If you walk along the waterfront, you'll see sleek new yachts. A tour boat slips past. You can hear guides telling audiences about pirates and old sailing ships.

Morehead City, about two miles from Beaufort, is a modern port. It is one of two important ports connecting North Carolina to the world. The other is Wilmington.

Downtown Wilmington fronts the Cape Fear River, which flows into the Atlantic Ocean only 25 miles away. *How has Interstate 40 encouraged recent growth there?*

Wilmington

Down the coast at Wilmington, you can see old cotton warehouses and markets where Africans began their lives as slaves. Still standing are taverns where people met to plan a revolution against the British. The Cape Fear Museum teaches about the Tidewater's past.

Wilmington shipyards built merchant ships and small navy craft to send out to the Atlantic and Pacific Oceans during World War II. The industry brought thousands of people to live in the Cape Fear area during the war. Some left after the war, but many stayed.

Wilmington is now the home of the U.S.S. *North Carolina,* "The Showboat." The battleship participated in every major naval battle in the Pacific during World War II. It was to be scrapped after the war, but North Carolina schoolchildren contributed nickels to help pay for the towing of the ship up the Cape Fear River to Wilmington. It is one of the city's favored tourist sites.

Thalian Hall, built in the 1850s, has been carefully restored and functions once again as a theater. Plays based on books by North Carolina writers have been produced there.

Wilmington has renewed its downtown. Its economy has grown partly because movie and TV companies make films there. Historic houses are used as movie sets.

Interstate 40 put Wilmington within easy reach of the Piedmont. Tourists flock there to go to the beach.

Keeping the Past Alive

Small towns dot the Tidewater west of the coast. Most once revolved around farming, fishing, or shipping products. Agriculture is no longer the only industry. In the northern Tidewater, people look to Norfolk, Virginia, for jobs.

Away from the coast, the Tidewater hasn't benefited as much from tourism. In a few places, older homes are transformed into bed-and-breakfast inns. These houses offer

CONNECTIONS

Geography & the Arts

Silk Batik

Flowing silk batik fabric plots the coast of North Carolina. Artist and small-plane pilot Mary Edna Fraser lives in Charleston, S.C. Her specialty is taking photo images of the coast and turning them into **batik**-dyed fabric.

Flying low to the water, she shoots her pictures. Her next step is to look at other images of the same area. She also travels over the land by car and foot.

Core Banks

Then she creates flowing silk banners out of these aerial images. Fraser makes batiks by putting melted wax in patterns on silk and then dyeing the unwaxed parts. North Carolina's coastline is often the theme of her shows. The Smithsonian Institution's National Air and Space Museum in Washington, D.C., displayed 50 of her pieces. People from all over the world saw North Carolina's coast done in silk batik.

Owners of older houses, such as this one in Bath, often open them as bed-and-breakfast inns. *Would you enjoy staying in an old home?*

visitors a place to stay and enjoy a family style meal. Many tourists enjoy staying in a house that might be 200 years old.

The Changing Inner Coastal Plain

What do you see if you come to the Inner Coastal Plain? Old wooden tobacco barns fall along the edges of fields. New aluminum curing barns gleam in the sun.

A few small towns may seem empty on weekends when people drive to Greenville or Raleigh to shop. On weekdays, downtowns stay busy as businesses serve local residents.

Many older, smaller farmhouses decay by the roadside. Off in the distance, you can see new subdivisions with many houses where once only one farmhouse stood.

In the fields you see huge new combines and fewer people taking care of tobacco, cotton, soybeans, or sweet potatoes. Machines do much of the work.

Livestock farms are another example of large-scale farming. Thousands of hogs, chickens, or turkeys can be raised and marketed by fewer people with the help of new farm machines.

Cities of the Inner Coastal Plain

Because fewer people farm, most people live in the cities of the Inner Coastal Plain (see map on page 237). Greenville, Rocky Mount, Wilson, and Kinston have grown in recent years. They have attracted industry, commerce, and educational institutions.

Fayetteville was a major town in colonial North Carolina. It was a port on the Cape Fear River. When the North Carolina Railroad bypassed Fayetteville in the 1850s, the town struggled through the rest of the 1800s. The Cape Fear and Yadkin Railroad connected Fayetteville to the Piedmont by 1900.

The city became important again when Fort Bragg was built in 1918. Land near the town was used for training soldiers. Farming became less important. People moved to Fayetteville to open stores and other businesses that served the military.

Both world wars led to growth in Fayetteville. The biggest boost in population occurred during World War II. Then, in the years of the Vietnam War, Fayetteville grew from 60,000 people in 1960 to 212,000 in 1970. People of Vietnam and other Asian countries settled here.

Fayetteville continues to grow, but not just because of the military. Its largest employer is a tire manufacturer.

The presence of the military changed Goldsboro, also. Seymour Johnson Air Force Base is a major employer. Goldsboro, like Greenville, Wilson, and Rocky Mount, has benefited from farm-related industries and has grown as a market town.

The Evans Metropolitan AME Zion Church in Fayetteville is a National Historic Site. The church is an example of the city's long history as an important town in the Coastal Plain. *What encouraged the growth of Fayetteville in the twentieth century?*

Preserving Natural Areas

Many communities in the Coastal Plain have state parks and recreation areas. Historic sites, such as Fort Macon and Somerset, try to preserve North Carolina's past. Other parks are simply for pleasure.

There are conflicts in the Coastal Plain about how land is used. Not everyone agrees land should be set aside for parks. Military bases want more land for training.

Wood duck boxes and ponds provide habitat for wildlife at the E. I. Dupont plant in Kinston. *Why is it important to preserve natural areas?*

Others want park land sold to individuals for development. Livestock waste and crop fertilizers drain into rivers, hurting natural areas. Some believe the environment will be permanently damaged.

Others believe pollution problems can be solved. Businesses and communities often work together to improve the environment. Clean air and water are necessary for good health. The E. I. Dupont Company in Kinston restored a natural area. Ponds, wild grasses, and trees attract birds and wildlife.

LESSON 2 REVIEW

Fact Follow-Up

1. Describe changes on North Carolina's Outer Banks.
2. How has Wilmington changed over the years?
3. What North Carolina towns and cities have been changed by military bases?
4. What are some conflicts about how land should be used in the Coastal Plain?

Think These Through

5. If you could choose to live on the North Carolina coast 200 years ago or today, which would you choose? Why?
6. What do you think is the biggest environmental challenge facing the Coastal Plain? Explain why.

LESSON 3

Economy of the Coastal Plain

The Coastal Plain of North Carolina holds many surprises. Leaf tobacco cures in bulk barns, and cucumbers become pickles in Mount Olive and Faison. Docks at Morehead City on the coast might be filled with large fish from deep ocean water. The variety of this region provides work for the people who live here.

LESSON PREVIEW

Key Ideas

- The land provides a living in the Coastal Plain.
- Towns and cities offer new jobs.

Yesterday's Workplaces

Two dusty roads once crossed at an intersection between Nashville and Rocky Mount. County farmers met at a general store that was the center of a small community called Langley Crossroads. The store sold fertilizer, gasoline, and food to nearby neighbors. It was also a place to greet friends and swap stories.

This type of country life, centered upon the seasons and rhythms of the land, is disappearing. Almost everyone once lived and worked in the countryside. The Tobacco Farm Life Museum in Kenly shows visitors the rural life of the past.

The Langley Brothers Store between Rocky Mount and Nashville was a place for farmers to gather to buy supplies and talk. *Why are these stores at rural crossroads disappearing?*

Agriculture

Eastern North Carolina is still a farming region, although fewer people have jobs in agriculture. The Coastal Plain counties raise more crops than counties in the Piedmont and the Mountains.

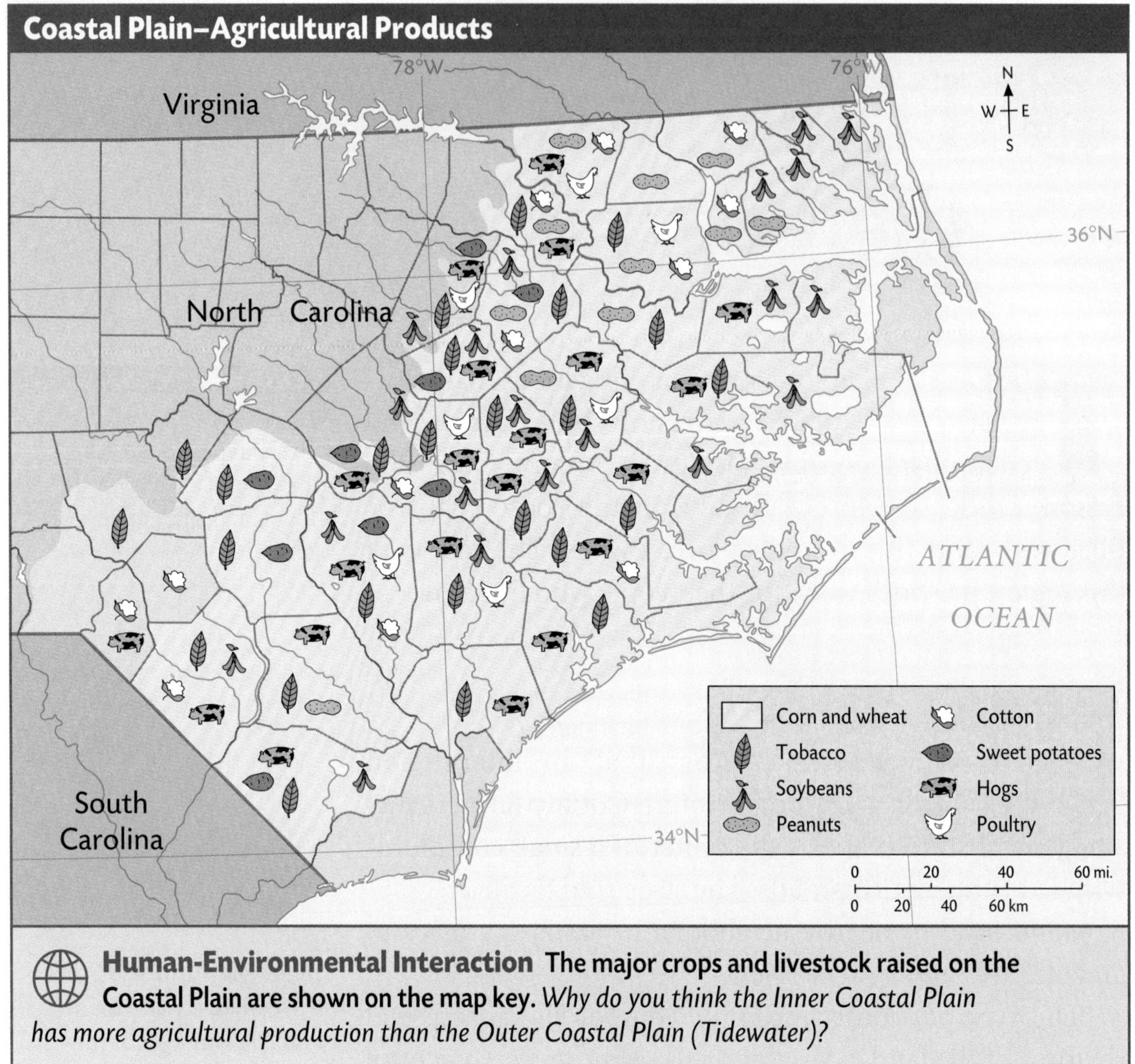

Human-Environmental Interaction The major crops and livestock raised on the Coastal Plain are shown on the map key. *Why do you think the Inner Coastal Plain has more agricultural production than the Outer Coastal Plain (Tidewater)?*

Tobacco The state still raises the largest tobacco crop in the nation. Farmers produced bright leaf tobacco worth more than $1 billion in 1993. Johnston, Pitt, Wilson, Nash, and Robeson Counties were among the top producers.

Cotton Again Cotton all but disappeared from the fields after the boll weevil pest destroyed crops in the 1920s. Also, after World War II, people wore clothes made from synthetic fibers. But fashion changed and many people today wear cotton jeans and T-shirts. The 1996 crop was the largest cotton harvest since the 1920s.

Soybeans Farm families across the Coastal Plain have turned to a wider variety of crops to make a living. A family today might grow a little tobacco and a lot of soybeans.

Soybeans have developed into an important ingredient for animal feeds, oils, and cereals. Farmers in Tidewater counties produce the most soybeans in North Carolina. Beaufort, Tyrrell, and Washington Counties grow more soybeans than any other part of the state.

Vegetables and Fruit Some farms have shifted to vegetable production. In Wayne County, farmers grow cucumbers for the pickle factories in Mount Olive and Faison. Farmers from across the Coastal Plain ship their crops in big trucks. Some buyers ship vegetables all the way to Canada. Campbell Soup Company processes vegetables at a factory it owns in Robeson County.

In Northampton, Hertford, and Bertie Counties, peanuts are a major crop. Coastal Plain peanut growers are the third largest producers in the United States.

In Johnston County, farmers lead the state in growing sweet potatoes. These end up on dinner tables across the country. More than one third of all sweet potatoes grown in the United States are grown in North Carolina, the leading producer in the country.

Corn-growing counties are found in the Tidewater area. Beaufort, Hyde, and Tyrrell counties produce the most corn in the Coastal Plain.

Fruit growers plant trees each year in the Sandhills. More than 50 years ago, farmers in Montgomery County began raising peaches to sell to passing motorists. Now Moore and Richmond Counties rival South Carolina and Georgia in peach production.

In the Carolina bays areas, particularly Bladen and Pender Counties, a notable kind of blueberry grows. The fruit is large, plump, and sweeter than blueberries grown in other parts of the nation. In Chadbourn, strawberries are a moneymaking crop.

North Carolina leads the United States in sweet potato production. *Where in the Coastal Plain are sweet potatoes grown (see map, page 252)?*

Livestock

Growing crops is an important part of North Carolina's agriculture. Even more important to the economy is the raising of livestock. Livestock, including turkeys, chickens, beef cattle, dairy cattle, and hogs, earn more than half of the money farmers make in North Carolina.

Leading livestock animals in the Coastal Plain are hogs and poultry, especially turkeys. *Where are poultry raised in the Coastal Plain (see map, page 252)?*

In the Coastal Plain, farmers mainly raise turkeys and hogs. Duplin, Sampson, and Onslow Counties raised more than 30 million turkeys in 1995.

Farmers in Sampson, Pitt, Greene, Bladen, Wayne, and Duplin Counties have started large hog farms. The farmers raise more than a million hogs in each county.

Hogs live in large buildings. The farmers often feed the pigs soybean meal that is locally grown. When the animals are ready for market, the meat may be processed in the state.

Manufacturing

In the Coastal Plain, people now have a wide variety of work opportunities. Industries from outside North Carolina have located in Coastal Plain towns. In the 1960s, E. I. Dupont built the first polyester manufacturing plant in the United States in Kinston.

Closer to the coast in the Tidewater, two other industries provide jobs. Processors prepare seafood for sale. Workers clean fish, shrimp, and crabs. Fresh seafood is sold all over the eastern United States. Some seafood is canned for sale to grocery stores.

Boatbuilders work in Chowan, Craven, Onslow, and New Hanover Counties and throughout the Tidewater. Custom boatbuilders in Carteret County create yachts for customers around the world.

Service Industries

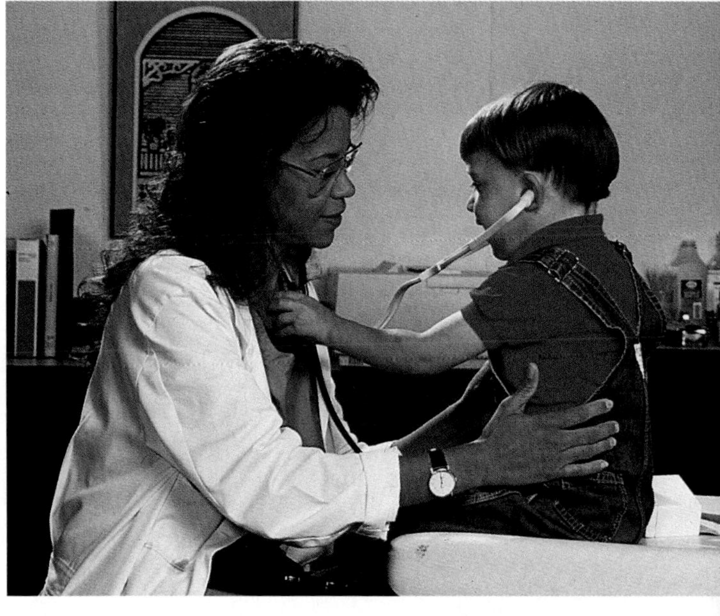

All counties have some type of service work, including education, restaurant and hotel services, office duties, tourism, and information processing. Many residents of the region work in service jobs at the military bases near Fayetteville, Jacksonville, and Goldsboro.

East Carolina University in Greenville employs more than 3,700 people in Pitt County. The ECU Medical Center trains doctors and nurses to serve in the region.

The East Carolina University Medical Center in Greenville is important to the health of Coastal Plain residents. *How else does the center serve the region?*

Along our southern coast in Wilmington, the North Carolina Film Studios makes movies and TV shows. State officials estimate that the movie industry has earned more than $300 million for North Carolina.

Recall that one of North Carolina's major industries is tourism. Coastal Plain beaches attract sailors and sunbathers. Its sounds attract hunters and fishermen. People employed in tourism work to provide food, entertainment, and places to stay for the tourists.

The economy of the Tidelands and the Inner Coastal Plain has changed the use of the land through the years. From a pick-your-own blueberry farm to a film studio, the region offers more opportunities for its people.

LESSON 3 REVIEW

Fact Follow-Up

1. What are some crops that Coastal Plain farmers have recently begun to grow?
2. What are some food processing industries of the Coastal Plain?
3. What are some important service jobs in the Coastal Plain?

Think These Through

4. In which industry of the Coastal Plain would you most like to work?
5. How is it possible to produce more goods with fewer workers?
6. Why are raising poultry and hogs major industries in the Coastal Plain?

Coastal Plain Culture

LESSON PREVIEW

Key Ideas

- Culture in the Coastal Plain is reflected in its traditions and festivals.
- Food of the Coastal Plain is different from other regions.
- Recreation and sports also show a people's way of life.

Key Terms

culture

New England has its clambake, Chesapeake Bay its steamed crabs, and Alaska its salmon. The Outer Banks has a traditional fish stew called muddle. Bankers, as the people who live there are called, make the stew with potatoes, onions, and whatever fish is on hand. Muddle warms the spirits during winter storms.

Want to see the Venus flytrap? Care to see a 2,000-year-old bald cypress? How about a bass tournament? decoys? a whalebone? All of these things can be seen in the Coastal Plain.

The food and sites of the Coastal Plain reflect the region's culture. **Culture** is a people's way of life. It is expressed through traditions, festivals, foods, sports, and recreation.

Tradition

If you visit someone on Harkers Island, east of Beaufort, they will greet you warmly and show you around. They might also wave happily when you leave. The islands off the coast offer their residents a feeling of isolation. The people enjoy leading their own life away from outsiders.

Harkers Island east of Beaufort is connected to the mainland by one road. *How does separation help preserve tradition in a place?*

The people of the Coastal Plain want traditions to continue. Always having a church bell ring on Sundays is special to those living in Plymouth. Weighing anchor to go shrimping at midnight is a pleasure to residents of Cedar Island. Helping a neighbor is important in every community.

Festivals

Small towns promote festivals that help create a neighborly feeling. Community festivals tell visitors about life in those towns, spotlighting local food, sports, and traditions.

Celebrations often are planned around the food grown in the Coastal Plain. The Strawberry Festival in Chadbourn is one of the more famous. Hertford has its Watermelon Festival and Spring Hope hosts the Pumpkin Festival. In the fall season, many towns hold sweet potato festivals.

The Azalea Festival in Wilmington is one of many festivals in the state that celebrate the flowers, food, history, and heritage of North Carolina. *What festivals does your town hold?*

Seafood festivals give people a chance to sample old favorites and try new tastes. Have some eel and octopus? The Seafood Festival in Morehead City draws quite a curious crowd to the waterfront.

There are even festivals to celebrate animals. In Benson there is a special weekend for mules! People bring mule teams for competition and parades. The event is a reminder of how important mules once were in helping farmers finish chores on their farms.

The Azalea Festival in Wilmington celebrates the beautiful azalea flowers. It also celebrates springtime. College students enjoy the Azalea Festival, which usually comes during their spring break.

Pork barbecue is a North Carolina tradition. Ways of cooking change from region to region, but it is loved statewide. *How is barbecue fixed where you live?*

Food

Food is a key ingredient at festivals. Every region has its own way of cooking special foods. Residents of eastern North Carolina eat the same kinds of food everyone eats—hamburgers and pizza, fried chicken and biscuits.

But you also will see plenty of barbecue. On the Coastal Plain, a whole pig is cooked long and slow over hot coals. The barbecued meat is then chopped, seasoned with hot sauce and vinegar, and served with boiled potatoes, cole slaw, and hot hushpuppies—cornmeal dough shaped into small balls and fried in deep fat. Barbecue suppers called "pig pickings" help communities raise money for schools, churches, and volunteer fire departments.

Up and down the coast, people choose their favorite seafood restaurants. Fish, shrimp, crab, and oysters fill the plates. Some seafood lovers make an annual trip to Calabash in Brunswick County. Raleigh residents have driven all the way to Morehead City or Wilmington to have a seafood platter for lunch.

WORD ORIGINS

Barbecue originally referred to roasting a whole hog, ox, or other large animal on a rack over a hickory wood fire. This method was described by French fur traders in the 1500s as cooking the animal from its ***barbe*** (whiskers) to its ***queue*** (tail). Today's modern word for barbeque is a combination of these two French words. Barbeque now describes both the method of cooking and the meat that is enjoyed by millions of North Carolinians.

Special Places

Residents of eastern counties point to people and places to show visitors what they like about their home.

Someone on the Outer Banks can proudly brag about a local lighthouse, the fishing, or the sunrises. A Kinston resident might take a visitor to see one of two remaining Confederate ironclad warships, the CSS *Neuse.*

A Hyde County resident can show you Lake Mattamuskeet. In Pender County you can see a Venus flytrap. In Martin County you can take a boat trip on the Roanoke River. Bertie County residents can show you a peanut field. In Bladen County you can see bald cypresses in a swamp.

In Jones County you can go to the North Carolina State University Teaching and Research Forest. In Brunswick County you can see the Plymouth gentian, a flower that also grows on Cape Cod in Massachusetts.

What would YOU do?

Guess what? Your family has decided to let you make the big decision this year. You get to say where the family will go on the coast for your vacation. What place will you choose?

You could think of where you like to spend your extra time. Inside or outside? Do you like water salty or fresh? Does everyone like seafood? How about sports? Does everyone in your family prefer to read?

There are lots of things to think about when it comes to vacation time.

What to Do for Fun!

Sailing or surfing? Golfing or hiking? Looking at wild birds or wildflowers? The Coastal Plain Region holds many fun things to do.

The state has more than 1,000 miles (1,610 km) of beaches. The quality and width of the beaches vary. North Carolina sand is not as white as in some states because of the ground-up shells and rocks that wash ashore.

Kure Beach, Atlantic Beach, and Emerald Isle draw people to fish, surf, swim, and sunbathe. People from Washington, D.C., and the Mid-Atlantic states crowd onto the Outer Banks each summer. Kite flying, hang gliding, and surf fishing are popular there.

White Lake in Bladen County has white sand and clear water. Lake Waccamaw is a popular lake for fishing and boating.

Gospel sings and chorus concerts reflect the culture of African Americans and descendants of Europeans living in the Coastal Plain. Native American members of the United Tribes of North Carolina meet every September to perform dances that remind them of the Green Corn ceremony.

Boating—in a fast motorboat, slow canoe, or smooth sailboat—is popular in the rivers, sounds, inlets, and the ocean of the Coastal Plain. *Where would you most like to go boating?*

Golfers enjoy the weather and landscape of courses at Pinehurst and other towns of the Coastal Plain. Golf course designer Tom Fazio of Hendersonville says "a golf course should belong to nature." *What does that statement mean?*

The Lure of Golf

Serious golfers believe that one of the best places to play the sport is in southeastern North Carolina. The weather and the land offer ideal conditions for golf.

Pinehurst, in the Sandhills, has drawn golfers since the turn of the century. Businessmen opened a course and hotel there, hoping to attract people from northern states during the winter.

Today, 30 courses around Pinehurst attract golfers. Pinehurst's World Golf Hall of Fame honors the finest golfers who ever played.

Golf's popularity has spread up and down the coast. Brunswick County has become a golfing center. Most of those new golf courses reflect a concern for the environment. Designers today are more aware of the dangers of chemicals that keep the links green.

LESSON 4 REVIEW

Fact Follow-Up

1. What is culture?
2. What are some important festivals of the Coastal Plain?
3. What are some fun things to do in the Coastal Plain?

Think These Through

4. How do festivals and food express culture?
5. How does the land of the Coastal Plain affect culture?
6. What site would you most like to visit in the Coastal Plain? Why?

Using Information for Problem Solving, Decision Making, and Planning

Using Our Fragile Land

Fragile is a word that describes something that is easily broken or ruined. Babies are fragile and should be handled carefully. So should tiny kittens or puppies. You may have been told that an antique (very old) treasure in your home is fragile and should be handled with care.

The environment in which all of us live is fragile as well. Only recently have we begun to realize that our actions can either help or hurt our fragile environment. During earlier times, people were more concerned with making a living than with any environmental damage they might have caused.

In any case, earlier generations "lived lightly on the land." There were few people and no modern machinery, so that the fragile environment was not seriously threatened.

Today, with more people, more roads, more factories, businesses and buildings, and more chemicals, such as fertilizers, the environment of the Coastal Plain is increasingly threatened. North Carolina's rivers run to the sea and carry with them the pollution put into the river by people upstream.

Coastal communities have some tough decisions to make. They need the jobs that tourism and economic development bring to the region, but their fragile environment is endangered. For every new business or industry that proposes to locate in a coastal community, community leaders are beginning to weigh the environmental consequences of allowing the business to locate.

The diagram below helps organize the arguments for and against a project that might affect the environment. What arguments for and against can you add?

Decision-Making Grid: Where to Build Refineries

Possible Positive Effects	**Possible Negative Effects**
1. New Jobs	**1.** Pollution
2. More people move here	**2.**
3. More houses and roads built	**3.**
4.	**4.**
5.	**5.**
6.	**6.**

Chapter 11 Review

LESSONS LEARNED

LESSON 1 Native Americans, Europeans, and Africans were the early settlers of the Coastal Plain. Their descendants have been joined by Latin Americans and retired people from other parts of the United States. The land of the Coastal Plain is home to many small cities, beach areas, crowded coastal towns, and farmland.

LESSON 2 The use of land in the Coastal Plain has changed through time. The Tidewater is more crowded and developed. The Inner Coastal Plain changed as agriculture changed. Wilmington and other coastal towns thrive through tourism. Fayetteville, Goldsboro, and Jacksonville have grown through the military bases located there.

LESSON 3 The economy of the Coastal Plain is still closely tied to agriculture. Tobacco, cotton, soybeans, vegetables, and livestock are the most important products. Manufacturing also offers jobs in textiles, food processing, and boatbuilding. Service jobs include tourism, education, and research.

LESSON 4 Coastal Plain culture can be discovered in the traditions, festivals, food, places to go, and fun things to do in the region.

TIME FOR TERMS

Latin Americans
migrant workers
culture
Hispanics
batik

FACT FOLLOW-UP

1. What groups of people live and have lived in the Coastal Plain Region?
2. How has the population of the Coastal Plain Region changed?
3. How has agriculture changed in the Coastal Plain Region?
4. What manufacturing industries are located in the Coastal Plain Region?
5. Name some of the major cities of the Tidewater and of the Inner Coastal Plain.
6. What are the most important service industries in the Coastal Plain Region?
7. How has the building of Interstate 40 changed the areas around Wilmington?
8. Where in the Coastal Plain Region are military bases located?
9. Why has cotton again become an important agricultural crop in the region?
10. In what agricultural crops does North Carolina rank high or lead the nation?

THINK THESE THROUGH

11. How has farm machinery changed the Coastal Plain Region?
12. What do you think is the biggest challenge facing the Coastal Plain Region? Explain why.
13. Why are some areas of the Coastal Plain Region growing in population while others are losing population?
14. In which service industry in the Coastal Plain Region would you most like to work? Why?
15. In which area of the Coastal Plain Region would you most like to live? Explain why.

16. Suppose you wanted to build a factory to make robots somewhere in the Coastal Plain Region. Where would you choose to build, and why?

SHARPENING SKILLS

17. Make a diagram to show some of the positive and negative effects of allowing a factory or large farm to locate on a river.
18. Should people living in the Coastal Plain be able to tell people living upstream how to use the water in rivers? Explain your answer.
19. What are some other decisions that leaders in the Coastal Plain must make?

PLACE LOCATION

Use the letters on the map to locate and name the places where the following can be found:

20. the Maritime Museum and the annual Seafood Festival.
21. Camp Lejeune, the United States Marine Corps base.
22. the North Carolina movie industry and the annual Azalea Festival.
23. Fort Bragg.
24. Seymour Johnson Air Force Base.
25. East Carolina University and the ECU Medical Complex.
26. site of many golf courses.
27. E. I. Dupont and CSS *Neuse.*

Reviewing Place Location

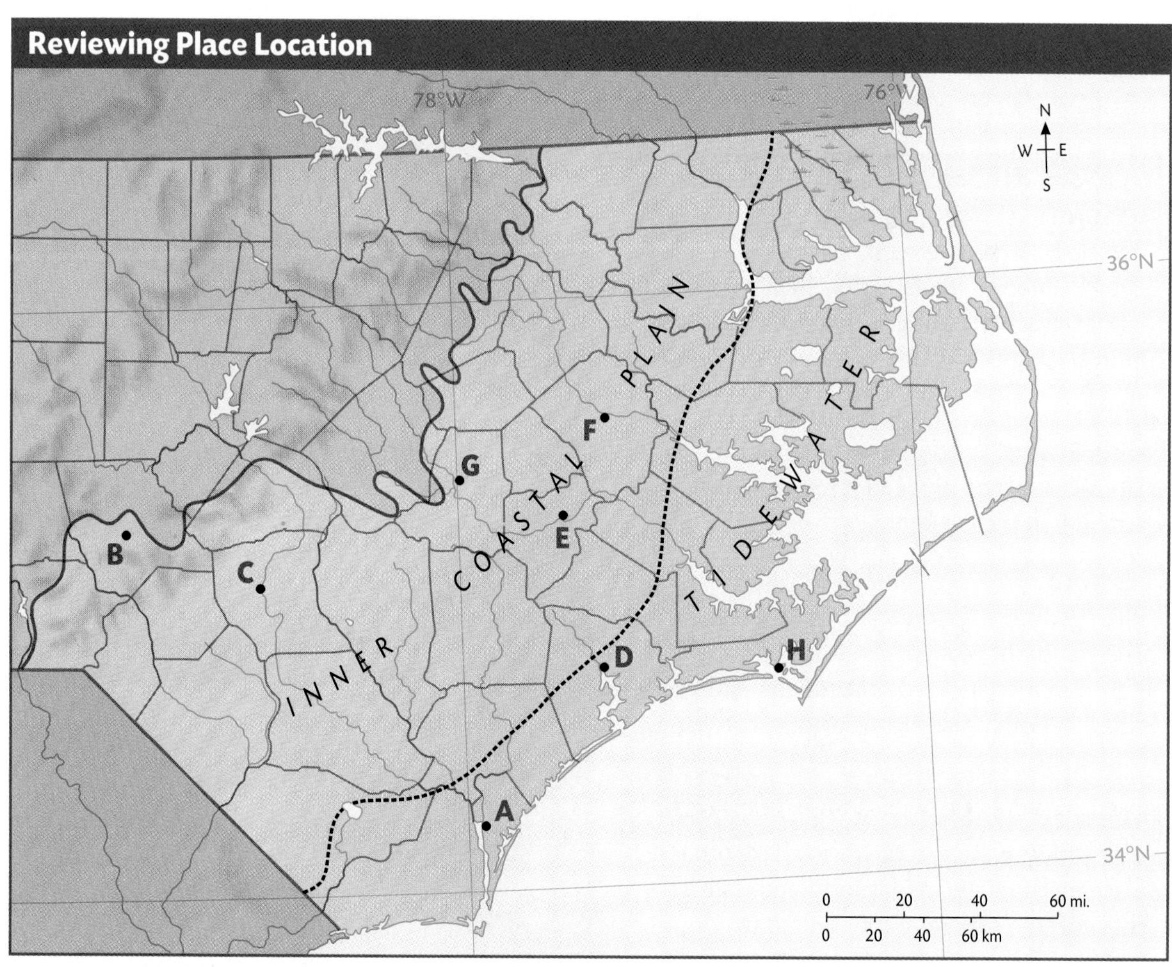

CHAPTER 12

The Piedmont

Hot-air balloons rise out of the mist. The reds, blues, and purples of the balloon canvasses gleam in the early morning light. Carried aloft by the heat of a gas burner, the balloons are guided by gentle winds. The passengers watch the rolling hills and the pine forests of the Piedmont.

Cars roll by on the interstate below. The balloonists over Rock Creek Road barely hear them. They see a few farms, industrial parks, then the cities of the Piedmont.

CHAPTER PREVIEW

Winston-Salem

North Carolina–Piedmont Region

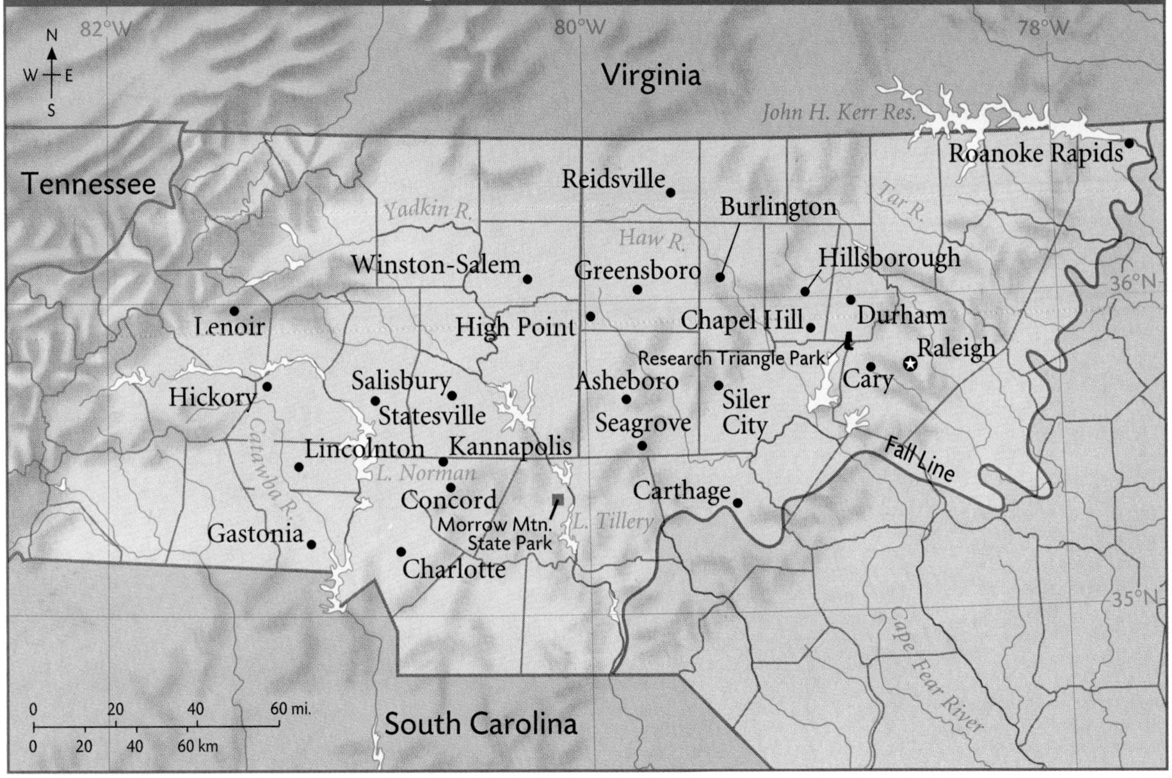

Virginia
Tennessee
South Carolina
John H. Kerr Res.
Roanoke Rapids
Reidsville
Burlington
Yadkin R.
Haw R.
Tar R.
Winston-Salem
Greensboro
Hillsborough
Lenoir
High Point
Chapel Hill
Durham
Research Triangle Park
Raleigh
Hickory
Salisbury
Asheboro
Siler City
Cary
Statesville
Seagrove
Catawba R.
Lincolnton
Kannapolis
L. Norman
Fall Line
Concord
Carthage
Morrow Mtn. State Park
L. Tillery
Gastonia
Charlotte
Cape Fear River
82°W
80°W
78°W
36°N
35°N
N S E W
0 20 40 60 mi.
0 20 40 60 km

International Stores

Have you ever had Mexican hot chocolate flavored with cinnamon? Have you ever worn a sari from India?

People from other countries who settle here want to have the food and clothing they have had all their lives. Sometimes there are enough people in a community to support a store that carries items from that country.

Are there any international stores in your community? What kinds?

People of the Piedmont

LESSON PREVIEW

Key Ideas

- Farming first brought people to the Piedmont. Now jobs in manufacturing, research, and education attract people.
- People from all over the world live in the Piedmont.

Key Terms

diversity, headquarters, sit-in

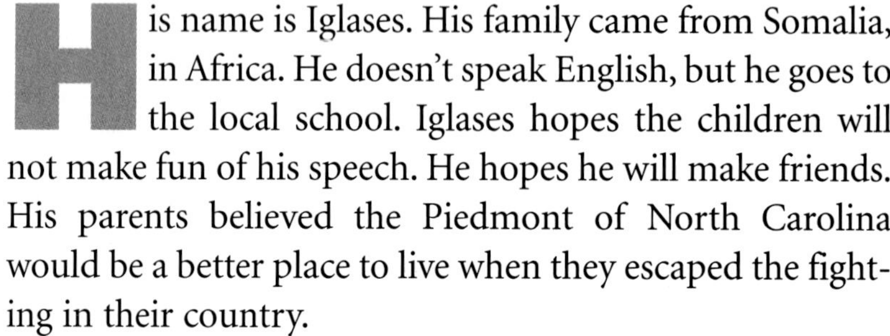

His name is Iglases. His family came from Somalia, in Africa. He doesn't speak English, but he goes to the local school. Iglases hopes the children will not make fun of his speech. He hopes he will make friends. His parents believed the Piedmont of North Carolina would be a better place to live when they escaped the fighting in their country.

New People, New Neighbors

From a hot-air balloon floating over the Piedmont the changing colors below look like the patches on a quilt. The different people who live in the Piedmont may also remind you of a many-colored quilt. The Piedmont has people from many places in the world. It is a region of great diversity. **Diversity** means having differing qualities.

Colonists began moving to the Piedmont during the 1700s. They came looking for good places to farm. Most stayed because the land and climate were good. The Piedmont gave its first settlers ways to improve their lives.

Today, the Piedmont's universities, research centers, and high-tech industries provide opportunities for people from all over the United States and the world. The jobs, a moderate climate, and attractive landscapes draw many families to the Piedmont.

Over the last 40 years, the population has changed everywhere in North Carolina. No region has changed more than the Piedmont.

This girl's family moved from Laos, a country in Southeast Asia, to High Point. Going to a new school can be scary, especially for children from other countries. *Why do their families move to the Piedmont?*

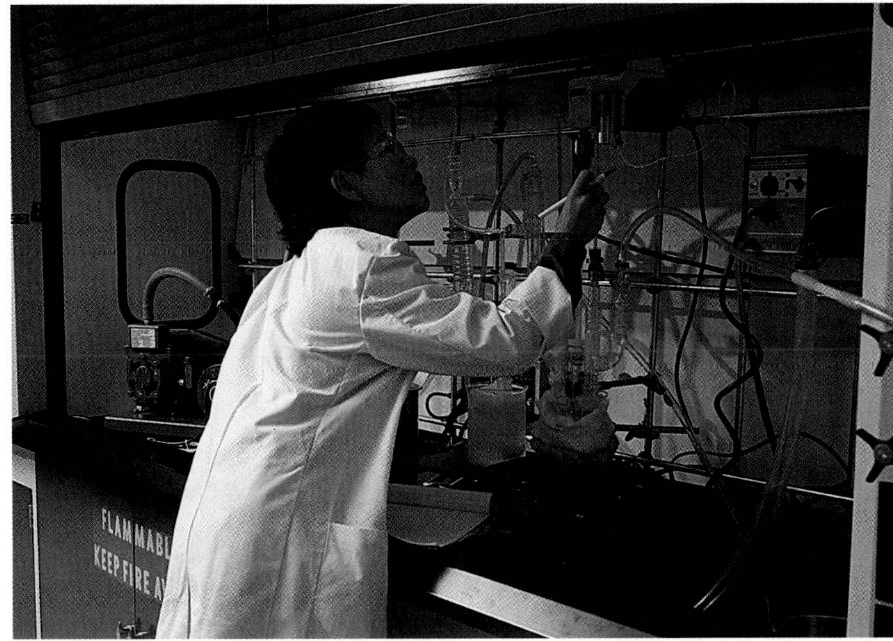

New people from different countries mean changes in the Piedmont. *What must newcomers learn when they move? What do people already here need to learn?*

The World Comes to the Piedmont

People from throughout the world have come to the Piedmont. Businesses—from Great Britain, Canada, Germany, and Japan—have built laboratories and factories. People from those countries run the businesses.

Students from the Middle East, Pakistan, India, China, and Korea study in the region's universities. Vietnamese from Southeast Asia have settled here. In the 1980s and 1990s, the number of Asian families jumped from 21,000 to more than 52,000. Most of these Asians live in the Piedmont.

Nearly 76,000 Latin Americans had come to live in North Carolina by 1990. Latin American families from Mexico, Central America, the Caribbean, and South America moved to the Coastal Plain and Piedmont. Construction workers moved from Texas after the building of houses and offices slowed there. They came to the Piedmont to work in its growing cities.

Other Latin American immigrants work at universities or in research. They find more jobs here than in their own country.

The Nation Comes to the Piedmont

People from other sections of the United States bring a great diversity to the Piedmont. Many new North Carolinians say they are from Virginia, South Carolina, Florida, and Texas. People from outside the South have also moved to the Piedmont, especially from California, New York, and New Jersey.

Many come to the Piedmont because their companies have moved their **headquarters**, or home office. Sometimes these companies move from states that are far away. They ask their workers to move as well. Have any of your parents

EYEWITNESS TO HISTORY

The Greensboro Sit-In

An important change in the Piedmont affected the entire country. In 1960, North Carolina did not treat African Americans and white citizens equally. African Americans were tired of waiting for changes to happen.

African Americans tried to exercise their rights as Americans with protests in the 1950s. In Montgomery, Alabama, African Americans led by Rosa Parks (left) and Martin Luther King, Jr. organized a bus boycott to protest segregated seating.

On February 1, 1960, four African American students (right) from North Carolina Agricultural and Technical College decided to make a difference. Worried, but determined, all four walked into a store and sat at a lunch counter.

had that experience?

Even rural Piedmont communities have new people moving into them. As cities grow larger, many people wish for more land or a more rural setting for their home. These people may choose to move outside a city and live in the countryside.

Winston-Salem is the headquarters for banking, textiles, tobacco, and communications companies. *How do companies with home offices in a region help that region grow?*

The biggest areas of growth have been in the Piedmont cities of Raleigh, Greensboro, Winston-Salem, and Charlotte. Since 1950 these cities have grown more quickly

It was against the law for African Americans to eat with whites in public. This law was unjust. These young men quietly took their seats. They asked for the same service as everyone else. They did not fight or yell when insulted. They sat quietly, refusing to move.

The four students were conducting a sit-in against segregation. A sit-in is a peaceful demonstration of sitting in the seats (above) or on the floor (right) of a place to protest the actions there. The four students were joined the next day by their classmates. Soon other college students joined the demonstration.

Similar sit-ins happened in other Piedmont cities. Some protestors were jailed (above), but the sit-ins spread to other states. The results were Civil Rights laws passed to guarantee equal treatment regardless of race.

Guides show visitors the exhibits in the North Carolina Museum of Art in Raleigh. *Have you been there? Is a museum in your town?*

than other cities in North Carolina during the second half of the twentieth century.

Retired persons often move to the Mountains and the Coastal Plain Regions. Many also make their way to the Piedmont. Cities there contain art museums, orchestras, and universities. Retirees have time to appreciate art shows, concerts, and university classes.

The Piedmont growth is part of a larger story of people moving into and around North Carolina. In fact, during the 1980s, more people moved into North Carolina than left it. This was the first time this had happened since its colonial days. You are living in a time that is as exciting as those early years.

LESSON 1 REVIEW

Fact Follow-Up

1. What attracts people to move to the Piedmont?
2. What are the largest cities of the Piedmont?
3. During the decade of the 1980s, something happened in North Carolina that had not happened since colonial times. What was it?
4. What were the sit-ins? Where did they begin?

Think These Through

5. Why are more people moving to the Piedmont than to other regions of North Carolina?
6. Do the same things attract people to the Piedmont today as in earlier times? Explain.

LESSON 2 Land Shapes Settlement

The Piedmont lies between the Coastal Plain and the mountains. If you are riding along I-40 toward the west, you will notice low rolling hills around Raleigh. As you ride still farther west, the land becomes hillier. West of Statesville, the hills change to mountains.

LESSON PREVIEW

Key Ideas

- The landforms of the Piedmont make it distinctive.
- The Piedmont attracted self-sufficient farmers as early settlers.
- Later, commercial farmers and manufacturers made the Piedmont home because of resources of water, timber, and transportation.

Key Terms

bottomland, commute

A Variety of Landforms

The Piedmont is a region between two major landforms. The land of the Piedmont ranges from nearly flat near the Coastal Plain to nearly mountainous along the Piedmont's western edge.

Some counties on the Piedmont's borders contain several landforms. Some of Harnett County is partly in the Coastal Plain. Part of its cropland comes from drained Carolina bays. Other areas of the county have Piedmont features. The land around Buies Creek rolls enough to have challenging golf courses.

From the highways of Interstate 40 you can see changing landforms as you cross regions. *How does the Piedmont's land change from the Coastal Plain to the Mountains?*

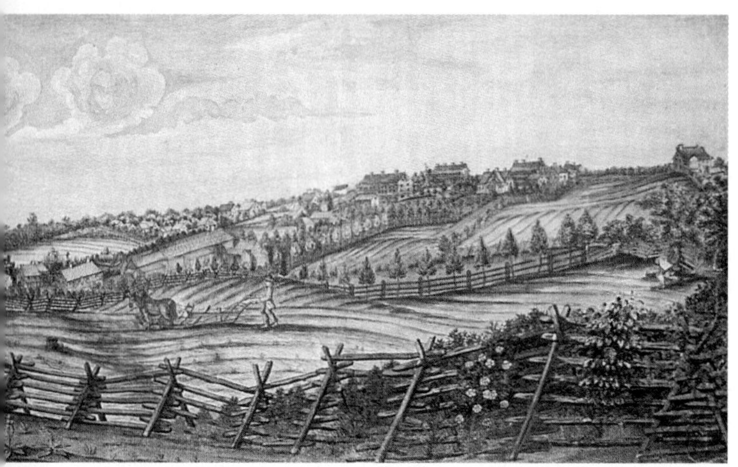

Early Piedmont settlers learned where the best places were to build homes, farm, and clear roads. *Where was good farmland?*

Wake County's eastern edge has some flat land of the Coastal Plain. The county's western edge has small hills. Much farther west, Lincoln County lies partly in the Piedmont and partly in the mountains. The land there begins to climb noticeably. It goes from 650 feet (195 m) above sea level to 1,480 feet (444 m) above sea level.

Early settlers found the Piedmont an attractive place to live. Forests provided game for food. Rivers and lakes held fish and provided water. The soil was good for farming. The temperature varied, but the climate was not too hot or too cold. Long growing seasons made farming rewarding.

Land Influences Life

Land formations in the Piedmont influenced where people settled. Hills and rivers encouraged early settlers to build homes close to each other. This gave the settlements safety.

Landforms also influenced where Piedmont settlers built farms and towns. Small river valleys were well suited for farming. **Bottomland**, flood plains along rivers, were natural places to clear fields to grow crops and graze animals. The bottomlands were fertile because the streams flooded regularly and left behind rich topsoil.

Farmers built homes on the ridges above streams. Roads along the ridge crests connected the settlements. Older roads often followed the natural patterns of the land. Curves and crooked streams forced roads one way and then another. You can see today where some roads and housing still follow the landforms. Train tracks also followed natural curves of the land. The Piedmont Crescent ran on tracks that curved around the Uwharrie Mountains.

People kept making better roads and finding easier ways to get around the countryside. As later settlers moved into the Piedmont, they found resources that supported manufacturing as well as farming.

Resources of the Land

Textile manufacturers settled in Piedmont counties that had water resources. Water provided power to run machinery. Water was needed to wash and dye the fabric.

Other manufacturers found materials they needed. Furniture manufacturers cut trees for wood. Textile mills bought local crops of cotton. Tobacco processors bought locally grown tobacco in the region.

Furniture making became North Carolina's third major industry. It grew in the late 1800s and early 1900s because of many hardwood trees and rivers to float logs and provide power. For those reasons, Hickory on the Catawba River became a major furniture manufacturing center. There are more than 50 furniture plants there today.

High Point grew to be an important furniture town after World War II. Today there are large furniture outlets and a modern furniture showplace. People from all over the world come to High Point to see North Carolina's furniture market.

Construction on the land—for highways, homes, and factories—changed the Piedmont as more people came. *How do people decide how to use the land?*

Good roads help trucks move resources to Piedmont factories where they are made into products sold worldwide. *What resources in the region help industry?*

Piedmont clay helped brick making become another big business. The clay found in the Piedmont made excellent bricks. Transportation helped the brick industry grow. Imagine how hard it would be to move thousands of bricks to a construction site without a train or large truck.

Power was needed for all these industries. The western Piedmont has rivers running through all its valleys. These rivers made a good source for hydroelectric energy. Lake Jordan and Kerr Lake, in the northern Piedmont, and Lake Tillery and Lake Norman, in the southern Piedmont, produce hydroelectric power and provide drinking water. All the lakes offer recreational facilities.

LIVING IN A COLONIAL INN

Voices From the Past

Built before the Revolutionary War, the Colonial Inn in Hillsborough was a wilderness tavern built along the Great Trading Path. Explorers stopped there as they headed west. Partially burned in 1768, the tavern was rebuilt as an inn.

It housed General Cornwallis in 1781. The inn must have heard the arguments and anger of British officers. Their army had been defeated at Guilford Courthouse. The Americans were winning their Revolutionary War.

A politician of the newly formed United States government stayed there in 1796. Aaron Burr stopped at the inn.

In 1865, Union General William T. Sherman stayed at the inn at the end of the Civil War. The inn heard the joyous shouts of the freed slaves and the quiet weeping of the families who lost loved ones in that war.

Today, the 11-bedroom inn allows you to stay close to this history. Dine in the room with the large table. If it is winter, the fireplace will be warm and inviting. The food will be served family style. Listen closely. The inn has many stories to tell you.

Transportation

Land development can increase flooding because paved parking lots do not absorb water from a heavy rain. *What are other problems of growth in the Piedmont?*

Residents of the 44 Piedmont counties travel on an interstate highway system with linking state roads. Some roads follow the paths of old trails. I-85 follows part of the route of the Great Trading Path.

Automobiles, good roads, and good weather allow people to live in one county and work in another. Most people are not bothered by having to **commute**, or drive to work, over 20 miles (32 km) or more. Traffic can be a problem when many people commute.

Many families in the Piedmont live in suburbs near large cities and commute only a short distance. Others prefer to live far from cities. They are willing to drive 30 miles (48 km) or more so they can enjoy a rural life.

Problems of Growth

People have moved so quickly into the Piedmont that schools cannot be built fast enough. Students in many schools are in temporary classrooms. Cities have trouble laying water and sewer lines to all the new houses. Even so, the Piedmont welcomes newcomers.

LESSON 2 REVIEW

Fact Follow-Up

1. Describe the landforms of the Piedmont Region.
2. Describe the transportation system of the Piedmont Region.
3. What are some problems facing the Piedmont Region today?
4. What natural resources are used by Piedmont industries today?

Think These Through

5. What do you think is the most important resource of the Piedmont Region? Why?
6. What do you think is the greatest challenge facing the Piedmont Region today? Why?

The Piedmont Economy

LESSON PREVIEW

Key Ideas

- The Piedmont economy is strong because of good transportation connections, important university and research facilities, and diverse cities.
- The Research Triangle Park and the cities of the Piedmont offer jobs in a wide variety of occupations.
- Airports in the Piedmont support the economy.

Key Terms

consumer

Lincolnton and applesauce. Winston-Salem and T-shirts. Gastonia and Christmas ornaments. Statesville and hot-air balloons. Greensboro and blue jeans. All these Piedmont towns make something that you might have seen, worn, or tasted. The Piedmont has a strong, varied economy. Let's see why.

Why the Piedmont?

Railroads, cotton, and a good water supply attracted textile mills years ago to the Piedmont. Timber drew the furniture industry. Today industry continues to come to the Piedmont. Since the 1950s, the Piedmont has been growing as a center for business, research in science and medicine, and university education. New sports franchises recently have come to the Piedmont. Both professional basketball and football teams are located in Charlotte.

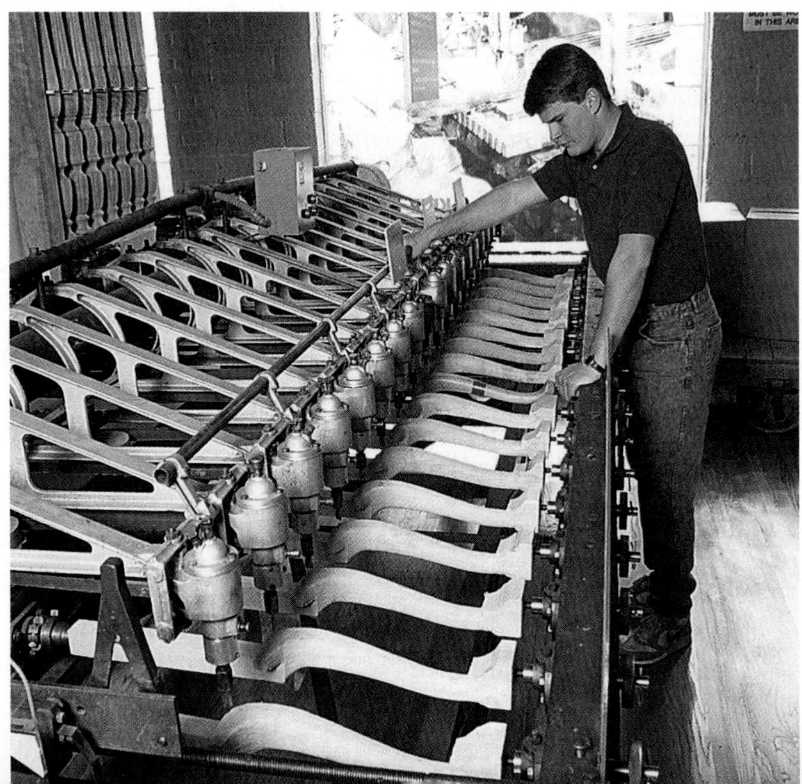

A furniture worker in High Point demonstrates an automatic lathe. This machine carves many pieces of wood at one time. *How did the Piedmont become a center of the furniture industry?*

When business leaders look for a new location, they look at the number of trained workers and the availability of resources. The Piedmont has a large population (see map below). This means there are many workers who can fill the new jobs that come to the area. The many universities help prepare students to work for companies who need well-educated workers. Good transportation to move resources also makes the Piedmont attractive to new industry.

Piedmont cities have varied populations. Businesses and government jobs are in each city. Some workers are downtown, but many more are located in areas far outside of town. Charlotte, Raleigh, Durham, Greensboro, and Winston-Salem have built new business centers outside of their downtown areas.

What would YOU do?

If you are going to college after high school, you have to decide which one. How would you make this decision? What would you need to think about?

Your parents would look at the cost. You might want to look at the school's location.

Maybe a special interest such as computers, history, or a sport will make you choose one school over another.

Major Piedmont Cities

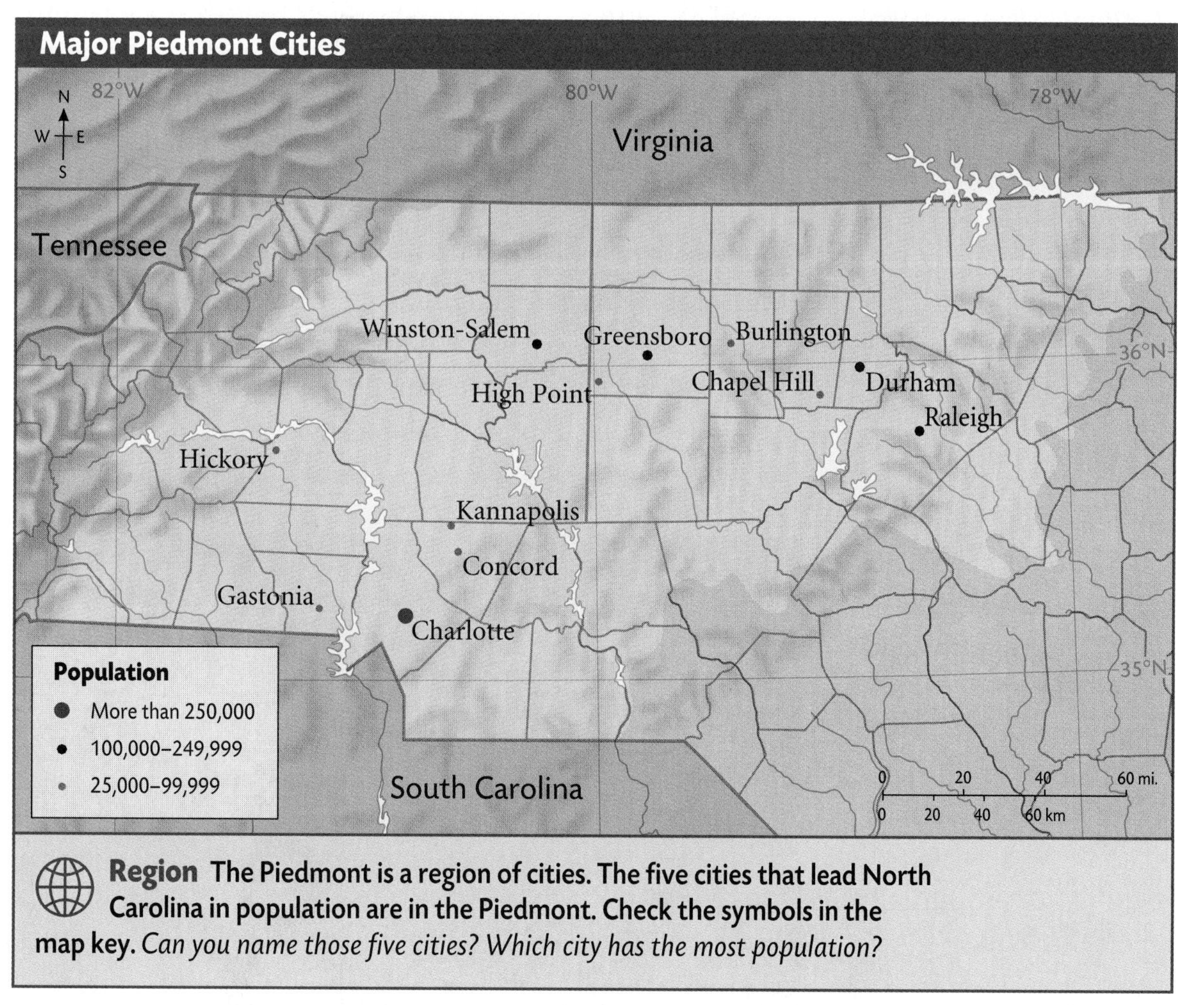

Region The Piedmont is a region of cities. The five cities that lead North Carolina in population are in the Piedmont. Check the symbols in the map key. *Can you name those five cities? Which city has the most population?*

Downtown Charlotte is filled with people who work in all sorts of jobs. *What are the major categories of jobs in the Piedmont?*

Jobs in the Piedmont

Whether they live in Charlotte—a city of almost 500,000—or in a town of less than 100,000 people, people in the Piedmont work in many kinds of jobs.

Research In the Research Triangle Park (RTP), centrally located among Raleigh, Durham, and Chapel Hill, more than 50 companies employ about 35,000 people as scientists, engineers, writers, and technicians. From RTP you can reach Duke University in Durham, North Carolina State University in Raleigh, and the University of North Carolina in Chapel Hill. Each has connections to the research companies at RTP. Duke, UNC, Bowman Gray in Winston-Salem, and East Carolina have nationally ranked medical schools.

North Carolina State University has leading research programs in engineering, veterinary science, and computer science. Wake Forest University in Winston-Salem and North Carolina A&T in Greensboro lead the state in making other important advances in science and technology.

Government Because Raleigh is the state capital, it is the home of the governor and thousands of other state workers. The state government is one of the largest employers in North Carolina. Many other state workers—public school teachers, university professors, and people who run state offices in cities and counties—live and work all over North Carolina.

These children are about to tour the governor's mansion in Raleigh, the state capital. *What other jobs do people have in state government?*

High Technology Many large companies place their headquarters in Charlotte, in Mecklenburg County. These companies include banks and insurance companies that handle millions of dollars every day. Banks rely on computer, telephone, and fax companies, which hire people to do jobs in communications.

Computer and communications specialists help these companies get their work done. High technology also serves the manufacturing industry. Computers run machines and plan work.

Manufacturing Guilford County has more manufacturing jobs than most counties. Three major textile mills operate in Greensboro: Blue Bell Corporation, Cone Mills, and Burlington Industries. Fieldcrest Cannon Mills in Cabarrus County also is a large employer.

Manufacturing has spurred the growth of Charlotte and its neighbor to the west, Gastonia. Dixie Yarns and Carolina Mills are two of the largest employers in Gastonia. R. J. Reynolds Tobacco Company still operates in Winston-Salem. Textile and other manufacturing companies employ many residents of Forsyth County. The Wake Forest University Medical School in Winston-Salem employs more than 13,000 people, including those in service jobs.

"Pick your own" farms give city dwellers a chance to pick fruit. You could pick blueberries or strawberries. *Why would some farmers have a farm of this kind?*

Agriculture "Pick your own" farms in all Piedmont counties are run by rural families. Fields of strawberries, peaches, blueberries, and other fruits and vegetables attract city people, who pick as much as they can buy.

Tobacco grows on farms in the Piedmont. Rabbits once dominated the market in Chatham County. Farmers there now raise dairy cattle, poultry, and hogs. Many Piedmont counties raise chickens. Union, Anson, Stanly, and Richmond County growers raise turkeys (see map, page 217).

Airports in the Piedmont are busy. People and products come from all over the world. *Can you name the three major airports?*

Timber and Furniture Lincoln and Montgomery Counties have lumber companies. These counties are near furniture manufacturers in High Point and Lexington.

High Point hosts the Southern Furniture Market. Buyers from New York and Los Angeles come to High Point twice a year to see the latest styles of furniture. Their visits mean money for hotels and restaurants.

The furniture bought at the market then is shipped by train, truck, and airplane to various stores across the country. In stores, the furniture will be sold to a **consumer**, a person who buys products.

Airports Work in offices, laboratories, classrooms, and factories influences how families live in the Piedmont. Planes carry passengers who speak at seminars and open new businesses. Universities host international conferences.

The Raleigh-Durham Airport serves Raleigh, Durham, and Chapel Hill. The Piedmont Triad International Airport serves Greensboro, High Point, and Winston-Salem. The Charlotte Douglas International Airport is North Carolina's largest airport. Airplanes offer quick transportation for goods and people.

With all that work, do the people of the Piedmont Region have time to relax? How do they play?

LESSON 3 REVIEW

Fact Follow-Up

1. What do businesses look for when they locate in a place?
2. What are the major businesses of the largest cities of the Piedmont?
3. What kinds of farming are found in the Piedmont?
4. Where are the region's major airports?

Think These Through

5. If you could choose to live in one of the major cities of the Piedmont, which would you choose? Explain why.
6. Why is the Piedmont a center for jobs in government? research?
7. How do airports support the economy of the Piedmont?

LESSON 4 Culture of the Piedmont

LESSON PREVIEW

Key Ideas

- Outdoor recreation is important to Piedmont residents.
- The region's cities offer a variety of cultural activities.
- Basketball, football, baseball, and stock car racing are popular sports.
- Fairs, festivals, and food reflect the culture of the Piedmont.

Key Terms

orchestra

Outdoor games take place during the spring, summer, and fall in the Piedmont. CASL, the Capital Area Soccer League, one of the largest soccer organizations on the East Coast, has 12,000 players from Wake County and surrounding areas. Boys and girls can begin to play at age four. The temperate climate for most of the year makes outdoors the best place to be.

Recreation

People of the Coastal Plain have the ocean, and mountain residents have the mountains for recreation. People of the Piedmont depend upon park lands, man-made lakes, and undeveloped areas for a break from city life.

The Eno River flows through Durham. Every Fourth of July, the Festival on the Eno draws more than 60,000 people to sing, dance, eat, and look at folk art. At other times, the Eno River State Park is a quiet place to hike.

People from Iredell, Lincoln, Catawba, Gaston, and Mecklenburg Counties play and live on Lake Norman.

The city of Statesville in Iredell County owns a lake. This lake and the surrounding area named Lakewood Park have an unusual attraction—24 lighted horseshoe courts.

For Piedmont people who enjoy rivers, Rockingham County offers four of them. The Dan, the Smith, the Mayo, and the Haw wind their way through the county. Farther south in Stanly County, Morrow Mountain State Park offers visitors a chance to play in Lake Tillery near the Pee Dee River.

Protected from hunting, the eagle makes its summer home on Piedmont lakes. *Where do eagles nest?*

The American Dance Festival in Durham includes dance performances, plays, movies, and concerts. *What event would you attend?*

Kerr Reservoir covers almost 50,000 acres (20,000 sq hm). The reservoir has 800 miles (1,288 km) of shoreline. It is located on the North Carolina-Virginia border.

Culture in the Cities

The cities offer different kinds of entertainment. All major Piedmont cities have a symphony orchestra. In an **orchestra**, 30 or more musicians perform music.

Art galleries, places where you can see and buy art, are found in larger Piedmont cities. The North Carolina Museum of Art in Raleigh, the Reynolda House Museum in Winston-Salem, and the Mint Museum of Art in Charlotte display paintings and sculpture.

Other types of museums tell the history of the Piedmont and North Carolina. The North Carolina Museum of Natural History and the Museum of History are in Raleigh.

Plays, movies, and musical concerts offer everyone something to do. Many of these activities also can be found on the coast and in the mountains. What makes them special in the Piedmont? There are more of them because there are more cities.

Sports

The people of the Piedmont love sports. The Carolina Panthers play football in the National Football League. The Charlotte Sting and the Charlotte Hornets are the women's and men's teams of the National Basketball Association. Hockey players skate for the Carolina Hurricanes.

Other popular sports are college football and basketball. The Atlantic Coast Conference includes four colleges from North Carolina: The Duke Blue Devils, the North

Carolina State Wolfpack, the University of North Carolina Tar Heels, and the Wake Forest Demon Deacons. Rivalries are especially strong in football and basketball.

Other universities across the Piedmont have teams that participate in the same sports. North Carolina Central University in Durham and North Carolina A&T in Greensboro are two mainly African American universities that participate in athletics.

Minor-league baseball is popular in the Piedmont. The Durham Bulls compete in a new stadium. The Carolina Mudcats play in Five County Stadium on the eastern edge of the Piedmont. Other teams are the Charlotte Knights, Greensboro Bats, Hickory Crawdads, Winston-Salem Wart Hogs, the Burlington Indians, and the Piedmont Boll Weevils of Kannapolis.

Nearly all communities sponsor baseball and softball games for young people. High school and middle school teams compete in soccer, field hockey, lacrosse, track and field, football, basketball, and baseball.

Stock car racing heats up the race tracks in North Carolina's Piedmont. Stock cars look like regular cars, but they have much more powerful engines.

Kids play baseball all over North Carolina. Piedmont cities organize softball and baseball teams. *Are there sports teams in your area?*

There are major races in the Piedmont sponsored by the National Association for Stock Car Auto Racing (NASCAR). The Winston Cup National 500 takes place in Charlotte in October. There are yearly races in Rockingham and North Wilkesboro. Richard Petty, Junior Johnson (both retired), and Dale Earnhardt are some famous drivers from North Carolina.

GAMES People Play

Ice Hockey Ice hockey as a southern sport? Yes. Every year ice hockey teams suit up in the Piedmont. Raleigh and Charlotte have professional teams. Greensboro and Hillsborough have rinks.

When the teams suit up, so do many children. Most ice hockey teams have teaching sessions for kids. Put on your ice skates and learn how to score a goal.

Fairs and Festivals

Raleigh offers a special treat once a year. For ten days in October, people from all over come to the North Carolina State Fair. Those from the Piedmont cities can see what their agricultural neighbors do. Large pumpkins, fat red hens, apple pies, and bawling calves get everyone's attention.

Rides, candy apples, and musical shows draw large crowds. Every evening at the close of the fair, fireworks burst across the sky.

Festivals and fireworks on the Fourth of July are ways people show how they enjoy where they live. Charlotte's Loch Norman Highland Games honor the Scottish heritage of the area.

The Piedmont celebrates its diversity with the African American Freedom Festival in Raleigh. *What are other ways to celebrate diversity?*

The State Fair in Raleigh offers fun for everyone in North Carolina. From animals to zithers, you can find it at the fair. *How far is the State Fair from your town?*

Greensboro holds crafts and performing arts festivals in the spring, summer, and fall. Winston-Salem plans an annual crafts fair every October.

Food

Because the Piedmont is in the South, people enjoy southern foods, especially fried chicken and corn on the cob. Sweet potatoes are served in the fall. Strawberries and peaches are favorite fruits in the summer.

Barbecue, smoked shredded pork served with a vinegar-based sauce, holds out as the favorite food in most eastern Piedmont counties. The farther west you go in the Piedmont, the more likely you are to see sliced barbecue with a tomato-based sauce.

Newcomers to the Piedmont bring new foods to their neighborhoods. Restaurants in the larger Piedmont cities serve Chinese, Mexican, Thai, German, and Italian food. Larger supermarkets are stocking shelves with foods popular in other countries. You can find Mexican, Asian, and Italian groceries in the region.

WORD ORIGINS

Cary once was called Pages' Tavern. When the railroad came, it became Pages' Siding. Incorporated in 1871, the town was named Carey in honor of an Ohio senator who sponsored Prohibition. The spelling changed to Cary in 1899. Cary lies just west of Raleigh.

Festivals celebrate a people's present way of life or a tradition from the past, such as the Carthage Buggy Festival. *Does your town have a festival that remembers the past?*

Favorite places to find some of this food are at local festivals in the Piedmont during the spring and fall. Chapel Hill has the Apple Chill Festival. Streets are blocked off for people to dance, hear music, and eat. Folk art and craftspeople show their wares on cloth-covered tables.

Cary, a city on the western edge of Raleigh, hosts the Cary Lazy Days. People from Raleigh and the surrounding smaller towns come to listen to music, eat all kinds of food, and view arts and crafts.

Siler City has a chicken festival to celebrate its large poultry production. Carthage in Moore County has its buggy festival to celebrate the buggies—horse-drawn wagons—made in that town at the turn of the century.

Food fairs specialize in one type of food. Raleigh has a Greek festival featuring Greek foods. Charlotte and Raleigh schedule Octoberfests every fall to celebrate German food and music. The Raleigh International Festival celebrates many cultures, so all kinds of dishes are served.

The Piedmont is so varied that most of its food changes from festival to festival and county to county, just like its landforms and people.

LESSON 4 REVIEW

Fact Follow-Up

1. What can people who live in the Piedmont do for recreation?
2. Describe sports in the Piedmont.
3. What are some special foods and celebrations in the Piedmont?

Think These Through

4. What do you think is the most interesting or important activity of the Piedmont? Explain why.
5. What activities of the Piedmont best show its diversity? Explain why.
6. Suppose you were trying to attract someone your age to come to live in the Piedmont. What would you tell them about the region? Why?

Acquiring Information From a Variety of Sources

Diversity

North Carolina's Piedmont is described in Chapter 12 as a region of great diversity. In fact, it is described as having the greatest diversity of any region in our state. Diversity means having differing qualities. A diverse region like the Piedmont has differences among its people, landforms, economy, and culture.

What are some of these noticeable differences? Lesson 1 describes the diversity of people who have come to live in the Piedmont Region. How many different groups of people have made their homes in the region?

When you have finished reviewing Lesson 1, list the diverse people of the Piedmont Region. At this point, you might like to use a web or spider chart to display your information. Here is an example of a spider chart using information from Lesson 1.

The diversity of landforms and land uses in the Piedmont is described in Lesson 2. Can you make a web chart for this? What would be a good title for this chart? What other kinds of diversity are described in the lesson?

Continue through Chapter 12, listing examples of diversity and constructing web charts. One of the most fun ways to make use of information from Lesson 3 is to make a sports chart. Can you make a web chart for sports in the Piedmont Region? What sports would the chart include?

When you have finished reviewing Chapter 12 and making your lists or charts, you can bring all the information together in a "giant" web chart titled "The Piedmont: Region of Diversity." This web chart will pull together all your lists and other web charts.

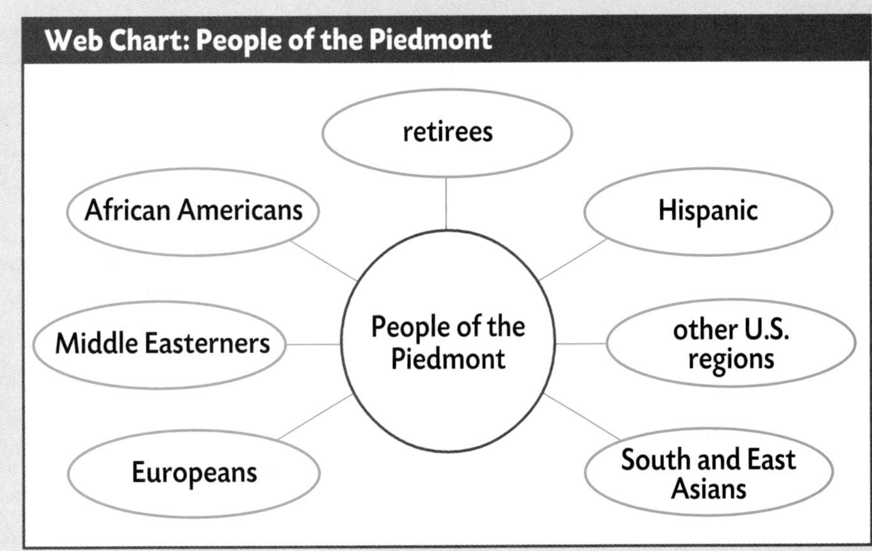

Chapter 12 Review

LESSONS LEARNED

LESSON 1 Agriculture once drew people to the Piedmont. Now jobs in manufacturing, research, and education draw people to the Piedmont from all over the United States and the world.

LESSON 2 Resources of water, timber, and transportation attracted settlers and businesses to the Piedmont. Settlers built homes and farms to adapt to the shape of rolling hills and river valleys.

LESSON 3 The Piedmont economy is strong. Jobs in manufacturing, research, education, government, and technology are supported by natural resources, research institutions, and universities.

LESSON 4 The culture of the Piedmont is changing as its population changes. Food reflects the international population. Festivals celebrate the diverse population. Piedmont residents can relax at recreation spots on rivers and lakes. The sports of basketball, baseball, and auto racing are popular in the Piedmont. Young people also have many choices of sports and educational programs.

TIME FOR TERMS

diversity
sit-in
commute
orchestra
headquarters
bottomland
consumer

FACT FOLLOW-UP

1. What groups of people have recently moved into the Piedmont?
2. What natural resources encourage growth in the Piedmont?
3. What environmental challenges face the Piedmont?
4. Why have many businesses chosen to locate in the Piedmont?
5. What recreational opportunities does the Piedmont offer?
6. What were some results of the Greensboro sit-ins?
7. What industries are located in the Piedmont?
8. How has the Research Triangle Park changed the Raleigh-Durham area?
9. How has improved transportation encouraged growth in the Piedmont?
10. How does the Piedmont change from east to west?

THINK THESE THROUGH

11. Suppose the Greensboro sit-ins and other demonstrations for civil rights had not happened. How would life be different?
12. Why is the Piedmont more diverse than other regions of North Carolina?
13. Why is population in the Piedmont growing more rapidly than in other North Carolina regions?
14. Suppose you were planning to build a theme park in the Piedmont. Where would you locate it? Explain why.

15. What makes the Piedmont most different from the Coastal Plain? Explain.

SHARPENING SKILLS

16. Construct a web chart showing diversity in the Coastal Plain. You will need to review Chapter 11 in order to do this.
17. What are some of the benefits of diversity?
18. Which people have brought the most diversity to North Carolina? Explain.
19. What one characteristic gives North Carolina most of its diversity? Explain.

PLACE LOCATION

Use the letters on the map to locate and name the following places:

20. the largest city in North Carolina, headquarters for major banks and other companies.
21. the site of a civil rights sit-in, the headquarters of textile mills, and one of the three cities of the Triad.
22. the home of Duke University and one of the three cities of the Triangle.
23. the home of the University of North Carolina and one of the Triangle cities.
24. the state capital, site of many museums, and one of the three cities of the Triangle.
25. the site of Wake Forest University, the headquarters of R. J. Reynolds, and one of the three cities of the Triad.
26. the site of the Southern Furniture Market and one of the three cities of the Triad.
27. the site of the headquarters for research companies and scientific organizations.
28. the site of many textile mills and the city west of Charlotte.

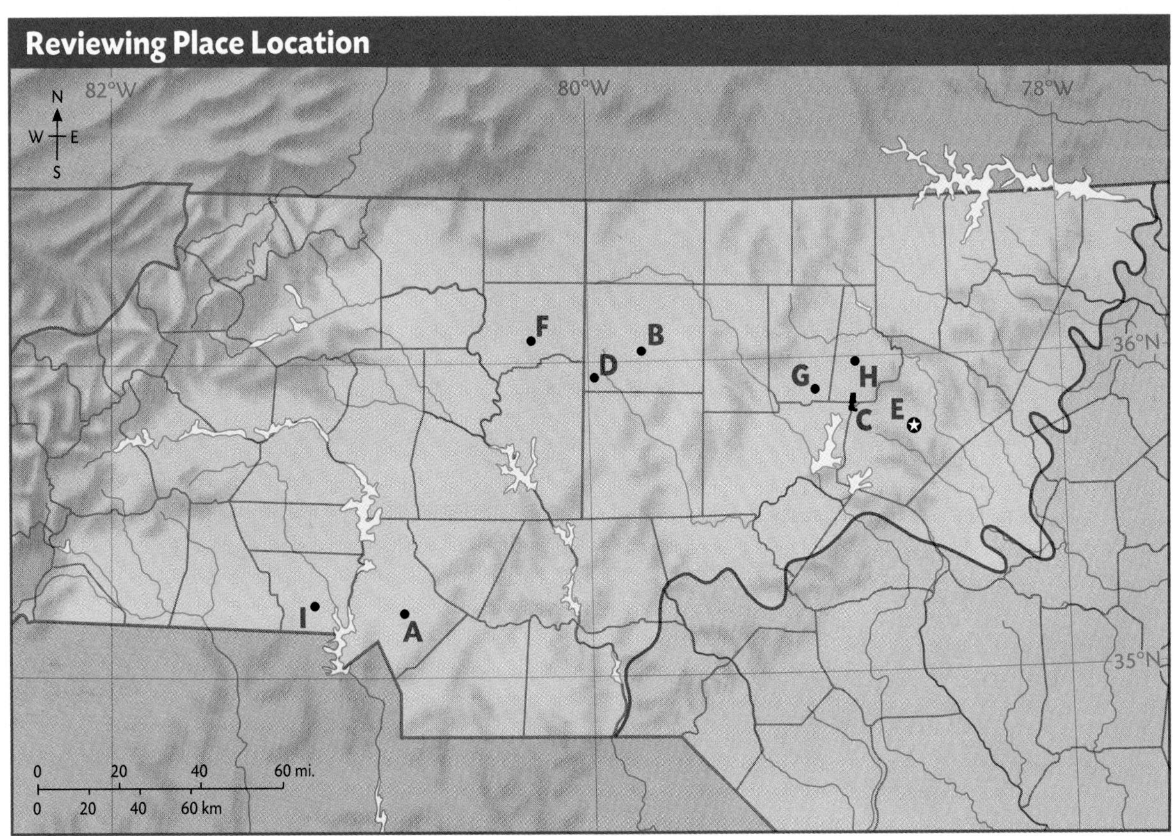

CHAPTER 13 Mountain Life Today

Standing on a mountain roadside you can hear the screams. Loud yells follow the screams. You scramble to the path to see what is going on. Dozens of people dressed in shorts and T-shirts, bathing suits and jeans wait in line. A large slick rock sends sliders slipping into a small natural pool.

Watch as they plop down, shivering with cold and excitement. Whoosh! Screech! They're off on Sliding Rock, a natural slide fueled by flowing water a few inches deep.

CHAPTER PREVIEW

LESSON 1
People of the Mountains
Many different people have lived in the Mountains Region.

LESSON 2
Land Shapes Communities
Mountain communities grew quickly after the railroad appeared. Other changes shaped life in the Mountains.

LESSON 3
The Economy of the Mountains
Work in the Mountains is shaped by the environment.

LESSON 4
Mountain Culture
People in the Mountains have fun in many ways.

Sliding Rock

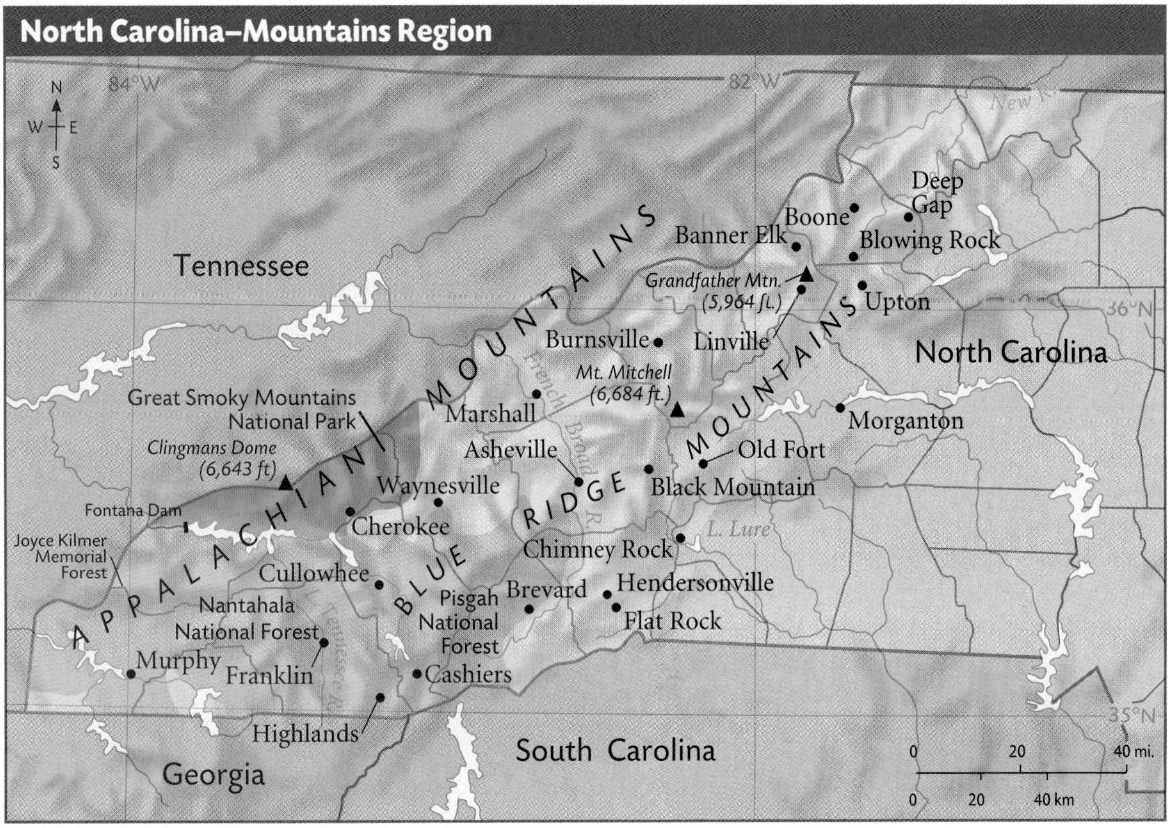

North Carolina–Mountains Region

84°W
82°W
36°N
35°N
N
W E
S
Tennessee
North Carolina
South Carolina
Georgia
APPALACHIAN MOUNTAINS
BLUE RIDGE MOUNTAINS
Great Smoky Mountains National Park
Clingmans Dome (6,643 ft)
Fontana Dam
Joyce Kilmer Memorial Forest
Nantahala National Forest
Murphy
Franklin
Highlands
Cashiers
Cullowhee
Cherokee
Waynesville
Pisgah National Forest
Brevard
Asheville
Marshall
Burnsville
Mt. Mitchell (6,684 ft.)
Black Mountain
Old Fort
Chimney Rock
L. Lure
Hendersonville
Flat Rock
Linville
Grandfather Mtn. (5,964 ft.)
Banner Elk
Boone
Deep Gap
Blowing Rock
Upton
Morganton
New R.
French Broad R.
L. Tennessee R.
0 20 40 mi.
0 20 40 km

Mountain Visitors

Families began coming to Asheville in the late 1800s to enjoy its cool summers. They were wealthy people who often had homes in New York and Florida. They could afford to travel to the mountains and stay for several weeks.

Famous people passed through the tall entryway of the Grove Park Inn after it opened in 1913. In 1918, three famous inventors—Henry Firestone (far left), Thomas Edison (second from left), and Henry Ford (second from right)—checked in.They strolled out to the balcony to enjoy the view. President Franklin D. Roosevelt spent a night at the Grove Park Inn in 1936.

People of the Mountains

LESSON PREVIEW

Key Ideas

- The Cherokee were the first settlers in the mountains.
- European settlers, mainly Scotch-Irish, moved to the mountains.
- More people began to move to the mountains after the railroads were built.
- The newest mountain residents come from all over the world.

Key Terms

Trail of Tears, religious retreat

George Caleb Bingham's painting of Daniel Boone at the Cumberland Gap shows the first European settlers of the Appalachians. *Who settled there before them?*

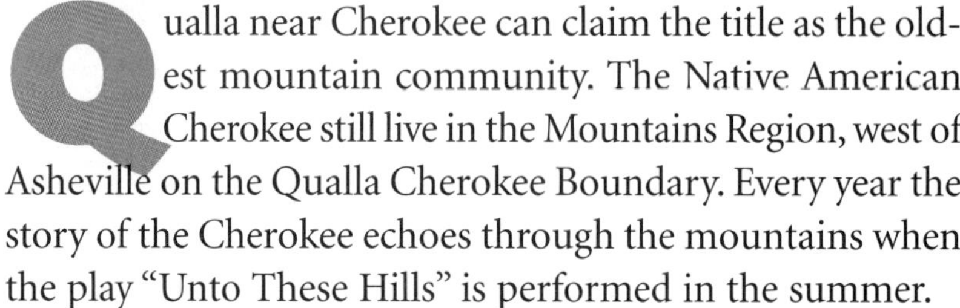

Qualla near Cherokee can claim the title as the oldest mountain community. The Native American Cherokee still live in the Mountains Region, west of Asheville on the Qualla Cherokee Boundary. Every year the story of the Cherokee echoes through the mountains when the play "Unto These Hills" is performed in the summer.

First Mountain Settlers

Native Americans in North Carolina have stayed in the same area for generations. In the Mountains Region, the Cherokee have lived in the same place since their ancestors first settled there. Some descendants of early European settlers still live in the Mountains.

European settlers came to the Mountains to find good land for crops and grazing animals. They hoped to make a new place for their children. German, Irish, and English families traveled from the North Carolina Coastal Plain. Others moved from central Pennsylvania to settle in mountain coves and hollows.

Rich plantation owners from Charleston, South Carolina, built summer houses at Flat Rock in Henderson County. The families at Flat Rock often spent entire summers there. They believed they were escaping the diseases caused by the hot air in the Tidewater swamps. We now know they really were avoiding mosquitoes that carried diseases.

New Residents of the Mountains

People still move to the Mountains for a better way of life. Some move from other parts of

Asheville grew quickly after a railroad tunnel connected it to the Piedmont. *Why did visitors often decide to settle in the Mountains Region?*

North Carolina and from other states to retire. As businesses relocate to the Mountains, employees are often asked to come along, too.

Many people have moved to the Mountains from other countries. Several hundred families from the Southeast Asian country of Laos in recent years moved to Marion and surrounding towns. These people come from a mountainous region. The Mountains of North Carolina remind them of their home country.

Latin American families have settled in the region. They might originally have come to help with crop production. Now they find employment in towns.

Railroads and Cars Bring Tourists

During the 1870s, many people stayed in Hickory, near the Brushy Mountains. Some wealthy families stopped in the cool Blue Ridge as they traveled between their homes in New York and Florida.

In the 1880s, the railroad cut a tunnel through the Blue Ridge Mountains. Asheville could then be reached by train. It quickly grew into a major tourist town. Today, some families from Florida escape the summer's heat and spend months in cooler Hendersonville. They return to Florida for the rest of the year when North Carolina experiences its winter months.

Railroads helped other towns attract visitors before there were automobiles. The Balsam Inn, near Waynesville, depended upon the train to bring in guests.

Beginning in about 1900, families took trains from Atlanta to homes at Highlands and Cashiers. Blowing Rock became a resort town for North Carolina Piedmont families.

Originally, families sought rest when they came to the Mountains. The slow pace of vacation contrasted with the

EYEWITNESS TO HISTORY

The Cherokee of North Carolina

Cherokee is a word that describes a Native American group who live in North Carolina and Oklahoma. The Cherokee also once lived in Tennessee, Georgia, Alabama, and South Carolina.

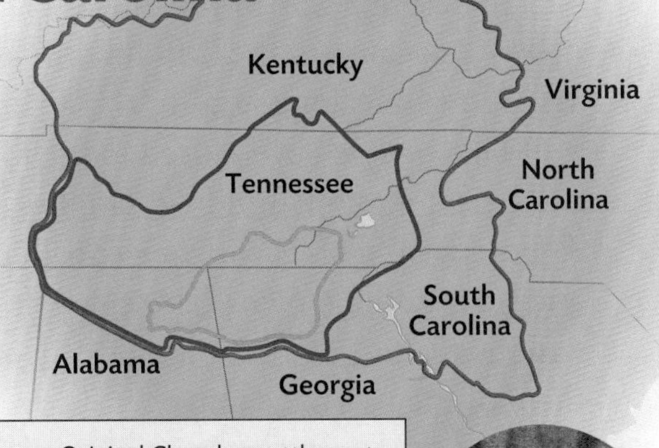

In the 1800s, the United States attempted to move all southeastern Native Americans to Oklahoma. More than 17,000 Cherokee from North Carolina, Georgia, and Tennessee were forced to walk (below). Native Americans called the walk the **Trail of Tears** because more than 4,000 Cherokee died during the 1,200-mile (1,932-km) trek.

Nearly 1,000 Cherokee refused to go. They hid in the highest mountains. The government allowed them to stay when Colonel William H. Thomas agreed to purchase land in Swain and Jackson Counties. This land was used to form the Qualla Reservation.

hustle of Charlotte, Atlanta, and other cities. Families hiked, swam, or played games. The cool evenings in such places as Lake Lure or Chimney Rock made sleep easier and daily life more comfortable.

When automobiles came along, people began traveling everywhere that decent roads could take them. Soon families from throughout the southeastern United States began to enroll their children in summer camps.

Today more than 100 camps in the Mountains Region offer horseback riding, sports, canoeing, crafts, and other recreation. Kids from many states come to our mountains each summer.

GAMES People Play

Fox and Geese is a game of tag in the snow. Shovel a circle 20 feet (6 m) in diameter. Make paths out from the circle in opposite directions. The Fox stands in the center. The Geese can go in any direction around the circle and on the paths. At the count of three, the Fox runs after the Geese. Tagged Geese are out of the game.

Europeans introduced the Cherokee to glass beads. The Cherokee made the beads into works of art. Each artist (left) uses patterns and colors to make unique pieces. Baskets (below) made from vines have intricate patterns. Plant dyes add color to the patterns. Cherokee patterns are easily recognized.

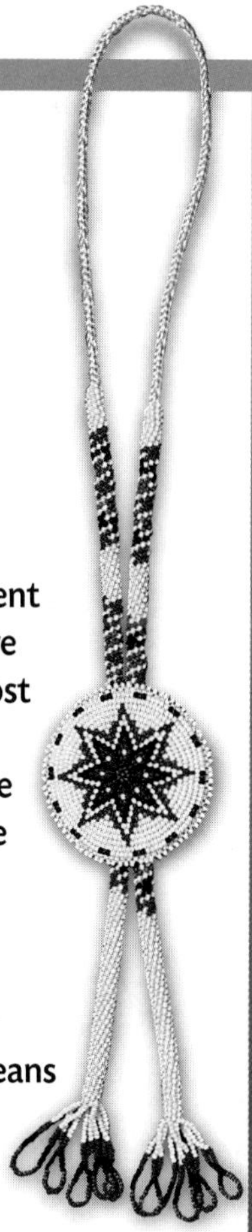

The town of Cherokee has made great progress in recent years. Its tourist businesses are important to the westernmost mountain area. Thousands of visitors come to Cherokee (left) every year. Some come to study the older ways of medicine, raising food, and making crafts. Others visit Oconaluftee Village to see how the Cherokee lived before Europeans came to North Carolina.

More than 6,000 Cherokee live there today. They are the largest Native American group living on a reservation east of the Mississippi River.

Lake Junaluska offers a change of scenery and a retreat setting for families.
Why are the Mountains a good place for religious retreats?

Mountain Retreats

People also use the Appalachian Mountains for religious retreats. A **religious retreat** is a time of quiet thought away from the pressures of daily life. Many churches have built retreat centers in the Mountains Region. The centers offer church members a place to stay and worship.

The Baptists at Ridgecrest, the Methodists at Lake Junaluska, the Episcopalians at Flat Rock and Valle Crucis, and the Presbyterians at Montreat operate large retreat centers. Youth programs take up much of the summer.

Mountain Sites

Finally, people today come to the Mountains to be outdoors. From Fontana Dam to Bat Cave to Linville Gorge, the Mountains refresh people and offer enjoyment.

Some visit the homes of famous people. Two great American writers had homes in the Mountains. Novelist Thomas Wolfe grew up in Asheville. Poet Carl Sandburg lived on a goat farm in Flat Rock. Their homes are now museums. Governor Zebulon Vance's birthplace in Weaverville is a popular attraction. Another favorite home is the Biltmore House, the largest private house in the United States. Cabins of early mountain settlers are open for tourists in Doughton Park near Blowing Rock.

LESSON  REVIEW

Fact Follow-Up

1. Why do Cherokees live in the Mountains Region?
2. Why did Europeans first move into the Mountains?
3. What in the Mountains has attracted people from other places to spend time there?

Think These Through

4. How important was the building of railroads to the Mountains? Explain.
5. Why are people moving into the Mountains today?
6. Why are religious retreats and summer camps located in the Mountains?

LESSON 2

Land Shapes Communities

Can you recognize a black bear's growl? a dulcimer's twang? a waterfall's thunder? a snowfall's silence? Fourth graders in the Mountains live closer to these sounds than young people anywhere else in the state.

LESSON PREVIEW

Key Ideas

- Mountain names often describe the land.
- The climate of the Mountains makes road maintenance difficult.
- Railroads and highways opened the Mountains to greater settlement.
- Asheville is the major city of the Mountains.

Key Term

cove

Learning from the Mountains

There is much to hear from both nature and people. Old folks tell stories of long ago. Mountain music has been heard for centuries. Cool air whistles new tunes through fir trees high on the ridges.

The names of mountains reveal their character. The sides of Glassy Mountain in Henderson County are so smooth that they remind people of glass. The Blue Ridge Mountains give off a bluish haze when seen from a distance. The Smoky Mountains have similar drifts of foggy haze.

Mountains are often named for their appearances. This is Whiteside Mountain. *Why do you think it was given that name?*

CONNECTIONS

Geography & Science

Tracking Footprints

If you took a hike on a mountain path, you might see tracks. Tracks tell you what type of animal or insect or person passed ahead of you on the trail. Imprints by feet, paws, or claws give you information about the creature ahead.

Daniel Boone tracked for food. You can track for fun. You have to know what to look for before you start.

A deep imprint might mean a large animal passed your way. Looking for certain types of tracks helps you tell what animal walked by earlier.

Look for animal droppings on the trail. Called "scat," droppings tell you what the animal ate. Deer, for example, leave droppings full of black seeds in autumn. Deer love persimmons, which are full of black seeds. You might find fur in the droppings of a fox.

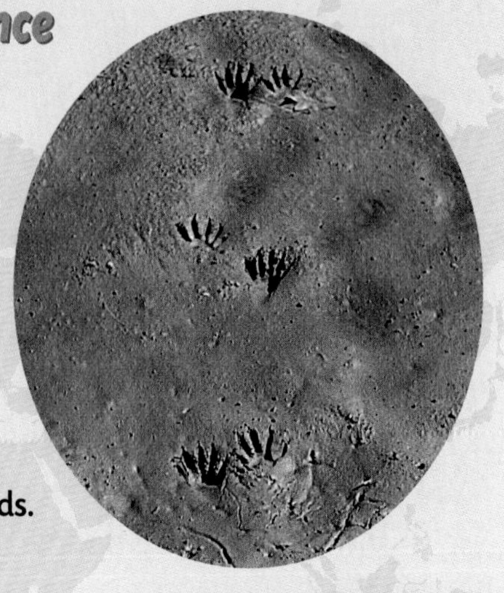

If you take a cast, a solid imprint, of the paw print, you can take it home to study or display. Make a square frame from a milk or beverage carton. Place the frame around the print.

Mix plaster of paris with water and pour the mixture into the print. Let the mixture harden. When you pick up the frame and turn it over, you can show people the tracks you have seen.

Adventures wait around every turn in the Mountains. Autumn leaves falling on the Appalachian Trail might look to hikers like bits of color spinning to earth. Rafters ride the rapids on the Nantahala River past steep cliffs. Skiers glide down snowy mountain trails. Shoppers seek quilts, wood carving, and honey to purchase.

Mountain Snow

It snows more in the Mountains than in the Piedmont and Coastal Plain. Fourth graders in the Mountains spend more time walking and playing in the snow.

In higher elevations, such as near Boone, snow and ice might be on the ground from January until March. That kind of weather is hard on people and roads. Severe cold damages pavement. Too much moisture from melting snow or heavy rains can cause cracks and holes. Mudslides and rockslides create danger for drivers.

Good roads in the Mountains have been the key to the region's growth. Roads gave mountain people more job choices and helped them sell more crops and other products. Roads also brought more people to the region because more people could safely drive there.

Mountain Spaces

For a long time mountain families lived in isolation because of the difficulty of building many roads in the Mountains Region. They farmed in coves between the high ridges of the Appalachian Mountains. A **cove** is a small opening between the ridges. Coves lead to large valleys cut by mountain streams.

Mountain families farmed for a living. They grew almost all of their own food, made their own tools, and "made do," as they called it, with what they had.

Crops grew in the valleys but did not do well on the barren rocky slopes. In some areas erosion had washed away all of the soil. As more people lived in the Mountains,

Crops grow on mountain farms where there is enough room to tend a field. *In what part of the Mountains did farmers find that kind of land?*

The improvement of roads in the Mountains Region changed the region. ***Why?***

land for farming grew scarcer.

In the early 1900s, many mountain families struggled to live well. Some moved to Piedmont towns, such as Greensboro or Gastonia, to work in the mills and factories. Some mountain towns, such as Globe and Upton, lost population.

Mountain Railroads

Railroads brought more people and businesses to the Mountains. Railroad building was hard in the region. Tons of rock had to be blown away by dynamite. If a train could not be built over or around a mountain, a tunnel was dug through the mountain. Many times the railroad companies built bridges for trains to cross valleys.

In the 1880s, the railroad lines reached the region. By 1895, you could travel through the Mountains from Morganton to Murphy (see map, page 193). When the trains put Asheville and other mountain towns in reach, the region was connected to the rest of the state.

Mountain Highways

During the 1930s, the economy all over the United States was poor. That meant many people in North Carolina lost their jobs. Government projects put some of these people back to work and improved North Carolina's transportation system.

During the 1930s, mountain residents worked for the federal government to build the Blue Ridge Parkway. The parkway project changed 470 miles (757 km) of mountain land into a highway. The Blue Ridge Parkway took 50 years to complete. Its final link, the Linn Cove Viaduct, was finished in 1987.

The parkway is one of the longest and most beautiful roads in the United States. You twist, backtrack, and curve from one ridge to another. Every few miles, a spectacular view makes you stop and look down thousands of feet.

Interstate 26 is a north-south route that connects Atlanta and other southeastern United States cities to the Appalachians. Interstate 77, another north-south route, is just east of the region.

In the 1950s and 1960s, the state government paved more roads in the Mountains. In the 1970s and 1980s, Interstate 40 made getting into the region easier. The interstates are important to its economy. Big trucks can easily haul freight in and out.

The good roads changed the way many mountain people lived. Folks in the coves now could drive to work in a nearby town. Younger people often moved from mountain communities into cities. They began doing the same work as North Carolinians were doing all over the state. The people there became less isolated.

Mountain towns became centers of trade and manufacturing, attracting even more residents. Today, more than half the mountain residents live in a town or city. Those living in a rural area can reach a town by car.

Linn Cove Viaduct was the last stretch built in the Blue Ridge parkway. People can see for miles from the road. *How many miles does the parkway cover?*

Asheville is the largest city of the "Land of the Sky," as the Mountains Region is called. *What helped Asheville grow?*

Mountain families now can choose to visit different parts of the Mountains or the Piedmont. These families have choices on where to spend their time and money.

Asheville

Good roads have helped make Asheville important to mountain residents. Asheville is the largest city in the Mountains Region. Large malls, shopping centers, and three large hospitals serve the general area.

Asheville is in many ways "the state capital of the Mountains." Many government agencies in Raleigh have a second office in Asheville to serve the needs of mountain residents. The governor even has a second residence there. There is a campus of the University of North Carolina at Asheville.

LESSON 2 REVIEW

Fact Follow-Up

1. Why do the Smoky Mountains and the Blue Ridge have those names?
2. What are transportation problems in the Mountains that other regions do not have?
3. What is the Blue Ridge Parkway?
4. Why is Asheville called the "state capital of the Mountains"?

Think These Through

5. Is transportation more of a problem to the Mountains than to the Piedmont or Coastal Plain? Explain.
6. Suppose you could choose to live in the Mountains in 1900 or today. Which would you choose? Explain your answer.
7. How has I-40 affected the Mountains?

LESSON 3 The Economy of the Mountains

LESSON PREVIEW

Key Ideas

- Mountain crafts are an important part of the economy.
- The chief agricultural products are poultry and dairy cattle, apples, and Christmas trees.
- Mountain residents work in the same jobs as all North Carolinians. The manufacturing of furniture and other wood products is important.
- Tourism is a vital part of the mountain economy.

Mountain artists display wood carvings, quilts, ceramic bowls, and tiny cloth dolls at the Southern Highland Folk Art Center near Asheville. These craftspeople use new and old tools to create art.

Woodworkers use electric band saws and drills and even lasers to cut wood. Yet the old ways of creating useful and decorative items still exist. Many carvers use hand tools to whittle small pieces of wood. Basket makers weave by hand. Quilters sew delicate patterns with needle and thread.

Mountain Workers Adapt to Change

The residents of the Mountains Region treasure their past. Preserving the old ways keeps alive the memories of how chores were done and how people entertained themselves. Today, residents of the region have adapted to newer ways of getting things done.

They also have taken the new jobs that are available in high-tech industries. Yet some people work part-time at regular jobs and part-time in the fields. Residents who have enough land still like to farm it.

Some people still operate small farms for crop production. They grow vegetables, fruit, or Christmas trees. Some raise dairy cattle or

Craftspeople make corn husk dolls, carve chairs, and sew quilts at the Southern Highland Folk Art Center. *What types of mountain crafts can you do?*

Livestock includes cattle, hogs, and poultry. Dairy and beef cattle are raised in the higher mountains. *Where in the Mountains is poultry (above) part of the economy?*

poultry. Most agriculture in the region takes full-time attention.

Raising Livestock

Mountain farmers earn money mainly in livestock. Beef cattle, dairy cattle, and poultry are the most important agricultural products of mountain counties. Farmers in Wilkes County and Alexander County raise both poultry and cattle. In the 1990s, Wilkes became one of North Carolina's top ten counties in farm income. Livestock production earned most of this money.

Cattle farms cover valleys in Ashe and Alleghany Counties. Farmers in Haywood and Buncombe Counties also raise thousands of head of cattle.

Growing Crops

Agriculture in western North Carolina varies. Many farmers raise corn, tobacco, and apples. Fruit, vegetables, and trees also grow well there.

Farmers in Henderson County raised more than 200,000 bushels of corn each year during the 1990s. Madison County is the only mountain county that annually produced more than 4 million pounds (1.8 million kg) of tobacco in the 1990s.

Apple orchards produce fruit for the nation. North Carolina grows more apples than 43 other states. Orchards produce more than 300 million pounds (135 million kg) of apples a year. Sales earn more than $20 million for North Carolina farmers.

Burke, Lincoln, and Henderson Counties are leading apple producers. Hendersonville hosts the annual Apple Festival over Labor Day weekend.

Roadside stands on mountain roads sell all sorts of

What would YOU do?

You must make a quilt that reflects North Carolina's heritage. You can use only one pattern.

A traditional pattern is bear claw. The pattern doesn't look like a real bear claw but represents it. Log cabin is another traditional pattern. Wedding ring, with large circles, symbolizes a ring.

How would you choose a pattern? Would you think of those shapes that are easy to make? Would you try animals, plants, or places?

apple products. Shoppers can buy North Carolina apple cider, apple pies, apple jelly and butter, and bags of apples. These roadside stands also sell items that families make by hand. Hooked rugs and such wooden toys as gee-haw whimmydiddles are popular items.

Forests Provide Jobs

Forests contribute in important ways to the economy of the mountains. Logging companies provide many jobs in Polk and other mountain counties. Workers cut down trees and haul timber.

Mountain tree farmers grow many of the Christmas trees you see on sale at holiday lots in Piedmont and Coastal Plain cities. North Carolina trees, particularly the Fraser fir, are popular Christmas trees throughout the East Coast of the United States. Fraser firs are dark green trees with short needles. Several times in the last few years the president and the first lady have decorated a North Carolina fir in the White House at Christmas.

Other trees become paper at mills in Haywood and Buncombe Counties. Mills make all sorts of paper products, including towels, stationery, sheets for computer printers,

GAMES People Play

Gee-haw whimmydiddle
If you have never played with a gee-haw whimmydiddle, it works this way. A mountain craftsperson carves notches into the side of an oak stick. A small piece of wood is nailed like a propeller at the end of the stick. You hold the gee-haw whimmydiddle in one hand and rub a second stick against the notches. What do you think happens? If you move the second stick fast enough, the propeller turns.

Gee-haw whimmydiddle

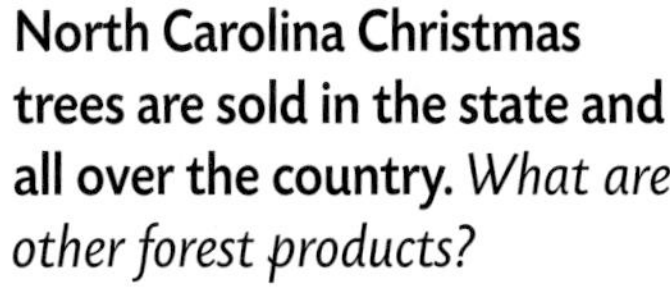

North Carolina Christmas trees are sold in the state and all over the country. *What are other forest products?*

and newsprint. A mill in Brevard manufactures the paper used in cigarettes.

Nearly every mountain county includes a factory that manufactures wood products. Furniture is a leading industry in Caldwell, Alexander, Rutherford, Mitchell, and Burke Counties. Furniture crafters turn trees into furniture throughout the Mountains.

Companies use timber to make paneling, beams, and boards for the building industry. Other wood products include sawdust and wood chips for plant mulch, and rosin and varnish to protect furniture. Turpentine, dyes, paint, and other chemicals also are made from trees.

Mountain Industries

The resources of the Mountains support the economy in other ways. Feldspar, mica, kaolin (white clay), and quartz are mined in the region.

Kaolin is used to make china. Feldspar is needed to manufacture electrical products. Mica is used in insulation. Granite, marble, limestone, and talc are dug from mountain quarries and used in construction.

The Canton Paper Mill in Haywood County uses timber to make paper. *What other jobs are related to mountain forests?*

Technology in industry has spread to the Mountains. *Why do you think a company would choose to open a factory in the region?*

Years ago, the Mountains lagged behind the rest of the state in other industries. Today, many industrial products are produced in the Mountains: textiles, transportation goods, food products, plastics, electronics, and telecommunications equipment.

Improving the Economy of the Mountains

For most of this century, mountain people made less money than any other North Carolinians. The United States government started programs in the 1960s to destroy poverty. Counties throughout the Appalachian Mountains, including those in North Carolina, were targeted for special attention.

A regional planning commission decided that the key to improving the mountain economy was to construct more roads. Roads from Waynesville through Murphy and from Asheville to Johnson City, Tennessee, were built. The completion of I-26 south of Asheville and roads from the southwest mountains leading to Georgia attracted more visitors.

Appalachian State University in Boone attracts many students. *What service jobs are found in colleges and universities?*

Service Industries

Service industries have become important to the economy of the Mountains. Service industries include tourism, education, medicine, and sales. Teachers work in a service job. So do doctors and sales clerks.

Appalachian State University in Boone is the largest university in the region. Other major colleges are the University of North Carolina at Asheville and Western Carolina University at Cullowhee.

Mountain residents increasingly make a living in service industries, especially by serving the needs of visitors through tourism. Tourism is the fastest growing part of service industries in the Mountains. Local families sometimes open parts of their homes to visitors. At bed-and-breakfasts, as they are called, guests sleep in family bedrooms. In the morning the hosts serve breakfast.

Mountain residents run hotels, some of which date back more than a century. The Nu-Ray Inn in Burnsville is a large white hotel built around the original log cabin constructed in the 1800s.

Mountain families also work at area landmarks, such as the Great Smoky Mountains National Park, the Biltmore House, and the area's ski resorts.

Tourism not only helps employ mountain people, it also helps them preserve their culture.

LESSON 3 REVIEW

Fact Follow-Up

1. What are the major agricultural products of the Mountains?
2. How are trees used in the Mountains?
3. List mineral resources found in the region. How are they used?
4. What service industries are located in the region?

Think These Through

5. If you could choose to live anywhere in the Mountains, where would you live? Why?
6. If you could choose to do any job in the region, what would it be? How would you prepare yourself to do that job?

LESSON 4
Mountain Culture

Music marks the culture of the Mountains. People all over the world recognize the sounds of the North Carolina mountains. The songs tell stories from the region about love and hate, work and disasters. The Smithsonian Institution has recorded mountain music.

LESSON PREVIEW

Key Ideas

- Music played on the fiddle, banjo, and dulcimer is a key element of mountain culture.
- Dancing, storytelling, and food are other important parts of mountain culture.
- The mountains themselves are the special attraction of the region.

Key Terms

reels, ballads, dulcimer, old-time music, bluegrass music, country music, clogging, tall tales, heritage, white water

Mountain Music

Mountain music goes back to the first settlers. Native Americans played reed flutes and drums.

European pioneers in the Mountains were Scotch-Irish who brought with them the stories and songs of their native lands. They also brought fiddles, the common word for violins. People who could play the fiddle were honored in the Mountains. Neighbors liked to get together to sing and dance. Music often provided the only entertainment.

The first songs were reels or ballads. **Reels** were lively tunes played for dancing. **Ballads** told stories, often sad ones, of people from the past. Ballads could also be love stories. Ballads were accompanied by a **dulcimer**, a stringed instrument held in the lap.

Over time, mountain music developed into three forms: **old-time music**, the original kind played with dulcimers and fiddles; **bluegrass music**, which used the banjo as the key instrument; and **country music**, which included a guitar.

A famous North Carolinian performs all three forms of mountain music. Doc Watson, from Deep Gap in Watauga County, has sung and played the traditional songs of North Carolina all over the world.

Bluegrass musicians start playing at a young age. *What instruments do you see?*

Dancing to mountain music is fun. Clog dancers need special shoes and lots of energy. It's a fast-paced, joyful way to dance. *Have you ever tried it?*

Hundreds of other mountain people also play and perform. They appear throughout the region and at fiddlers' festivals each year. At fiddlers' festivals, groups compete for prizes and trophies. The fiddlers' festival at Union Grove in Iredell County has been held every Memorial Day since 1924.

Classical music also fills the Mountains each summer. Brevard in Transylvania County holds one of the most famous festivals of classical music in the country. There you can hear orchestras perform.

Mountain Dancing

If there is music, there must be dancing. Folk dancing, square dancing, and clogging call for strong legs and lots of fiddle music. Square dancing has formal patterns which a "caller" sings out over the music. The four or eight people in the circle make the patterns in rhythm to the music.

Folk dancing might include some patterns from square dancing. You do not need a partner to folk dance. Some forms of folk dance have existed since the first settlers arrived.

Clogging has definite patterns and partners, but it also has a particular rhythmic stomp by the dancers. Their feet make music just like the fiddles and banjos.

WORD ORIGINS

Clogging doesn't refer to stopping up drains. Although the word means to block something, it is also the name of a dance. The name comes from the Middle English word for clog, which means "block of wood." The shoes once worn for the dance were wooden clogs that made thunderous sounds on wooden planks. Today, cloggers use steel taps on their shoes.

Telling Stories

When people aren't playing music or dancing, they might be over in the corner listening to stories. Jackie Torrence of Boone tells tall tales. **Tall tales** involve characters who can do the impossible. These stories ask you to give up your doubts and enjoy the story.

The most famous tall tales are the Jack stories, which mountain people have told for centuries. You have probably heard "Jack and the Beanstalk."

Other stories are told by the Cherokee, such as the legend of young lovers at Blowing Rock. Mountain people

believe that these stories should have a moral, or a lesson, that people should learn in the end.

Blowing Rock gets its name from a legend. Legends are memories of stories that get told and retold. *Do you know the Blowing Rock legend or other mountain legends?*

Food

The most famous restaurants and inns in the Mountains serve their meals family style. That means everyone sits around a table and the food is passed around, just like at home. There is plenty to eat.

Large bowls of mashed potatoes, sweet potatoes, corn, and beans are placed on the table. Fried chicken and biscuits with honey might be served. Usually cakes and pies are for dessert. No one has to leave the table feeling hungry.

Places of Heritage

The true heritage of the region rests upon its rocky slopes. **Heritage** is a gift from the past in the form of memories, stories, songs, and traditions.

The slopes and peaks of the mountains are a treasure to many people. From the peak of Mount Mitchell, visitors

White water! Getting wet is part of the fun as rafters row down the roaring Nantahala River. *What special equipment do rafters wear?*

can see the Great Smoky Mountains in North Carolina and Tennessee. Nearby Grandfather Mountain stands nearly as tall. This mountain is famous for its animals, vegetation, and the mile-high swinging bridge.

The most visited place in the Mountains, the Great Smoky Mountains National Park, attracts millions of people each year. Hiking is popular there. Linville Gorge, one of the rockiest places in the state, also attracts hikers.

Tourists visit the Nantahala National Forest in the westernmost part of the state. There they go white-water rafting on the Nantahala River. **White water** is the part of a stream that goes through rocks. The water bounces into so many bubbles that the sunlight makes it appear white. Sliding Rock attracts thrill seekers willing to slide down slick rock into a cold pool of water. Rafters and canoeists go down the New River in Ashe County.

North Carolina's Mountains burst with adventure and beauty. Its people are energetic and friendly. The people of North Carolina are the most important resource of the state.

LESSON 4 REVIEW

Fact Follow-Up

1. What are some varieties of mountain music? What instruments are used in each?
2. What are tall tales?
3. What are some important tourist attractions in the Mountains Region?

Think These Through

4. Why do you think the Mountains developed a special kind of music while the Piedmont did not?
5. Are tall tales and folktales found only in the Mountains? Explain your answer.
6. Why do the writers of the book say that "the true heritage of the region rests upon its rocky slopes"? Do you agree with this statement? Why?

The Five Themes of Geography: Place

Using Geography's Themes: Human Characteristics of Place

Earlier, when you studied about North Carolina's regions in Chapter 3, you learned about the **physical characteristics of place**. You will recall some of those physical characteristics: landforms, bodies of water, climate, soils, and natural resources. Turn to the chapter and review what you learned about the physical characteristics of place.

All places where people live have **human** characteristics as well. **Human characteristics of place** are those characteristics that people and their activities bring to a place.

Look at the picture of someone skiing. The ski slope has been built on a mountainside (a physical characteristic), but skiing and the ski tows are human characteristics—placed on the mountain by people.

Since human characteristics of a place are created by people, then all the things people do and build are part of the human characteristics of places where they live.

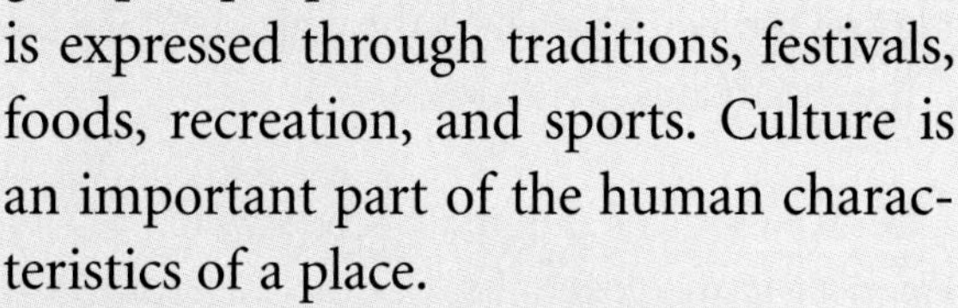

Music and other forms of entertainment are part of a place's culture. Culture is the ways of life of a group of people. Culture is expressed through traditions, festivals, foods, recreation, and sports. Culture is an important part of the human characteristics of a place.

Other cultural characteristics are language, religion, and education. People's homes and clothing can display other signs of tradition.

Review Chapter 13 and list as many human characteristics of place in the Mountains as you can. When you have finished, compare your list with a classmate's.

Can you group any of the human characteristics of the Mountains under titles or categories? For example, what might be grouped under the title "Music"? What other categories can you form? Make a web chart like the one to the left. Show categories of human characteristics and list examples.

The Mountains, Human Characteristics

Human Characteristics of the Mountains
Dance
Festivals
Buildings
Music
Sports
Crafts

Chapter 13 Review

LESSONS LEARNED

LESSON 1 The Mountains Region was first settled by Native Americans, and is still represented by the Cherokee. Scotch-Irish were the first European settlers. Railroad construction brought more people to the region. Today, new residents are attracted to the mountains for their beauty and resources.

LESSON 2 Mountains define the region. Mountain names often describe their appearances. The Mountains Region changed with railroads and improved roads, both attracting more settlers. Asheville is the major city of the mountains.

LESSON 3 The mountain economy is similar to the economies of other regions in manufacturing and service jobs, including tourism. Crafts and livestock raising are unique parts of the economy. Other crops include apples and Christmas trees.

LESSON 4 The culture of the Mountains is expressed through music, dancing, and tall tales. Recreation and heritage are offered by the mountains themselves.

TIME FOR TERMS

Trail of Tears
cove
ballads
old-time music
country music
religious retreat
reels
dulcimer
bluegrass music
clogging
tall tales
white water
heritage

FACT FOLLOW-UP

1. How has improved transportation changed the Mountains?
2. What natural resources of the region have encouraged the development of industry?
3. What are some special challenges faced by people living in the region?
4. How are agricultural products of the Mountains like and different from those of the Coastal Plain?
5. How are service industries of the Mountains like and different from those of the Piedmont?
6. Compare the diversity of population in the Mountains in 1900 with its diversity today.
7. How have tourist attractions in the Mountains changed over the years?
8. What are the physical characteristics of place in the Mountains?
9. What are the human characteristics of place in the Mountains?
10. How does the Mountains Region show the geographic theme of Human-Environmental Interaction?

THINK THESE THROUGH

11. Is the Mountains Region more like the Piedmont or more like the Coastal Plain? Explain your answer.

12. What do you think is the greatest challenge facing the Mountains? Explain why.
13. Suppose you wanted to start your own business in the Mountains. What business would you choose? Explain why.
14. What do you think is the greatest strength of the Mountains? Explain why.
15. Has isolation been more important for the Mountains or for the Coastal Plain? Explain your answer.

SHARPENING SKILLS

16. Make a web chart showing the human characteristics of the Piedmont or Coastal Plain Region.
17. Make a web chart showing the human characteristics of the county where you live.
18. Is it possible to describe the human characteristics of a place as large and diverse as North Carolina? Why or why not?
19. Why are both physical and human characteristics important in describing the Mountains? Explain your answer.

PLACE LOCATION

Use the letters on the map to locate and name the following places:

20. site of the Grove Park Inn and Biltmore House, the chief city of the mountains.
21. site of Ocanaluftee Village.
22. site of Appalachian State University.
23. site of Western Carolina University.
24. site of apple orchards, home of the Apple Festival.
25. site of white-water rafting and Sliding Rock.

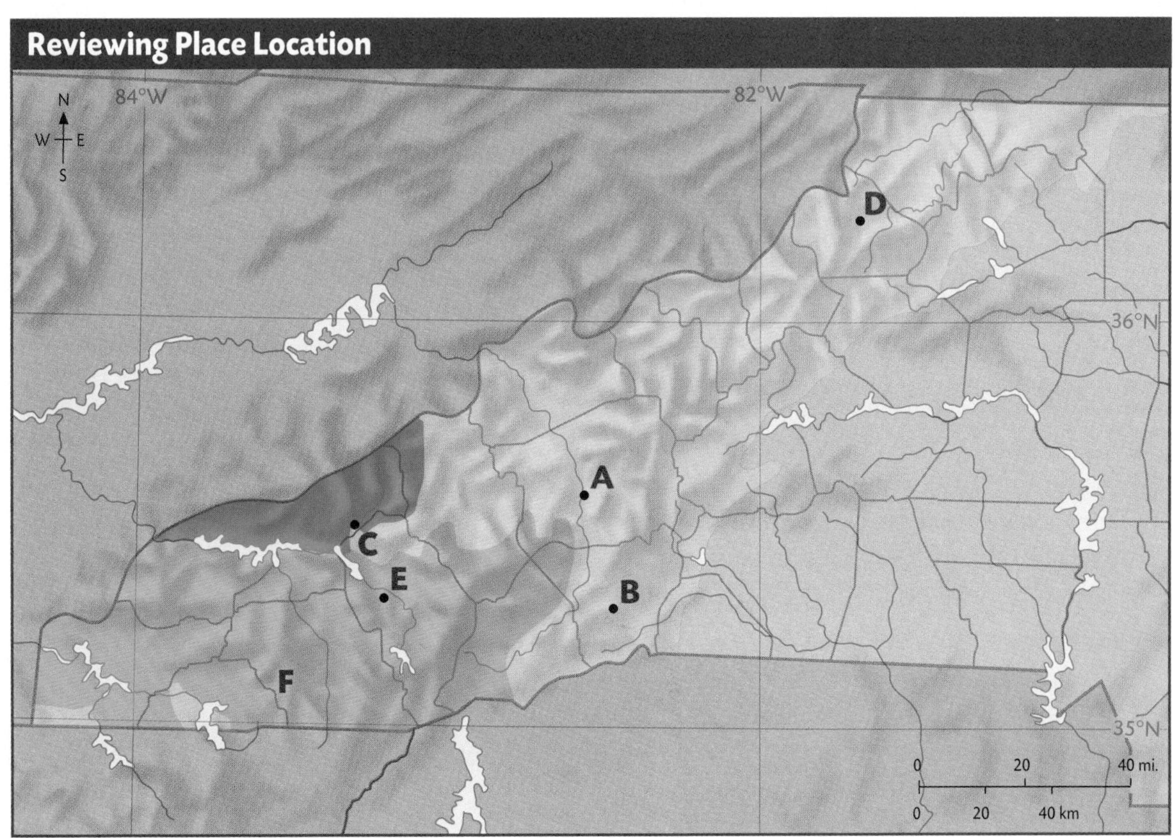

North Carolina Today and Tomorrow

As one of 50 states in the United States, North Carolina is governed by the United States Constitution. The state follows the Constitution in its plan of government and protects the rights of its citizens.

The freedom Americans enjoy gives them the opportunities to prepare for the future. North Carolina's future shines brightly because of its natural resources, technology, education, and people.

UNIT PREVIEW

CHAPTER 14
Government of the United States
Our nation's symbols show our nation's ideals. The United States Constitution is our plan of government.

CHAPTER 15
How North Carolina Governs
The government of North Carolina, like the federal government, contains three branches. State and local governments serve the people of North Carolina.

CHAPTER 16
North Carolina in the Twenty-First Century
North Carolina will continue to lead in education, research, and technology. Protecting the environment will be an important part of the future.

North Carolina students at the state capitol in Raleigh.

CHAPTER 14

Government of the United States

John Paul Jones

More than 200 years ago, a United States naval vessel sailed into a French harbor. John Paul Jones, a hero of the American Revolution, was in command. A bright, new flag—red, white, and blue—flew from his ship, the U.S.S. Constitution.

When the French caught sight of the flag, their sailors fired a cannon salute. This was the first time that our nation's flag was formally recognized by another country.

U.S.S. Constitution *in battle.*

CHAPTER PREVIEW

LESSON 1
Our Nation's Symbols
The flag, the "Star-Spangled Banner," and other symbols represent the people, land, and principles of the United States.

LESSON 2
The Constitution Expresses National Ideals
The Constitution is our plan of government.

LESSON 3
Limiting Power of the National Government
The Bill of Rights and the three branches of government limit the power of government.

Star-Spangled Banner

by Francis Scott Key

Oh! say, can you see, by the dawn's early light,
What so proudly we hailed at the twilight's last
gleaming?
Whose broad stripes and bright stars, through
the perilous fight,
O'er the ramparts we watched were so gallantly
streaming?
And the rockets red glare, the bombs bursting
in air,
Gave proof through the night that our flag was
still there.
Oh! say, does that star-spangled banner yet
wave
O'er the land of the free and the home of the
brave?

Pledge of Allegiance

I pledge allegiance
to the flag of the United
States of America and to
the republic for which
it stands, one nation,
under God, indivisible,
with liberty and justice
for all.

Baseball and North Carolina

North Carolina has played an important part in baseball, our national pastime. Captured Union soldiers played it at the Confederate prison in Salisbury during the Civil War (above). State universities organized teams after the war. Several cities now have minor-league baseball teams, including Durham, Asheville, Kinston, Raleigh, Goldsboro, and Winston-Salem. Many North Carolinians played in the Major League. Some are members of the Baseball Hall of Fame. Enos "Country" Slaughter of Roxboro played for the St. Louis Cardinals. Gaylord Perry of Williamston won 314 games and won the Cy Young Award twice.

Our Nation's Symbols

LESSON PREVIEW

Key Ideas

- The flag is a symbol of the land, people, government, and ideals of the United States.
- Other symbols of our country are our national anthem, "Uncle Sam," and the eagle.
- The ideals of our country were first written down in the Declaration of Independence.
- After independence, leaders wrote the Constitution to create a fair government that guaranteed freedom.

Key Terms

Stars and Stripes, "Star-Spangled Banner," symbols, democracy, Declaration of Independence, Constitution

Can you imagine the excitement that John Paul Jones and his men felt when they heard the French cannon fire? The United States had begun to fight for independence from England two years earlier. The battle for independence was not over, but already one of Europe's most powerful nations had recognized the United States as an independent nation.

The Flag

The most popular name for our flag is the **Stars and Stripes**. The 50 white stars represent the states of the United States. The 13 stripes stand for the original American colonies.

The Stars and Stripes symbolizes the land, the people, the government, and the ideals of the United States. This is why the flag is honored wherever it is shown.

On special occasions people rise to pledge allegiance—or loyalty—to our flag and nation. We also sing a song about our country and our flag called the "**Star-Spangled Banner**." The song is our national anthem. The words, written by Francis Scott Key, represent our love for the United States of America.

The Importance of Symbols

We cannot touch a government the way we can touch a flower or an animal. Symbols represent the United States. Our national anthem and our flag are important symbols of our country.

Symbols represent or stand for other things. A school's mascot is a symbol of the school.

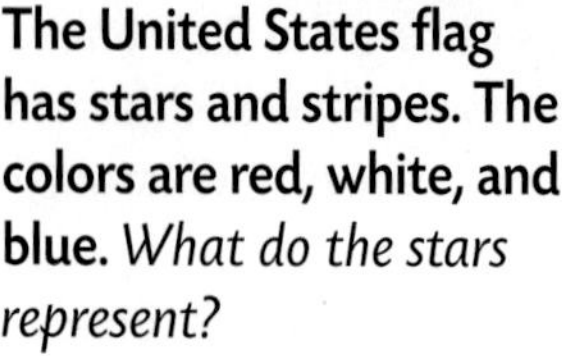

The United States flag has stars and stripes. The colors are red, white, and blue. *What do the stars represent?*

The American bald eagle stands for the United States. The eagle is a strong and brave bird. *Why do you think we use it for our symbol?*

Other Symbols of the Country

Have you ever heard of "Uncle Sam"? He is not a real person. On posters he is the man dressed up in red, white, and blue, usually with a white beard and a top hat. He represents the United States, also.

The eagle in full flight with wings spread and talons sharp and gleaming is also a symbol of the United States. The eagle, the national bird, represents our nation's spirit.

What Our Symbols Mean

We show respect for our nation's symbols. We stand to say the Pledge of Allegiance with our hands over our hearts. We stand to sing our national anthem. We stand when the flag goes by in a parade. Many people salute the flag. These signs of respect are not for the cloth in a flag flying from a pole. These signs of respect are for our country.

Our national symbols represent the land of the United States. Like most Americans, North Carolina residents think of themselves as citizens of their state and nation.

The flag and other symbols help us remember the sacrifices made by Americans who protect our country. Our symbols stand for people who died to keep our country free. They also represent people who sacrificed to protect the country from threats to freedom at home.

This is a statue honoring U.S. Marines who fought during World War II. They raised the flag after a battle at Iwo Jima, an island in the Pacific Ocean. *Why is the flag an important part of this statue?*

Our national symbols represent freedom. Our freedoms are admired by people outside the United States. Many people in countries all over the world do not have the freedoms that citizens in the United States enjoy. Yet many want these freedoms. They want the freedom to choose the kind of work they want to do. They want freedom to worship as they please. They want the freedom to speak freely.

The flag, the anthem, and the eagle stand for important ideals that go back to the founding of our nation. We read about those ideals in the Declaration of Independence.

WORD ORIGINS

We live in a **democracy**. We are a nation of people who rule themselves. Democracy means rule by the people. The word comes from the Greek words ***demos***, which means "people," and ***kratein***, which means "to rule."

The Declaration of Independence

The **Declaration of Independence** is a document that announced the colonies independent of England. In the declaration, Thomas Jefferson described the ideals that would guide the new country.

He wrote that the purpose of government is to make sure citizens had the rights of "life, liberty, and the pursuit of happiness." To make certain citizens have these rights, a government has only powers that are given to it by the people.

Our nation still holds firm to these beliefs. They are written into our **Constitution**, the plan for the government of the United States.

Writing the Constitution

After winning independence, the United States wanted a government strong enough to hold the states together. The people also wanted to limit the powers of that government so that freedom would be preserved.

In the spring of 1787, 55 delegates met in Philadelphia to write a document that reached both goals. Under the leadership of James Madison and George Washington of Virginia, and Benjamin Franklin of Pennsylvania, the delegates wrote the Constitution.

***Signing of the Declaration of Independence* shows representatives of the colonies declaring freedom from England.** *What else does the declaration mean to our country?*

LIVING IN A NATIONAL PARK

Touring with a Park Ranger

If you and your family wanted an outdoor vacation, you might go to the Great Smoky Mountains National Park or the Cape Hatteras National Seashore. Park rangers work for the United States government to help visitors learn about national parks.

Denise, a park ranger in the Great Smoky Mountains National Park, waits to take visitors on walks. She will help them identify the 120 species of native trees. She will warn not to feed the bears. Deer and raccoons wander through the campsites looking for leftover food.

Denise will tell you to pack up food carefully. The rangers want the animals to stay wild in the park.

Some scientists study wolves in the Great Smoky Mountains National Park. A few can make wolf calls. When the wolves hear them, they call back. You will not be able to see the wolves, but you will hear their "singing" deep in the forests.

Sam, a park ranger at the Cape Hatteras National Seashore (left), also takes visitors on walks. He shows them shells and dunes. He helps visitors understand how wind and waves change the islands.

People come to study at national parks and seashores. Scientists study plants and animals and how erosion changes islands.

At the Cape Hatteras National Seashore, scientists study the movement of the tide and how it affects the beaches and sounds of the Outer Banks. They learn how islands slowly move toward land as sand gets washed off the beach and builds up in the sound.

The writers wanted a fair government that guaranteed freedom. The Constitution of the United States contains those guarantees.

LESSON  REVIEW

Fact Follow-Up

1. Name some of our nation's symbols.
2. For what does our national flag stand?
3. What is the meaning of "democracy"?
4. What is the Declaration of Independence?

Think These Through

5. What do you think is our most important national symbol? Explain why.
6. What is the importance of the Declaration of Independence? How is it a symbol?
7. How do you show respect for our country?

LESSON 2

The Constitution Expresses National Ideals

Alexander Hamilton and Thomas Jefferson were as different as two men could be. Jefferson owned a plantation in Virginia. Hamilton was a merchant in New York.

Hamilton and Jefferson argued about who should vote. Jefferson believed that everyone should have a chance to choose their leaders. Hamilton wanted only the educated and wealthy to make those choices.

Despite those arguments, both wanted the new government of the United States to work. They both believed that the nation's government should be strong. Both also believed that the new constitution must protect the people's freedom.

Jefferson and Hamilton argued furiously over many issues. They also shared beliefs that kept them working together for a good government.

LESSON PREVIEW

Key Ideas

- The Constitution is our plan of government.
- The Constitution established a republic.

Key Terms

republic, federal system

The writing of the United States Constitution took time. Representatives from the new states argued about some details. *What shared beliefs did they agree upon?*

Three Principles of the Constitution

Our Constitution has withstood wars and economic depressions. Now more than 200 years old, the Constitution is still going strong.

The United States Constitution is a good plan for government. It is built on three key principles:

We the People of the United States, in
insure domestic Tranquility, provide for the common defence, promote the general Welf
and our Posterity, do ordain and establish this Constitution for the United States of Am

Article. I

Section. 1. All legislative Powers herein granted shall be vested in a Congress of the Un
of Representatives.

Section. 2. The House of Representatives shall be composed of Members chosen every sec
in each State shall have Qualifications requisite for Electors of the most numerous Branch of the St

No Person shall be a Representative who shall not have attained to the Age of twenty fi
and who shall not, when elected, be an Inhabitant of that State in which he shall be chosen.

This is how the beginning of the Constitution reads. Notice how large the first three words are. *Why are those words important?*

First, the government of the United States is responsible to the people. The government has only the power that the people choose to give it. The first three words of the Constitution describe the source of the government's power: "We the People." Because the people rule, the government is a democracy.

Second, the government of the United States is a **republic**. That means citizens make laws by electing leaders.

Third, the United States has a **federal system** of

EYEWITNESS TO HISTORY

Voting in North Carolina

The people of the United States decide who will be their leaders by voting. There was a time when not all adult North Carolinians could vote. Amendments were added to the Constitution of the United States to give more citizens the right to vote. North Carolina's Constitution of 1868 guaranteed that all men had the right to vote. The Fifteenth Amendment to the Constitution of the United States, adopted in 1870, gave voting rights to all African American men.

Extending the Right to Vote: Time Line of Key Events

1870
The Fifteenth Amendment gives voting rights to African American men.

1898
In the Wilmington Race Riot, a mob of whites burns the Daily Record newspaper office owned by an African American.

1860 | 1870 | 1880 | 1890 | 1900 | 1910

1868
North Carolina's Constitution guarantees the voting rights of all men, regardless of race or how much property they own.

By 1880s
Many state laws keep African American men from voting.

1890s
Gertrude Weil and the North Carolina Equal Suffrage Association begin working for the voting rights of women.

government. This means the national government shares power with the states. The United States was begun, the Constitution writers remind us, "to form a more perfect Union."

LESSON 2 REVIEW

Fact Follow-Up

1. What are the three key principles of the United States Constitution?
2. What does the term "a government of limited powers" mean?
3. What is a "federal system" of government?

Think These Through

4. Why do we have a federal system of government in the United States?
5. Do you think eighteen-year-olds should have the right to vote? Why?
6. Why is the right to vote important to citizens?

By the 1880s, North Carolina and other states were passing laws and finding ways to make it impossible for African Americans to vote. In the Wilmington Race Riot in 1898, a mob burned the Wilmington *Daily Record* newspaper office owned by an African American. Between 11 and 30 African Americans were killed in the riot.

The North Carolina Equal Suffrage Association began working for women's right to vote in the 1890s. The Nineteenth Amendment giving women the right to vote became law in August 1920.

1971
The Twenty-sixth Amendment guarantees voting rights to United States citizens over the age of 18.

1920	1930	1940	1950	1960	1970

1920
The Nineteenth Amendment passes, giving voting rights to women.

1964
The Twenty-fourth Amendment passes, banning poll taxes, which had prevented many African Americans from voting.

1965
The Voting Rights Act of 1965 outlaws state laws that kept African Americans from voting.

Limiting Power of the National Government

LESSON PREVIEW

Key Ideas

- The Constitution preserves individual freedoms by limiting the power of government.
- The Constitution established three branches of government to limit the power of each.
- The Constitution established a federal system of government.

Key Terms

Bill of Rights, checks and balances, legislative branch, Congress, judicial branch, Supreme Court, president, executive branch, federal government, state government

What would YOU do?

Taxes pay for services. The federal government takes taxes from people's income to pay for the military, the government, and parks. People grumble about taxes.

If you wanted to be taxed less, what services would you do without? Should we do without national parks? Do we need to pay for the military?

Would you give up representation to save tax dollars?

At first, some states would not accept the Constitution. North Carolina was one of those states. After Congress passed a Bill of Rights, North Carolina voted for the Constitution. The **Bill of Rights** best expresses how the people's rights are protected.

The Bill of Rights

The Bill of Rights keeps the government from taking away the freedom of individuals. The Bill of Rights is written into the first ten amendments to the Constitution. Here is what they say:

The government cannot tell someone how or how not to worship God. The government cannot stop people from saying or printing what they think. Anyone can criticize the government. A group can gather peacefully to debate what the government does. All citizens have the right to own guns.

No soldier or police officer can enter your house or be housed on your property without your permission. If police do enter, they must have an order from a judge.

No one has to go to trial just because one person accuses another of a crime. A grand jury has to meet and decide if that person should be tried.

No one tried and found not guilty can be tried again for the same crime. A jury chosen from the people decides cases before a judge. No one shall be beaten to get a confession. Guilty people must not be punished in a cruel way.

Rights not listed in the Constitution are kept by the people. Powers not given the national government nor forbidden by the states are held by the people.

The Bill of Rights limits the power of government by strengthening the rights of individuals. The majority rules in deciding issues of government through voting. But the Constitution makes sure that individual rights are not taken away.

The men who wrote the Constitution wanted to make sure that no one person, state, or part of government could have all the power. Congress established three branches of government to help keep any person or group from becoming too powerful.

GAMES **People Play**

Memory Games Schoolchildren play memory games that help them remember facts. Some play a game where they are asked to name all the states of the nation. In North Carolina students can play a memory game where they name all 100 counties. Another game is a Geography Bee. Students are asked to remember facts about the landforms and people of the state. What games do you play in your school?

Three Branches of Government

The writers of the Constitution said that its purpose was to "secure the blessings of liberty to ourselves." The three branches of government were designed to help guarantee liberty.

The Constitution keeps a single branch of government from having more power than the other branches. Through a system of **checks and balances** the three branches of government have checks over the other two. The chart on page 330 shows how one branch can check, or stop, the actions of another branch.

The three branches are called the legislative, the executive, and the judicial.

The heads of each branch are located in Washington, D.C. The abbreviation *D.C.* stands for the District of Columbia, a special city set aside to be the headquarters of the national government. *Why were three branches established?*

Branches of the United States Government

	Legislative	**Executive**	**Judicial**
Building	U.S. Capitol	White House	Supreme Court
Purpose	**Make laws**	**Carry out laws**	**Interpret laws**
Leaders	**535 members (435 in the House; 100 in the Senate) of Congress**	**President**	**9 justices of the Supreme Court**

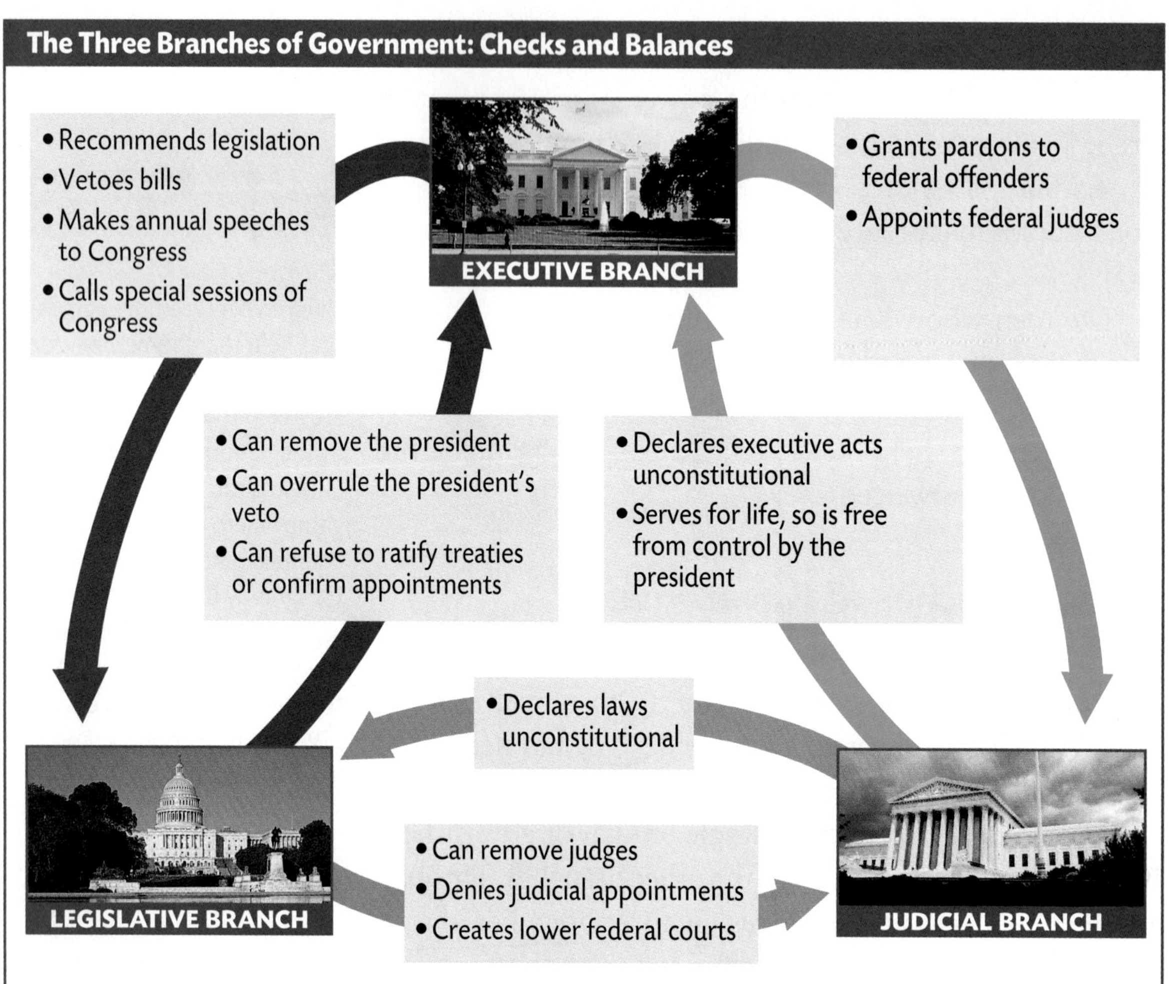

The chart above shows how the system of checks and balances works among the three branches of government. *Why did the writers of the Constitution try to balance power among the branches?*

Legislative Branch The Capitol Building houses the **legislative branch** of government. Legislative means law-making.

Congress is our name for the legislative branch of government. There are two houses in Congress, the Senate and the House of Representatives.

Each state elects two senators. A senator serves six years. Each state elects people to the House of Representatives based on the size of the state's population. There are 100 senators and 435 representatives in the House.

Congress passes laws for the nation. Some laws say how much money will go to the federal government. Congress decides how that money will be spent.

Judicial Branch The Supreme Court Building houses the **judicial branch**. Judicial means judging. This branch judges whether laws made by Congress are fair and follow the Constitution.

If someone has a disagreement about a law or believes a law is unfair, he or she may take that argument to court. If the law is a federal law or the disagreement is between states, the United States **Supreme Court** will hear the argument.

Since the Supreme Court cannot try every argument, there are 13 federal courts of appeal. There are 95 federal district courts, including three in North Carolina. The judges of all these courts are appointed by the president. All must be approved by the Senate.

Executive Branch The White House, on Washington's Pennsylvania Avenue, is where the **president** lives. The president heads the executive branch of the government. The **executive branch** carries out the laws passed by Congress.

The president is the commander in chief of the armed forces. The president represents our country when visiting other countries. The president recommends new laws to Congress.

The vice president replaces the president if the president dies or cannot perform official duties. The vice president

At the opening session of Congress, new members are sworn into office. *In which branch of government is Congress?*

The federal courthouse in Charlotte (top) and the post office in Whittier (bottom) show the federal government at work in North Carolina. *Why do you think state governments do not run post offices?*

also votes in the Senate in order to break a tie vote to pass a bill into law.

The Federal System

The Constitution established a federal system of government in the United States. The **federal government** makes laws for the entire nation. Each state has a **state government** that makes state laws. The federal and state governments share the power to govern the people.

In every state there are county, city, and village governments. These local governments also have a direct effect on the people they govern. They provide services, such as police protection and garbage collection, that state and federal governments cannot provide without spending too much money.

The federal government provides for the defense of the country. It makes treaties with other countries and controls trade. It decides how foreigners can become citizens. The federal government also sets up post offices and courts. It prints and coins money.

State governments share the powers of collecting taxes, borrowing money, and providing for the welfare and safety of citizens. State powers also are those not given to the national government. You will learn how North Carolina carries out those powers in the next chapter.

LESSON 3 REVIEW

Fact Follow-Up

1. What are some of the rights guaranteed by the Bill of Rights?
2. What is the system of checks and balances?
3. What are the jobs of the legislative branch?
4. What are the duties of the president?
5. List some powers of the federal government.

Think These Through

6. Of all the rights given in the Bill of Rights, which do you think is most important? Why?
7. Should the Congress ever be able to tell the president what to do? Explain.
8. Should the vice president have other jobs? Why?

Participating Effectively in Civic Affairs

Contacting Elected Officials

Have you ever thought about what it means to be a "good" citizen? We often think of good citizens as paying taxes, voting, and obeying all the laws.

You cannot vote yet; so how can you be an effective citizen? Even if you cannot vote, public officials are interested in your opinions. As a future voter, you are important! And you need to start right now to practice effective citizenship.

Effective citizens take action. They gather information about civic issues. They let elected officials know how they feel.

In order to do these things, you will need two very important skills: the skill of making a business telephone call and the skill of writing a business letter. Effective citizens use telephone calls and letters to inform themselves and to express their opinions.

Making a telephone call to an elected official is different from calling a friend. When you're calling a public official, you need to remember four important things:

1. Ask permission from your parents.
2. Identify yourself. This means giving your name and the town where you live. Identify yourself as a fourth-grade student in _________School.
3. Tell why you are calling. If you are calling to ask for information, be as specific as you can about the information you want. If you are calling to express your opinion, explain your opinion.
4. Remember to say thank you and, if asked, to give your address and telephone number.

Make some notes and write down a list of questions before making a telephone call to an elected official. Think of an issue, plan a telephone call, and practice your telephone call with a classmate. Remember to follow the four steps above.

Effective citizens are often letter writers. They write letters to ask public officials for information or to express their opinions. Often they write letters to the editor of their local newspaper so other citizens will know how they feel about public issues.

Ask your teacher to show you the correct way to write a business letter. Then, write a three-paragraph letter using the four steps of a business telephone call to ask for information or express an opinion.

You can write to one of North Carolina's senators or to your Congressional representative. Send the letter to their e-mail address on your computer or mail it to the address in your local telephone directory.

Chapter 14 Review

LESSONS LEARNED

LESSON 1 Our nation has many symbols, including the flag, the national anthem, and "Uncle Sam." We respect these symbols because they represent the land and people of the United States. The Declaration of Independence and the Constitution express our national ideals and created a system of government for the people of the United States.

LESSON 2 The Constitution spells out our plan of government. The Constitution establishes our national government and limits its power. The government is a republic system of elected officials. It is a federal system that shares power with the states.

LESSON 3 The powers of the national government are limited through guarantees of individual freedoms in the Bill of Rights. Powers of the three branches of government—legislative, executive, and judicial—are limited. No single branch can dominate the nation's government.

TIME FOR TERMS

Stars and Stripes
symbols
Declaration of Independence
federal system
checks and balances
Congress
"Star-Spangled Banner"
democracy
Constitution
republic
Bill of Rights
legislative branch
judicial branch
Supreme Court
executive branch
state government
president
federal government

FACT FOLLOW-UP

1. Why does our nation have symbols?
2. What does it mean for citizens to have a government of limited powers?
3. Describe the system of checks and balances.
4. How are the number of representatives from each state to the House of Representatives decided?
5. What amendments to the Constitution gave more people the right to vote?
6. What are freedoms in the Bill of Rights?
7. Why did North Carolina at first not accept the Constitution?
8. What is the job of the judicial branch of government?
9. What is the job of the executive branch of government?
10. What is the job of the legislative branch of government?

THINK THESE THROUGH

11. If you could make another symbol for our nation, what would it be? What colors would you use? What animals, people, or places would you use?
12. If you had to give up one of the rights guaranteed by the Bill of Rights, which one would it be? Explain why.
13. Are there any new symbols for our nation?

What are they? Explain your answer.

14. Should people under the age of eighteen be allowed to vote? Give reasons for your answer.
15. What responsibilities go along with having the right to vote?
16. Imagine that we had no Bill of Rights. How would our nation be different?
17. Imagine that there were no checks and balances among the three branches of government. How would our nation be changed?
18. Why does the national government, and not the state governments, have the power to make agreements with other countries?

SHARPENING SKILLS

19. Suppose you want to add an additional national holiday, such as a special day to honor children. Write a letter to your representative asking for support.
20. Why do members of Congress say they appreciate letters from citizens?
21. Is it more effective to write a letter to a member of Congress or to make a telephone call? Give reasons for your answer.
22. What are other ways to contact your elected representatives?
23. With your classmates choose an issue that is important in your community. Write a letter to the editor of your local newspaper stating your point of view.

PLACE LOCATION

Use the letters on the grid below to answer the following questions:

24. Which of the three branches makes laws?
25. Which of the three branches carries out laws?
26. Which of the three branches interprets laws?
27. Which branch contains 435 members of the House of Representatives and 100 members of the Senate?
28. Which branch is led by the president?
29. Which branch is led by the nine justices of the Supreme Court?
30. Which branch represents our country in visits to other countries?
31. Which branch has federal and district courts located in states?
32. Which branch decides how money will be spent by the federal government?
33. Which branch appoints judges?
34. Which branch has two members elected from each state?
35. Which branch decides how to interpret the law in disputes between states?

Branches of the United States Government

	Legislative	**Executive**	**Judicial**
Building	U.S. Capitol	White House	Supreme Court
Branch	a	b	c

CHAPTER 15

How North Carolina Governs

North Carolina's flag snaps in the wind over the legislative building in Raleigh, our state capital. Adopted in 1885, our flag's red, white, and blue colors match the colors of the United States flag. Both flags have flown over the state capitol building since 1885. Our flags remind us of our loyalty to our country and our state.

CHAPTER PREVIEW

LESSON 1
Government in North Carolina
Like the federal government, North Carolina has three branches of government.

LESSON 2
The General Assembly in North Carolina
The General Assembly is responsible for making laws in North Carolina.

LESSON 3
Local Governments
North Carolina has two kinds of local government—counties and municipalities.

Making a Mark in Journalism

Four men from North Carolina have shaped television news. When television first began, Edward R. Murrow helped set the style for news reporting. The Greensboro native had broadcast from London on CBS Radio during World War II. After the war, Murrow (right) started television shows about history and current events.

David Brinkley, born in Wilmington, was one of TV's first newscasters. He worked for ABC and NBC in important news jobs.

Charles Kuralt, also born in Wilmington, attended UNC-Chapel Hill. His *On the Road* show on CBS took him to every part of America. Kuralt also hosted a popular Sunday morning news show.

Roone Arledge, reared in Hendersonville, led ABC's sports coverage of the Olympics before becoming president of ABC News.

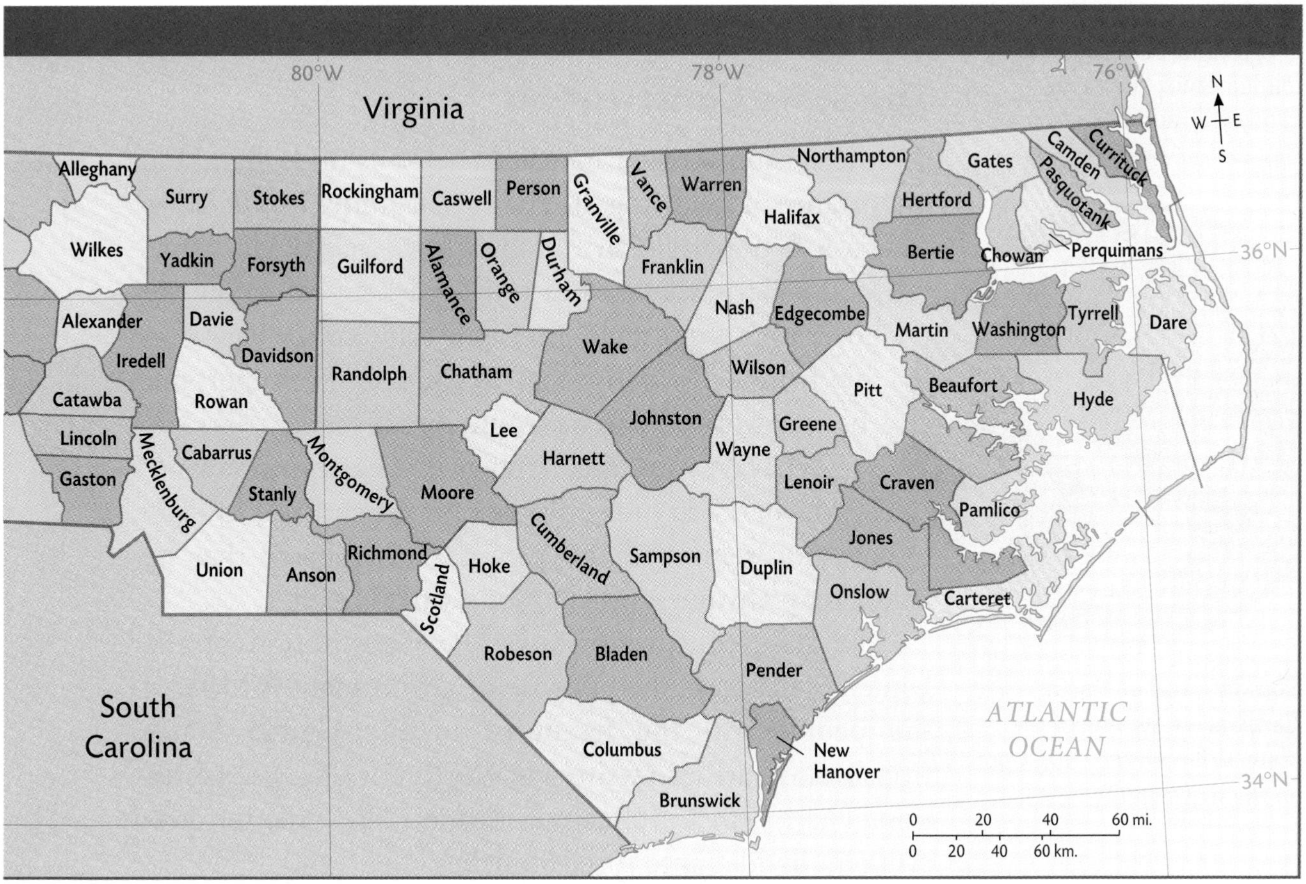

80°W
78°W
76°W
N
W E
S
36°N
34°N
Virginia
South Carolina
ATLANTIC OCEAN
Alleghany
Surry
Stokes
Rockingham
Caswell
Person
Granville
Vance
Warren
Northampton
Gates
Camden
Currituck
Pasquotank
Hertford
Halifax
Wilkes
Yadkin
Forsyth
Guilford
Alamance
Orange
Durham
Franklin
Bertie
Chowan
Perquimans
Alexander
Davie
Iredell
Davidson
Randolph
Chatham
Wake
Nash
Edgecombe
Martin
Washington
Tyrrell
Dare
Wilson
Pitt
Beaufort
Hyde
Catawba
Rowan
Lincoln
Lee
Johnston
Greene
Wayne
Harnett
Gaston
Mecklenburg
Cabarrus
Stanly
Montgomery
Moore
Lenoir
Craven
Pamlico
Jones
Union
Anson
Richmond
Scotland
Hoke
Cumberland
Sampson
Duplin
Onslow
Carteret
Robeson
Bladen
Pender
Columbus
Brunswick
New Hanover
0 20 40 60 mi.
0 20 40 60 km.

Government in North Carolina

LESSON PREVIEW

Key Ideas

- The state constitution says that its purpose is to serve the people.
- The three branches of state government are legislative, executive, and judicial.
- The governor carries out state laws through state divisions.
- Courts interpret state laws.

Key Terms

General Assembly, governor, bills, budget, veto, pardon, misdemeanor, civil cases, felony, jury, appeal

Dogwoods, cardinals, and the nickname "Tar Heels" all represent North Carolina and its people. The dogwood and the cardinal are naturally found in the woods of the state. The Tar Heels name says something about our history and our belief in ourselves as a people of courage.

The state seal of North Carolina has the words "Esse quam videri" written upon it. This is the state's motto. The Latin words mean "to be rather than to seem." The motto reflects North Carolinians' honesty and integrity.

The state seal of North Carolina is a symbol of the state. *What do the Latin words on the seal mean?*

The State Constitution

A television show of the 1960s helps us understand the importance of following the law. In *The Andy Griffith Show,* set in a fictional North Carolina town called Mayberry, Deputy Barney Fife once put a parking ticket on the governor's windshield. Everyone told Barney he was in big trouble for doing that to someone so important. Barney worried that he would lose his job.

What do you think happened? The governor came to Mayberry to praise Barney for doing his duty. The governor reminded the people of Mayberry that he more than anyone needed to follow the law.

The state constitution, like the Constitution of the United States, says the purpose of government is to serve the people. All the freedoms in the United States Constitution are also written in North Carolina's constitution. The North Carolina constitution also calls for government divided into three branches.

Three Branches of Government

The legislative branch of North Carolina government is called the **General Assembly**. The General Assembly makes the state's laws.

The executive branch is led by the governor. The **governor** is the chief executive of North Carolina. The governor's job is to carry out state laws. The governor is elected by the people.

The judicial branch decides if people are following the law. Judges run different types of courts. Citizens sit on juries in most cases.

Andy Griffith (right), from Mount Airy, N.C., starred on TV as Sheriff Andy Taylor. Don Knotts played Barney, his deputy in the make-believe town of Mayberry, N.C. *Did Barney get in trouble for giving the governor a ticket?*

The Governor

The governor of North Carolina heads the executive branch. The governor represents the state to visitors and officials of other governments.

The governor presents **bills** (proposed laws) and a budget to the legislative branch. The **budget** is the plan for how much money the state will spend and how it will spend it.

A governor of North Carolina can **veto**, or reject, bills approved by the legislative branch. With a vote of three fifths of its members, the General Assembly can override a

The governor of North Carolina lives in the governor's mansion in Raleigh. *Which branch of state government is headed by the governor?*

veto by the governor. That means the veto is canceled. Bills become laws after the General Assembly passes them and the governor accepts them. He or she must see that laws of the state are carried out by the state agencies within the executive branch.

A governor can pardon a prisoner. **Pardon** means that a person can be set free from prison by order of the governor.

The lieutenant governor runs the sessions of the state senate in the General Assembly and represents the state when asked to do so by the governor. If the governor dies or has to leave office during a term, then the lieutenant governor becomes governor.

EYEWITNESS TO HISTORY

Flying the Flag of North Carolina

The flags of North Carolina have always reflected the state's history. The symbols that the designers put on the flags showed the ideals important to the state when the flags were made.

In 1861, when North Carolina seceded from the Union, the state did not have a flag of its own. Members of the General Assembly accepted a design (right) submitted by artist William Jarl Browne.

Manly's battery flag

It had a red field crossed by white bars, and a white star set on a blue patch in the flag's center. Adopted in 1861, it was the flag North Carolina troops first carried into battle during the Civil War. Later, troops from the state carried a flag into the battle at Bentonville (left) that looked like the Confederate flag.

Bentonville battle flag, Civil War

Administrative Divisions

The governor runs the state government. He or she does this by directing the divisions of state government that carry out the laws of the state.

The Division of Crime Control and Public Safety runs state prisons through the Department of Corrections. The division also ensures highway safety through the Highway Patrol Department.

The state auditor checks how each state office spends its money. The superintendent of public instruction heads the department that sets standards for schools.

The commissioner of agriculture oversees the effort to

In 1885, a new flag was adopted. The date of the Halifax Resolves, April 12, 1776, became the date under the star. People liked this date because it showed that North Carolina was the first state to ask for freedom from the English.

Some people have asked that the Mecklenburg Declaration date be removed because of its uncertain historical accuracy. Can you think of another date that might belong on our state flag?

keep food and fuel safe for us. The commissioner of labor oversees the health and safety of workers in North Carolina.

A State Highway Patrol trooper directs traffic. The highway patrol is part of the executive branch of state government. Its job is to keep roads safe. *Does your town have a highway patrol station?*

Some of these commissioners and department heads are elected by the people. Others are appointed by the governor. All work under the governor but report to the people.

The executive branch of state government employs more than 180,000 people. The state runs offices in every major town. These offices include the highway patrol station and the driver's license office. North Carolina's employment office helps people locate available jobs.

The Judicial Branch

North Carolina's courts system is the the third branch of our state's government. Like many other state offices, courts are located in each of our 100 counties. Courts are nearby so people can more easily settle important questions.

Courts help people settle arguments. Courts have the duty to decide if a person, business, or even government office has broken any state laws.

Several kinds of courts make up the judicial branch. District courts decide guilt or innocence in criminal cases. These district courts listen to cases involving property disagreements. They also hear cases involving violations called misdemeanors. A **misdemeanor** is a crime that is not very serious. Persons found guilty of a misdemeanor are not punished severely.

Superior courts listen to two kinds of cases. One kind involves conflicts over large amounts of property or money. These are called **civil cases**. Superior courts also listen to criminal cases called felonies. A **felony** is a serious crime such as armed robbery or murder. Punishment of guilty people in such cases may be severe.

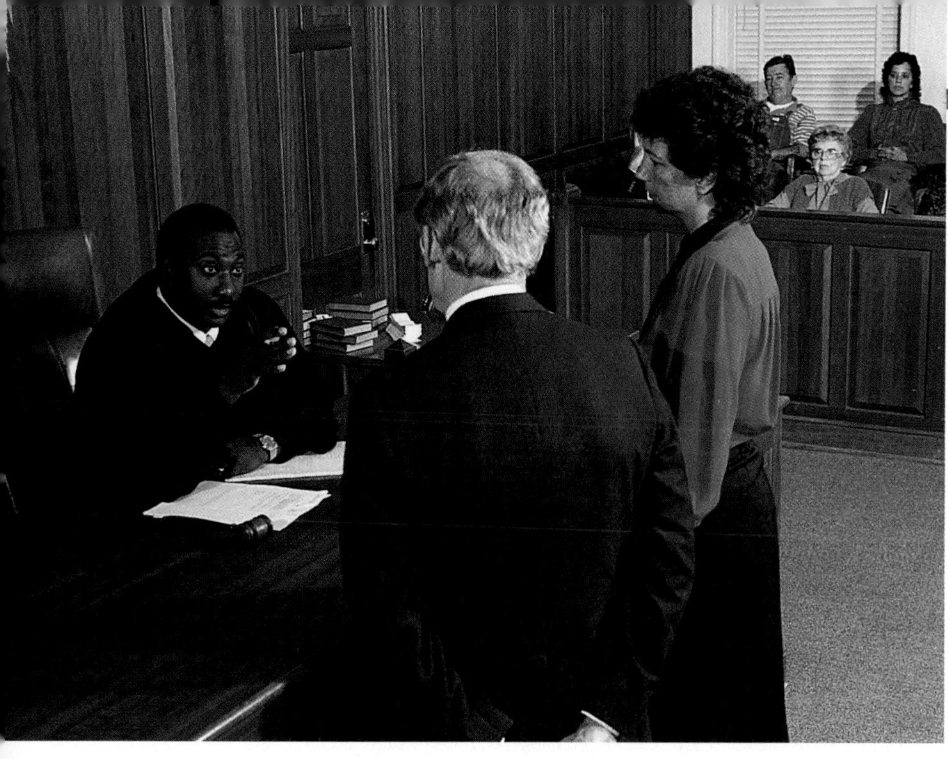

During a trial, a judge makes sure the lawyers on both sides follow the law while presenting their cases. Judges in North Carolina sit in district courts, superior courts, courts of appeal, and the Supreme Court of North Carolina. *Which court handles misdemeanors?*

A jury sits in most superior court cases. A **jury** is a group of citizens that listen to both sides of a case. The jury then decides if a person is guilty or not.

North Carolina has two higher courts that listen to and decide on appeals from district and superior courts. An **appeal** comes to these courts when someone believes that the law was not applied correctly in their case. Through an appeal the person hopes that the first decision will be changed.

One of these higher courts is called the North Carolina Court of Appeals. The other is called the Supreme Court of North Carolina. The supreme court is our state's highest court.

LESSON 1 REVIEW

Fact Follow-Up

1. What are some symbols of North Carolina?
2. How are the constitutions of North Carolina and the United States alike?
3. What are some of the jobs of the executive branch of government in North Carolina?
4. Describe the judicial system in North Carolina.

Think These Through

5. How are the United States and North Carolina judicial systems alike and different?
6. How are the jobs of the president of the United States and the governor of North Carolina alike?
7. Do we need a State Highway Patrol? Explain your answer.

The General Assembly in North Carolina

LESSON PREVIEW

Key Ideas

- The General Assembly passes state laws in North Carolina.
- The General Assembly is made up of two houses, the House of Representatives and the Senate.
- A bill is introduced then goes to a committee. If the committee gives the bill a favorable recommendation, the General Assembly votes to pass the bill into law.

Key Terms

Senate, House of Representatives, page

The General Assembly meets in Raleigh to pass state laws. *What are the two houses in the General Assembly?*

Are you ready for an exam? This one has three questions, but all have the same answer. What part of North Carolina's government decides how much money may be spent on the textbooks in your classroom? decides the number of days in each school year? decides on the money the state will pay for teachers' salaries?

The answer? The General Assembly, the name of North Carolina's legislature, or lawmaking body.

The General Assembly is Important

Everyone in North Carolina is affected by questions that the General Assembly decides. How much money should people pay in state taxes? How old should a young person be before he or she can apply for a driver's license? And you and your classmates can add many more questions if you try.

The General Assembly meets every year in Raleigh. Its organization is the same as the United States Congress. One legislative body has 50 members and is named the **Senate**. The other chamber, the **House of Representatives**, has 120 members.

Every member of the General Assembly is elected from districts from all over North Carolina. This means that through their senators

Central Piedmont Community College in Charlotte is one of almost 60 community colleges in the state. The General Assembly created community colleges with a law passed in 1963. *Is there a community college near where you live?*

and representatives our state's people have a voice in the General Assembly's decisions.

Making Bills into Law

The General Assembly cannot change North Carolina's constitution. It may vote for a change to the state's constitution through an amendment. The amendment must be approved by a vote of the people before it becomes part of the constitution.

The General Assembly can remove a law. It also may approve new laws. This is how our legislature makes important decisions for the state.

An idea for removing an old law or making a new one may come from almost anywhere. The governor might propose it. A citizen may ask that the legislature act on some troubling question. Only a member of the Senate or House of Representatives, however, may turn the idea into a bill. Each bill then must be introduced in either the House or Senate. This is the first step of long and careful consideration that is summarized in the chart on page 346. Each time it meets, the General Assembly may consider 1,000 bills or more. Only a few become law.

The lieutenant governor and Speaker of the House work together to run the General Assembly. They appoint legislators to serve on committees. Committees conduct hearings on bills.

Committees work with specific types of legislation. There are committees on banking, education, crime, highways, and the budget. Special committees can be set up to investigate such matters as health care or day-care centers.

Bills that make it through the committees are sent "to the floor." This is when the bill appears in the legislative chamber, a room large enough to seat all the members. In the chamber, members debate the bill. They can vote to change, defeat, or pass the bill.

Once the General Assembly votes to pass a bill, it is sent to the governor. If the governor does not veto the bill, it becomes law. If the governor vetoes the bill, it still can become law if three fifths of the General Assembly vote to override the governor's veto. The secretary of state publishes the laws passed in the state.

Working for State Government

You can affect the laws passed by the General Assembly. You can learn about the bills legislators are considering. If you disagree with a bill, you can write your legislator and

How Bills Are Made
1. A new law is needed.
2. A bill is introduced in the House of Representatives and the Senate with a first reading.
3. Committees of both houses conduct hearings on the bill.
4. The bill is sent "to the floor," where it is read again.
5. On the floor, members from both houses debate the bill.
6. The bill is read a third time before a vote is taken to defeat or pass the bill.
7. Once the bill is passed and approved by the governor, it becomes law.

This chart shows the way bills become law in North Carolina. How many steps are there? *Which branch of state government makes laws?*

CONNECTIONS

Geography & Language Arts

State Poet Sam Ragan

North Carolina has a state poet. He or she is called our poet laureate.

Sam Ragan was named poet laureate by Governor Jim Hunt in 1982. Before he became our poet laureate, Mr. Ragan had already served as a state official. In 1972-73, he led the Department of Art, Culture, and History in North Carolina. We call it the Department of Cultural Resources today.

Sam Ragan was a great cultural resource himself. Most of his life he was a writer, a state leader, and a teacher. He died in 1996.

He was our third poet laureate. The first was Arthur Talmage Abernethy from Burke County. James Larkin Pearson of Wilkes County was the second. Mr. Ragan grew up on a farm in Granville County.

By the time he started the fourth grade in a rural schoolhouse, young Sam knew he wanted to be a writer. At college in Wilson, North Carolina, he kept on writing stories and poems.

Then he got a job as a newspaper reporter. Soon World War II began, and he served in the Pacific Ocean as a soldier. Not long after the war ended, Mr. Ragan became an editor of *The News and Observer,* a famous Raleigh newspaper. Many days he put one of his poems into this paper. His readers were glad to see them. Some readers later asked Mr. Ragan to teach them how to write poems. He started a class for poets at NCSU. Many students enrolled.

Mr. Ragan owned and edited *The Pilot* in Southern Pines. He ran a place for writers called Weymouth Center. He also published five books of poetry. One is called *The Tree in the Far Pasture.* Another is *To the Water's Edge.* His students have published their own poems in many books and magazines. Every June he hosted a poetry festival.

Sam Ragan wanted all of us to read and write poetry. His wife and two daughters are writers also. He said that all writing is a kind of reporting.

What do you think? Did his poems make him a good newspaper editor? How did they help him teach other writers? How did poems make him a famous state official?

Here is one of his poems.

Where Does a Poem Come From?

Where does a poem come from?
No one knows.
Bits and pieces are lodged within
From days, months, years, lifetimes,
And then something nudges them
Into the sunlight.
You suggest and imply,
Something happens.
A poem is written a long time
Before it goes down on paper.

–*from* Collected Poems of Sam Ragan, *1990, St. Andrews Press, Laurinburg, North Carolina.*

Young people work as pages in the North Carolina General Assembly. They stand in front of the speaker's podium ready to run errands for members of the legislature. Some pages are the sons or daughters of elected representatives. *Would you like to be a page someday?*

ask him or her not to vote for it.

The Legislative Services Commission distributes bills, provides computer and copying services, and helps legislators with research. A young person can work for the commission as a page. A **page** serves as a messenger to the General Assembly. Pages are rising seniors in high school who take time away from school to do this job.

Perhaps you can be a page when you become a teenager. You will have to be willing to work hard. You will need to know about North Carolina government to do well.

LESSON 2 REVIEW

Fact Follow-Up

1. What is the name of North Carolina's legislative branch of state government?
2. What are some jobs of the legislature?
3. How can you affect the work of the North Carolina General Assembly?
4. Who was the North Carolina state poet? Do you think you would like his job? Why?

Think These Through

5. Does the North Carolina General Assembly have too much power? Explain your answer.
6. Is there a system of checks and balances in North Carolina? Explain your answer.
7. Imagine that you are a page in the North Carolina General Assembly. What would be the most interesting part of your job? Why?

LESSON 3 Local Governments

Did you know the county you live in has something to do with knights, castles, ladies, and lords? The word county goes back to the days of knights and castles in Europe. A count lived in a castle and ruled an area called a county. The count's rule usually extended as far as someone could ride a horse in a day. That's around 20 miles (32 km). If you look closely at North Carolina's counties, you will see that many extend 20 miles north to south and 20 miles east to west.

LESSON PREVIEW

Key Ideas

- There are two kinds of government in North Carolina—county and municipal.
- County governments serve counties.
- Municipal governments serve cities or towns.

Key Terms

county, municipal, county seat, zoning

Two Kinds of Local Government

North Carolina has two forms of local government: county and municipal.

A **county** government serves the people of a county. North Carolina has 100 counties. Not all counties were created at the same time. Some counties on the coast go all the way back to the 1600s. Hoke County, created in 1911, gave North Carolina its 100th county.

Municipal governments serve towns or cities. Counties, cities, and towns all provide basic services for their citizens.

WORD ORIGINS

The word **municipal** is an appropriate word in a democracy. A democratic government is a government of the people. Democratic governments are designed to serve their people. Because *municipal* comes from French words meaning "to undertake service," municipal governments really do serve towns or cities.

What Counties Do

A **county seat** is the town or city where the county government conducts its business. You have learned about several county seats. Hillsborough is the county seat of Orange County. Manteo is the county seat of Dare County. Murphy is the county seat of Cherokee County. What is the name of your county seat? See the county chart on pages 389 to 393.

In a courthouse, trials are held, fines are paid, and people buy licenses. The clerk of court keeps records for all the

Bryson City is the county seat of Swain County. Before the courthouse was renovated most county business was conducted there. *What are some of the services provided by a county?*

decisions that are made in court.

The register of deeds keeps records for all the property owned by people in the county. The deed to your home is filed here. This proves who owns the home.

The register's office also keeps birth certificates and issues marriage licenses. You and your parents could receive a copy of your birth certificate there.

Other county offices may be in the courthouse or nearby buildings. The tax collector and the tax assessor work there. The tax assessor figures fair taxes on property. The collector collects the taxes for the county.

Usually the sheriff works in the jail next to the courthouse. The sheriff's office includes deputies and a jailer, the person who keeps the jail running.

County offices also include a department of social services. County offices have a school system to administer the local public schools, and a health department, where the public can get medical treatment. Many counties run hospitals, libraries, parks, and museums.

The Orange County Commissioners hold a public meeting in Hillsborough, the county seat. *Why is it important for county commissioners to listen to the citizens of the county?*

We elect a county commission every two or four years to represent our interests. The commission sets the tax rate on property. The commission also decides how much money will go to local schools and other agencies. Commissioners hire people to direct the various agencies. In many places, a county manager oversees the people who do the county's work.

Sheriff John Baker runs the sheriff's department in Wake County. The sheriff's office is in Raleigh, the county seat. *What does a sheriff do?*

Towns and Cities

About half of all North Carolinians live in a town or city. Their communities have received permission from the state legislature to set up local governments. Most places with fewer than 10,000 people are considered to be towns. Cities are places with more than 10,000 people.

Usually a city council governs a city. It is elected by the people. The city council sets the tax rate and performs the same duties for the city as the commission does for the county. Like the county, the city often hires a manager to run daily activities.

Another elected city official is the mayor. He or she heads the city council. The mayor also represents the city at all kinds of events.

Cities collect garbage and treat sewage. They maintain and clean the streets. Some run their own libraries. Others, such as Fayetteville and Greensboro, manage their own local history museums. Most important, all cities provide police and fire protection for all citizens.

Almost all cities have planning and zoning departments. **Zoning** is the way city governments plan how the city will grow. For example, zoning may work to put commercial buildings near one another, usually along the major streets. That type of zoning keeps residential areas quieter and less congested by preventing businesses from locating there.

Another type of zoning may mix houses, apartments, and businesses. That way people would be near grocery

What would YOU do?

Recycling trucks pick up cans and newspapers in many neighborhoods. Businesses buy used cans, glass, and newspapers. Who pays for the pick up? Taxpayers do. It is part of a city or county budget. Would you choose to vote for recycling? Why? How could you let your county commissioners know you think recycling is important?

Children listen to a tour guide describe the Native American exhibit at the Museum of the Cape Fear in Fayetteville. The museum is partly paid for by the city. *What other services do city governments provide?*

stores or service stations and other things they need.

Finally, most cities have citizens serve on commissions to make decisions about their communities. The zoning commission, for example, recommends changes and enforcement of the zoning rules. Other commissions oversee the work of libraries, historic sites, museums, or parks. Commissions are made up of volunteer citizens who give their time to help make their communities work better.

LESSON 3 REVIEW

Fact Follow-Up

1. How does county government serve the people of a county?
2. Who are the elected leaders of county government?
3. Who are the elected leaders of a town or city?
4. What does a city government do?

Think These Through

5. Are there too many North Carolina counties today? Give reasons for your answer.
6. How are county and municipal services alike and different?
7. Why do you think it is important for a city to have a zoning department?

Participating Effectively in Civic Affairs

Fourth Graders Pass Legislation

Participation in government is not just for adults. Students at Elvie Street Elementary School in Wilson (below) proved that in 1995 when they succeeded in getting the sweet potato declared the North Carolina state vegetable.

When the students studied the state symbols of North Carolina, they realized that we have an official state seashell, flower, bird, mammal, and even a dog. The General Assembly had not picked a state vegetable. The Elvie Street Elementary School students decided to change that with the help of their teacher, Celia Ashe Batchelor.

They researched the food crops grown in North Carolina and learned that our state produces many vegetables—including cucumbers, peanuts, and potatoes. But North Carolina produces more sweet potatoes than any other state. When they had this piece of information, the students went to work.

They contacted their representatives in the North Carolina General Assembly and suggested that North Carolina's state vegetable should be the sweet potato.

The students also talked with their parents and friends and got the entire community of Wilson behind their efforts.

Legislators became convinced that these fourth graders were serious. Even if the students were too young to vote, their parents and other interested citizens in Wilson were voters. Elected political officials want to please voters if they can.

While the General Assembly was meeting in Raleigh, the students' idea for making the sweet potato the official state vegetable was introduced as a bill.

The students and the people of Wilson worked hard to convince their legislators to pass the bill. They wrote letters, made telephone calls, and sent faxes.

The students were successful! From their experience they learned to be prepared by doing research. They learned how to contact elected officials with the help of adults. They never gave up.

Chapter 15 Review

LESSONS LEARNED

LESSON 1 Symbols of North Carolina represent the people and government of the state. The constitutions of the United States and of North Carolina both serve the people. There are three branches of state government. The governor heads the executive branch and proposes the state budget. The judicial branch includes district, superior, and supreme courts.

LESSON 2 The legislative branch is the General Assembly. The General Assembly passes state laws through the House of Representatives and the Senate. Young people can work to get bills passed.

LESSON 3 County governments serve counties. Municipal governments serve cities or towns in North Carolina. They are run by mayors and city councils. Citizens can serve on commissions to make decisions about their communities.

TIME FOR TERMS

General Assembly
bills
veto
misdemeanor
felony
appeal
House of Representatives
county
county seat
governor
budget
pardon
civil cases
jury
Senate
page
municipal
zoning

FACT FOLLOW-UP

1. How are the symbols of North Carolina and the United States alike and different?
2. How are the North Carolina General Assembly and the United States Congress alike and different?
3. Compare the job of a member of the General Assembly and a member of Congress.
4. Compare our state and national judicial systems.
5. In what ways are the constitutions of North Carolina and the United States alike and different?
6. How are county and municipal governments alike?
7. How many counties are there in North Carolina?
8. How is county government affected by the actions of state government?
9. What is the purpose of zoning?
10. How can citizens influence the actions of county and state governments?

THINK THESE THROUGH

11. Why is it important for the governor to have veto power? Explain.
12. Which of the three branches of state government is the most powerful? Give reasons for your answer.
13. Why must all state constitutions go along with the Constitution of the United States?

14. What service of county or municipal government is most important to your own family? Explain why.
15. What are some ways that you can influence how county or municipal governments work?
16. What changes would you try to make in your town if you were mayor?
17. If you could make one change in how the government of North Carolina operates, what would it be? Explain why.
18. If you were the state poet, what would you write about in your poems?

SHARPENING SKILLS

19. If you wanted a law passed by the General Assembly, what would you do first?
20. Imagine that your class is working to get a law passed by the General Assembly. Make a list of all the people and groups you should contact to help you.
21. Why was it important that the fourth graders at Elvie Street Elementary School were prepared before asking their representatives for help?
22. Why do you think some people are successful in having laws passed by the General Assembly while others are not?
23. What kinds of laws are the most important for the General Assembly to pass?

PLACE LOCATION

Using the map on page 337, name the counties in which the cities shown below appear:

24. Raleigh.
25. Wilmington.
26. Asheville.
27. Charlotte.
28. Manteo.
29. Hillsborough.
30. Greenville.
31. Fayetteville.
32. Concord.
33. Boone.
34. What is the westernmost county in North Carolina?
35. What is the southernmost county in North Carolina?
36. What is the easternmost county in North Carolina?

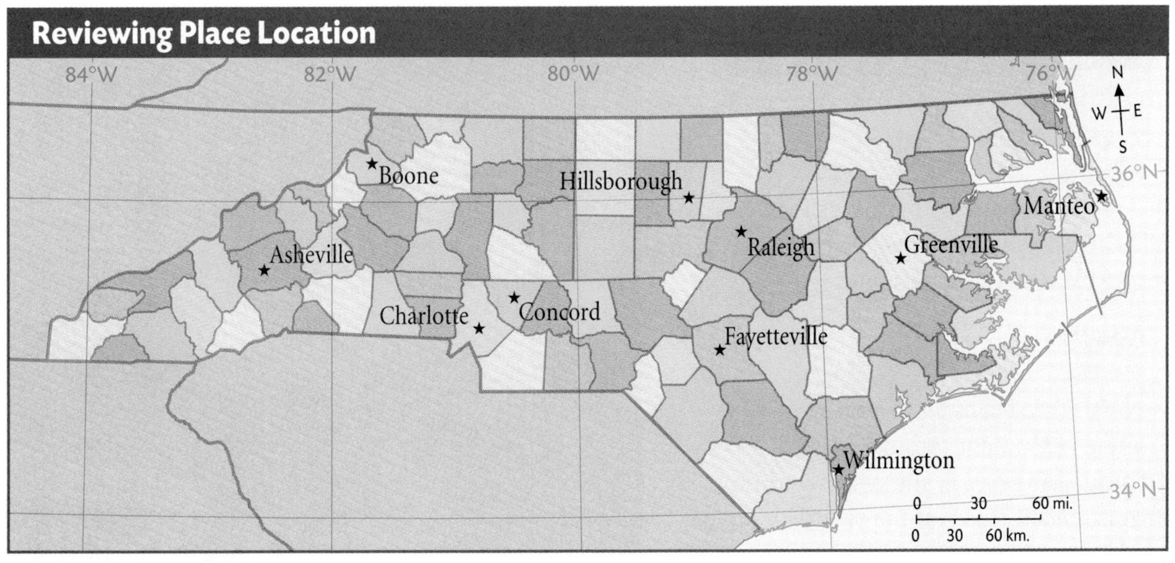

CHAPTER 16

North Carolina in the Twenty-First Century

Walk in the door and make a choice. Do you go for the static electricity exhibit, where your hair will fly all over your head? How about the laser display? Maybe you would rather pan for gold?

Discovery Place in Charlotte is a special museum. Old and new ways to work and play wait for you. You can look at fossils or catch a hint of the future. All you have to do is choose.

CHAPTER PREVIEW

LESSON 1

North Carolina's Role in the Future

Population changes, new roles for high technology, and a changing economy give clues to the state's future.

LESSON 2

Protecting the Environment

North Carolinians protect their heritage and environment through parks, forests, land trusts, and preserves. You must become part of the efforts.

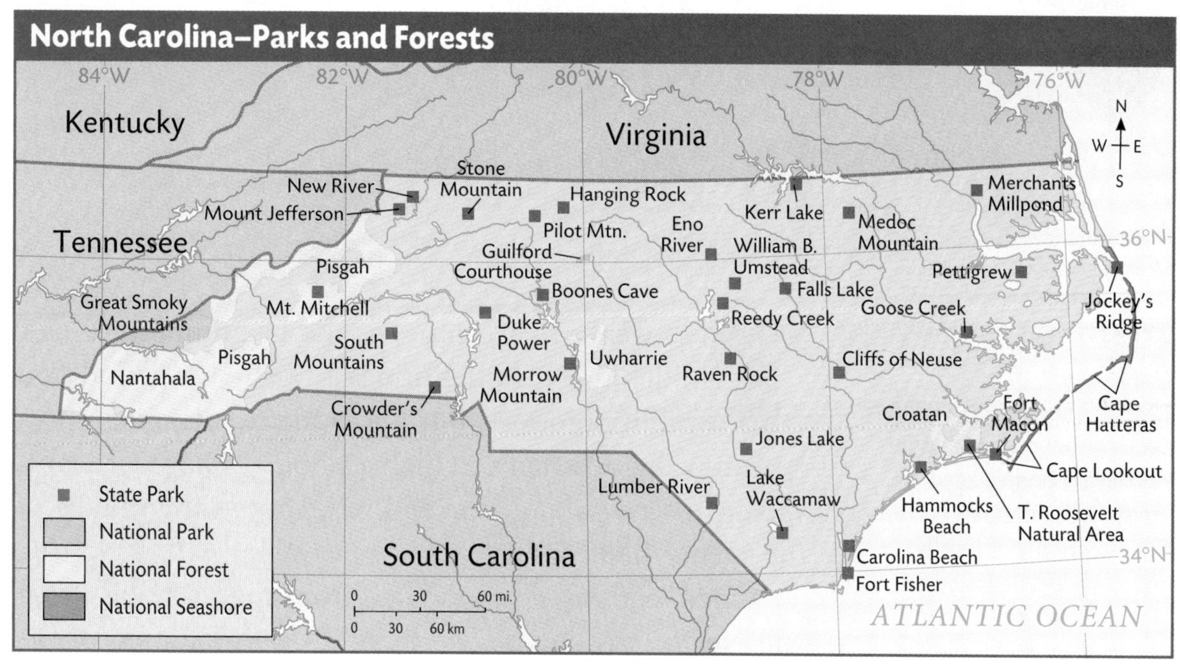

Global Transpark

If you ride along U.S. Highway 70 near Goldsboro, you will see a Global Transpark sign. The Global Transpark is an idea for the future, much like the Research Triangle Park was a 1950s idea for the present.

Global Transpark (see drawing, below) will be a place to move goods quickly around the world. First, Global Transpark planners will develop good highway, air, and rail transportation. Then manufacturing firms will build factories on the site.

With transportation and manufacturers in one place, North Carolina goods will move quickly to markets around the world.

Discovery Place in Charlotte

North Carolina's Role in the Future

LESSON PREVIEW

Key Ideas

- North Carolina's population will continue to increase, especially people aged sixty-five and older.
- The economy of North Carolina will be based on high technology in industry, agriculture, and trade.
- Research will continue to play an important role in the future of North Carolina.

Key Terms

millenium, retraining centers, foreign trade zone

The twenty-first century is the beginning of a new millenium. A **millenium** is a 1,000-year period. You will live most of your life in the twenty-first century. You will graduate from high school, a college, or a university. After working, you will retire about the middle of the twenty-first century.

What year will you graduate from high school? What will North Carolina be like then? To get a glimpse of the future, look at the course North Carolina has taken in the recent years of this century.

Population

North Carolina has more people than 40 other states in the United States. It continues to grow rapidly because of the numbers of people moving into the state.

Americans move. People move from city to city and state to state as they try to improve their lives. More people are moving into North Carolina than are moving out of the state.

A retired person spends time caring for her flower garden. Many retirees want to move to North Carolina after a life of work. ***Why?***

Many come for jobs in research and high technology. They enjoy their work, the mild climate, and the nearness of the beach and mountains. Thousands of people also retire here every year.

Microchips are tested in a clean room at MCNC in Research Triangle Park. High-technology industries will grow in the future. *What skills will workers of the future need to work in these jobs?*

The fastest growing part of the population of North Carolina is the group of people aged sixty-five and older. By 2010, there will be more than 1.2 million people in North Carolina over sixty-five. As in the rest of the United States, the population of the state is becoming older. In the next century there will be more people in older age groups (aged forty-five and up) than in younger age groups (under forty-five).

Some people in that oldest age group will have worked here and then decided to retire here. Others in that group will have worked elsewhere and come to retire here. Nearby medical facilities, museums, orchestras, golf courses, and shopping centers attract retirees to North Carolina.

High Technology

High-technology products and services will continue to provide jobs for North Carolina citizens. High-technology industries will offer more jobs as computers become a larger part of every industry.

It is difficult to predict what new products will be needed. Textiles, manufacturing, and food processing will continue to be part of North Carolina's economy. The workers in those industries will have to be well educated and highly trained. Machines will do more tasks than humans. People will have to know how to run those machines.

The computer will play a larger role in every business. Manufacturing, advertising, and distribution will be aided by computer technology. The continued wave of high technology will carry North Carolina into the twenty-first century.

Computers also will be in almost everyone's home. Radios were important to families in the 1930s. TVs were commonplace in homes during the 1950s and 1960s. Computers will become a part of the furniture in most homes.

North Carolina is already a leader in making products for the information age. Manufacturing of telephones, faxes, and computers will continue as important parts of the state's economy. High-tech manufacturing of transportation equipment will grow as an industry.

GAMES People Play

Computer games of the future—what will they be like? Not many computer games can be played outside. What might an outside computer game look like? What would it do? Virtual Reality is like a computer game, but usually for one person wearing a headset. Could someone design a Virtual Reality room? Would you like to be that designer?

A Changing Economy

Agriculture in North Carolina will continue to change. Tobacco manufacturing is slowing down. Farmers look for other crops to grow while increasing yields of corn and soybean crops. Research and computers will help farmers with these needs.

Central Piedmont Community College in Charlotte, other community colleges, and state universities are teaching students to work in high-technology jobs. *Why is education important to the future?*

Farm machinery runs by computer chips. A year's plan for crop production can be kept on a computer. Dairy and cattle farmers can keep track of feed for their animals by computer.

As agricultural jobs change with manufacturing, people have to learn new skills. Community colleges throughout the state provide classes to teach the technological skills that workers will need. North Carolina also works with private companies to build **retraining centers** where workers can learn new skills. A center in Cleveland in Rowan County is one example.

People can learn a new skill at any age. Workers over the age of sixty-five may retire from one job and begin another. *What other changes will occur as the state population ages?*

Because people will work to an older age, many will need training as they change jobs during their lifetime. A young woman might start as a salesperson after high school. Then she might go to nursing school. After working as a nurse, she might become a supervisor in a retirement home. Or she may leave the health care industry and return to sales.

An Aging Work Force

An aging population will affect the economy of North Carolina. State tax dollars will be spent on services for an aging population. There will be choices about how tax dollars are spent.

Do we build schools or more retirement homes? Do we build more hospitals or parks? Should the state concentrate on providing services for the elderly? What will the young children born after 2000 need? With government money going to the elderly, will more children live in poverty? These are questions that will have to be answered.

The service industries that serve people aged sixty-five and older will grow.

Advertising will focus on the needs of older people. Tourism will be geared to meet the desires of aging couples instead of families. Fast-food restaurants might offer other types of food.

Trade

North Carolina has been connected to the rest of the United States and the world for many years because of its trade. It has long been a major exporter of agricultural products—especially tobacco and cotton—and textiles.

More recently, North Carolina has enjoyed success in encouraging foreign companies to build factories and laboratories here. These companies have brought new jobs and tax dollars to the state and local governments.

North Carolina set up foreign trade zones near airports in our largest cities as a way to attract international trade. A **foreign trade zone** is an area where goods brought from another country can be stored, bought, and sold without paying high taxes.

The state also has improved the state ports in

Ships docked in Morehead City (below) and Wilmington bring cargo from other countries. *How does foreign trade help the economy of North Carolina?*

Wilmington and Morehead City to help large ships dock there. These ships carry huge containers full of cargo that are lifted from the ships and placed onto railroad cars or trucks. Then the products are moved quickly throughout the eastern and southern United States.

LIVING IN THE FUTURE

Predicting North Carolina's Future

What will the future look like? We all wonder about life 10 or 20 years from now. Some people wonder about life in 50 or 100 years.

Let's imagine what types of transportation you're going to use in 50 years.

Will there be only the hum of electric cars? Can you imagine how much quieter the world might be without the roar of the gasoline engine?

Let's imagine the kind of electricity you might use. Will it be solar panels on every home? Will new dams designed to produce hydroelectricity be built? Will exploration in outer space mean more understanding of energy from the sun?

What kinds of food will you eat? Will any of it be fresh? Will it all come from a different part of the country? Will you still eat pizza? What about new varieties of fruit and vegetables? You might eat a *peachlle,* a combination of peach and apple. Or will it be called a *papple?*

What new inventions will you use? Maybe you will invent some new tools to do work. Maybe you will think of new toys or games.

What will your school be like? Will your children go to a building to be with other students their age? Will they stay at home and learn with a computer and other tools of technology that have not yet been imagined?

Whatever the future holds, you will be an important part of it. What kind of work would you like to do? Your work will contribute to the quality of life in North Carolina.

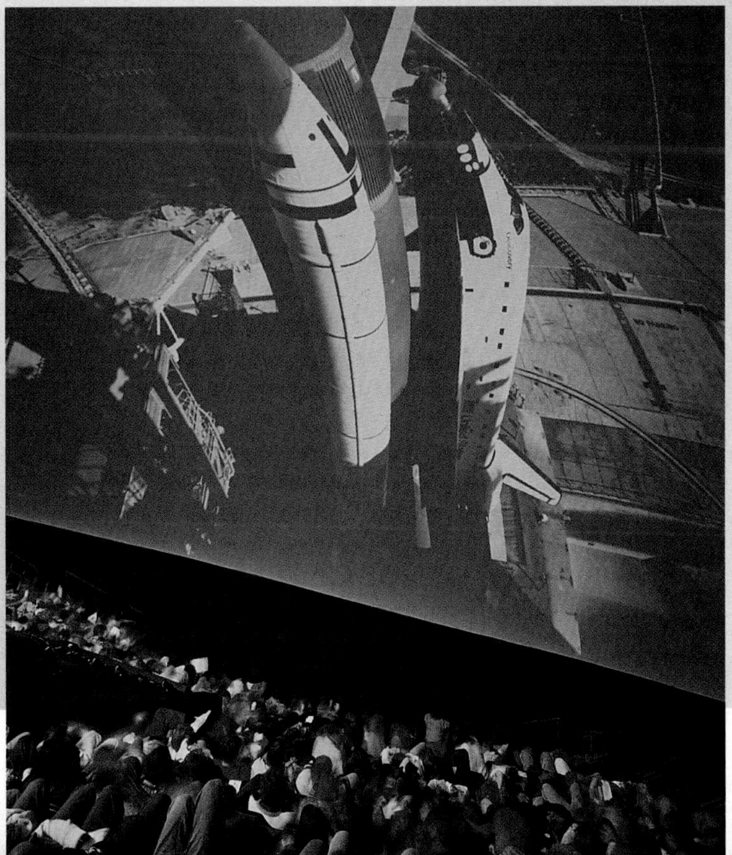

Discovery Place, Charlotte

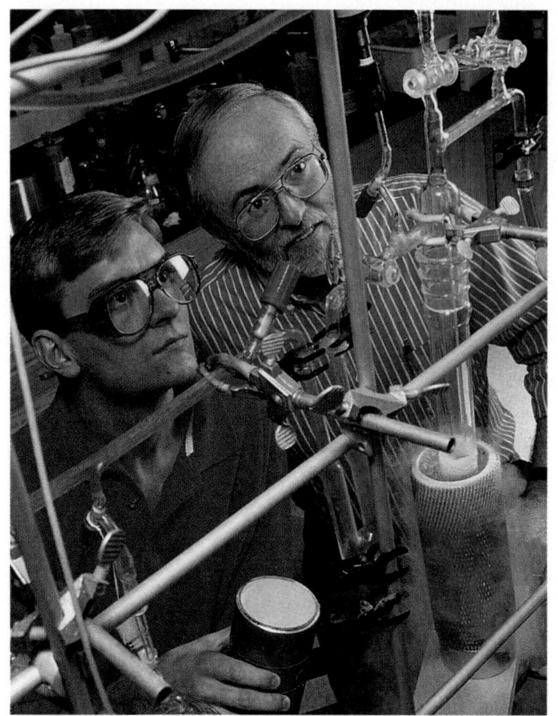

Two Wake Forest University scientists conduct research. *Why are university research centers and the Research Triangle Park important to the future of North Carolina?*

Agriculture

High technology will affect farming, too. Products grown by the farmers of the 1990s will still be grown in North Carolina in the twenty-first century. Climate makes crop production favorable. The tools farmers use will help them be even more productive. Laboratory research also will increase crop yields.

Soybeans, sweet potatoes, peanuts, and cotton will be a greater part of the agricultural dollar earned in North Carolina. Farms that raise livestock will continue to expand as fewer acres of tobacco are farmed. Hogs and poultry will be raised throughout North Carolina.

Research

North Carolina will continue to lead the country and the world in research. Because of its head start in building the Research Triangle Park in the 1950s, the state will continue to attract top scientists.

Working with state and private universities, researchers will begin to solve some tough problems. Medical cures and discoveries in environmental science will improve life for North Carolinians and people throughout the world.

LESSON  REVIEW

Fact Follow-Up

1. Describe North Carolina's population.
2. What are retraining centers? Why are they needed?
3. What are foreign trade zones?

Think These Through

4. Will research be more important to North Carolina in the future than it has been in the past? Explain your answer.
5. Imagine that you are sixty-five years old. What kind of life will you want to be leading at that age?
6. What changes will need to be made in North Carolina for an aging population?

LESSON 2

Protecting the Environment

When the Cape Hatteras Lighthouse was built in the late 1800s, it stood almost half a mile from the beach. Because of storms and waves, the ocean now comes close to lapping at the base of the famous lighthouse.

For years, concerned citizens have worked together to "Save the Light" because the Cape Hatteras Lighthouse is a symbol of all the state's resources. By showing interest in saving the lighthouse, North Carolina shows concern for other resources, both natural and human-made.

LESSON PREVIEW

Key Ideas

- Many parts of the state's natural environment are preserved through the efforts of citizens.
- Preserving buildings in cities helps preserve the past in North Carolina.

Key Terms

land trust, bird sanctuary, greenway, scenic byways, historic preservation

Preserving Natural Environments

All take pride in the majesty of mountain peaks. Yet trees in the Appalachian Mountains are dying from acid rain. People enjoy the rivers and lakes of the Piedmont. Yet water is a threatened resource there because of the many people in the region. Most appreciate the spray of ocean surf. Yet the coast suffers from overcrowding, overbuilding, and offshore pollution. The Coastal Plain also struggles with animal waste and fertilizers in rivers.

The people of North Carolina will decide together how the beaches and sounds of the Coastal Plain, rivers

North Carolinians are proud of Cape Hatteras Lighthouse. Some are working to save it by moving it back from the waves. *Why should we save signs of our state's past?*

and lakes of the Piedmont, and mountain trees can be preserved. The government will play an important role, but citizens are taking the lead in protecting the environment.

Preserving Parks and Forests

The state and federal governments work together to protect parts of North Carolina. The state has set aside 34 park and recreation areas (see map, page 357). The federal government runs national parks, national forests, and two national seashores in North Carolina. The map on page 357 shows their locations.

EYEWITNESS TO HISTORY

Sending Messages to the Future

People often want to leave messages to people in the future. Since pieces of paper might get lost, people have found another way to communicate. They bury time capsules. On an important day, such as July 4th or the day that marks an anniversary, churches, businesses, and towns often bury time capsules. The capsules are filled with items that would tell citizens of the future about life when the capsule was buried.

The Daily Tar Heel

Clinton Calls for Courage to Change America

President Hails UNC's Persistence

N.C. Officials Greet Clinton at RDU

The University's newspaper was put in a capsule.

In 1993-94, The University of North Carolina and the town of Chapel Hill celebrated their bicentennials, their 200th anniversaries of their foundings. One part of the festivities was the burial of time capsules at each entrance to the city.

Chapel Hill Mayor Ken Broun and schoolchildren pose with a time capsule.

Preserving the Coastal Plain

North Carolinians have worked together to save the Cape Hatteras Lighthouse and other resources of the Coastal Plain. Parts of the Outer Banks are protected within the Cape Lookout National Seashore, Cape Hatteras National Seashore, and Pea Island Wildlife Refuge.

Two hurricanes in 1996 battered the coast. The damage forced residents to ask questions about rebuilding on fragile islands. The hurricanes destroyed homes, businesses, and dunes. Beaches were swept away and pushed onto roadways.

Coastal Plain rivers are a major water resource. Keeping those streams clean involves the entire state.

The United States Postal Service issued a stamp (below) in honor of the university's bicentennial. President Bill Clinton attended the celebration in October 1993.

Time capsule

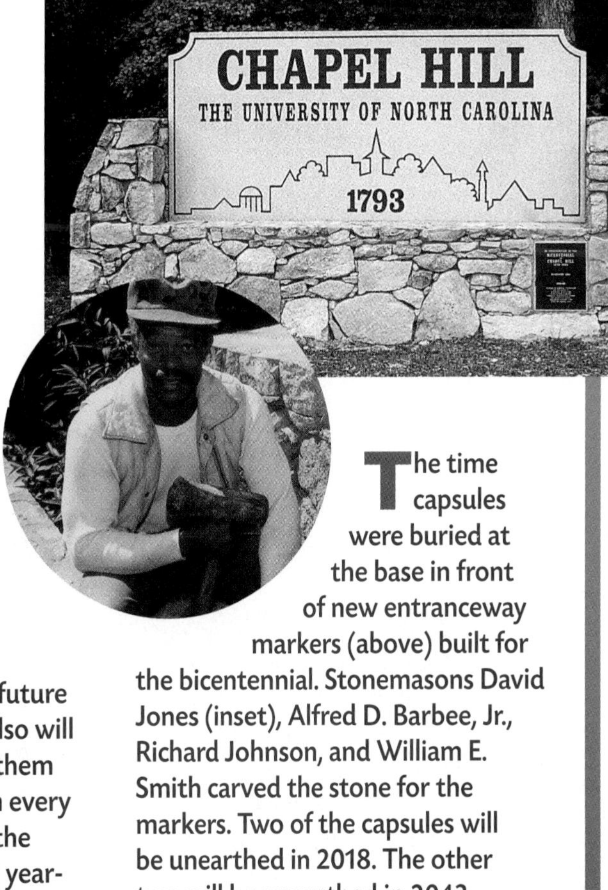

The time capsules were buried at the base in front of new entranceway markers (above) built for the bicentennial. Stonemasons David Jones (inset), Alfred D. Barbee, Jr., Richard Johnson, and William E. Smith carved the stone for the markers. Two of the capsules will be unearthed in 2018. The other two will be unearthed in 2043.

Time capsules will give people of the future a special look at our present. They also will tell them what people who lived before them thought about their time. Students from every school in Chapel Hill collected items for the four time capsules. They included school yearbooks, T-shirts, copies of local newspapers, and letters to schoolchildren of the future.

Preserving the Piedmont

Massive building for newcomers who need homes and roads changes the natural land of the Piedmont. Citizens in the Piedmont have come together to form land trusts. A **land trust** is an organization that helps people find ways to conserve their land from unnecessary development.

People have given acreage along the South River, a tributary of the Black River, to protect it from development. Others have given more land to existing preserves. One land trust works to keep the environment natural in the Yadkin-Pee Dee River valley.

What would YOU do?

When you are an adult, you might want to tell fourth graders about the state you knew when you were a child. One way to do that would be to make a time capsule now about North Carolina.

What would you put in your time capsule to tell about your life here?

What would you tell future fourth graders about your life in North Carolina?

Preserving the Mountains

People of the Mountains Region have worked to keep the beauty that attracts so many visitors. One of the most important preserved areas is the Joyce Kilmer Memorial Forest, deep in Graham County within the Nantahala National Forest. The Kilmer forest has some of the oldest trees in the United States.

Keeping mountains free from air pollution and acid rain requires cooperation among people from North Carolina and other states. Parks, forests, and land trusts help keep mountains from overdevelopment.

The New River in the mountains became a "scenic river." This means that the river is protected. *Why is it necessary to protect a river?*

Pretty Pond Bay in Robeson County is a preserve of the Nature Conservancy. *How does the Conservancy preserve natural areas in North Carolina?*

The Nature Conservancy

The Nature Conservancy has worked to raise money to buy land to protect it from development. Some of the last forest land on the Outer Banks, the Nags Head Woods, was saved by the Nature Conservancy.

Green Swamp, a pocosin near Wilmington, has also been preserved. The Conservancy also owns preserves on Black River in Bladen and Pender Counties and Roanoke River in Martin County.

Preserving Towns and Cities

Inside our towns and cities, citizens are acting to make communities more open to nature. A town can declare itself a **bird sanctuary**. This means birds cannot be killed within its boundaries.

A few towns have greenways. A **greenway** is a narrow park space that allows people to walk or bicycle from point to point. **Scenic byways** are 1,500 miles of highways that provide travelers with pretty drives between North Carolina towns.

WORD ORIGINS

An animal sanctuary protects animals from hunting or other dangers. A city or a park can be a sanctuary for birds and animals. **Sanctuary** is from the Latin word ***sanctus***, which means "sacred" or "holy." Sacred places are places set aside for worship. Bird sanctuaries are places set apart for birds.

The citizens of Washington, North Carolina, and other communities work to preserve their old buildings. *Why is it important to keep these older places?*

Houses, stores, churches, and schools are also preserved as part of the town's heritage. The effort to keep buildings preserved in a historically accurate way is **historic preservation**.

North Carolina is one of the leading states in historic preservation. Citizens in many communities work together to restore and protect historic neighborhoods.

Franklinville, in Randolph County, can spend historic preservation funds to keep up its old mill houses instead of letting the wood rot. Downtowns in Wadesboro, Washington, and Salisbury revive their main streets. The beauty of their local communities shines again. The heritage of North Carolina will be preserved for fourth graders of the future.

The state has preserved many historic sites. You have read about some North Carolina Historic Sites such as Bennett Place, Fort Fisher, Bath, CSS *Neuse,* Brunswick Town, Reed Gold Mine, and Somerset Place. They are run by the North Carolina Department of Cultural Resources.

LESSON 2 REVIEW

Fact Follow-Up

1. What North Carolina resources and landmarks are in danger?
2. What is a land trust? What is its purpose?
3. Why do many towns and cities want bird sanctuaries and greenways?
4. What is meant by historic preservation?

Think These Through

5. Of all the North Carolina resources you have learned about this year, which is most important to you? Explain why.
6. Of all the North Carolina landmarks you have learned about this year, which is most important to you? Explain why.
7. What do you think will be the greatest problem facing North Carolina in the next 20 years? Explain why.
8. How is your community preserving North Carolina resources and landmarks for the future?

Demonstrating Skills in Constructive Interpersonal Relationships and Social Participation

Resolving Conflicts

Chapter 16 is about North Carolina's future. You learned about some of the challenges facing our state in the years to come. And you learned about some of the things you as a North Carolinian will need to do to help our state and its people be successful in the future.

There are many things we cannot know about the future, but there are some things that we know already. One thing that we already know is that there will be conflict or disagreement.

People will come into conflict over the use of scarce resources, over how tax dollars should be spent, over which groups in our society should be helped by government. As a citizen of North Carolina, these issues will be yours to help resolve.

In resolving conflicts, the first step is to make sure you know exactly what the disagreement or conflict is. As you resolve conflicts, it might be helpful to use a diagram or chart like the one above. Notice how the chart above shows two sides to a conflict.

Decision-Making Grid: Resolving Conflicts

Side A	Side B
1.	1.
2.	2.
3.	3.
4.	4.
5.	5.

Once you know both sides of the conflict, you can list their points of view to help both sides understand one another. They should learn the points of view of each side.

The third step in resolving conflicts is to examine the interests of each side. In other words, why does Side A want what it wants? What are Side A's interests in this conflict? To get answers to these questions, you will need to read about or talk with people on both sides of the conflict.

Next, try to find some points on which both sides agree. If people on opposite sides of a conflict can agree on one point, they can then sometimes work out their disagreements. Ask questions like "Can we agree on this point?" and "Would this action or option satisfy both sides?"

Perhaps if both sides sit down together and try to find areas of agreement, they can solve the conflict.

Remember the steps:

1. State what the conflict is.
2. State the points of view of both sides.
3. Examine the interests of both sides.
4. Try to find areas of agreement.

The Future of North Carolina: A Letter to Fourth Graders

Dear Fourth Grader in North Carolina,

You learned about your local community a year ago in the third grade. Next year you will learn about the United States and all of the Western Hemisphere. In the next grades you will explore the rest of the world.

In the eighth grade, you will study North Carolina once again. By that time, both you and North Carolina will have changed.

As a fourth grader or eighth grader, you are part of a changing North Carolina. As you grow, you can give back to the state that gives you so much.

How? You can care about your school and work to improve it. You can be a good neighbor. You can help your parents to be even better citizens. You can learn to recycle. You can take care of our land as often as you are able. You can read newspapers, books, and magazines that talk about our state. You can learn what things there are to do.

Most of all, you can try to be a leader in North Carolina. North Carolina has become the state it is because of the work and energy of many people. This work has been with us since the days of the Lost Colony. It never ends. Your energy and enthusiasm can go a long way to making North Carolina an even better state.

Where would you most like to help someday? Would you work to protect the environment? Would you help out as a volunteer in a hospital? Would you want to serve in a public office?

Education is the best way to guarantee the success of North Carolina. Education will be the key to your success in the future. Education will help prepare you for the changes you will see in North Carolina and yourself.

There are simple ways to prepare for the future today.

Read about North Carolina and other topics that interest you. Through reading you learn about the world around you. And reading also helps you learn to think.

Thinking is important, because a successful person of the future will need to know how to solve problems. Problem solving is not taught as a subject. But in Language Arts, Social Studies, Math, Art, Music, and Science, your teachers instruct you how to solve problems. Problem solving can be used in any subject and in any life situation.

North Carolina needs good thinkers and good problem solvers like yourself.

Welcome to the future.

Sincerely,

Your North Carolina Ancestors

Chapter 16 Review

LESSONS LEARNED

LESSON 1 It is difficult to predict the future, but some characteristics of the future are present now. North Carolina will have an aging population and an economy based on research and high technology in agriculture, industry, and trade.

LESSON 2 Citizens are leading efforts to preserve the natural environment and historically important buildings and neighborhoods in each region of North Carolina. They have organized land trusts, greenways, and historic preservation districts. The future of North Carolina is dependent upon today's fourth graders.

TIME FOR TERMS

millenium	retraining centers
foreign trade zone	land trust
bird sanctuary	greenway
scenic byways	historic preservation

FACT FOLLOW-UP

1. What is the fastest-growing group in North Carolina's population?
2. How does North Carolina rank with other states in population?
3. In what ways will an aging population affect the North Carolina economy?
4. How are community colleges important to the North Carolina economy?
5. What are foreign trade zones? How do they help the state?
6. What agricultural changes are predicted for the future?
7. What environmental resources are endangered?
8. What groups are working to preserve the natural environment of North Carolina?
9. How are towns and cities working to save historic landmarks?
10. How will technology shape North Carolina's future?

THINK THESE THROUGH

11. How will more elderly people in the state affect state services and resources?
12. What will be the importance of education in North Carolina's future?
13. What do you think will be the greatest environmental issues in North Carolina's future? Explain why.
14. Do you think land trusts are a good idea? Explain your answer.
15. How do citizens groups help the environment?
16. Should state governments pass more laws to protect the environment? Explain your answer.
17. How will the future of North Carolina help you decide the kind of work you want to do when you are an adult?
18. What do you think was the best advice given to you in the letter from your ancestors? Why?

19. How will reading, thinking, and problem solving prepare you for the future?
20. What are some of the things you can do to help North Carolina have a bright future?
21. What do you think is the single greatest challenge facing North Carolina? Explain why.

SHARPENING SKILLS

22. Choose a classroom, school, or community conflict. Make a chart showing two sides of the the conflict and the arguments of each side.
23. Why is it important to have correct information when people are trying to resolve conflicts?
24. Which conflicts seem to you to be easiest to resolve? Explain why.
25. Why is it useful to put yourself into the other person's shoes when you are trying to resolve a conflict with that person?
26. Are there some conflicts that cannot be resolved? Explain your answer.

PLACE LOCATION

Use the letters on the map, the map on page 357, and a state highway map to locate the following places. For each place, give the relative location of its closest city.

27. Great Smoky Mountains National Park.
28. Guilford Courthouse National Park.
29. Cape Hatteras National Seashore.
30. Cliffs of the Neuse State Park.
31. Carolina Beach State Park.
32. Pilot Mountain State Park.
33. New River State Park.
34. Morrow Mountain State Park.
35. Lake Waccamaw State Park.
36. Nantahala National Forest.
37. Merchants Millpond State Park.
38. William B. Umstead State Park.
39. Mount Mitchell State Park.
40. Jockey's Ridge State Park.
41. Goose Creek State Park.
42. Pisgah National Forest.
43. Kerr Lake State Park.

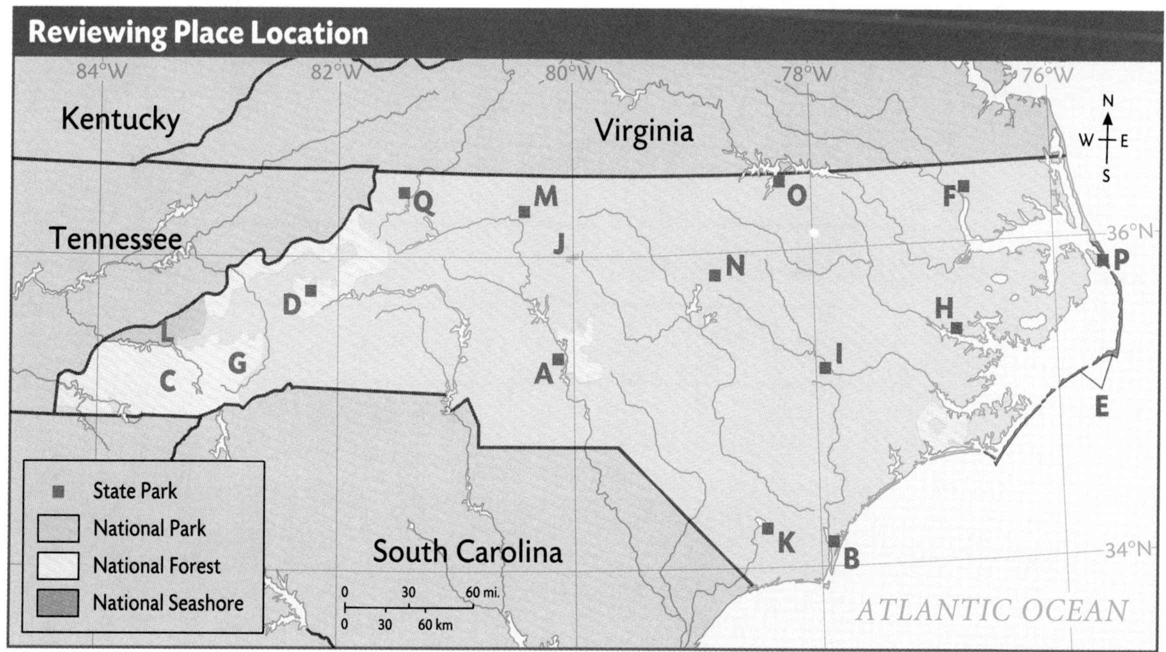

Appendix

Atlas

Atlas Key

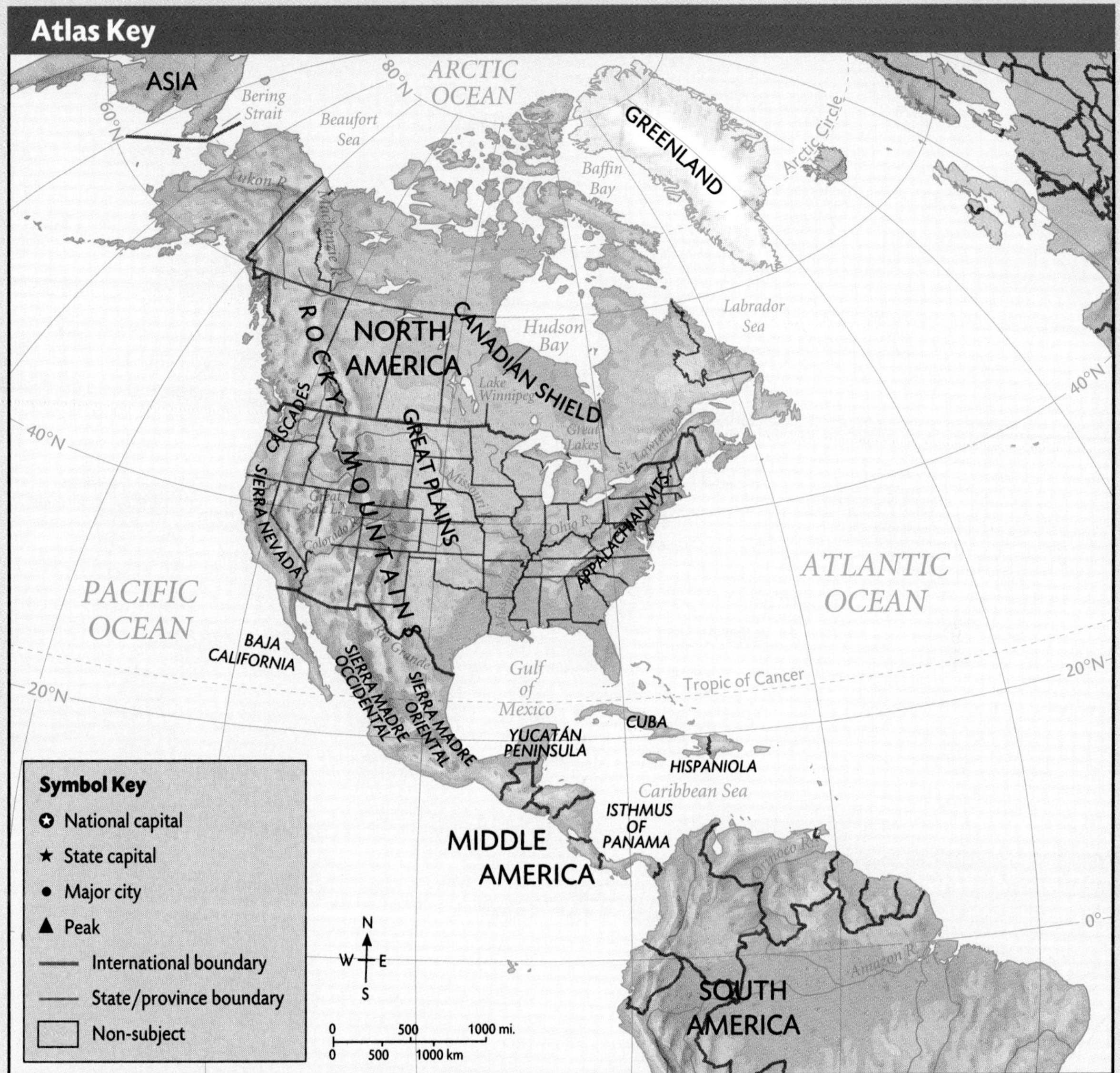
ASIA
Bering Strait
Beaufort Sea
ARCTIC OCEAN
GREENLAND
Baffin Bay
Arctic Circle
Yukon R.
Mackenzie R.
Labrador Sea
Hudson Bay
NORTH AMERICA
ROCKY MOUNTAINS
CANADIAN SHIELD
Lake Winnipeg
Great Lakes
St. Lawrence R.
CASCADES
GREAT PLAINS
SIERRA NEVADA
Great Salt L.
Missouri R.
Colorado R.
Ohio R.
Mississippi R.
APPALACHIAN MTS.
ATLANTIC OCEAN
PACIFIC OCEAN
BAJA CALIFORNIA
Rio Grande
SIERRA MADRE OCCIDENTAL
SIERRA MADRE ORIENTAL
Gulf of Mexico
Tropic of Cancer
CUBA
YUCATÁN PENINSULA
HISPANIOLA
Caribbean Sea
ISTHMUS OF PANAMA
MIDDLE AMERICA
Orinoco R.
Amazon R.
SOUTH AMERICA
80°N
60°N
40°N
20°N
0°
Symbol Key
National capital
State capital
Major city
Peak
International boundary
State/province boundary
Non-subject
N
W
E
S
0 500 1000 mi.
0 500 1000 km

World–Political

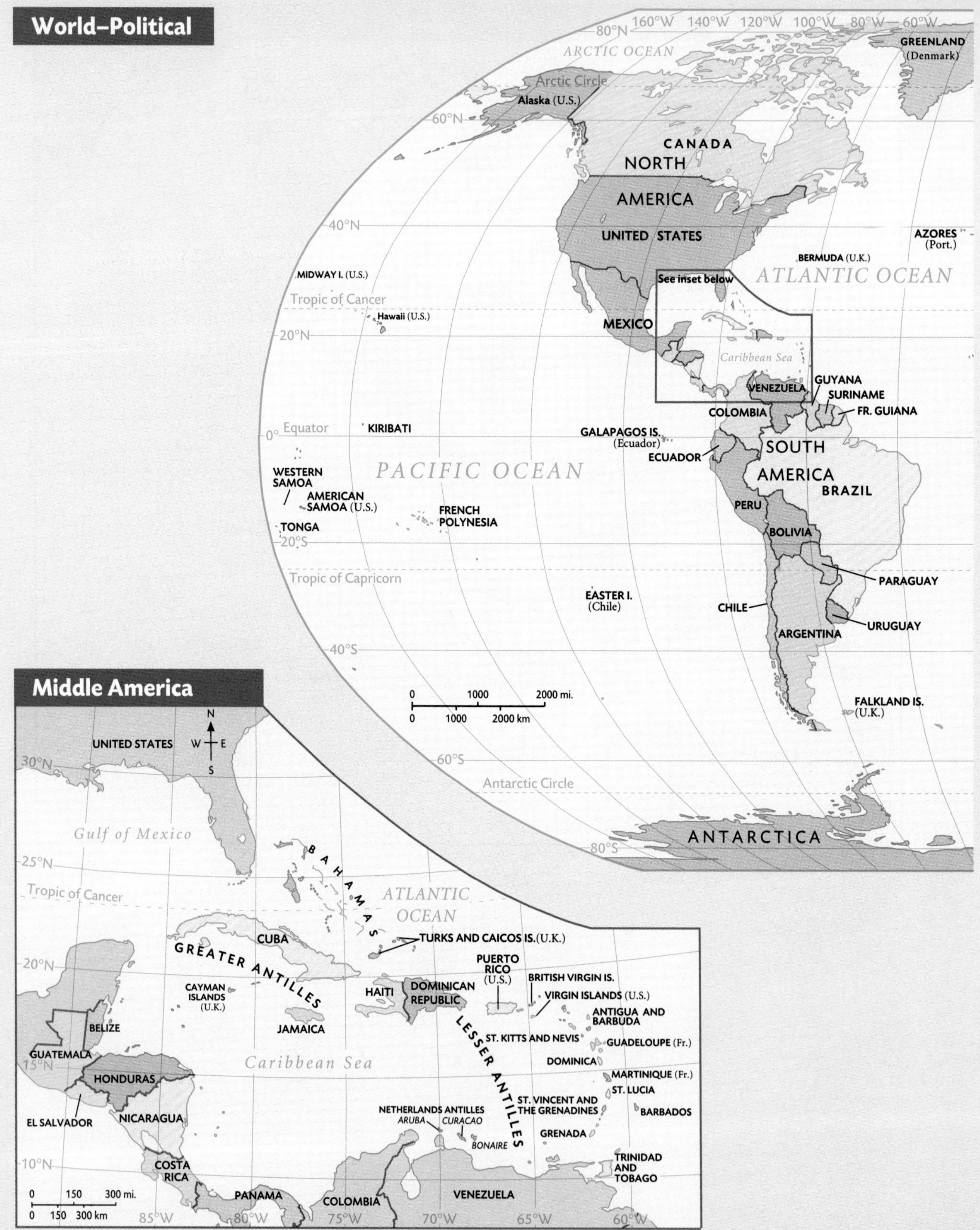

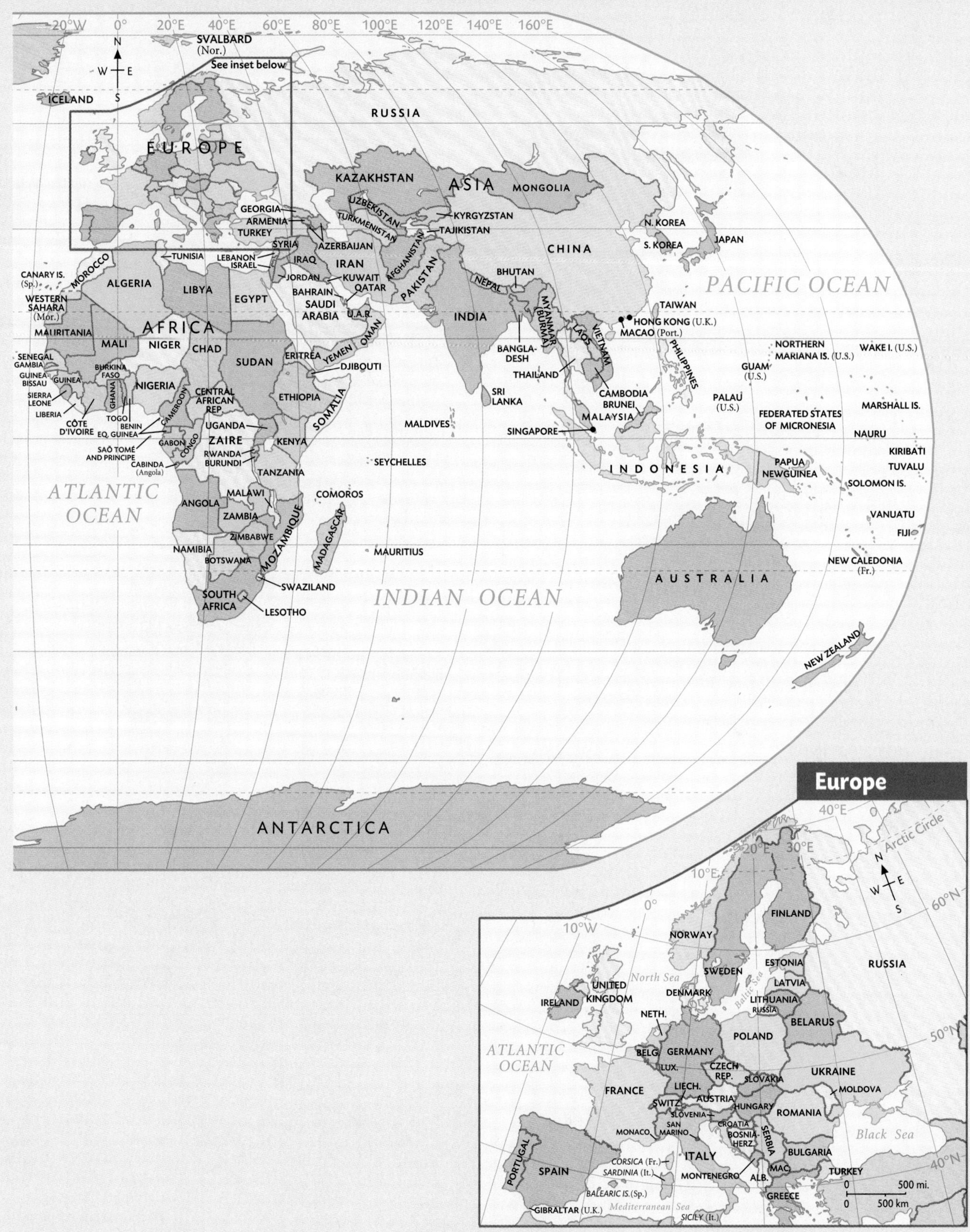

SVALBARD (Nor.)
See inset below
ICELAND
RUSSIA
EUROPE
KAZAKHSTAN
ASIA
MONGOLIA
GEORGIA
ARMENIA
TURKEY
UZBEKISTAN
TURKMENISTAN
KYRGYZSTAN
TAJIKISTAN
AZERBAIJAN
N. KOREA
S. KOREA
JAPAN
CHINA
SYRIA
TUNISIA
LEBANON
ISRAEL
IRAQ
IRAN
AFGHANISTAN
CANARY IS. (Sp.)
MOROCCO
ALGERIA
LIBYA
EGYPT
JORDAN
KUWAIT
BAHRAIN
QATAR
SAUDI ARABIA
U.A.E.
PAKISTAN
NEPAL
BHUTAN
PACIFIC OCEAN
WESTERN SAHARA (Mor.)
MAURITANIA
AFRICA
MALI
NIGER
CHAD
SUDAN
ERITREA
YEMEN
OMAN
INDIA
MYANMAR (BURMA)
LAOS
VIETNAM
TAIWAN
HONG KONG (U.K.)
MACAO (Port.)
PHILIPPINES
NORTHERN MARIANA IS. (U.S.)
WAKE I. (U.S.)
SENEGAL
GAMBIA
GUINEA-BISSAU
GUINEA
BURKINA FASO
GHANA
NIGERIA
DJIBOUTI
BANGLA-DESH
THAILAND
GUAM (U.S.)
SIERRA LEONE
LIBERIA
CÔTE D'IVOIRE
TOGO
BENIN
EQ. GUINEA
CAMEROON
CENTRAL AFRICAN REP.
ETHIOPIA
SOMALIA
SRI LANKA
CAMBODIA
BRUNEI
MALAYSIA
PALAU (U.S.)
FEDERATED STATES OF MICRONESIA
MARSHALL IS.
UGANDA
MALDIVES
SINGAPORE
SAO TOMÉ AND PRINCIPE
GABON
CONGO
ZAIRE
KENYA
NAURU
RWANDA
BURUNDI
CABINDA (Angola)
SEYCHELLES
KIRIBATI
TANZANIA
INDONESIA
PAPUA NEWGUINEA
TUVALU
ATLANTIC OCEAN
MALAWI
COMOROS
SOLOMON IS.
ANGOLA
ZAMBIA
MOZAMBIQUE
MADAGASCAR
VANUATU
FIJI
ZIMBABWE
NAMIBIA
BOTSWANA
MAURITIUS
NEW CALEDONIA (Fr.)
SWAZILAND
AUSTRALIA
SOUTH AFRICA
LESOTHO
INDIAN OCEAN
NEW ZEALAND
ANTARCTICA
Europe
Arctic Circle
FINLAND
NORWAY
ESTONIA
RUSSIA
North Sea
SWEDEN
LATVIA
UNITED KINGDOM
DENMARK
Baltic Sea
LITHUANIA
RUSSIA
IRELAND
NETH.
BELARUS
POLAND
ATLANTIC OCEAN
BELG.
GERMANY
LUX.
CZECH REP.
UKRAINE
SLOVAKIA
FRANCE
LIECH.
MOLDOVA
SWITZ.
AUSTRIA
HUNGARY
ROMANIA
SLOVENIA
CROATIA
SAN MARINO
MONACO
BOSNIA-HERZ.
SERBIA
Black Sea
BULGARIA
PORTUGAL
CORSICA (Fr.)
ITALY
SPAIN
SARDINIA (It.)
MONTENEGRO
ALB.
MAC.
TURKEY
500 mi.
500 km
BALEARIC IS. (Sp.)
GREECE
GIBRALTAR (U.K.)
Mediterranean Sea
SICILY (It.)

World–Physical

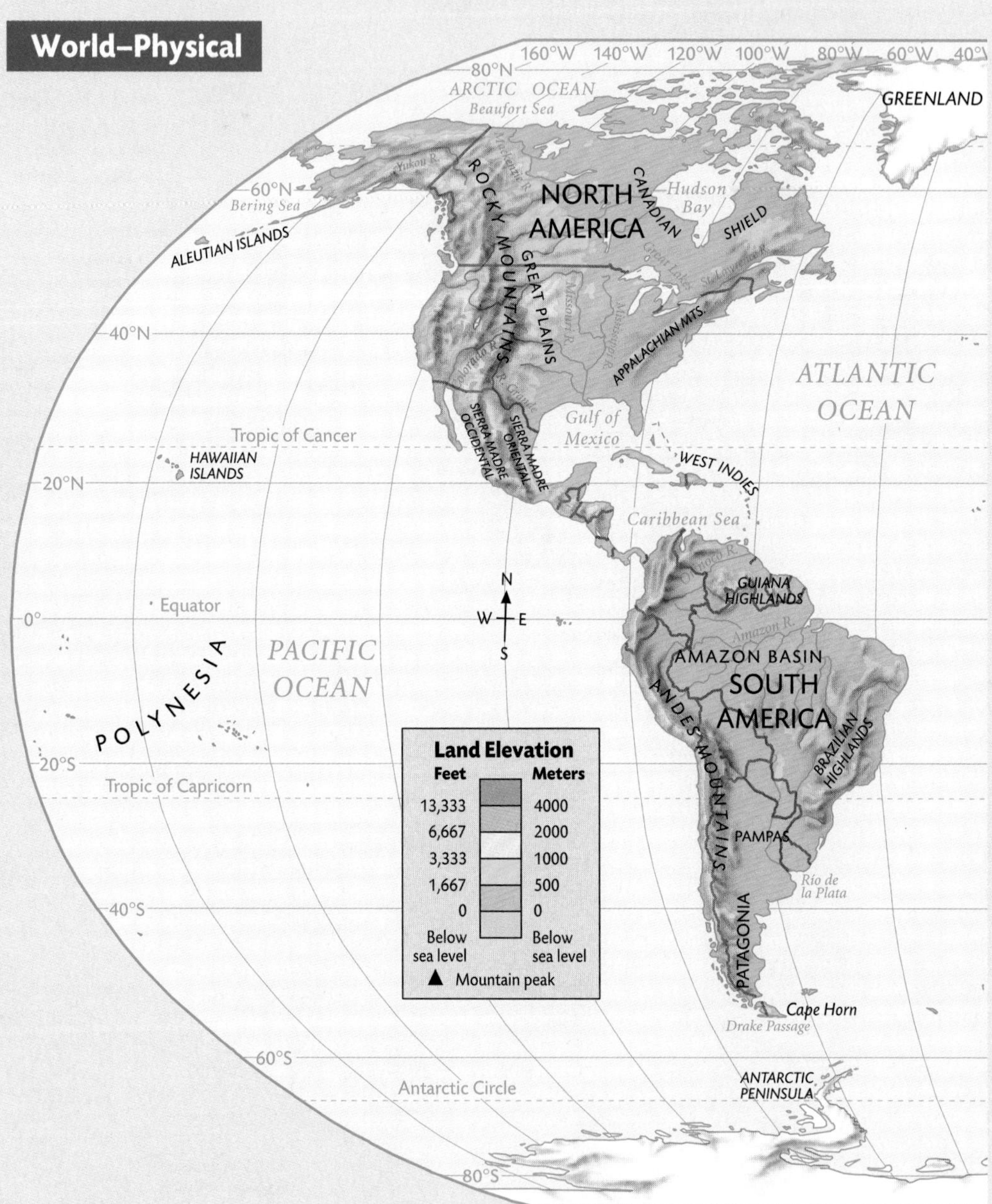

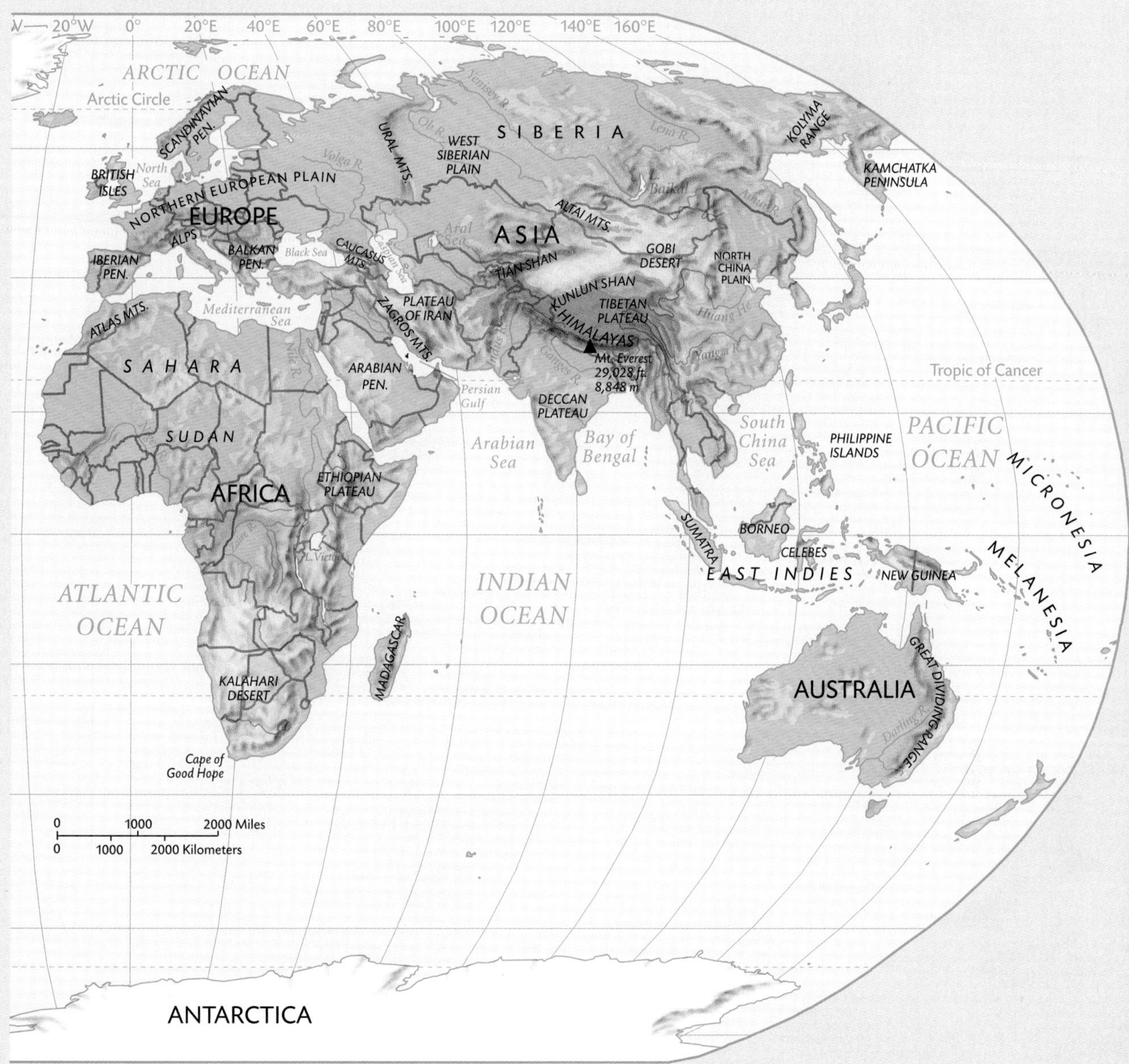

20°W
0°
20°E
40°E
60°E
80°E
100°E
120°E
140°E
160°E
ARCTIC OCEAN
Arctic Circle
SCANDINAVIAN PEN.
BRITISH ISLES
North Sea
NORTHERN EUROPEAN PLAIN
EUROPE
ALPS
BALKAN PEN.
IBERIAN PEN.
Black Sea
CAUCASUS MTS.
Caspian Sea
Aral Sea
URAL MTS.
WEST SIBERIAN PLAIN
SIBERIA
KOLYMA RANGE
KAMCHATKA PENINSULA
ALTAI MTS.
ASIA
GOBI DESERT
NORTH CHINA PLAIN
TIAN SHAN
KUNLUN SHAN
TIBETAN PLATEAU
HIMALAYAS
Mt. Everest 29,028 ft. 8,848 m
PLATEAU OF IRAN
ZAGROS MTS.
Mediterranean Sea
ATLAS MTS.
SAHARA
ARABIAN PEN.
Persian Gulf
DECCAN PLATEAU
Tropic of Cancer
Arabian Sea
Bay of Bengal
South China Sea
PHILIPPINE ISLANDS
PACIFIC OCEAN
MICRONESIA
SUDAN
ETHIOPIAN PLATEAU
AFRICA
SUMATRA
BORNEO
CELEBES
EAST INDIES
NEW GUINEA
MELANESIA
ATLANTIC OCEAN
INDIAN OCEAN
MADAGASCAR
KALAHARI DESERT
GREAT DIVIDING RANGE
AUSTRALIA
Cape of Good Hope
0 1000 2000 Miles
0 1000 2000 Kilometers
ANTARCTICA

Western Hemisphere–Political

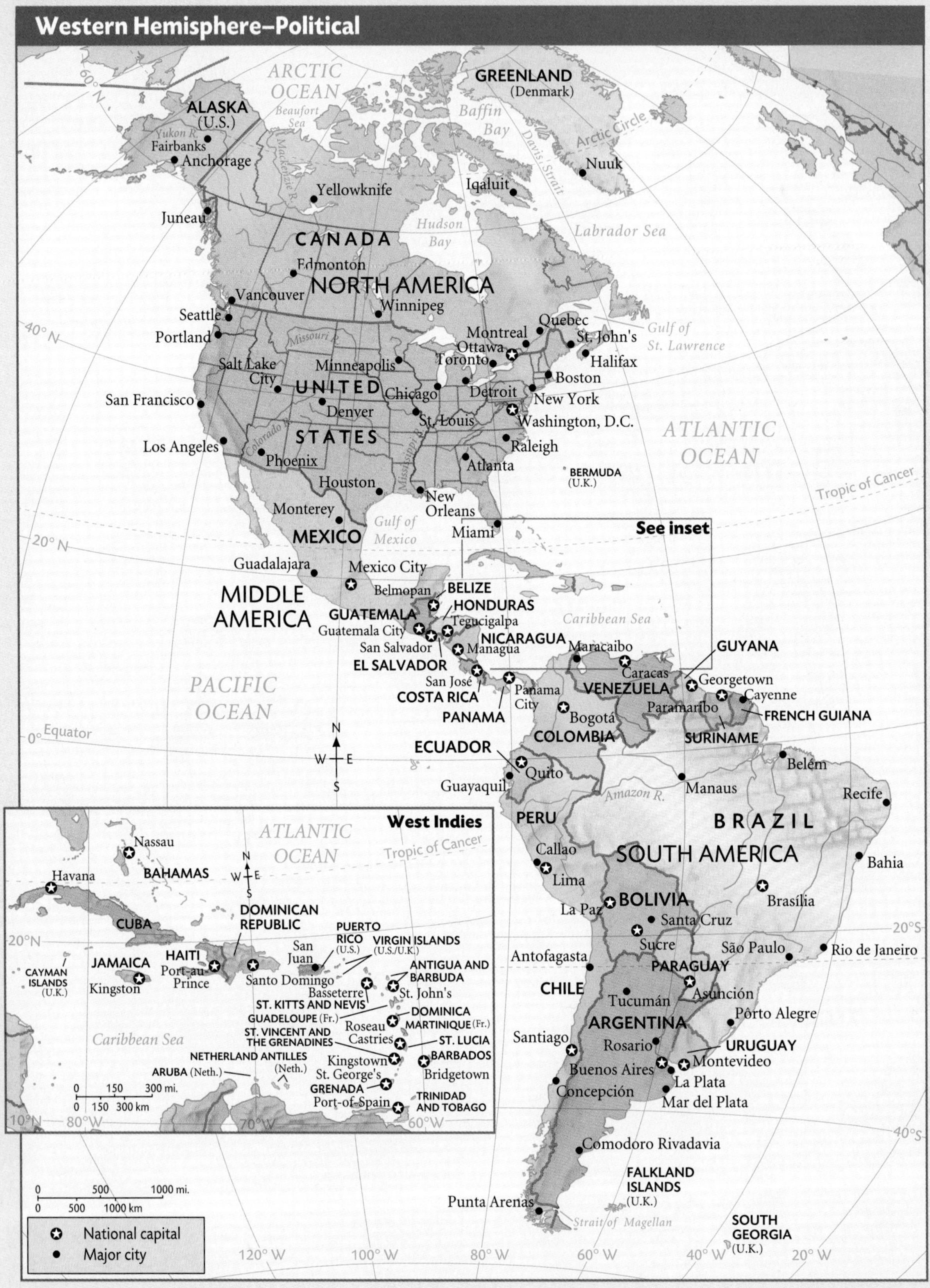

Western Hemisphere–Physical

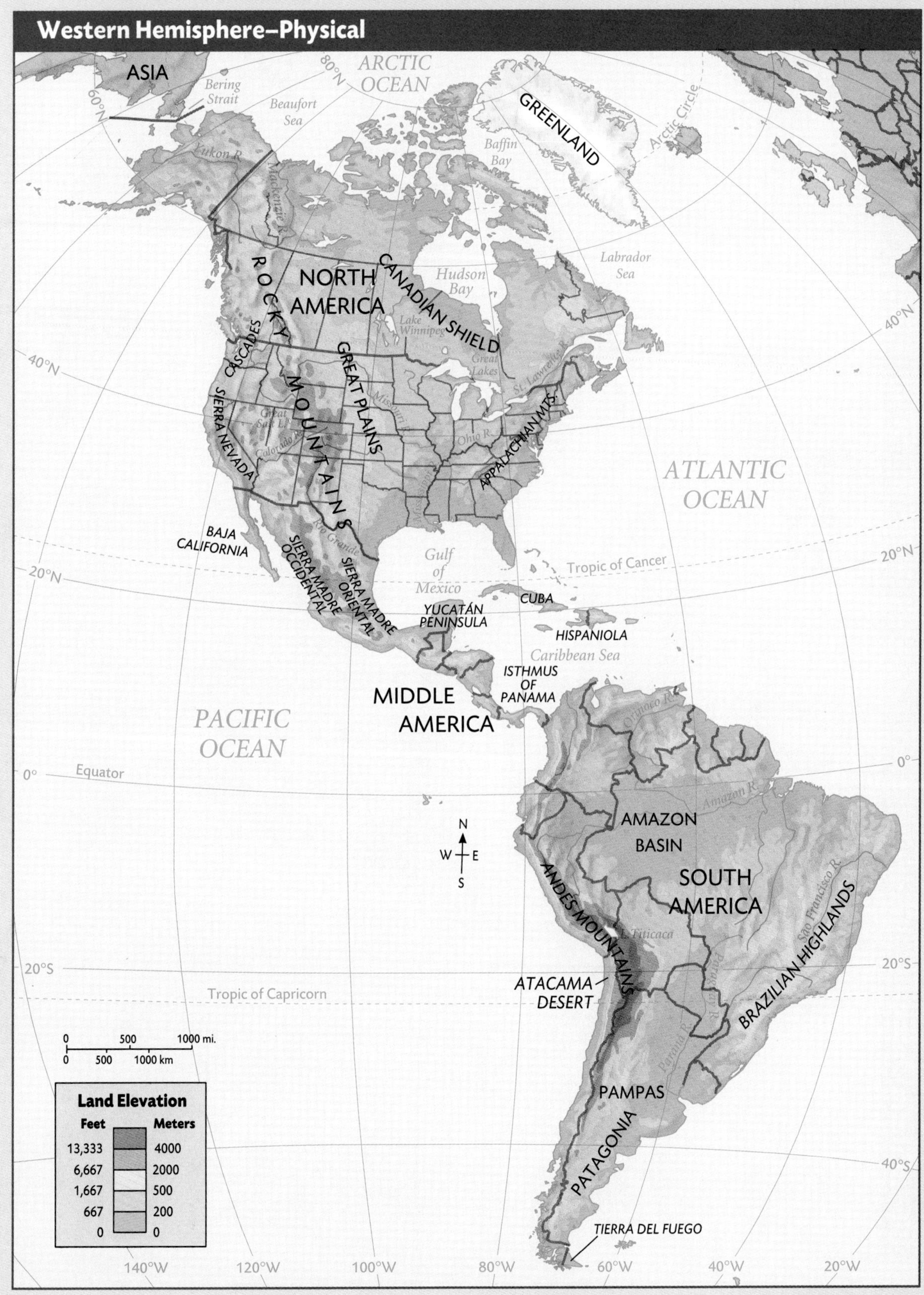

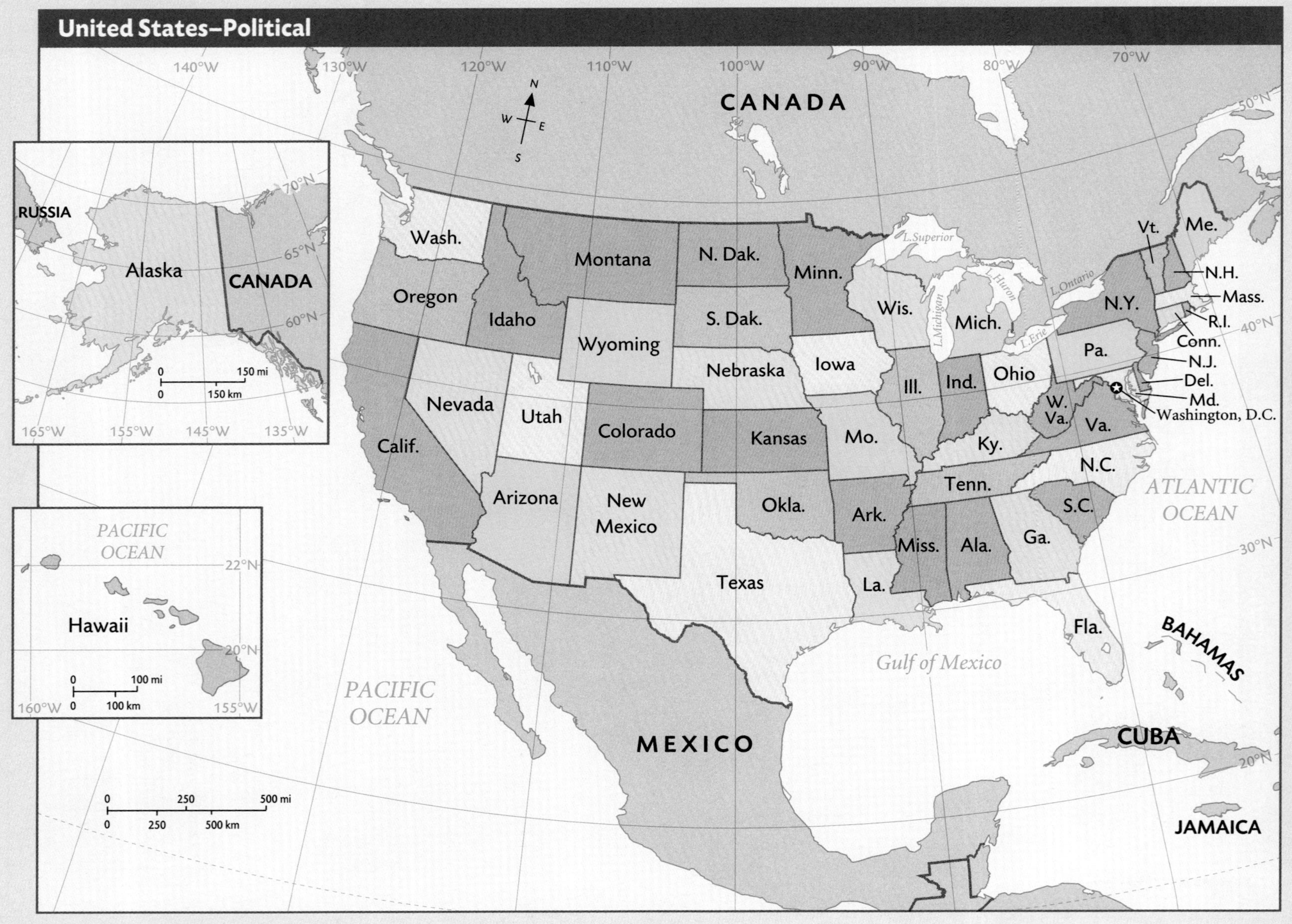
United States–Political
CANADA
MEXICO
CUBA
BAHAMAS
JAMAICA
ATLANTIC OCEAN
PACIFIC OCEAN
Gulf of Mexico
L. Superior
L. Michigan
L. Huron
L. Erie
L. Ontario
Wash.
Oregon
Calif.
Nevada
Idaho
Montana
Wyoming
Utah
Arizona
Colorado
New Mexico
N. Dak.
S. Dak.
Nebraska
Kansas
Okla.
Texas
Minn.
Iowa
Mo.
Ark.
La.
Wis.
Ill.
Mich.
Ind.
Ohio
Ky.
Tenn.
Miss.
Ala.
Ga.
Fla.
S.C.
N.C.
Va.
W. Va.
Pa.
N.Y.
Vt.
N.H.
Me.
Mass.
R.I.
Conn.
N.J.
Del.
Md.
Washington, D.C.
N
S
E
W
50°N
40°N
30°N
20°N
70°W
80°W
90°W
100°W
110°W
120°W
130°W
0
250
500 mi
0
250
500 km
RUSSIA
CANADA
Alaska
70°N
65°N
60°N
140°W
135°W
145°W
155°W
165°W
0
150 mi
0
150 km
PACIFIC OCEAN
Hawaii
22°N
20°N
155°W
160°W
0
100 mi
0
100 km

United States–Physical

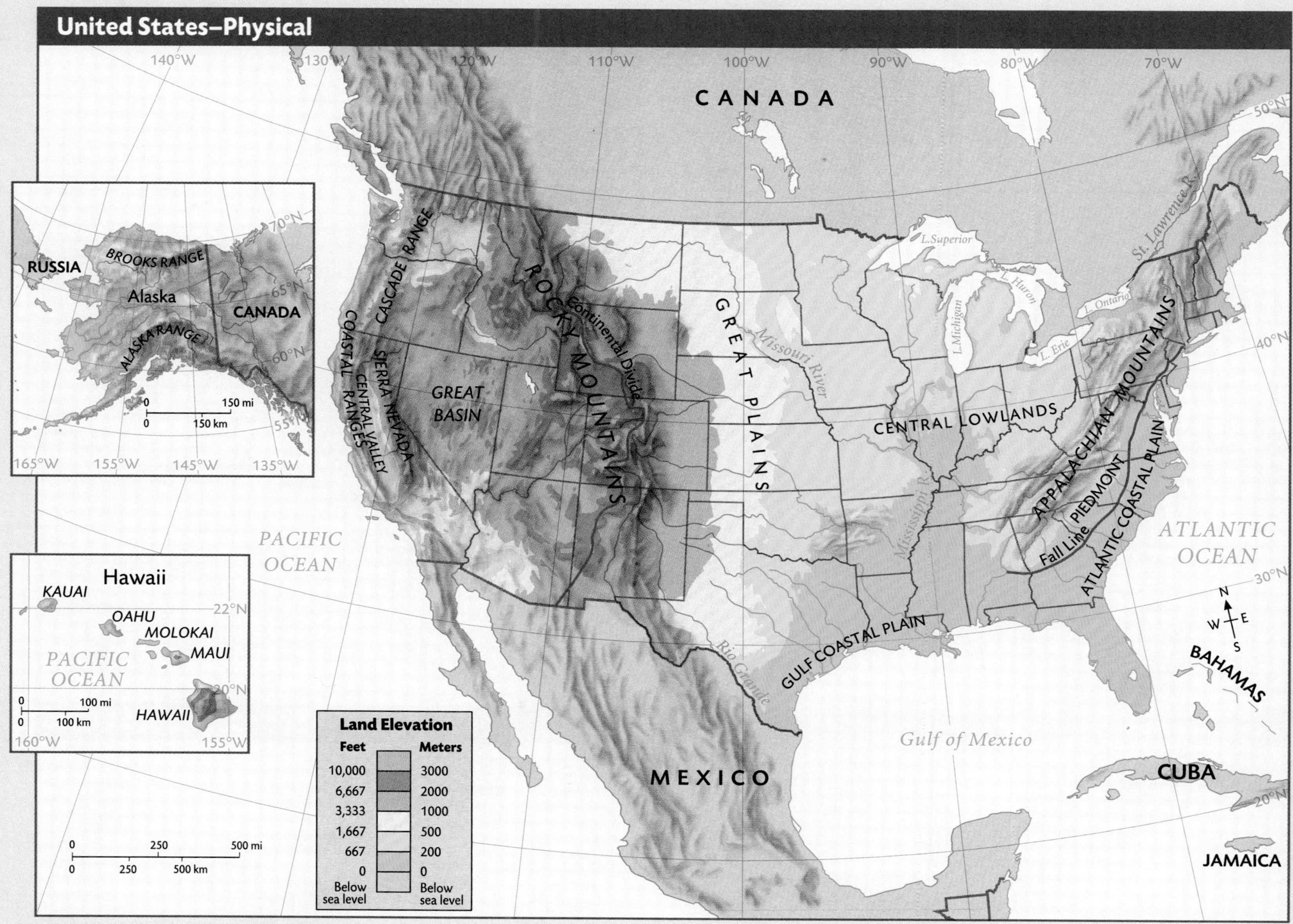

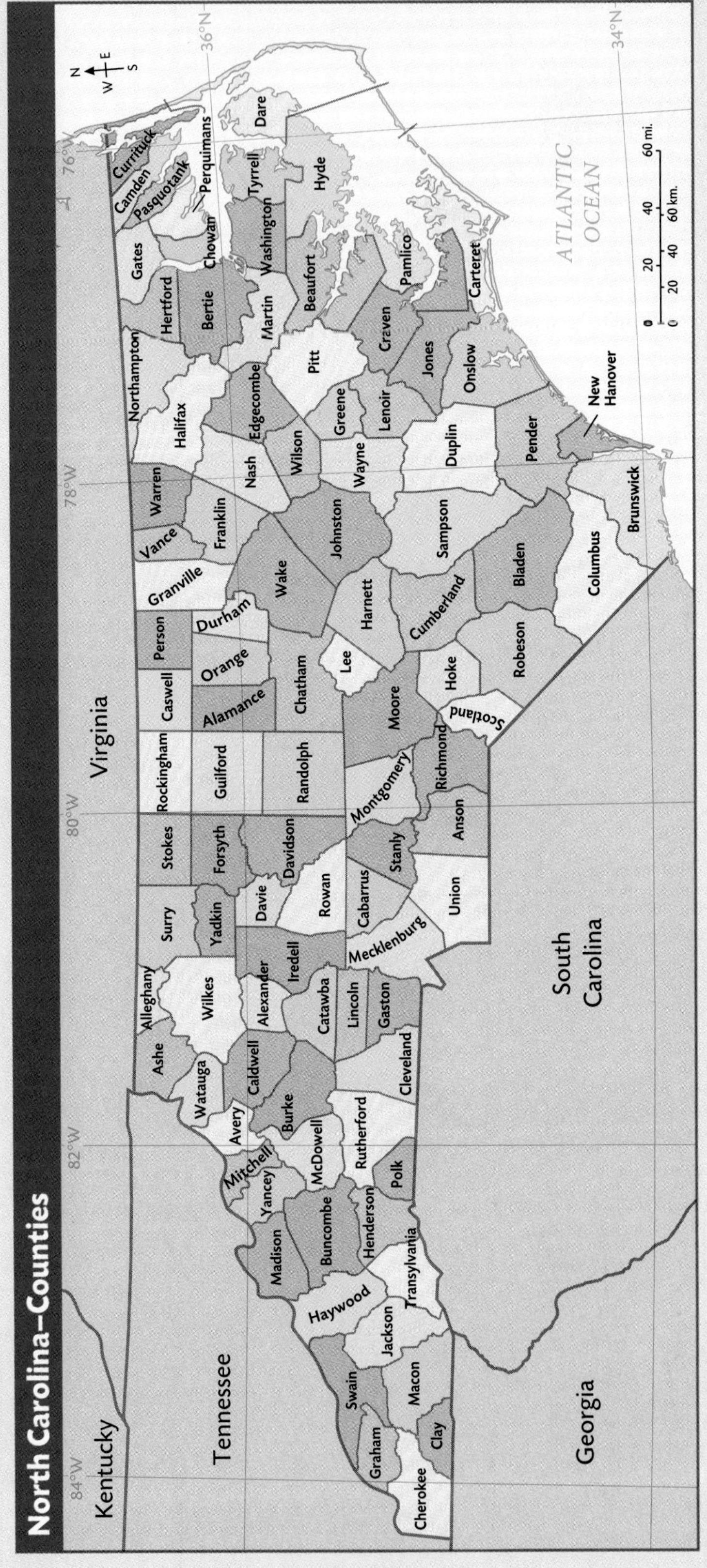
North Carolina–Counties
Kentucky
Tennessee
Virginia
South Carolina
Georgia
ATLANTIC OCEAN
N
E
S
W
84°W
82°W
80°W
78°W
76°W
36°N
34°N
0
20
40
60 mi.
0
20
40
60 km.
Currituck
Camden
Pasquotank
Perquimans
Dare
Tyrrell
Hyde
Gates
Chowan
Washington
Hertford
Bertie
Martin
Beaufort
Pamlico
Carteret
Northampton
Halifax
Edgecombe
Pitt
Craven
Jones
Onslow
Nash
Wilson
Greene
Lenoir
Wayne
Duplin
Pender
New Hanover
Warren
Vance
Franklin
Johnston
Sampson
Bladen
Brunswick
Columbus
Granville
Wake
Harnett
Cumberland
Robeson
Person
Durham
Orange
Caswell
Alamance
Chatham
Lee
Moore
Hoke
Scotland
Rockingham
Guilford
Randolph
Montgomery
Richmond
Anson
Stokes
Forsyth
Davidson
Stanly
Union
Surry
Yadkin
Davie
Rowan
Cabarrus
Mecklenburg
Alleghany
Wilkes
Alexander
Iredell
Catawba
Lincoln
Gaston
Ashe
Watauga
Caldwell
Burke
Cleveland
Avery
McDowell
Rutherford
Polk
Mitchell
Yancey
Buncombe
Henderson
Madison
Transylvania
Haywood
Jackson
Swain
Macon
Graham
Clay
Cherokee

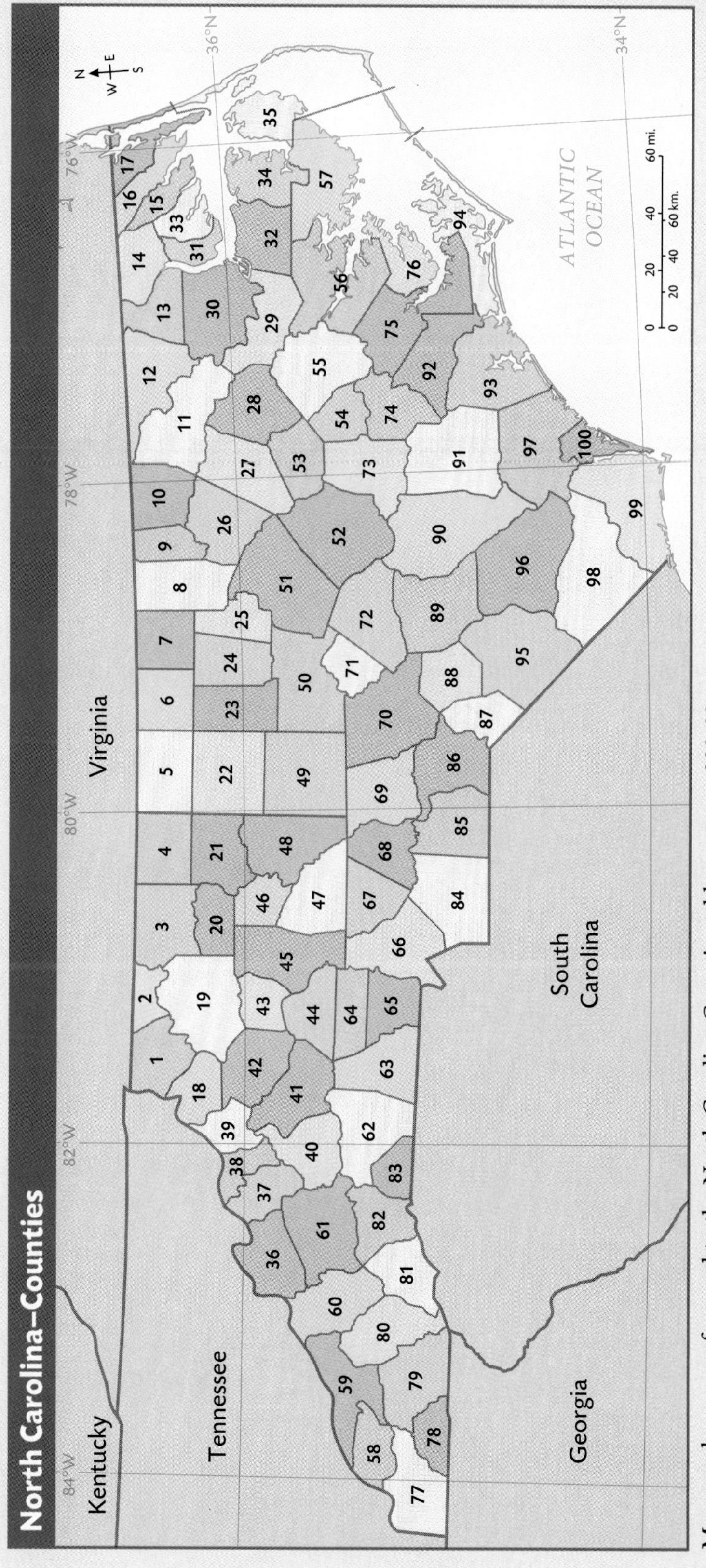

Map numbers are referenced to the North Carolina Counties table on pages 389-93.

North Carolina–Political/Physical

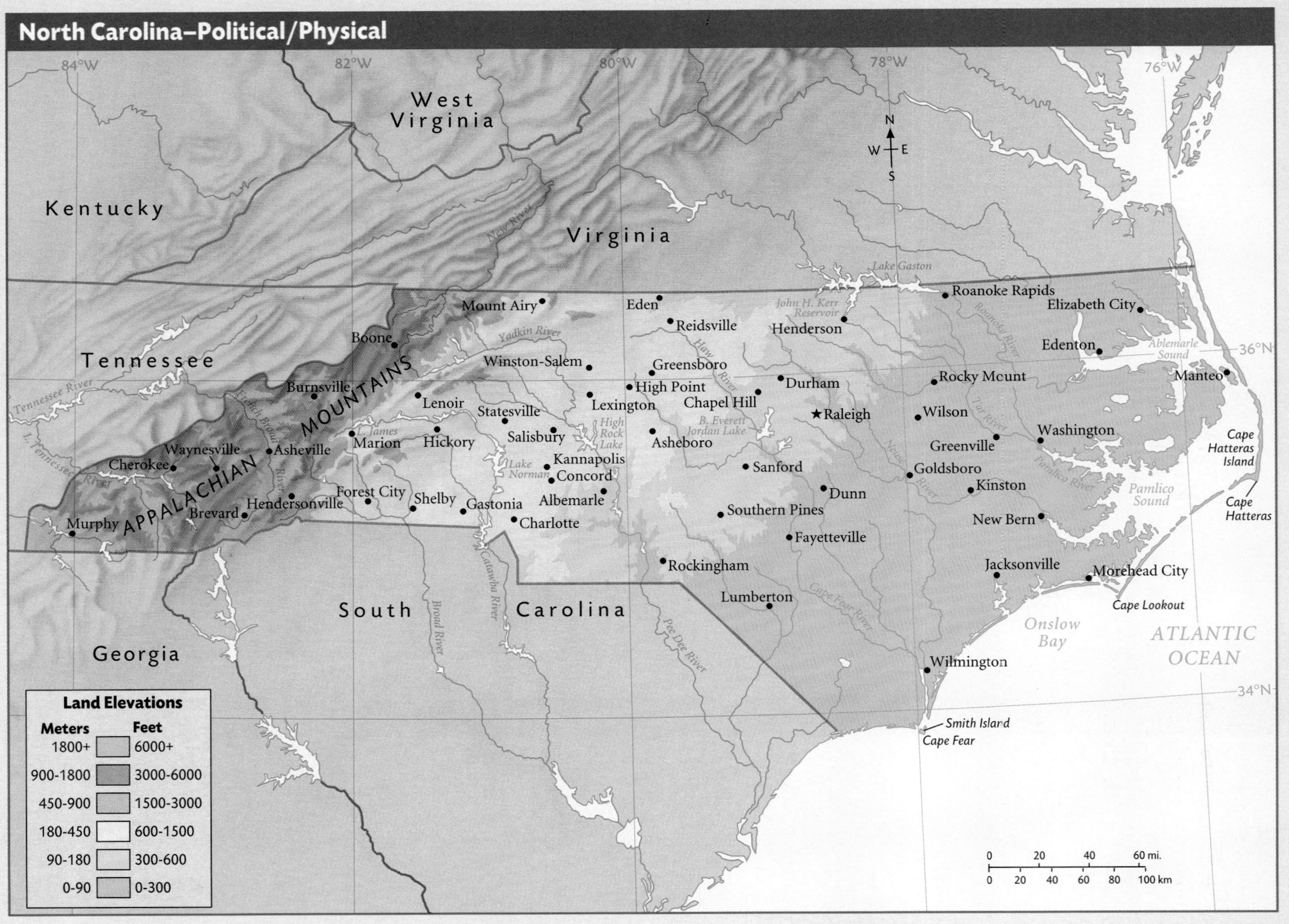

Name	Named For	Land Area (sq miles)	Of Interest	County Seat	Number on Map (p. 387)
Alamance	Great Alamance Creek (Native American name)	434	Cane Creek Mountains	Graham	23
Alexander	William J. Alexander	255	First emerald mine	Taylorsville	43
Alleghany	Native American name for the Alleghany and Ohio Rivers	230	Name means "a fine stream"	Sparta	2
Anson	George, Lord Anson	533	First soil conservation district in U.S.	Wadesboro	85
Ashe	Samuel Ashe	427	Once called the lost province	Jefferson	1
Avery	Waightstill Avery	247	Highest county seat east of the Rockies	Newland	39
Beaufort	Henry Somerset, Duke of Beaufort	831	Historic Bath	Washington	56
Bertie	James and Henry Bertie	693	2,000-year-old cypress tree	Windsor	30
Bladen	Martin Bladen	879	7 lakes that are part of the Carolina bays	Elizabethtown	96
Brunswick	Town of Brunswick	873	Plymouth gentian grows here	Bolivia	99
Buncombe	Edward Buncombe	645	Biltmore Estate	Asheville	61
Burke	Thomas Burke	506	Gold mined in the 1800s	Morganton	41
Cabarrus	Stephen Cabarrus	360	Reed Gold Mine, the country's first gold mine	Concord	67
Caldwell	Joseph Caldwell	476	Grandfather Mountain	Lenoir	42
Camden	Charles Pratt, Earl of Camden	239	Dismal Swamp	Camden	16
Carteret	Sir John Carteret	532	Croatan National Forest	Beaufort	94
Caswell	Richard Caswell	435	Flue-cured tobacco process begun here	Yanceyville	6
Catawba	Catawba Native Americans	406	Heart of the furniture industry	Newton	44
Chatham	William Pitt, Earl of Chatham	707	Largest eastern summertime home of the bald eagle	Pittsboro	50

Name	Named For	Land Area (sq miles)	Of Interest	County Seat	Number on Map (p. 387)
Cherokee	Cherokee Native Americans	454	Cherokee Reservation	Murphy	77
Chowan	Chowan Native Americans	180	Smallest county in the state	Edenton	31
Clay	Henry Clay	213	Formed in 1861	Hayesville	78
Cleveland	Benjamin Cleaveland	466	Mineral springs	Shelby	63
Columbus	Christopher Columbus	939	Lake Waccamaw	Whiteville	98
Craven	William, Lord Craven	725	Tryon Palace and gardens	New Bern	75
Cumberland	William Augustus, Duke of Cumberland	661	Fort Bragg and Pope Air Force bases	Fayetteville	89
Currituck	Native American word for 'wild goose'	273	Currituck Beach Lighthouse at Corolla	Currituck	17
Dare	Virginia Dare	388	Wright Brothers National Memorial	Manteo	35
Davidson	William Lee Davidson	546	High Rock Lake, Lake Thom-a-Lex Reservoir	Lexington	48
Davie	William R. Davie	264	Yadkin River	Mocksville	46
Duplin	Thomas Hay, Lord Duplin	822	Goshen Swamp	Kenansville	91
Durham	Durham, NC, which was named for Durham, England	299	Bennett Place	Durham	25
Edgecombe	Richard Edgecumbe	511	Tar River, home of freshwater mussels	Tarboro	28
Forsyth	Benjamin Forsyth	424	Old Salem	Winston-Salem	21
Franklin	Benjamin Franklin	494	Laurel Mill	Louisburg	26
Gaston	William Gaston	358	Schiele Museum	Gastonia	65
Gates	Horatio Gates	343	Merchants Millpond State Park	Gatesville	14
Graham	William A. Graham	289	Joyce Kilmer Memorial Forest	Robbinsville	58
Granville	John Carteret, Earl Granville	542	Oldest tobacco market in NC	Oxford	8
Greene	Nathanael Greene	269	Habitat for peregrine falcon and alligator	Snow Hill	54

Name	Named For	Land Area (sq miles)	Of Interest	County Seat	Number on Map (p. 387)
Guilford	Francis North, Earl of Guilford	651	First steam cotton mill in NC	Greensboro	22
Halifax	George Montagu, second Earl of Halifax	722	Historic Halifax, called NC's cradle of history	Halifax	11
Harnett	Cornelius Harnett	606	Steep bluffs and ravines formed by rivers	Lillington	72
Haywood	John Haywood	543	Shining Rock Wilderness Area	Waynesville	60
Henderson	Leonard Henderson	382	Straddles the Eastern Continental Divide	Hendersonville	82
Hertford	Francis Seymour Conway, Earl of Hertford	356	Chowan River, Meherrin River	Winton	13
Hoke	Robert F. Hoke	381	Carolina bays	Raeford	88
Hyde	Edward Hyde	634	Lake Mattamuskeet, a national wildlife refuge	Swan Quarter	57
Iredell	James Iredell	591	Lake Norman	Statesville	45
Jackson	Andrew Jackson	496	Great Smoky Mountains Railway	Sylva	80
Johnston	Gabriel Johnston	795	Bentonville Battleground	Smithfield	52
Jones	Willie Jones	467	Hoffman Forest, NCSU's teaching forest	Trenton	92
Lee	Robert E. Lee	255	Large coal deposits	Sanford	71
Lenoir	William Lenoir	391	75 miles of the Neuse River	Kinston	74
Lincoln	Benjamin Lincoln	308	Lake Norman	Lincolnton	64
Macon	Nathaniel Macon	517	Gem mines	Franklin	79
Madison	James Madison	456	685 miles of open streams	Marshall	36
Martin	Josiah Martin	481	Roanoke River; home of black bears	Williamston	29
McDowell	Joseph McDowell	442	Gateway of the mountains	Marion	40
Mecklenburg	Queen Charlotte's German hometown	542	1800s gold-mining capital of the country	Charlotte	66
Mitchell	Elisha Mitchell	220	Mount Mitchell	Bakersville	38

Name	Named For	Land Area (sq miles)	Of Interest	County Seat	Number on Map (p. 387)
Montgomery	Richard Montgomery	488	Uwharrie National Forest	Troy	69
Moore	Alfred Moore	705	World Golf Hall of Fame	Carthage	70
Nash	Francis Nash	552	The Country Doctor Museum	Nashville	27
New Hanover	House of Hanover	194	U.S.S. *North Carolina* Battleship Memorial	Wilmington	100
Northampton	James Compton, Earl of Northampton	539	Produces most peanuts in the state	Jackson	12
Onslow	Arthur Onslow	756	New River, Camp Lejeune	Jacksonville	93
Orange	William V of Orange	398	North Carolina Botanical Gardens	Hillsborough	24
Pamlico	Pamlico Sound	341	Swing bridges and ferries	Bayboro	76
Pasquotank	Pasquotank Native Americans	229	Blackbeard's home	Elizabeth City	15
Pender	William D. Pender	857	Venus flytrap	Burgaw	97
Perquimans	Perquimans Native Americans	261	Yaupon grows here	Hertford	33
Person	Thomas Person	400	Copper once mined here	Roxboro	7
Pitt	William Pitt, Earl of Chatham	656	A steamboat route in 1847 on the Tar River	Greenville	55
Polk	William Polk	234	Pearson's Falls	Columbus	83
Randolph	Peyton Randolph	801	North Carolina Zoological Park	Asheboro	49
Richmond	Charles Lennox, Duke of Richmond	477	National Railroad Museum	Rockingham	86
Robeson	Thomas Robeson	944	Lumber River	Lumberton	95
Rockingham	Charles Watson-Wentworth, second Marquis of Rockingham	572	Four rivers—Dan, Smith, Mayo, Haw	Wentworth	5
Rowan	Matthew Rowan	517	NC Transportation Museum	Salisbury	47
Rutherford	Griffith Rutherford	566	Chimney Rock, Lake Lure	Rutherfordton	62
Sampson	John Sampson	963	Largest NC grower of cucumbers and peppers	Clinton	90

Name	Named For	Land Area (sq miles)	Of Interest	County Seat	Number on Map (p. 387)
Scotland	Country of Scotland	317	Carolina bays; eastern green tiger salamander habitat	Laurinburg	87
Stanly	John Stanly	399	Uwharrie Mountains	Albemarle	68
Stokes	John Stokes	459	Hanging Rock State Park	Danbury	4
Surry	County of Surrey, England	537	Pilot Mountain; the world's largest open-faced granite quarry	Dobson	3
Swain	David L. Swain	530	Clingmans Dome	Bryson City	59
Transylvania	Latin words *trans* ("across") and *sylva* ("woods")	379	Land of the waterfalls, Pisgah Forest	Brevard	81
Tyrrell	Sir John Tyrrell	399	Albemarle Sound, Alligator River, Lake Phelps	Columbia	34
Union	the union of this county from parts of two others	643	Once home of Waxhaw Native Americans	Monroe	84
Vance	Zebulon B. Vance	249	Kerr Lake; tungsten once mined here	Henderson	9
Wake	Margaret Wake	864	Westernmost site of eastern cedar trees; state capital	Raleigh	51
Warren	Joseph Warren	443	Kerr and Gaston Lakes; White Sulphur Springs	Warrenton	10
Washington	George Washington	336	Cypress trees in Pettigrew State Park	Plymouth	32
Watauga	Watauga River	320	Name means "beautiful water"	Boone	18
Wayne	Anthony Wayne	555	Wilmington and Weldon Railroad created Goldsboro	Goldsboro	73
Wilkes	John Wilkes	765	50 miles of Blue Ridge Parkway	Wilkesboro	19
Wilson	Louis D. Wilson	373	Titanium is mined here	Wilson	53
Yadkin	Yadkin River	335	Yadkin River, Yadkin River Bluffs	Yadkinville	20
Yancey	Bartlett Yancey	311	Black Mountains (tallest in the eastern U.S.)	Burnsville	37

City	County	Region	1993 Population	Rank (by Population)
Asheville	Buncombe	Mountains	68,474	9
Burlington	Alamance	Piedmont	42,273	17
Cary	Wake	Piedmont	65,912	10
Chapel Hill	Orange	Piedmont	43,539	16
Charlotte	Mecklenburg	Piedmont	469,809	1
Concord	Cabarrus	Piedmont	35,468	19
Durham	Durham	Piedmont	148,129	5
Fayetteville	Cumberland	Coastal Plain	93,219	6
Gastonia	Gaston	Piedmont	57,181	12
Goldsboro	Wayne	Coastal Plain	47,992	15
Greensboro	Guilford	Piedmont	193,298	3
Greenville	Pitt	Coastal Plain	56,307	13
Havelock	Craven	Coastal Plain	21,042	27
Hickory	Catawba	Piedmont	30,058	21
High Point	Guilford	Piedmont	71,791	8
Jacksonville	Onslow	Coastal Plain	75,069	7
Kannapolis	Cabarrus	Piedmont	34,423	20
Kinston	Lenoir	Coastal Plain	25,729	22
Monroe	Union	Piedmont	21,273	26
New Bern	Craven	Coastal Plain	21,696	24
Raleigh	Wake	Piedmont	249,332	2
Rocky Mount	Nash	Coastal Plain	55,952	14
Salisbury	Rowan	Piedmont	24,543	23
Statesville	Iredell	Piedmont	21,655	25
Wilmington	New Hanover	Coastal Plain	62,256	11
Wilson	Wilson	Coastal Plain	40,232	18
Winston-Salem	Forsyth	Piedmont	165,750	4

Source: North Carolina Office of State Planning

Year	Name	Home County
1776–80	Richard Caswell	Dobbs (now Lenoir)
1780–81	Abner Nash	Craven
1781–82	Thomas Burke	Orange
1782–84	Alexander Martin	Guilford
1784–87	Richard Caswell	Dobbs (now Lenoir)
1787–89	Samuel Johnston	Chowan
1789–92	Alexander Martin	Guilford
1792–95	Richard Dobbs Spaight	Craven
1795–98	Samuel Ashe	New Hanover
1798–99	William R. Davie	Halifax
1799–1802	Benjamin Williams	Moore
1808–10	David Stone	Bertie
1810–11	Benjamin Smith	Brunswick
1811–14	William Hawkins	Warren
1814–17	William Miller	Warren
1817–20	John Branch	Halifax
1820–21	Jesse Franklin	Surry
1821–24	Gabriel Holmes	Sampson
1824–27	Hutchins G. Burton	Halifax
1827–28	James Iredell	Chowan
1828–30	John Owen	Bladen
1830–32	Montfort Stokes	Wilkes
1832–35	David L. Swain	Buncombe
1835–36	Richard Dobbs Spaight, Jr.	Craven
1836–41	Edward B. Dudley	New Hanover
1841–45	John M. Morehead	Guilford
1845–49	William A. Graham	Orange
1849–51	Charles Manly	Wake
1851–54	David Reid	Rockingham
1854–55	Warren Winslow	Cumberland
1855–59	Thomas Bragg	Northampton
1859–61	John W. Ellis	Rowan
1861–62	Henry T. Clark	Edgecombe
1862–65	Zebulon B. Vance	Buncombe
1865	William W. Holden*	Wake
1865–68	Jonathan Worth	Randolph
1868–71	William W. Holden*	Wake

Year	Name	Home County
1871–74	Tod R. Caldwell	Burke
1874–77	Curtis H. Brogden	Wayne
1877–79	Zebulon B. Vance	Mecklenburg
1879–85	Thomas J. Jarvis	Pitt
1885–89	Alfred M. Scales	Rockingham
1889–91	Daniel G. Fowle	Wake
1891–93	Thomas M. Holt	Alamance
1893–97	Elias Carr	Edgecombe
1897–1901	Daniel L. Russell	Brunswick
1901–5	Charles B. Aycock	Wayne
1905–9	Robert B. Glenn	Forsyth
1909–13	William W. Kitchin	Person
1913–17	Locke Craig	Buncombe
1917–21	Thomas W. Bickett	Franklin
1921–25	Cameron Morrison	Mecklenburg
1925–29	Angus W. McLean	Robeson
1929–33	O. Max Gardner	Cleveland
1933–37	J. C. B. Ehringhaus	Pasquotank
1937–41	Clyde R. Hoey	Cleveland
1941–45	J. Melville Broughton	Wake
1945–49	R. Gregg Cherry	Gaston
1949–53	W. Kerr Scott	Alamance
1953–54	William B. Umstead	Durham
1954–61	Luther B. Hodges	Rockingham
1961–65	Terry Sanford	Cumberland
1965–69	Dan K. Moore	Jackson
1969–73	Robert W. Scott	Alamance
1973–77	James E. Holshouser, Jr.	Watauga
1977–85	James B. Hunt, Jr.	Wilson
1985–92	James G. Martin	Iredell
1992–	James B. Hunt, Jr.	Wilson

* First term is appointment to office by Andrew Johnson under his plan of Reconstruction. Second term he was impeached and removed from office in 1871.

1776–1835 Governors elected to two houses of the General Assembly to one-year terms.

1826–68 Governors elected by qualified voters to two-year terms.

Since 1868 Governors elected to four-year terms.

North Carolina's symbols represent what North Carolinians think about the state. The state seal contains figures and a phrase in Latin, "Esse Quam Videri," which means "to be rather than to seem." North Carolina's early leaders believed this represented the people's spirit of honesty and integrity. The General Assembly has passed laws making a few animals, minerals, and plants official symbols of North Carolina.

State seal

The Eastern Box turtle was named the state reptile in 1979. The box turtle lives in swampy, woodland areas of the Coastal Plain.

State flag

Dogwood

Because of our coastline we have a state shell. The Scotch Bonnet was chosen in 1965 as the official state seashell.

The dogwood is North Carolina's official state flower. In 1941 the General Assembly gave the plant that honor.

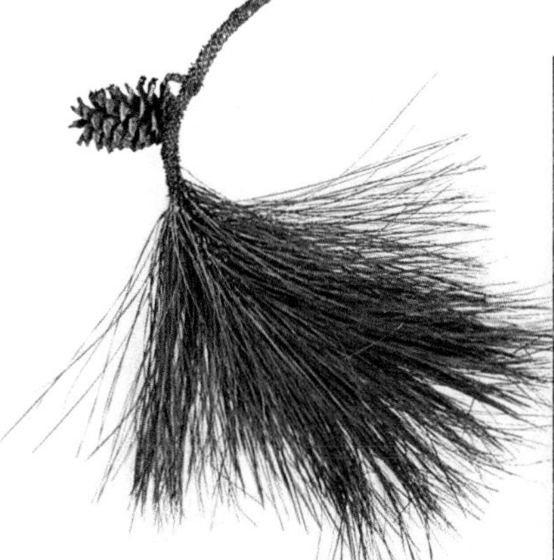

The state tree is the longleaf pine tree. The General Assembly chose it in 1963.

The cardinal became North Carolina's official bird in 1943.

The North Carolina General Assembly also has adopted the following as official state symbols:

Vegetable: sweet potato
Precious gem: emerald
Fish: channel bass
Boat: shad boat
Beverage: milk
Dog: plott hound
Rock: granite
Mammal: gray squirrel
Colors: red and blue
Song: "The Old North State"
Nicknames: The Tar Heel State, The Old North State
Motto: *Esse quam videri,* "To Be Rather Than To Seem"

Emeralds

North Carolina's honey bee was named the state insect in 1973. Some people think the insect represents how hard North Carolinians work.

DICTIONARY OF GEOGRAPHIC TERMS

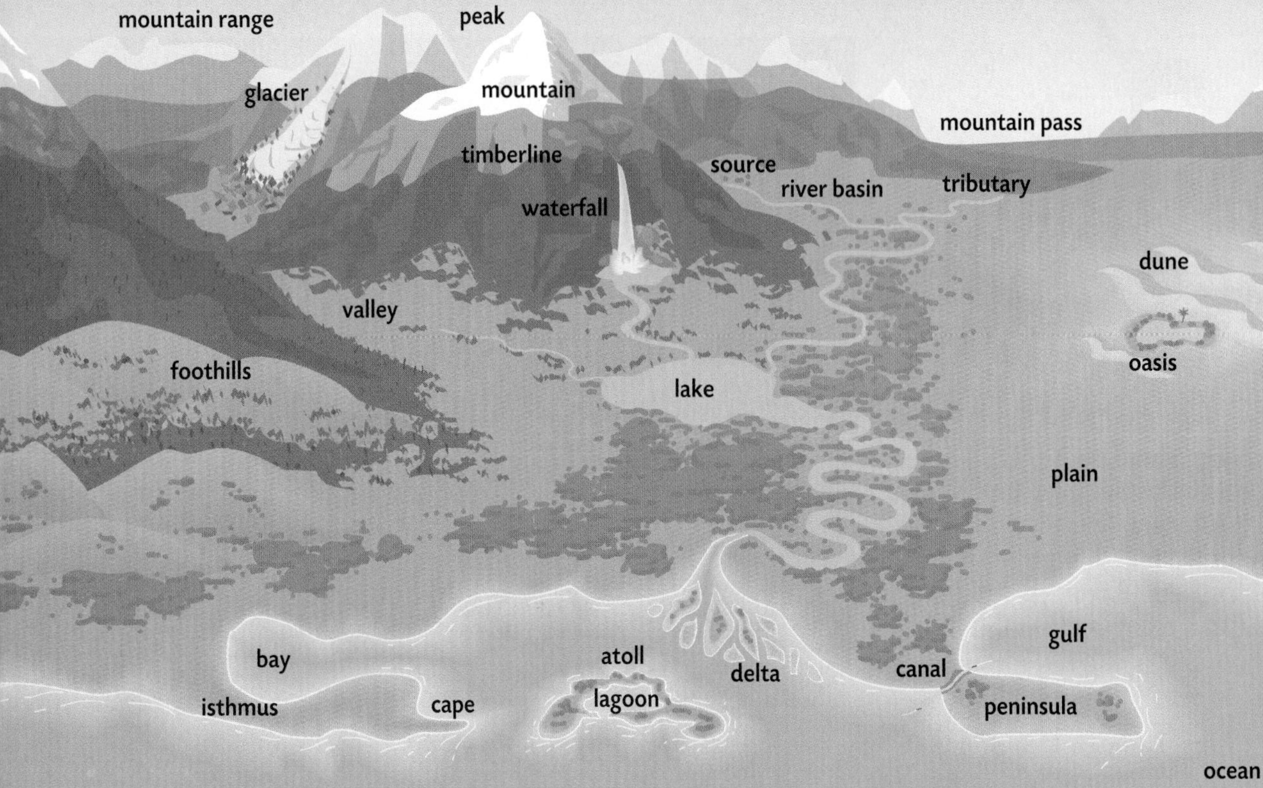

archipelago (ar·kee·PELL·ah·goh) A large group or chain of islands.

atoll A ring-shaped coral island or string of islands surrounding a lagoon.

basin An area of low-lying land surrounded by higher land. *See also* **river basin**.

bay Part of an ocean, sea, or lake extending into the land. Usually smaller than a gulf.

beach The gently sloping shore of an ocean or other body of water, especially that part covered by sand or pebbles.

butte (beyoot) A small, flat-topped hill. A butte is smaller than a plateau or a mesa.

canal A waterway built to carry water for navigation or irrigation. Navigation canals usually connect two other bodies of water.

canyon A deep, narrow valley with steep sides.

cape A projecting part of a coastline that extends into an ocean, sea, gulf, bay, or lake.

cliff A high, steep face of rock or earth.

coast Land along an ocean or sea.

dam A wall built across a river to hold back the flowing water.

delta Land formed at the mouth of a river by deposits of silt, sand, and pebbles.

desert A very dry area where few plants grow.

dune A mound, hill, or ridge of sand that is heaped up by the wind.

fjord (fyord) A deep, narrow inlet of the sea between high, steep cliffs.

foothills A hilly area at the base of a mountain range.

glacier (GLAY·sher) A large sheet of ice that moves slowly over some land surface or down a valley.

gulf Part of an ocean or sea that extends into the land. A gulf is usually larger than a bay.

harbor A protected place along a shore where ships can safely anchor.

hill A rounded, raised landform, not as high as a mountain.

island A body of land completely surrounded by water.

isthmus (ISS·muss) A narrow strip of land bordered by water that connects two larger bodies of land.

lagoon A shallow body of water partly or completely enclosed within an atoll. Also, a shallow body of sea water partly cut off from the sea by a narrow strip of land.

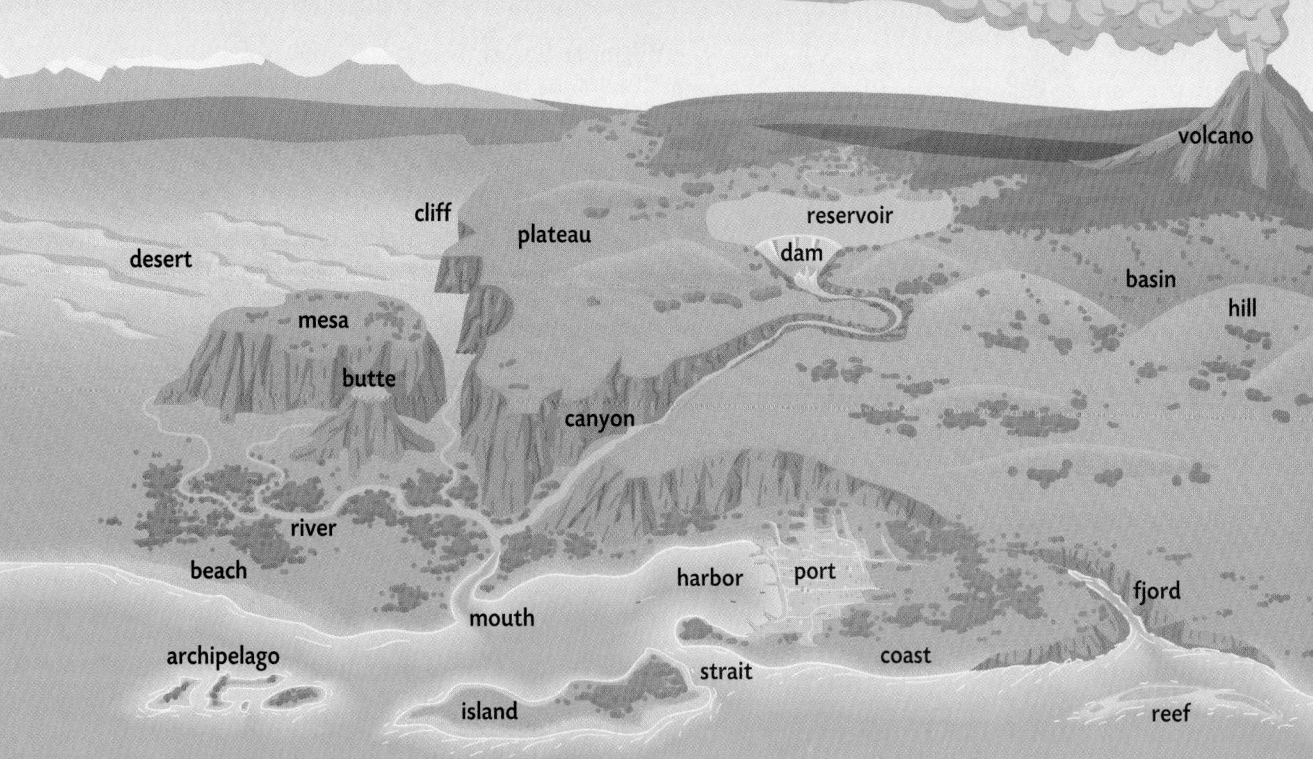

lake A body of water surrounded by land.
mesa A high, flat landform rising steeply above the surrounding land. A mesa is smaller than a plateau and larger than a butte.
mountain A high, rounded or pointed landform with steep sides, higher than a hill.
mountain pass An opening or gap through a mountain range.
mountain range A row or chain of mountains.
mouth The place where a river empties into another body of water.
oasis A place in the desert made fertile by a steady supply of water.
ocean One of the earth's four largest bodies of water. The four oceans are really a single connected body of salt water that covers about three fourths of the earth's surface.
peak The pointed top of a mountain or hill.
peninsula A body of land nearly surrounded by water.
plain A large area of flat or nearly flat land.
plateau A high, flat landform that rises steeply above the surrounding land. A plateau is larger than a mesa or a butte.
port A place where ships load and unload goods.
reef A ridge of sand, rock, or coral that lies at or near the surface of a sea.
reservoir A natural or artificial lake used to store water.
river A large stream of water that flows across the land and usually empties into a lake, ocean, or other river.
river basin All the land drained by a river and its tributaries.
sea A large body of water partly or entirely surrounded by land. Another word for ocean.
source The place where a river or stream begins.
strait A narrow waterway or channel connecting two larger bodies of water.
timberline An imaginary line on mountains above which trees do not grow.
tributary A river or stream that flows into a larger river or stream.
valley An area of low land between hills or mountains.
volcano (vol·KAY·no) An opening in the earth through which lava, rock, gases, and ash are forced out.
waterfall A flow of water falling from a high place to a lower place.

A

Albemarle Sound Tidewater sound of northeastern North Carolina, 52 miles (84 km) long, 5 to 14 miles (8 to 23 km) wide.

Alligator River Coastal Plain river that rises in Hyde County, flows east to north, and empties into Albemarle Sound.

Appalachian Mountains Largest mountain chain in eastern North America. Stretches from Alabama to Canada. In North Carolina, includes the Blue Ridge, Black, and Great Smoky Mountains.

Appalachian Trail A marked footpath of about 2,050 miles (3,300 km) that extends from Maine to Georgia. About 200 miles (322 km) of the trail are in North Carolina.

Asheboro Piedmont city and county seat of Randolph County. Site of North Carolina Zoological Park.

Asheville Largest city of the Mountains Region. County seat of Buncombe County.

Atlantic Beach Atlantic Ocean coastal town on the eastern end of Bogue Banks.

Atlantic Ocean One of the world's largest bodies of water, marking North America's east boundary. North Carolina has 328 miles (528 km) of coast along the Atlantic.

B

Banner Elk Mountain ski resort town in northeast Avery County.

Bath Oldest town in North Carolina, settled in 1690. Located in the Tidewater in central Beaufort County.

Beaufort Coastal town built on the site of a Native American village. County seat of Carteret County.

Belhaven Coastal Plain town in east Beaufort County.

Benson Town in southwest Johnston County on the fall line between the Coastal Plain and the Piedmont.

Bentonville Site of Civil War battle, bloodiest ever in North Carolina. Located in Johnston County.

Biltmore Estate Large private home on the southern outskirts of Asheville in Buncombe County. Built for the Vanderbilt family in 1895 and open to tourists.

Biltmore Forest Forest of 11,000 acres (4,400 sq hm) on the Biltmore Estate. Gifford Pinchot, first American-trained forester, planned and directed the planting of the forest.

Black Mountains Mountain range from Buncombe-Yancey county line northeast to south-central Yancey County. Peaks include Mount Mitchell and Potato Knob.

Blowing Rock Mountain town in southern Watauga and northern Caldwell Counties.

Blue Ridge Mountains Eastern portion of the Appalachian Mountains. Highest peaks are in the Black Mountains of North Carolina.

Blue Ridge Parkway Scenic road and park along the crest of the Blue Ridge Mountains. Goes from Shenandoah National Park in Virginia to Great Smoky Mountains in North Carolina and Tennessee.

Bodie Island One of the Outer Banks, in eastern Dare County. Bounded on the south by Oregon Inlet.

Bogue Banks Barrier island in southern Carteret County forming one of the Outer Banks. Fort Macon is located at the eastern end.

Bogue Sound Sound along the southern edge of Carteret County. Empties into the Atlantic Ocean through Bogue Inlet.

Boone Mountain city in Watauga County named for Daniel Boone. Site of Appalachian State University. County seat of Watauga County.

Brevard Mountain town and county seat of Transylvania County.

Brunswick Colonial-era town settled on Cape Fear River in Brunswick County. Now state historic site.

Brushy Mountains Low mountain range crossing southern Wilkes, northern Alexander, and eastern Caldwell Counties.

Burlington Piedmont city in central Alamance County. North Carolina Railroad built repair shops here around 1851.

Buxton Coastal town on Hatteras Island in Dare County.

C

Camp Lejeune Marine base in southern Onslow County. Covers 173 square miles (450 sq km).

Cane Creek Piedmont creek that rises in southwest Alamance County and flows into the Haw River. Site of Quaker Meeting House (1751).

Canton Mountain city on the Pigeon River in eastern Haywood County.

Cape Fear River formed by junction of Deep and Haw Rivers on the Chatham-Lee county line. Flows into the Atlantic Ocean.

Cape Hatteras Easternmost point in North Carolina. Located at the tip of Hatteras Island in southeast Dare County.

Cape Lookout The southernmost tip of Core Banks in Carteret County.

Carolina bays Oval-shaped shallow lakes of uncertain origin in southeast North Carolina. White Lake is a Carolina bay.

Carrot Island A marshy island about 1.5 miles (2.4 km) long, southeast of Beaufort in southern Carteret County.

Carthage Piedmont city and county seat of Moore County. Hosts an annual buggy festival.

Cary Piedmont city in western Wake County founded as a tavern site, later a railroad town.

Cashiers Mountain resort town in southern Jackson County.

Catawba River Piedmont river that flows from Caldwell County southeast to form Lake Norman before flowing into South Carolina.

Cedar Island Large island in northeast Carteret County between West Bay and Core Sound.

Chapel Hill Piedmont city in Orange County that is the site of the University of North Carolina. Forms the Triangle with Durham and Raleigh.

Charlotte Largest city in North Carolina. Located in the Piedmont. County seat of Mecklenburg County.

Cherry Point Marine Air Station Marine base in southeast Craven County on Neuse River.

Cherokee Mountain town in eastern Swain County.

Cherokee Indian Reservation. *See* Qualla Reservation

Chimney Rock A mountain resort town in western Rutherford County.

Chowan River Coastal Plain river formed on Hertford-Gates county line. Flows southeast into the Albemarle Sound.

Clingmans Dome Highest peak in the Great Smoky Mountains at 6,642 feet (1,993 m). Named for Thomas L. Clingman.

Coastal Plain Landform region of eastern North Carolina. Extends inland 100 to 150 miles (161 to 242 km) from the Atlantic Ocean to the fall line of the rivers flowing out of the Piedmont.

Concord Piedmont city and county seat of Cabarrus County.

Core Sound Sound between the mainland and the Outer Banks from Cape Lookout to Pamlico Sound.

Croatan Sound Sound that connects Albemarle and Pamlico Sounds between Roanoke Island and the mainland of Dare County.

Croatoan Island Hatteras Inlet divides this portion of the Outer Banks into two islands: a southern portion of Hatteras Island and a portion of Ocracoke Island.

Cullowhee Mountain town in west-central Jackson County. Home of Western Carolina University.

Currituck Coastal Plain town and county seat of Currituck County.

Currituck Sound The sound between Currituck Banks to the east and the mainland of Currituck County to the west.

D

Dan River Piedmont river that flows southeast from Virginia into Stokes County and Rockingham County, then northeast back into Virginia.

Deep River Piedmont river formed in southwest Guilford County. Meets the Haw to form the Cape Fear River in southeast Chatham County.

Dismal Swamp Coastal Plain swamp, lake, and cypress area about 30 miles (48 km) long and 10 miles (16 km) wide. Partially in Gates, Pasquotank, Camden, and Currituck Counties.

Dismal Swamp Canal Canal that connected the waters of Elizabeth River in Virginia with the Pasquotank River.

Durham Piedmont city and county seat of Durham County. Forms the Triangle with Chapel Hill and Raleigh.

E

Edenton Early colonial capital located where the Chowan River flows into the Albemarle Sound. Incorporated in 1722. County seat of Chowan County.

Elizabeth City Coastal Plain city and county seat of Pasquotank County.

England One independent country that is part of the United Kingdom of Great Britain and Northern Ireland. Located in the British Isles in northwestern Europe. Homeland of first European explorers and colonists of North Carolina.

Eno River Piedmont river that rises in northern Orange County and flows southeast into western Durham County to join the Flat River to form the Neuse.

F

Fairntosh Community in northern Durham County named for plantation owned by Duncan Cameron. Site of former post office named Stagville.

Fayetteville Coastal Plain city located on the Cape Fear River. Once called Cross Creek and Campbellton. County seat of Cumberland County.

Fontana Dam Hydroelectric dam that forms 30-mile (48-km)-long Fontana Lake in Graham and Swain Counties in western North Carolina. The dam is the highest in eastern United States.

Fort Dobbs State historic site in central Iredell County. Fort used by English settlers in battles against the Cherokee during the French and Indian War.

Fort Fisher State historic site at the southern tip of New Hanover County. Site of Confederate fort that protected blockade-runners entering the Cape Fear River during the Civil War.

French Broad River Mountain river formed in Transylvania County. Flows northeast into Henderson County, then northwest into Buncombe and Madison Counties before flowing into Tennessee.

G

Gastonia Piedmont city and county seat of Gaston County.

Georgia Southeast state of the United States. Borders North Carolina to the southwest.

Goldsboro Coastal Plain city east of the Neuse River. County seat of Wayne County.

Grandfather Mountain Mountain landmark at junction of Avery, Caldwell, and Watauga Counties. 5,964 feet (1,789 m) high.

Great Britain. *See* England

Great Dismal Swamp. *See* Dismal Swamp

Great Smoky Mountains Mountain range of the Appalachian Mountains. Lies along the North Carolina-Tennessee state line. Clingmans Dome is highest peak.

Great Trading Path. *See* Trading Path

Great Wagon Road. *See* Wagon Road

Greensboro Piedmont city in central Guilford County. Forms the Triad with Winston-Salem and High Point. County seat of Guilford County.

Greenville Coastal Plain city in Pitt County. Site of East Carolina University. County seat of Pitt County.

Guilford Courthouse Site of Revolutionary War battle in present-day Greensboro in Guilford County.

Gulf of Mexico Large body of water south of the United States. Influences the climate of North Carolina through wind currents and the Gulf Stream.

Gulf Stream Warm current in the Atlantic Ocean that flows north out of the Gulf of Mexico along the east coast of the United States. Comes close to Cape Hatteras before flowing northeast away from the coast.

H

Halifax City on Roanoke River settled during colonial times as important "backcountry" town. County seat of Halifax County.

Hanging Rock State Park Park in central Stokes County in the Sauratown Mountain range.

Harker's Island Island in southeast Carteret County between Core Sound and Bogue Sound.

Hatteras Inlet An inlet from the Atlantic Ocean into Pamlico Sound. Lies between Hatteras Island and Ocracoke Island.

Hatteras Island Island of the Outer Banks east of Dare County.

Haw River Piedmont river that rises in northeast Forsyth County and flows northeast, then southeast into Jordan Lake.

Henderson Piedmont city and county seat of Vance County.

Hendersonville Mountain city and county seat of Henderson County.

Hickory Piedmont city in northwest Catawba County.

Highlands Resort Mountain town in southeast Macon County, 3,838 feet (1,151 m) high. Receives the most precipitation in North Carolina.

High Point Piedmont city in southwest Guilford County. Forms the Triad with Greensboro and Winston-Salem. Highest point, 960 feet (288 m), on the North Carolina Railroad.

Hillsborough Town founded during colonial times as important backcountry settlement on the Eno River. County seat of Orange County.

I

Inner Coastal Plain Western part of the Coastal Plain Region. Noted for its fertile farmland.

Intercoastal Waterway Waterway inland from the Atlantic Ocean that flows south from Massachusetts to Florida. 308 miles (496 km) are in North Carolina.

J

Jacksonville Coastal Plain city in central Onslow County on the New River, adjacent to Camp Lejeune. County seat of Onslow County.

Jockey's Ridge A sand dune 138 feet (41 m) high on Bodie Island, north of Nags Head. Highest coastal sand dune on the Atlantic and Gulf Coasts.

Joyce Kilmer Memorial Forest 3,840-acre (1,536-sq hm) mountain forest within the Nantahala National Forest in western Graham County.

Jugtown Piedmont community in northwest Moore County. Hand-turned pottery is made there.

K

Kannapolis Piedmont city of southern Rowan and northern Cabarrus Counties. Founded as a company mill town by Cannon Mills.

Kenly Coastal Plain town in eastern Johnston County. Home of the Tobacco Farm Life Museum.

Kill Devil Hills Town on Bodie Island in eastern Dare County near site of Wright Brothers' first flight.

Kings Mountain Mountain range about 3 miles (5 km) long in southeast Cleveland and southwest Gaston Counties extending into South Carolina. Site of important Revolutionary War battle.

Kinston Coastal Plain city and county seat of Lenoir County.

Kitty Hawk Community in eastern Dare County. Near Kill Devil Hills, site of Wright Brothers' first flight.

L

Lake Lure Mountain resort in western Rutherford County on the Broad River.

Lake Mattamuskeet Coastal Plain lake in central Hyde County covering about. 30,000 acres (12,000 sq hm).

Lake Norman Piedmont lake of 32,510 acres (13,004 sq hm) on the Catawba River formed by the dam at Cowan's Ford.

Lake Phelps 16,000-acre (6,400-sq hm) fresh-water lake in eastern Washington County and western Tyrrell County on the Coastal Plain.

Lake Waccamaw A natural Coastal Plain lake in northeast Columbus County, 5 miles (8 km) long and 3 miles (5 km) wide.

Lenoir Piedmont city and county seat of Caldwell County.

Lexington Piedmont city and county seat of Davidson County.

Lincolnton Town and county seat of Lincoln County. Ramseur's Mill, site of Revolutionary War battle, is on the northern outskirts.

Linville Falls Mountain waterfall in northwest Burke County on Linville River. Water drops 90 feet (27 m).

Linville Gorge Linville River flows through this in northwest Burke County. The only National Forest Wilderness in the east.

Lumber River Coastal Plain river formed on the Moore-Richmond county line. Flows into the Little Pee Dee River in South Carolina.

Lumberton Coastal Plain city and county seat of Robeson County.

M

Manteo Roanoke Island town settled in 1865. County seat of Dare County.

Morehead City Coastal Plain city in south-central Carteret County on Bogue Sound and Newport River.

Morganton City and county seat of Burke County.

Mountains Region Mountainous region of western North Carolina.

Mount Mitchell Highest peak (6,684 feet; 2,005 m) in the eastern United States. Located in southern Yancey County among the Black Mountains.

Mount Olive Coastal Plain city in Wayne County.

Mount Pisgah Mountain on the Buncombe-Haywood line. Can see North Carolina, South Carolina, Georgia, Tennessee, and Virginia from its peak (5,721 feet; 1,716 m).

Murphy Mountain town settled in 1830. County seat is in central Cherokee County.

N

Nags Head Town on Bodie Island facing the Atlantic Ocean.

Nantahala Gorge Deep canyon of the Nantahala River in northeast Graham and southwest Swain Counties.

Nantahala National Forest Western North Carolina national forest in parts of Cherokee, Clay, Graham, Jackson, Macon, Swain, and Transylvania Counties.

Nantahala River Mountain river that rises in southwest Macon County and flows northwest to the Clay-Macon county line.

Nashville Coastal Plain city and county seat of Nash County.

Neuse River Piedmont river formed in western Durham County by the junction of the Eno and Flat Rivers.

New Bern Coastal Plain city founded by the Swiss in colonial times where the Trent and Neuse Rivers flow into Pamlico Sound. County seat is in central Craven County.

New River Mountain river formed on the Ashe-Alleghany county line by the junction of North Fork and South Fork New River. Flows northeast and northwest into Virginia and West Virginia.

New River Coastal Plain river that rises in northwest Onslow County near Jones county line. Flows southeast across the county.

North Wilkesboro City in south-central Wilkes County across the Yadkin River from Wilkesboro. Formerly called Mulberry Fields.

O

Ocracoke Inlet Inlet from the Atlantic Ocean into Pamlico Sound. Lies between Ocracoke Island and Portsmouth Island.

Ocracoke Island Island of the Outer Banks in southeast Hyde County.

Oregon Inlet Inlet flowing from the Atlantic Ocean into Pamlico Sound in eastern Dare County between southern tip of Bodie Island and northern tip of Pea Island.

Outer Banks Low, narrow barrier islands extending more than 175 miles (282 km) on the eastern coast of North Carolina.

P

Pamlico River Coastal Plain river that is the lower course of the Tar River after it enters Beaufort County. Flows 33 miles (53 km) southeast and empties into Pamlico Sound.

Pamlico Sound Tidewater sound in eastern North Carolina, separated from the Atlantic Ocean by the Outer Banks. Largest sound on the East Coast of the United States.

Piedmont Central landform region of North Carolina that extends from the fall line on the east to the Blue Ridge. Elevation from 500 to 1,500 feet (150 to 450 m).

Piedmont Crescent A crescent-shaped area of the Piedmont that follows the route of the North Carolina Railroad and Interstate 85. Crosses Wake, Durham, Orange, Alamance, Guilford, Randolph, Forsyth, Davidson, Rowan, Cabarrus, Mecklenburg, Gaston, and Lincoln Counties.

Pilot Mountain 2,700-foot (810-m) mountain in southeast Surry County.

Pinehurst Coastal Plain city in southern Moore County known for golf courses.

Pisgah National Forest Western North Carolina national forest in parts of Avery, Buncombe, Burke, Caldwell, Haywood, Henderson, Madison, McDowell, Mitchell, Transylvania, Watauga, and Yancey Counties.

Q

Qualla Reservation Mountain home of the eastern band of the Cherokee Tribe. Covers 63,000 acres (25,200 sq hm) in Swain and Jackson Counties.

Queen Anne's Creek Creek that rises in southern Chowan County and flows southwest into Edenton Bay.

R

Raeford Coastal Plain city and county seat of Hoke County.

Raleigh State capital. Forms Triangle with Durham and Chapel Hill. County seat of Wake County.

Ramseur's Mill. *See* Lincolnton.

Reidsville Piedmont city of southern Rockingham County. Early backcountry settlement.

Research Triangle Park 5,000-acre (2,000-sq hm) area in southeast Durham and western Wake Counties containing offices and laboratories of government agencies, research companies, and corporations.

Roanoke Canal Canal dug to bypass the Upper and Lower Falls of the Roanoke River.

Roanoke Island Island in eastern Dare County 11 miles (18 km) long and 2 1/4 miles (3.6 km) wide. Site of Fort Raleigh.

Roanoke River Piedmont and Coastal Plain river formed in Montgomery County, Virginia. Flows southeast into North Carolina in Warren County. Empties into Albemarle Sound.

Rocky Mount Coastal Plain city in eastern Nash and western Edgecombe Counties. Near the falls of the Tar River.

Rutherfordton Mountain city and county seat of Rutherford County.

S

Salem Piedmont city founded by Moravians in Forsyth County. Joined with Winston in 1913 to form Winston-Salem.

Salisbury Piedmont city and county seat in east-central Rowan County. Founded near the intersection of the Great Trading Path and the Great Wagon Road as a backcountry settlement.

Salter Path Coastal Plain community on Bogue Banks.

Sandhills Rolling hills between Cape Fear and Pee Dee Rivers of sandy soil and longleaf pine trees.

Scotland Formerly independent country now part of the United Kingdom of Great Britain and Northern Ireland. Located in the British Isles north of England. Homeland of Scottish Highlanders and Scotch-Irish settlers of the backcountry of North Carolina.

Seagrove Town in southern Randolph County known for pottery.

Siler City Piedmont city in western Chatham County. Home of the Chicken Festival.

Somerset Coastal Plain plantation on Lake Phelps. Descendants of Somerset slaves have reunions here.

South Carolina Southeast state of the United States. Borders North Carolina to the south.

Southern Pines Coastal Plain resort town in southern Moore County.

Spencer Town in eastern Rowan County founded as Spencer Shops, construction yard for the Southern Railroad.

Statesville Piedmont city and county seat of Iredell County. Early backcountry settlement.

T

Tar River Piedmont and Coastal Plain river that rises in west-central Person County and flows southeast through Granville, Franklin, Nash, Edgecombe, and Pitt Counties. Becomes the Pamlico River in Beaufort County.

Tennessee Southeast state of the United States. Borders North Carolina to the west.

Tidewater The eastern portion of the Coastal Plain that includes the eastern mainland, sounds, and islands.

Town Creek Native American settlement on the Pee Dee River in Montgomery County. Mound there was site of Native American ceremonies.

Trading Path Backcountry trading route from the 1600s that linked the Piedmont and the Mountains to Virginia. Built along a Native American trade route.

Trent River Coastal Plain river that rises in Lenoir County and flows southeast across Jones County and into Craven County, where it joins the Neuse River in New Bern.

Triad Informal name of the three Piedmont cities of High Point, Greensboro, and Winston-Salem.

Triangle Informal name of the three Piedmont cities of Chapel Hill, Durham, and Raleigh.

Tryon Palace State historic site in New Bern, central Craven County. Home of Governor Tryon, 1770. First capitol building in North Carolina.

U

Uwharrie Mountains Hills of the Piedmont that extend northeast to southwest across Randolph, Montgomery, and Stanly Counties. Altitude not higher than 1,800 feet (540 m). Site of North Carolina Zoological Park.

V

Virginia Southeast state of the United States. Borders North Carolina to the north.

W

Wagon Road Land route of colonial times that connected the Piedmont backcountry to Virginia and South Carolina. Built along a Native American trading path.

Washington Coastal Plain city founded in 1776. First city named for George Washington in the United States. County seat of Beaufort County on Pamlico River.

Washington, D.C. Capital city of the United States. Located in eastern United States north of Virginia and south of Maryland. Site of the White House, Supreme Court, and United States Capitol.

Waynesville Mountain city and county seat of Haywood County.

Weldon Town in Halifax County on Roanoke River. The northern end of the Wilmington-Weldon Railroad.

Weymouth Woods 433-acre (173-sq hm) forest southeast of Southern Pines in southeast Moore County.

White Lake Coastal Plain Carolina bay in east-central Bladen County. Covers 1,068 acres (427 sq hm).

Wilkesboro City and county seat of Wilkes County on the Yadkin River. Located on the border between the Piedmont Region and the Mountains.

Williamston Coastal Plain city on the Roanoke River. County seat of Martin County.

Wilmington Coastal Plain city on the Cape Fear River that is North Carolina's largest port. County seat of New Hanover County.

Wilson Coastal Plain city and county seat of Wilson County.

Winston Formerly an independent city in central Forsyth County. Joined with Salem to form Winston-Salem in 1913.

Winston-Salem Coastal Plain city formed in 1913 by joining Winston and Salem. Forms Triad with Greensboro and High Point. County seat of Forsyth County.

Y

Yadkin River Mountains and Piedmont river that rises in Watauga County near Blowing Rock and flows southeast into Caldwell County, where it turns northeast to flow through Wilkes County. Two branches flow southeast to join the Pee Dee River in Anson, Montgomery, and Stanly Counties.

Z

Zebulon Town in eastern Wake County.

This glossary will help you pronounce and understand the meanings of the Key Terms in this book. The page number at the end of the definition tells where the word or phrase first appears.

A

abolitionists Those who favored doing away with slavery. (p. 160)

absolute location The unique spot on earth where a particular place is located, using coordinates of longitude and latitude. (p. 20)

agriculture The science of farming. (p. 60)

Algonkian (al•GAHN•kee•uhn) Tidewater Native Americans, including the Croatan, Pamlico, Secotan, and Pasquotank. (p. 87)

anthropologists (an•throw•PAH•loh•jists) Scientists who study human beings. Collectors of early Native American stories. (p. 98)

Appalachian Mountains Largest mountain range in the eastern United States. Stretches from Virginia and West Virginia to Alabama. (p. 12)

appeal Legal proceeding that results when someone believes a court's decision has not applied the law correctly (p. 343)

archaeologists (ar•KAY•oh•loh•jists) Scientists who study the remains (fossils, artifacts, and monuments) of past human life. (p. 82)

Archaic people (ar•KAY•ik) Descendants of the Paleo-Indian people. Lived 8,000 B.C. to 1,000 B.C. (p. 83)

artifacts Objects of the past, such as arrowheads and pottery, discovered by archaeologists. (p. 82)

assembly A group of citizens elected to pass laws. North Carolina colonists organized assemblies to protest English laws. (p. 115)

atlatl (aht•LAH•tul) Spear-thrower used by early Native Americans. (p. 84)

auction A sale of property to the highest bidder. (p. 186)

axis An imaginary line that runs through the earth between the North Pole and the South Pole. (p. 26)

B

backcountry Any area far enough away from the North Carolina coast to make communication and trade difficult during European settlement. Examples in the early 1700s were Cross Creek (later Fayetteville), Hillsborough, and Halifax. (p. 122)

balds Treeless fields on the peaks of the Appalachian Mountains. Laurel and rhododendron grow well here. (p. 72)

ballads Sentimental songs that tell a story. (p. 309)

barrier islands Islands near an ocean shore that are separated from the shore by a sound. An example is the Outer Banks. (p. 55)

barter To trade by exchanging one commodity for another. Money is not used. (p. 142)

batik (baa•TEEK) A fabric printed by coating with wax the parts not to be dyed. (p. 247)

Battle of Bentonville The only major Civil War battle fought in North Carolina (1865). (p. 167)

Bill of Rights The first ten amendments to the United States Constitution, which guarantee the rights of the individual. (p. 328)

bills Proposed laws. (p. 339)

bird sanctuary A place (usually a town or a park) designated as a safe haven for birds. (p. 369)

blockade A string of ships that blocks other ships from entering an enemy's port. (p. 164)

blockade-runners Fast ships that supplied the Confederacy during the Civil War. (p. 165)

Blue Ridge Parkway Part of a two-lane road running along the Blue Ridge Mountains from Virginia to Cherokee, North Carolina. (p. 68)

bluegrass music Form of mountain music that uses the banjo as the key instrument. (p. 309)

bolls The white, fluffy balls of the cotton plant. (p. 189)

borrow To receive something with the intention of returning the same. (p. 176)

bottomland Fertile flat areas along rivers. (p. 272)

brackish Describes a mixture of salt and fresh water, found especially in the sounds along the North Carolina coast. (p. 57)

bright leaf Flue-cured tobacco best grown in the sandy soil of eastern North Carolina. It was originally grown along the North Carolina-Virginia border, growing well in the Inner Coastal Plain and eastern Piedmont. (p. 185)

budget The plan submitted by the governor to the legislative branch indicating how much money the state will spend and how it will spend it. (p. 339)

burley Air-cured tobacco grown primarily in the mountains and western Piedmont. (p. 185)

C

camp meeting Religious tradition of neighbors putting aside work and spending a long weekend together in worship. (p. 144)

canopy The uppermost spreading branch layer of a forest. Other trees, bushes, and shrubs grow well in the protective shade underneath, providing a good habitat for wildlife. (p. 39)

cardinal directions The directions north, south, east, and west. (p. 7)

Carolina bays Shallow lakes of unknown origin southeast of the Sandhills. (p. 62)

census A count of the United States population taken every ten years. (p. 211)

checks and balances Provisions of the Constitution that keeps any one branch of the government from having more power than the other two. (p. 329)

chop To remove excess cotton plants. (p. 189)

civil cases Cases heard in superior court involving disputes over money or property. (p. 342)

clans Large groups of related families. (p. 97)

climate The average weather (temperature, wind velocity, precipitation) at a place over time. (p. 26)

clogging A dance in which the performer wears clogs (shoes or sandals with thick wooden soles) and beats out a rhythm on the floor. (p. 310)

clubbing Early system of farmers traveling together to take their harvests or animals to distant markets. (p. 143)

Coastal Plain A major landform of North Carolina and the South. Mostly fertile flat or gently sloping land that extends inland from the Atlantic Ocean and the Gulf of Mexico. (p. 12)

Coastal Plain Region One of the three regions of North Carolina. The area between the Piedmont and the ocean. (p. 54)

colonists The settlers of a colony, who maintain ties to their parent country. (p. 109)

colony An area settled in one country by people from another country. (p. 109)

Committees of Correspondence Committees formed throughout the American colonies to collect information about taxes and other laws passed in England that affected the colonies. (p. 135)

commute To travel back and forth regularly to work (as between a suburb and a city). (p. 275)

Confederate States of America (Confederacy) The name of the independent government formed by the seceding Southern states in 1861. (p. 162)

Congress The legislative branch of the United States. (p. 330)

conifers Evergreen, cone-bearing trees. Coniferous forests are the major plant resource of North America. (p. 39)

Constitution The plan for the national government of the United States, which specifies a strong, fair national government with principles that guarantee freedom. (p. 323)

consumer Any person who buys products. (p. 280)

continents The seven main landmasses of the world. (p. 20)

convention A meeting of citizens who gather for a common purpose. (p. 152)

Convention of 1835 A political meeting during which a new North Carolina constitution was written that increased the powers of the legislature and gave eastern and western North Carolina equal representation. (p. 152)

cooperatives Businesses owned by and operated for the benefit of those using their services. Poor farmers after the Civil War, for example, bought supplies together and sold their crops as a group. (p. 178)

council The group of leaders of a Native American community. (p. 97)

council houses Large Native American thatch-covered buildings where ceremonies were held and guests slept. (p. 96)

country music Form of mountain music that uses the guitar. (p. 309)

county A land division of local government within a state. North Carolina has 100 counties. (p. 349)

county seat The city or town in a county where the county government conducts its business. (p. 349)

cove A small opening between mountain ridges leading to large valleys cut by mountain streams. (p. 299)

culture A way of life expressed through traditions, festivals, foods, sports, and recreation. (p. 256)

D

deciduous forests Dense growths of trees in temperate climates. These trees shed their

leaves every autumn. Examples are maple, birch, and oak. (p. 39)
Declaration of Independence July 4, 1776, document declaring the American colonies free and independent of England. (p. 322)
degree (°) Unit of measurement indicating distance between lines of latitude and longitude. Also, a unit of temperature expressed in Fahrenheit (F) or Centigrade (C). (p. 21)
delegates Leaders who represent the people in making important decisions. (p. 138)
democracy Rule by the people. The United States is a nation ruled by its people. (p. 322)
denim The sturdy dark blue cotton cloth used to make blue jeans. (p. 190)
diversity Distinct, differing qualities. (p. 266)
drovers People in the 1800s who moved livestock to market. (p. 140)
dulcimer A lap-held stringed instrument played by plucking or strumming. (p. 309)

E

Eastern Hemisphere The half of the earth east of the prime meridian. (p. 24)
Edenton Tea Party 1774 meeting where a petition was signed by 50 women supporting the First Continental Congress's vote to stop all trade with England. (p. 137)
elevation The height of land above sea level. (p. 12)
Emancipation Proclamation President Abraham Lincoln's order on New Year's Day, 1863, to free all slaves in the Confederate states under Union control. All North Carolina slaves were eventually freed in 1865. (p. 169)
Equator Imaginary line circling the earth halfway between the North and South Poles, dividing the earth into two hemispheres. (p. 20)
evergreen forests Dense growths of trees in temperate climates. These trees keep their needlelike leaves all year. Examples are the pine, fir, and spruce. (p. 39)
executive branch Carries out laws passed by Congress. Headed by the president. (p. 331)

F

fall line Line where the streams come down from the hilly Piedmont into the flatter Coastal Plain. (p. 63)
federal government The national government, which makes laws for the nation. (p. 331)
federal system A system where the national government and the states share power. (p. 326)
felony A crime, such as murder or burglary. Punishment is more severe than for a misdemeanor. (p. 342)
fibers Strands of cotton, flax, or wool. (p. 142)
Five Themes of Geography Location, Place, Human-Environmental Interaction, Movement, and Region. (p. 4)
foreign trade zone An area where goods bought from another country can be stored, bought, and sold without paying high taxes. (p. 362)
forestry The science of developing, caring for, or cultivating forests. (p. 71)
free people of color Those few African Americans in the mid-1800s who were not slaves. They had either bought their freedom or been granted it by their former owners. (p. 149)

G

game A name for wild animals and fish used for food. (p. 86)
General Assembly Legislative branch of North Carolina's government that makes the state laws. (p. 339)
ginseng root Aromatic herb valued as a medicine. Protected under North Carolina law. (p. 93)
global grid Imaginary lines of latitude and longitude on maps that help you find the absolute location of any place. (p. 20)
Good Roads Movement North Carolina road-building program in the 1920s. The state paid for roads connecting every county seat. (p. 225)
governor Chief executive in North Carolina, who makes sure that state laws are carried out. (p. 339)
Great Trading Path Old Native American trail used by backcountry settlers. Connected the Piedmont to the Mountains Region, Virginia, and South Carolina. (p. 123)
Great Wagon Road Old Native American trail used by backcountry settlers. Connected the Piedmont to Virginia and South Carolina. (p. 123)
Green Corn ceremony Annual early Native American ritual of cleansing bodies (by fasting), homes, and minds. Occurred in late summer, when the corn crop was ripening. (p. 100)

greenway A narrow space in a park or in and around a city for people to walk or bicycle safely. (p. 369)

H

habitat A place where a plant or an animal naturally lives. (p. 38)

Halifax Resolves 1776 document signed by North Carolina delegates urging all the colonies to declare independence from England. (p. 138)

headquarters A company's home office. (p. 268)

heritage A gift from the past in the form of memories, stories, songs, and traditions. (p. 311)

hiddenite A green emerald found only in North Carolina. (p. 44)

Hispanics Latin Americans who speak Spanish. (p. 240)

Historic (Period) The time when the history of Native Americans was first written, when the Europeans came to North America. (p. 87)

historic preservation The effort by the state and citizen groups to preserve historical houses and other structures. (p. 370)

House of Representatives One of two houses of the North Carolina legislature. (p. 344)

hub The center of an airline transportation network, where an airline directs most of its traffic. (p. 226)

Human–Environmental Interaction One of the Five Themes of Geography. Answers the questions "How does the environment affect the humans in a place?" and "How do humans affect the environment in a place?" (p. 103)

humid subtropical Describes North Carolina's climate. A type of temperate climate that brings mild and rainy winters, humid springs, and hot, humid summers. (p. 27)

husquenaw (HUH•skwee•naw) A time of intense trial and discipline for early Native American teenage boys and girls in eastern North Carolina. (p. 100)

hydroelectricity Electricity produced through water movement. (p. 47)

I

Inner Coastal Plain Part of the Coastal Plain Region. Flat like the Outer Coastal Plain (Tidewater) but with a higher elevation and more fertile soil. (p. 54)

intermediate directions The directions between the cardinal directions: southeast, southwest, northeast, and northwest. (p. 8)

Iroquoian (EAR•ah•quoy•uhn) A Native American language family of eastern North America, including the Cherokee and Tuscarora. (p. 87)

J

judicial branch The branch of government on the state and national levels which interpret laws passed by the legislative branch. (p. 330)

jury Twelve citizens picked from the community who serve at a trial and are sworn to give a verdict based on the evidence presented in court. (p. 343)

K

key A section of a map containing the meanings of the map's symbols. (p. 12)

Ku Klux Klan A post-Civil War secret society that supported white supremacy. (p. 174)

L

land trust An organization that helps people find ways to protect their land from unnecessary development. (p. 368)

landform A physical feature of the land. (p. 11)

landmark Reference point used to find a place. (p. 5)

Latin Americans People of the Western Hemisphere who live south of the United States and speak Spanish, Portuguese, or French. (p. 240)

latitude Distance north or south of the Equator, expressed in degrees (°). (p. 20)

legislative branch Congress, which passes our country's laws. (p. 330)

livestock Animals raised on farms: beef and dairy cattle, hogs, and poultry. (p. 218)

Location One of the Five Themes of Geography. Answers the question "Where is a place?" (p. 4)

longitude Distance east or west of the prime meridian, expressed in degrees (°). (p. 23)

Lords Proprietors English owners of the new colony of Carolina (1663), now present-day North Carolina and South Carolina. (p. 114)

Lost Colony Ill-fated colony begun on Roanoke Island in 1587. Sometime between then and 1590, every inhabitant disappeared. (p. 111)

Loyalists Colonists who sided with England in the American Revolution. (p. 137)

M

map scale A divided line on a map showing the length used to represent the real measurements of the area on the map. (p. 33)
meridians Any lines of longitude west or east of the prime meridian. (p. 23)
migrant workers People who move regularly in order to find work, especially in harvesting crops. (p. 240)
militia A body of citizens organized for military service. (see Regulators) (p. 135)
mill village Community near the textile mills where workers lived. (p. 201)
millenium A 1,000-year period of time. (p. 358)
mint United States Treasury building where gold and silver are weighed and pressed into coins. Charlotte was the site of the nation's first mint. (p. 44)
misdemeanor A crime not considered serious. No jury sits in judgment. (p. 342)
Mountains Region One of the three regions of North Carolina. The area west of the Piedmont. (p. 54)
Movement One of the Five Themes of Geography. Answers the question "How are people, goods, and ideas moved within and to a place?" (p. 129)
municipal One of two forms of local government (the other is county) in North Carolina. Serves towns or cities. (p. 349)

N

naval stores Building materials for ships, including tar, turpentine, and tree trunks. Early moneymaking crops in the Carolina colonies. (p. 118)
North Carolina Railroad Opened in 1856, ran from Goldsboro to Charlotte. Led to the growth of Wilson, Raleigh, Durham, Greensboro, and Salisbury as important farm markets. (p. 153)
Northern Hemisphere The half of the earth north of the Equator. (p. 21)

O

ocean current A strong stream of water running through the ocean. (p. 29)
old-time music Original mountain music. (p. 309)
orchestra A group of 30 or more performing musicians. (p. 282)
Outer Banks Huge sand ridges in the Atlantic Ocean east of the North Carolina mainland. The ridges form barrier islands that extend along the North Carolina coast. (p. 55)
Outer Coastal Plain Also called the Tidewater. Part of the Coastal Plain Region. (p. 54)

P

page A messenger—usually a teenager on summer vacation—for legislators. (p. 348)
Paleo-Indian people (PAY•lee•oh) North Carolina's first settlers (10,000 B.C.-8,000 B.C.). (p. 83)
panning Washing earth or gravel in a round, shallow container (pan) in search of metal, usually gold. (p. 45)
parallels Any lines of latitude north or south of the Equator. (p. 21)
pardon The act of setting a person free from prison. The president and state governors have this power. (p. 340)
Parliament The lawmaking body of Great Britain. (p. 135)
Patriots Colonists who wanted to be independent of England. (p. 138)
peat The compressed layers of tissue from decayed plants used to enrich garden soil. Dug up in the Pamlico Sound area. (p. 43)
pemmican Native American food mixture of grease, dried meat, and dried persimmon. (p. 91)
Piedmont A major landform stretching from Virginia to Alabama. Hilly, rolling countryside that lies between the Coastal Plain Region and the Mountains Region. (p. 12)
Piedmont Crescent The area between Raleigh and Charlotte marked first by the crescent-shaped curve of the North Carolina Railroad and later by Interstate 85. (p. 65)
Piedmont Region One of the three regions of North Carolina. The area between the Coastal Plain and the mountains. (p. 54)
Pine State, the North Carolina nickname. (p. 118)
Place One of the Five Themes of Geography. Answers the questions "What are a place's

physical characteristics?" and "What are the human characteristics of a place?" (p. 49)

plantation A large farm specializing in the growing and selling of a profitable crop. (p. 117)

plateau (pla•TOW) A mostly level landform that is higher than nearby areas. (p. 63)

pocosin (POW•cuh•sin) A type of Tidewater swamp. Often described as "a swamp upon a hill." (p. 59)

precipitation Moisture that falls from the sky as mist, rain, hail, sleet, or snow. (p. 29)

prehistoric Before history was written. (p. 83)

president Head of the executive branch of the United States government. (p. 331)

prime meridian Line of longitude (0°) from which longitude east and west is measured. (p. 23)

Q

quarry (KWAR•ee) An excavation site for obtaining stone, slate, or limestone. There are more than 100 quarries in North Carolina. (p. 46)

quarters Group of cabins where slaves lived. Typically one-room log dwellings. (p. 147)

R

rain shadow effect The blocking by high peaks of winds carrying precipitation across mountains. Land across the mountains, away from the wind direction, receives less precipitation. (p. 31)

raising Early custom started in the 1800s whereby farmers got together and helped put up the framework of a house or a barn in a single day. This was followed by a celebration of food and dancing. (p. 142)

Reconstruction Reorganization of the defeated states after the Civil War. (p. 173)

reels Lively Scotch-Irish dancing tunes. (p. 309)

Region One of the Five Themes of Geography. Answers the question "How do places in an area share similar characteristics?" (p. 74)

Regulators Backcountry settlers who opposed the taxes set by the English government. Fought Governor William Tryon's militia at Alamance Creek in 1771. (p. 134)

relative location Approximate location of a place found by using nearby references. (p. 4)

religious retreat A time of quiet thought away from daily pressures. (p. 296)

republic Form of government in which people elect their leaders by voting. The United States government is a republic. (p. 326)

research Careful study and experimentation to discover facts. (p. 229)

reservoirs Lakes dug to hold water for hydroelectric dams or to be pumped to homes and businesses. (p. 47)

retraining centers Places provided by private companies where workers learn new skills. (p. 361)

rural Refers to the country, country people or life, or agriculture. (p. 65)

S

sacred Holy. (p. 99)

Sandhills Rolling ridges of sand far inland, remnants from a time when the ocean covered the area before the Ice Age. The area includes such cities as Fayetteville, Southern Pines, and Raeford. (p. 61)

scenic byways More than 1,500 miles of highways that provide travelers with pretty drives between North Carolina towns. (p. 369)

"Scott Roads" North Carolina road-building program in the late 1940s. Thousands of miles of dirt roads were paved. (p. 225)

secede (suh•SEED) To withdraw from something. The South seceded from the Union. (p. 162)

segregation The separation or isolation of a race, class, or ethnic group by discrimination. (p. 200)

Senate One of two houses of the North Carolina legislature. (p. 344)

service industries Production or profit-making enterprises that help people and businesses, such as tourism, restaurants, banks, and schools. (p. 223)

sharecropping Financial arrangement where former slaves and poor white farmers rented farmland and shared a portion of the harvest with the landowners. (p. 171)

Siouan (soo•yuhn) Early Native Americans of the Piedmont. Largest tribe was the Catawba. (p. 87)

sit-in An organized peaceful demonstration against a business that practiced segregation.

Effective method of protest in the 1950s and 1960s. (p. 269)

slaves People owned as property. The major source of labor on plantations where Africans were brought to this country against their will. (p. 118)

sound A body of water that lies between the mainland and coastal (barrier) islands. Examples are the Pamlico and Albemarle Sounds. (p. 56)

Southern Hemisphere The half of the earth south of the Equator. (p. 21)

"Star-Spangled Banner" National anthem of the United States. (p. 320)

Stars and Stripes Popular name for the United States flag. (p. 320)

state government Makes state laws. Shares power with the federal government. (p. 331)

stockades Fences of half-round posts that protected early Native American villages. (p. 95)

suburb Residential area on the outskirts of a city or large town. (p. 65)

Supreme Court Highest court in the United States. Determines whether laws passed by Congress follow the Constitution. (p. 331)

swamp A low, wet Tidewater area with poor soil, characterized by forests of pine, scrub oak, and cypress. (p. 58)

symbols Anything that stands for something else. Our national anthem and flag are important symbols of our country. (p. 320)

T

tall tales Oral stories featuring characters who can do the impossible. (p. 310)

Tar Heel State, the North Carolina nickname. (p. 118)

temperate A moderate climate characterized by a variety of temperatures and rainfall. (p. 27)

textile Woven or knitted cloth. Also refers to businesses that make cloth. (p. 188)

Tidewater Also called the Outer Coastal Plain. The area along the coast where waters rise and fall each day from ocean tides. (p. 54)

Trail of Tears The forced walk of many Cherokee from North Carolina, Georgia, and Tennessee to a new reservation in Oklahoma. More than 4,000 Cherokee died on the journey. (p. 294)

Triad Informal name for the area formed by High Point, Greensboro, and Winston-Salem. (p. 64)

Triangle Informal name for the area formed by Raleigh, Durham, and Chapel Hill. (p. 64)

U

Underground Railroad A system of cooperation among antislavery people before 1863 by which runaway slaves were secretly helped to reach the North or Canada. (p. 160)

Union The United States. (p. 162)

urban The opposite of rural. Refers to areas in and around a city. (p. 65)

V

veto The executive branch's rejection of a bill passed by the legislative branch. The president and state governors have this power. (p. 339)

W

weirs Native American fishing traps. (p. 91)

Western Hemisphere The half of the earth west of the prime meridian. (p. 24)

white water Frothy water—the part of a stream that goes through rocks. (p. 312)

wigwams Native American huts having a framework of poles covered by bark or animal hides. (p. 95)

Wilmington and Weldon Railroad Opened in 1838. Helped Coastal Plain farmers move their goods to Wilmington and later helped supply Confederate troops with goods brought to Wilmington by blockade-runners. (p. 153)

Woodland people Native Americans who lived in eastern North Carolina almost 2,000 years ago. (p. 85)

Z

zoning The way city governments plan how their cities will grow. (p. 351)

O

P

CREDITS

...nted

..., Inc.: 22, 24(left), 25, 49, 74, 75, 88, 102, 103, 128, 129, 155, 179, 203, 215, ...3, 261, 287, 326-7, 329, 331, 335, 346, 371; **Precision Graphics:** 6, 8, 11, 14, 21, ...(right), 26, 31, 56, 70-1, 109, 125, 167, 194, 228-9, 240-1, 294.

Photographs

APS—Aerial Photography Services; **JA/NCSU**—Jim Alchediak/North Carolina State University, **MKP**—Mike Kesselring Photography; **MMA**—Mint Museum of Art, Charlotte, North Carolina; **NCC**—N. C. Collection, UNC-Chapel Hill Library; **NCT**—North Carolina Division of Travel and Tourism; **NH/NCSU**—Neal Hutcheson/North Carolina State University; **OCEDC**—Orange County Economic Development Commission; **TRI**—Transparencies, Inc.

1, APS, (insets) APS; **2 & 3,** NCT; **4,** NH/NCSU; **5,** Simon Griffiths Photography; **6,** The Granger Collection; **6-7,** The Granger Collection; **7,** (inset) The Granger Collection, (tr) State Archives of N. C., (br) NCC; **9,** NCT; **11,** Richard Parker/Photo Researchers; **12,** NCT; **18,** Science Source/Photo Researchers; **18-19,** NCSU Computer Graphics Center, Courtesy of Dr. Heather Cheshire; **19,** AP/Wide World Photos; **22,** (l) The Granger Collection, (br) Special Collections, East Carolina University Library; **22-23,** Hispanic Society of America; **23,** (tr) "Map of North & South Carolina" (1896), NCC, (br) NASA, (inset) Intergraph Corporation; **27,** NCT; **30,** (l) MKP, (r) JA/NCSU (fern specimen courtesy of the William Lanier Hunt Arboretum, N. C. Botanical Garden, Chapel Hill); **36,** Melissa McGaw/N. C. Wildlife Resources Commission; **36-37,** Simon Griffiths Photography; **37,** White House Photography Office; **38,** Simon Griffiths Photography; **39,** APS; **40,** NH/NCSU; **41,** (t) JA/NCSU (pine specimen courtesy of Paula Otto and Dr. Robert Weir, NCSU College of Forest Resources), (b) "Land of the Sky" quilt, Southern Highland Craft Guild; **42,** NCT; **43,** Melissa McGaw/N. C. Wildlife Resources Commission; **44,** (bl, br) NCC, (tr) State Archives of N. C., (inset) MMA; **45,** (tr) N. C. Museum of History, (mr) Simon Griffiths Photography, (bl) MMA; **46,** APS; **47,** Simon Griffiths Photography; **48,** NCT; **52,** (inset) Ruth Harris; **52-53,** NCT; **53,** State Archives of N. C.; **54, 57, 58 & 59,** NCT; **60,** NCSU Visual Communications; **61,** JA/NCSU; **62,** Melissa McGaw/N. C. Wildlife Resources Commission; **63,** NH/NCSU; **66,** NCT; **67,** (l) NCT, (r) Jugtown Pottery stoneware, Ackland Art Museum, UNC-Chapel Hill; **68,** NCT; **70 & 71,** NCC; **70-71,** APS; **72 & 73,** MKP; **78-79,** David Latham/N. C. Division of Archives and History; **80 & 80-81,** Simon Griffiths Photography, Courtesy of the Schiele Museum of Natural History; **81,** Archive Photos; **83, 84, 85, 86, 88 & 89,** Images courtesy of Dr. David S. Phelps, Archaeology Laboratory, Institute for Historical and Cultural Research, East Carolina University; **90,** British Library; **91,** Trustees of the British Museum; **92,** JA/NCSU; **93,** Dr. David Phelps/ECU Archaeology Laboratory; **94,** The Granger Collection; **95,** Bridgeman/Art Resource, Courtesy of the Trustees of the British Museum; **96,** NCT; **97,** NCC; **98,** Dr. David Phelps/ECU Archaeology Laboratory; **99 & 100,** Trustees of the British Museum; **101,** Rick Hill; **102,** Simon Griffiths Photography; **103,** NCT; **106-107,** Dare County Tourist Bureau; **107,** NCC; **108,** Trustees of the British Museum; **109,** NCC, Courtesy of the Trustees of the British Museum; **110,** (t) NCT, (b) The Granger Collection; **111,** (t) Trustees of the British Museum, (b) NCC; **112,** N. C. Historic Sites; **114,** (l) N. C. Museum of History, (r) State Archives of N. C.; **115,** Simon Griffiths Photography; **116,** NCC; **117,** Arents Collection, The New York Public Library, Astor, Lenox and Tilden Foundations; **118,** NCC; **119,** William Russ/NCT; **121,** East Carolina Manuscript Collection, East Carolina University; **124 & 125,** Filson Club Historical Society; **124-125 & 126,** NCT; **127,** N. C. Historic Sites; **132,** (l) Bridgeman/Art Resource, Courtesy of the Guildhall Art Gallery, London; **132-133,** The Granger Collection; **133,** (inset) NCT; **135,** NCC; **136,** (l) Tryon Palace Historic Site and Gardens, (m) NCT, (r) Simon Griffiths Photography; **137,** NH/NCSU, Courtesy of Tryon Palace Historic Site and Gardens; **138,** N. C. Historic Sites; **139,** Independence National Historical Park; **140 & 141,** Simon Griffiths Photography; **142,** NCC; **143,** Simon Griffiths Photography; **144 & 145,** N. C. Historic Sites; **147,** (l) State Archives of N. C., (inset) NCC; **148,** Southern Historical Collection; **149,** N. C. Museum of History; **150,** Courtesy of the Mariners' Museum, Newport News, Virginia; **152,** NCC; **152-153,** "First Railroad Town on the Mohawk & Hudson Road," by E. L. Henry, Albany Institute of History & Art, Albany, New York; **153,** (inset) State Archives of N. C.; **154,** State Archives of N. C.; **155,** (l) NCT, (r) APS; **158,** N. C. Museum of History; **158-159 & 159,** State Archives of N. C.; **161,** (l) The Bettmann Archive, (r) Courtesy of the Warner Collection of Gulf States Paper Corporation; **163,** Courtesy of William S. Powell; **164,** Southern Historical Collection, UNC-Chapel Hill Library; **165,** (t, b) State Archives of N. C.; **166,** (l) State Archives of N. C., (t) Underwater Archaeology Unit, N. C. Department of Cultural Resources; **166-167,** Courtesy Bermuda National Trust Collection, Bermuda Archives; **167,** State Archives of N. C.; **168,** Naval Historical Foundation; **169,** State Archives of N. C.; **170,** NCC; **171,** (t) NCC, (b) JA/NCSU; **172,** State Archives of N. C.; 173, The Bettmann Archive; **174,** N. C. Museum of History; **175,** Simon Griffiths Photography, Courtesy of Duke Homestead State Historic Site; **176 & 176-177,** NCC; **177 & 178,** State Archives of N. C; **182,** (t) Rhode Island Historical Society, (b) Culver Pictures; **183,** (l) Becky Johnson/Duke Homestead State Historic Site, (r) State Archives of N. C.; **184,** State Archives of N. C.; **185,** NCC; **186,** Duke University Special Collections Library; **187 & 188-189,** NCC; **189,** (inset) State Archives of N. C., (r) NCC; **190-191,** NCC; **191,** Cone Mills Corporation; **193 & 195,** NCC; **196 & 197,** State Archives of N. C.; **198,** NCC; **199,** Southern Historical Collection; **200,** (l) State Archives of N. C., (b) Photography Collection, University of Maryland-Baltimore County; **200-201,** Photography Collection, University of Maryland-Baltimore County; **201,** (b) NCC, UNC-Chapel Hill Library, (r) Photography Collection, University of Maryland-Baltimore County; **202,** (t) State Archives of N. C., (inset) NCC; **206-207,** Henry Ossawa Tanner, "The Banjo Lesson," (1893), oil on canvas, Hampton University Museum, Hampton, Virginia; **208,** (t) The Granger Collection; **208-209,** State Archives of N. C.; **209,** NCSU College of Textile Engineering, Chemistry and Science; **210-211,** State Archives of N. C.; 211, (inset) JA/NCSU, Courtesy of the U. S. Bureau of the Census; **212,** NCC; **213 & 214,** State Archives of N. C.; **215,** NH/NCSU; **216,** Simon Griffiths Photography; **217,** NCSU Visual Communications; **218,** MKP; **219,** Duke University Special Collections Library; **220,** NCT; **221,** State Archives of N. C.; **223,** Jim Stratford/Burlington Industries; **224,** (inset) State Archives of N. C., (r) OCEDC; **226,** Simon Griffiths Photography; **227,** Linda Hambourger/ NCSU College of Humanities and Social Sciences; **228,** (l, m) State Archives of N. C., (r) NCSU Engineering Publications; **229,** (l) Courtesy of Dan Tucker, NCSU Biomedical Communications, (b) NCSU Mars Mission Research Center, (r) NCSU Engineering Publications; **231,** Billy Barnes/TRI; **232,** APS; **236,** NCT; **236-237,** NCT; **237,** drawing by Bill Ballard, Courtesy of the N. C. Division of Archives and History; **238,** David Latham/N. C. Historic Sites; **239,** Courtesy of Debra Jacobs, Waccamaw Siouan Development Association; **240,** (l, ml) APS, (r, mr) NCT; **241,** NCT; **242,** Simon Griffiths Photography; **243 & 244,** NCT; **245,** (t) NCC, (inset) NCT; **246,** Joe Swift; **247,** "Core Banks," by Mary Edna Fraser, batik on silk, courtesy of the artist; **248,** N. C. Historic Sites; **249,** NH/NCSU; **250,** Photos by Jim Stratford/Black Star, Courtesy of E. I. du Pont Corporation; **251,** Courtesy of Lynne Welborn; **253,** N. C. Sweet Potato Commission; **254,** Simon Griffiths Photography; **255,** East Carolina University Medical Center; **256,** NH/NCSU; **257,** Joe Swift; **258,** Joe Webb; **259 & 260,** NCT; **264,** NCT; **264-265,** APS; **265,** NH/NCSU; **266,** Patsy Hill, Allen Jay Elementary School, High Point, N. C.; **267,** Jon F. Silla/TRI; **268,** (l, br) UPI/Bettmann, (tr) State Archives of N. C.; **269,** (tr) APS, (ml, mr, b) State Archives of N. C.; **270,** N. C. Museum of Art; **271,** OCEDC; **272,** Museum of Early Southern Decorative Arts, Winston-Salem, N. C.; **273,** (t) OCEDC, (b) Chapel Hill/Orange County Visitors Bureau; **274,** Chapel Hill/Orange County Visitors Bureau; **275,** Erin Wall/Chapel Hill News; **276,** NCT; **278,** (t) Jane Faircloth/TRI, (b) Simon Griffiths Photography; **279,** Simon Griffiths Photography; **280,** Dolan/TRI; **281 & 282,** NCT; **283 & 284,** Simon Griffiths Photography, **285,** NH/NCSU; **286,** Pinehurst Area Convention & Visitors Bureau; **290,** Asheville/Buncombe County Tourist Development Authority; **290-291,** NCT; **291,** Ewart M. Ball Collection, Ramsey Library, UNC-Asheville; **292,** The Granger Collection; **293,** NCC; **294,** (l) "The Trail of Tears," by Robert Lindneux, Woolaroc Museum, Bartlesville, Oklahoma, (inset) NCC; **294-295,** MKP; **295,** (l) NCT, (inset, r) N. C. Museum of History; **296,** Lake Junaluska Assembly, United Methodist Church; **297,** MKP; **298,** N. C. Wildlife Resources Commission; **299,** Simon Griffiths Photography; **300,** Peter Garcia; **301,** NCT, **302,** APS; **303,** Southern Highland Craft Guild; **304,** Tyson Foods ; **305,** (b) Simon Griffiths Photography, (t) JA/NCSU; **306,** MKP; **307,** N. C. Department of Commerce; **308,** Appalachian State University News Bureau; **309 & 310,** MKP; **311,** APS; **312,** Simon Griffiths Photography; **313,** MKP; **316-317,** Lisa Christensen/NCSU Visual Communications; **318,** The Granger Collection; **318-19,** Courtesy of the New Haven Colony Historical Society; **319,** Courtesy of H. G. Jones; **320,** MKP; **321,** The Granger Collection; **322,** Tony Stone Images; **322-323,** "Signing of the Declaration of Independence," by John Trumbull, Yale University Art Gallery; **324,** M. Booher/ TRI; **325,** "Signing the Constitution," by T. L. Rossiter, Independence National Park Historical Collection; **326,** (t) The Granger Collection, (m) JA/NCSU, Courtesy of the League of Women Voters of North Carolina, (bl, br) NCC; **327,** (l) State Archives of N. C., (r) Duke University Archives; **329, 330 & 335,** U. S. Capitol photo (E. C. Stangler/ Photophile), White House photo (Bettmann), Supreme Court photo (Martin Jeong/UPI/-Bettmann); **331,** Ron Edmonds/AP/Wide World Photos; **332,** (t) Jane Faircloth/TRI, (b) MKP; **336,** Jane Faircloth/TRI; **337,** AP/Wide World Photos; **338,** JA/NCSU; **339,** (t) Culver Pictures, (b) Governor's Office, State of North Carolina, Courtesy of Vicki Nizen; **340,** N. C. Museum of History; **341,** Lisa Christensen/NCSU Visual Communications; **342,** Public Information Office, N. C. Highway Patrol, Courtesy of Sgt. W. S. Hunter; **343,** Billy Barnes/TRI; **344,** Principal Clerk's Office, General Assembly of the State of North Carolina, Courtesy of Denise Weeks; **345,** Central Piedmont Community College; **347,** Jan Hensley; **348,** Carlyle Teague/Tobacco Stabilization Board; 350, (l) MKP, (r) OCEDC; **351,** Wake County Sheriff's Department, Courtesy of Sheriff John Baker; **352,** Walton Haywood/Museum of the Cape Fear, Fayetteville, N. C.; **353,** N. C. Sweet Potato Commission; **356 & 356-357,** Jane Faircloth/TRI; **357,** N. C. Global Transpark Authority; **358,** Courtesy of the Forest at Duke, Durham, N. C.; **359,** MCNC, Courtesy of Dr. Tom Krakow; **360-361,** Central Piedmont Community College; **361,** Courtesy of the Forest at Duke; **362,** NCT; **363,** Jane Faircloth/TRI; **364,** Will & Deni McIntyre/Wake Forest University; **365,** NCT; **366,** JA/NCSU, Courtesy of the Office of the Bicentennial Observance, UNC-Chapel Hill; **366-367,** Pat Chancer/Frank Porter Graham Elementary School, Chapel Hill, N. C.; **367,** (l) Sam Roman Oertwig, (inset-left) JA/NCSU, (inset-right) Ross Taylor/Chapel Hill News, (r) Sam Roman Oertwig; **368,** Ken Taylor/N. C. Wildlife Resources Commission; **369,** J. M. Lynch/North Carolina Nature Conservancy; **370,** City of Washington, N. C., Courtesy of Bob Boyette; **372 & 373,** OCEDC.